MILLER'S
Collectables
PRICE GUIDE

MILLER'S
Collectables
PRICE GUIDE

General Editor
Madeleine Marsh

1999–2000
(Volume XI)

MILLER'S COLLECTABLES PRICE GUIDE 1999-2000

Compiled, edited and designed by
Miller's Publications Ltd
The Cellars, High Street
Tenterden, Kent TN30 6BN
Telephone: 01580 766411
Fax: 01580 766100

General Editor: Madeleine Marsh
Editorial & Production Co-ordinator: Sue Boyd
Editorial Assistants: Catherine Carson-Parker, Jo Wood
Production Assistants: Gillian Charles, Léonie Sidgwick, Caroline Bugeja
Designers: Kari Reeves, Shirley Reeves
Advert Designer: Simon Cook
Photographic Co-ordinator & Advertising Executive: Elizabeth Smith
Advertising Assistants: Jill Jackson, Melinda Williams
Indexer: Hilary Bird
Additional photography: Ian Booth, Roy Farthing, David Merewether,
Robin Saker, Dennis O'Reilly

First published in Great Britain in 1999
by Miller's, a division of Mitchell Beazley,
imprints of Octopus Publishing Group Ltd
2-4 Heron Quays, London E14 4JB.

© 1999 Octopus Publishing Group Ltd

Reprinted 2000

A CIP catalogue record for this book is
available from the British Library

ISBN 0-75370-331-9

Illustrations and film output: CK Litho, Whitstable, Kent
Colour origination: Pica Colour Separation, Singapore
Printed and bound by Printer Portuguesa Industria Gráfica Lda.

Miller's is a registered trademark of
Octopus Publishing Group Ltd

HOW TO USE THIS BOOK

It is our aim to make this guide easy to use. In order to find a particular item, turn to the contents list on page 7 to find the main heading, for example, Jewellery. Having located your area of interest, you will see that larger sections have been sub-divided by subject or maker. If you are looking for a particular factory, maker, or object, consult the index, which starts on page 486.

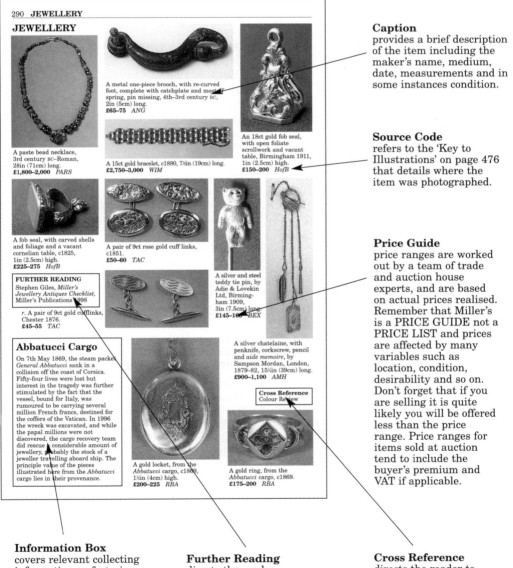

290 JEWELLERY

JEWELLERY

A paste bead necklace, 3rd century BC–Roman, 28in (71cm) long.
£1,800–2,000 *PARS*

A metal one-piece brooch, with re-curved foot, complete with catchplate and mount spring, pin missing, 4th–3rd century BC, 2in (5cm) long.
£65–75 *ANG*

A 15ct gold bracelet, c1880, 7½in (19cm) long.
£2,750–3,000 *WIM*

An 18ct gold fob seal, with open foliate scrollwork and vacant table, Birmingham 1911, 1in (2.5cm) high.
£150–200 *HofB*

A fob seal, with carved shells and foliage and a vacant cornelian table, c1825, 1in (2.5cm) high.
£225–275 *HofB*

A pair of 9ct rose gold cuff links, c1851.
£50–60 *TAC*

FURTHER READING
Stephen Giles, *Miller's Jewellery Antiques Checklist*, Miller's Publications 1998.

r. A pair of 9ct gold cufflinks, Chester 1876.
£45–55 *TAC*

A silver and steel teddy tie pin, by Adie & Lovekin Ltd, Birmingham 1909, 3in (7.5cm) long.
£145–165 *BEX*

Abbatucci Cargo
On 7th May 1869, the steam packet *General Abbatucci* sank in a collision off the coast of Corsica. Fifty-four lives were lost but interest in the tragedy was further stimulated by the fact that the vessel, bound for Italy, was rumoured to be carrying several million French francs, destined for the coffers of the Vatican. In 1996 the wreck was excavated, and while the papal millions were not discovered, the cargo recovery team did rescue a considerable amount of jewellery, probably the stock of a jeweller travelling aboard ship. The principle value of the pieces illustrated here from the *Abbatucci* cargo lies in their provenance.

A silver chatelaine, with penknife, corkscrew, pencil and *aide memoire*, by Sampson Mordan, London, 1879–82, 15¼in (39cm) long.
£900–1,100 *AMH*

Cross Reference
Colour Review

A gold locket, from the *Abbatucci* cargo, c1869, 1½in (4cm) high.
£200–225 *RBA*

A gold ring, from the *Abbatucci* cargo, c1869.
£175–200 *RBA*

Caption
provides a brief description of the item including the maker's name, medium, date, measurements and in some instances condition.

Source Code
refers to the 'Key to Illustrations' on page 476 that details where the item was photographed.

Price Guide
price ranges are worked out by a team of trade and auction house experts, and are based on actual prices realised. Remember that Miller's is a PRICE GUIDE not a PRICE LIST and prices are affected by many variables such as location, condition, desirability and so on. Don't forget that if you are selling it is quite likely you will be offered less than the price range. Price ranges for items sold at auction tend to include the buyer's premium and VAT if applicable.

Information Box
covers relevant collecting information on factories, makers, care, restoration, fakes and alterations.

Further Reading
directs the reader towards additional sources of information.

Cross Reference
directs the reader to where other related items may be found.

ACKNOWLEDGEMENTS

We would like to acknowledge the great assistance given by our consultants who are listed below. We would also like to extend our thanks to all the auction houses, their press offices, dealers and collectors who have assisted us in the production of this book.

STEVE TOMLIN
Reclamation Services Ltd,
Cat Brain Quarry,
Painswick Beacon,
Gloucestershire GL6 6SJ
(Architectural Salvage)

POM HARRINGTON
100 Fulham Road,
London SW3 6HS
(Books)

ADRIAN HARRINGTON
64A Kensington Church Street,
London W8 4DB
(Books)

LEO HARRISON
Stand J20/21,
Gray's Mews Antiques Market,
1–7 Davies Street,
London W1Y 2LP
(Fishing Books)

JANET DAVIS
Dragonlee Collectables,
Maidstone,
Kent
Tel: 01622 729502
(Noritake Ceramics)

MICHEL BACH
The French Glasshouse,
P14/16 Antiquarius,
135 Kings Road,
London SW3 4PW
(Royal Copenhagen Ceramics)

POPPY COLLINSON
Fraser's Autograph Gallery,
399 The Strand,
London WC2R OLX
(Autographs)

JIM BULLOCK
Romsey Medal Centre,
5 Bell Street,
Romsey,
Hants SO51 8GY
(Military Medals)

A. HARRIS
Tel: 09561 46083/0181 905 3745
(Newspapers)

PAUL WANE
Tracks,
PO Box 117, Chorley,
Lancashire PR7 2QZ
(Rock & Pop)

KERRY TAYLOR
Sotheby's,
34–35 New Bond Street,
London WIA 2AA
Tel: 0171 293 5000
(Spice Girls)

PATRICK BOGUE
Onslow's Auction House,
The Old Depot, The Gas Works,
2 Michael Road,
London SW6 2AD
(Titanic Memorabilia)

DIANA APSIMON
Tel & Fax: 01235 812708
(Stevengraphs)

PAUL RAMSBOTTOM
Rambo's Tattoo Studio,
42 Shude Hill,
Manchester M4 1EY
(Tattooing Memorabilia)

GAVIN PAYNE
The Old Granary,
Battlesbridge Antique Centre,
Nr Wickford,
Essex SS11 7RF
(Telephones)

STEVEN PHILIPS
Identity, Portobello Green Market,
London W11
(Vivienne Westwood)

WAYNE MAXTED
The Computer & Games Exchange,
65 Notting Hill Gate Road,
London W11 3JS
(Computer & Video Games)

CONTENTS

INTRODUCTION

As the new millennium dawns, our passion for collecting seems to grow ever stronger. In this new edition of *Miller's Collectables Price Guide* we have sections dedicated to the 1950s, 1960s and 1970s, and for the first time, the 1980s, exposing demand for Margaret Thatcher mementos and other memorabilia from the decade of the 'Yuppie'. In Rock & Pop, we look at Spice Girls items; they will certainly be 'old Spice' by the 21st century, but will they also be collectable? In Toys we check out the market for vintage, computer and video games – are our children just wasting their youth zapping aliens or could they be playing on the collectables of the future?

The passage of time can transform the most mundane object into something sought after and surprisingly valuable. Our Architectural Salvage section looks at the expanding market for reclaimed bricks and roof tiles, and in a new feature on Newspapers, we explore the history of these everyday, ephemeral items, beginning with 17th-century Civil War journals and including such later rarities as the first *Daily Mail*. In Railwayana, we show two, apparently ordinary, Victorian train tickets: once used, these little pieces of pasteboard were literally rubbish and tended to be thrown away. As such very few early tickets appear on the market, and these particular examples fetched the astonishing sum of over £600 each at auction.

Rarity is one factor that makes an object collectable, another is condition. In Books we illustrate a first edition of *The Hound of the Baskervilles* by Arthur Conan Doyle. In poor condition this might be worth around £200, in a good condition, the value could shoot up by an extra £1,000. But this particular example is remarkable in that it still has its original dust jacket. Only two other copies with dust jackets are believed to exist, and this single volume sold for over £80,000, a result that even Sherlock Holmes, the great detective, could not have anticipated!

Pottery and porcelain are always among the favourite objects in *Miller's Collectables Price Guide*, and subjects covered this year include Burleigh Ware, Royal Copenhagen, Torquay Pottery and Noritake. We celebrate the centenary of Clarice Cliff's birth with a look at her colourful tableware and talk to two painters (now both in their eighties) from her original 1930s team, known as the 'Bizarre girls'.

Ceramics, glass and metalware have long been among the most common items in the home and have a very broad collecting base. Other subjects, however, are far more esoteric; tattooing is certainly one of the most unusual topics ever featured in a Miller's guide. The objects shown in this new section range from pictures of tattooed ladies to Victorian tattooing implements, celebrating a popular ancient craft that is once again the height of fashion.

Equally fashion conscious is our feature devoted to Vivienne Westwood, one of Britain's most famous and controversial designers. Vintage examples of her work are already being snapped up by collectors and ripped relics from the punk generation, can now be worth three- and four-figure sums. Other collectables illustrated this year range from the tragic (Titanic Memorabilia) to objects created purely for fun. We tell the story of the Smurfs and tune in to TV soap memorabilia, from *Dallas* autographs to *Coronation Street* mugs. We also chart our relationship with 'man's best friend', with a section on the collectable dog.

The earliest objects in this guide are small antiquities dating from centuries before Christ, and we end the Colour Review with Collectables of the Future. Every year we ask you to send in your suggestions for this page, and this year's winners are sisters and young collectors Anna and Karen Booth (aged 12 and 10), who scored a double whammy by nominating both Kinder Surprise eggs and the Spice Girls. Send us your ideas for next year's Collectables of the Future, and the winning entrant will receive a free copy of *Miller's Collectables Price Guide*.

Thank you for sharing your collecting passions with us, and if there are any other subjects you would like to see included in future guides please let us know. We look forward to collecting with you in the 21st century, and, as ever, happy hunting!

ADVERTISING & PACKAGING

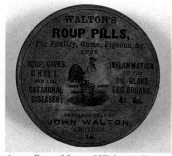

A cardboard box of Walton's Roup Pills, c1840, 2¼in (5.5cm) diam.
£20–25 *INC*

A Belleek Belgravia Dairy Company Ltd jug, First Period, c1858, 3¼in (8.5cm) high.
£260–300 *DeA*

r. An early Delft-style ointment pot, inscribed 'Poor Man's Friend, Price 1/1½', and 'Prepared only by Dr Roberts, Bridport', minor base chip, c1900, 1½in (4cm) high.
£250–300 *BBR*

This is only the second such example recorded.

An Ogden's Cigarettes mahogany cabinet, c1880, 30in (76cm) high.
£800–900 *GBr*

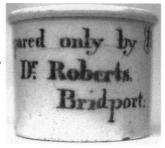

A Wm R. Adams earthenware microbe killer bottle, c1890, 12in (30.5cm) high.
£25–35 *WAB*

An enamel dairy jug, inscribed 'Use Llewellin's Victory Churn', some damage, early 20thC, 8in (20.5cm) high.
£65–75 *B&R*

A Mason's OK sauce advertising penknife, c1920, 2¾in (7cm) long.
£35–45 *WAB*

r. A box of Lux soap powder, unopened, 1920s, 4in (10cm) high.
£8–10 *MRW*

A wooden Natural Cherry Tipped Whiffs cigar box, 1920s, 8¼in (21cm) wide.
£28–32 *WEE*

A wooden Superfine Chocolate box, 1920–30, 16in (40.5cm) long.
£30–40 *WEE*

A wooden Cadbury's Chocolate box, late 1920s, 12in (30.5cm) long.
£30–40 *BBR*

A mirror in the form of a tennis racket, advertising Pinguin, c1930, 14½in (37cm) high.
£80–100 *MLa*

A cardboard box of CWS Wheatsheaf Night Lights, complete with contents, 1930s, 6¼in (16cm) long.
£5–6 *HUX*

A Viyella knitting yarn cardboard box, complete with wool, c1935, 3¾in (9.5cm) wide.
£4–6 *HUX*

A cast iron bench, inscribed 'Butlin's, For your comfort, No charge', restored, 1940s, 72in (183cm) long.
£120–150 *JUN*

A collection of advertising bowls measures, 1940s, 2in (5cm) wide.
£12–15 each *CHU*

A container of Mirro bathroom cleaner, unused, 1950s, 9in (23cm) high.
£10–12 *HUX*

A collection of 6 Robertson's Golly figures, including lollipop lady, traffic warden, soldier, astronaut, pilot and sailor, 1960s, 3in (7.5cm) high.
£60–70 *BBR*

r. A Belfast Sparkling Water neon advertising clock, 1940s, 12in (30.5cm) high.
£400–500 *EKK*

Brooke Bond

Brooke Bond was founded by Arthur Brooke, who opened his first shop in Manchester in 1869, selling tea, coffee and sugar. He added 'Bond' to the company name simply because it sounded good.

Once the preserve of the upper-classes, tea was becoming an increasingly popular and affordable drink in the second half of the 19th century. The firm prospered and was soon supplying grocers across Britain. Arthur Brooke died in 1918, but Brooke Bond continued unabated, and in 1930 PG Tips was launched, its most famous brand. 'PG' came from the Latin *pre geste*, meaning to aid digestion, while 'Tips' referred to the fact that only the top and most tender parts of the tea plant are used in the blend.

Some 70 years on, PG Tips is still Britain's number one brew, with advertising playing a huge part in this success. The famous PG Tips chimps first appeared on British television in 1956, the brainwave of a copywriter who had seen a chimps' tea party at a local zoo. Today, these commercials are the longest running advertising campaign in British TV history. Many famous personalities, including Cilla Black, Peter Sellers, Donald Sinden and Kenneth Williams, have supplied the voice-overs, and the 'Mr Shifter' advertisement, in which the chimps remove the piano, has been shown over 2,000 times.

Over the years Brooke Bond has produced trade cards and a wide range of promotional material, which now attracts a growing number of collectors.

A Brooke Bond cut-out booklet, for the Bird Portrait series of cards, one of 4 in series, 1957, 4¾in (12cm) wide.
£30–40 *FMu*

A Brooke Bond PG Tips 400-piece wooden jigsaw puzzle, depicting the chimp family, late 1950s/early 1960s, 18in (46cm) wide.
£25–30 *FMu*

The chimps for this advertising campaign were trained by animal trainer Molly Baden.

A selection of Brooke Bond pin badges, late 1960–70s.
£3–8 each *FMu*

A Brooke Bond 'D' ironstone china cup and saucer, by Sampson & Bridgewood, early 1970s, 3in (7.5cm) high.
£15–20 *FMu*

A selection of Brooke Bond quarter pound tea packets, with advertising cards, 1972–77.
£10–15 *FMu*

A collection of Brooke Bond Olympic Greats tea cards, set of 40, 1979.
£8–10 *LCC*

A set of Brooke Bond Pyramid Power tea cards, set of 45, 1996.
£4–5 *LCC*

r. A set of 3 Brooke Bond Chimp dolls, 1982, 13¾in (35cm) high.
£20–25 each *FMu*

Coca-Cola

The famous Coca-Cola formula was invented in 1886 by Dr John Pemberton, an Atlanta pharmacist. The brown syrup, mixed with still water, was first sold as a 'temperance drink' and a patent medicine that would 'cure all nervous affectations'. By accident, a patient was given a dose mixed with carbonated water. The taste was dramatically improved, and by the 1890s Coca-Cola was being promoted as a fun and refreshing soft drink.

Vast amounts of advertising material have been produced over the years. The red-and-white logo is famous worldwide as is the distinctive bottle, first trademarked in 1960. Coca-Cola items attract legions of collectors and there is even a Coca-Cola museum in Elizabeth Town, Kentucky, USA. Rare pieces can fetch high prices, but buyer beware – many vintage items have been reproduced, in particular tin trays.

A Tiffany gold-plated 'fantasy' brass belt buckle, advertising Coca-Cola, Atlanta, USA, marked Tiffany foundry, 1970–80s,
£160–190 *PC*

A Coca-Cola tin tray, worn condition, c1900, 6in (15cm) wide.
£14–16 *JoC*

r. Two Coca-Cola tin trays, 1937 and 1938, 12in (30.5cm) high.
£180–220 each *SMAM*

A Coca-Cola freestanding metal sign, 1950s, 24in (61cm) high.
£60–85 *COB*

Display Figures

A plaster rabbit, walking, holding a pipe, the orange-suited animal with green bow and black boots, on a circular base, c1910, 11¼in (28.5cm) high.
£60–80 *P(B)*

A Japanese plastic window display figure, 1962, 8in (20.5cm) high.
£30–35 *DAC*

An American Sy Rocco waiter display figure, 1920s, 8in (20.5cm) high.
£125–135 *Bar*

A plaster duck, with spotted hat and flower-trimmed bib, 1990s, 13in (33cm) high.
£25–30 *PC*

Enamel Signs

An Evans' Pastilles enamel advertising sign, c1905, 11 x 24in (28 x 61cm).
£80–90 *JUN*

A Quaker Oats enamel advertising sign, c1910, 34 x 24in (86.5 x 61cm).
£150–200 *JUN*

A Wills's Flag cigarettes enamel advertising sign, c1920, 36 x 24in (91.5 x 61cm).
£150–180 *JUN*

l. A Macdonald's tobacco enamel advertising sign, gilt, black and colours on white, gilt border, 1920–30s, 30 x 22in (76 x 56cm).
£550–650 *P(C)*

A Leventhall's Pure Dairy Butter enamel advertising sign, c1920, 15 x 29in (38 x 74cm).
£175–200 *B&R*

A Black Cat cigarettes enamel advertising sign, the top half showing the head of a black cat with black and yellow eyes, with an open packet of cigarettes beneath, white and yellow ground, 1930s, 35¾ x 24in (91 x 61cm).
£120–150 *P(C)*

r. A KB radio double-sided enamel advertising sign, c1930, 20 x 13in (51 x 33cm).
£70–90 *JUN*

A double-sided enamel advertising sign, inscribed 'A British Co', 1920–30s, 3 x 21in (7.5 x 53.5cm).
£15–25 *COB*

Posters & Display Cards

A Colman's Mustard poster, c1860–80, 25 x 20in (63.5 x 51cm).
£180–220 *INC*

A cardboard advertising shop display sign for McMichael Twin Supervox radio, c1934, 20 x 39in (52 x 99cm).
£50–100 *OTA*

A J. & G. Campbell Ltd Dublin Whiskey enamel advertising sign, c1870–80, 24 x 30in (61 x 76cm).
£250–300 *HON*

A Wardonia cardboard advertising sign, 1930s, 23 x 16in (58.5 x 40.5cm).
£40–50 *JUN*

A Thomas Bradford & Co cloth-backed advertising sign, 1880s, 33 x 27in (83.5 x 68.5cm).
£350–400 *JUN*

A Burdall's multi-coloured show card, featuring 3 of their products, 1930–40s, 12 x 9½in (30.5 x 24cm).
£40–50 *BBR*

A Hornby Trains shop display sign, 1920s, 19 x 5¾in (50 x 14.5cm).
£120–140 *RAR*

l. A cardboard advertising sign for Scientific Palmistry, 1930s, 10¾ x 18in (27.5 x 45.5cm).
£12–15 *SAF*

A Hornby shop display card, 1930s, 8½ x 6in (21.5 x 15cm).
£60–80 *RAR*

A Robin Starch show card,
1930s, 15in (38cm) wide.
£30–40 *MRW*

An ARP cardboard poster,
inscribed 'Serve to Save', 1938,
15 x 10in (38 x 25.5cm).
£45–55 *PC*

An Ovaltine Chuckles
cardboard shop display sign,
1940s, 12in (30.5cm) high.
£25–35 *HUX*

A Hornby Speed Boats shop
display poster, 1934,
17 x 13in (43 x 33cm).
£200–220 *RAR*

A cardboard poster,
advertising the Royal Marines
Searchlight Tattoo, 1938,
10 x 7in (25.5 x 18cm).
£10–15 *COB*

A Nestlé's cardboard
shop display sign, 1950s,
8in (20.5cm) wide.
£8–10 *HUX*

A Jay Vinegar cardboard
display poster, 1930s,
11 x 17in (28 x 43cm).
£15–25 *COB*

A Max Factor cardboard
shop display sign, 1940s,
11½in (29cm) high.
£5–7 *MRW*

A Ceresan cardboard
shop display sign, 1950s,
15in (38cm) high.
£4–6 *MRW*

r. A Tri-ang illuminated shop
sign, c1955, 15in (38cm) wide.
£275–325 *JUN*

Soap & Talcum Powder

A cardboard container of Fuller's Earth, 1880–90, 2¼in (5.5cm) high.
£60–80 *INC*

A bar of Little Peter soap, 1920s, 7¾in (20cm) wide.
£40–45 *HUX*

A box of Hudson's soap extract, unopened, 1920s, 8½in (21.5cm) high.
£6–10 *MRW*

A tin of Boots Sun-Tan Talcum Powder, 1930s, 5½in (14cm) high.
£14–16 *HUX*

In the 1920s and '30s, and through the influence of designers such as Coco Chanel and Jean Patou, a bronzed skin became fashionable. Women were wearing less restrictive clothes and leading a more active lifestyle. Patou, who introduced the shorter tennis skirt at Wimbledon and fashionable sportswear, was among the first to manufacture suntan lotion, and other producers soon followed suit. The attraction of this orange suntan powder tin lies in the way it captures the vogue of the period.

A tin of Helex Healing Powder, 1920s, 2in (5cm) high.
£20–25 *INC*

A tin of Vinolia Violet Powder, c1920, 4¾in (12cm) high.
£12–15 *HUX*

A tin of My Secret Talcum Powder, by E. Mella, Lesound Pivert, 1920s, 7½in (19cm) high.
£25–30 *HUX*

A pack of Morny Shaving Soap, 1930s, 4¼in (11cm) square.
£12–15 *PC*

A bar of Energol Trim soap, Italian, 1970s, 2in (5cm) wide.
25–50p *TRE*

l. A packet of Bibby Best Soap, 1930s, 6in (15cm) wide.
£12–15 *HUX*

Tins

l. A Huntley & Palmers Court biscuit tin, c1870, 8¼in (21cm) wide.
£180–200 *WAB*

A Huntley & Palmers biscuit tin, entitled 'Wagon', 1870s, 7¼in (18.5cm) wide.
£150–200 *WAB*

This tin is inscribed on its base 'received the Grand Prize from the 1878 Paris Exhibition'. Huntley & Palmers won this award for their products and recorded it on their tins. This provides a helpful clue for dating. A tin bearing this inscription must have been produced in or after 1878, but before any other major shows (for example the Paris Exhibition of 1890) at which the firm also won prizes.

A Victory V tin, in the form of a chest of drawers, c1900, 10in (25.5cm) high.
£145–165 *AnS*

A McVitie & Price oatcakes tin, depicting people who have been awarded the Victoria Cross, c1890, 5½in (14cm) high.
£180–200 *WAB*

A Champion's Mustard tin, depicting Little Red Riding Hood, c1890, 6in (15cm) wide.
£45–65 *WAB*

A McVitie & Price oatcakes tin, depicting nursery rhymes, c1890, 5in (12.5cm) high.
£130–150 *WAB*

A tin of glove powder, c1890, 4½in (11.5cm) high.
£30–40 *INC*

This powder was used for puffing into gloves to prevent sticking.

l. A MacFarlane Lang biscuit tin, in the form of a chest of drawers, c1900, 7in (18cm) high.
£120–150 *WAB*

A Farrow & Co mustard tin, depicting children, Boston, USA, c1900, 3¼in (8.5cm) high.
£90–100 *WAB*

A Huntley & Palmers boulle-pattern tin, c1903, 7in (18cm) wide.
£85–100 *WAB*

A MacFarlane Lang biscuit tin, in the form of a nest of eggs, c1908, 5¼in (13.5cm) diam.
£350–400 *WAB*

A Turnwright's toffee tin, in the form of a fire bucket, worn condition, c1910, 11in (28cm) high.
£15–20 *CPA*

A Huntley & Palmers biscuit tin, in the form of an artist's palette, c1910, 9½in (24cm) long.
£170–190 *WAB*

A Huntley & Palmers biscuit tin, with 'embroidery' pattern, c1911, 8½in (21.5cm) wide.
£150–200 *WAB*

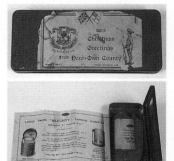

A combination candlebox tin, 1914–18, 6½in (16.5cm) long.
£65–85 *WAB*

These tins were presented to the Huntingdon regiments in WWI.

A Huntley & Palmers biscuit tin, in the form of a shell, c1914, 8in (20.5cm) wide.
£175–200 *WAB*

A Huntley & Palmers biscuit tin, in the form of a pencil case, c1912, 8in (20.5cm) long.
£100–130 *WAB*

A tin of Matabele Mixture tobacco, by The Tobacco Company of Rhodesia and South Africa Ltd, c1920, 5¼in (13.5cm) wide.
£80–90 *WAB*

Two Lyons tea tins, 1920s, 5½in (14cm) high.
l. **£25–35**
r. **£55–75** *WAB*

Two of a set of four tins, the full set included a box with a mirror, one with a calendar, another with a thermometer, and the rarest tin with an egg-timer.

A tin of Health Salts, 1920s, 3½in (9cm) high.
£20–25 *INC*

A Mackintosh's toffee tin, in
the form of a casket, c1920,
15½in (39.5cm) wide.
£20–25 *UTP*

A Cremona Nursery
Toffee tin, decorated
with various nursery
rhyme characters, 1920s,
8½in (21.5cm) wide.
£20–30 *MRW*

A Sharp's Super-Kreem
toffee tin, in the form
of a drum, 1920s,
4in (10cm) high.
£20–25 *INC*

A Hignett's Pilot Flake tobacco tin,
c1920, 5½in (14cm) wide.
£30–40 *WAB*

l. A Nut Joy
toffee tin,
1920s, 5in
(13cm) high.
£25–30 *INC*

r. A Star
gramophone
needles tin,
c1920, 1¾in
(4.5cm) wide.
£10–20 *WAB*

A Fry's Malted Milk
Cocoa tin, in the form
of a pencil sharpener,
1920s, 1in (2.5cm) high.
£20–25 *INC*

r. A Hawley's Milk
Sugar tin, c1930,
5in (13cm) high.
£8–10 *UTP*

A Cadbury's Dairy Milk
Chocolate tin, in the form
of a milk churn, 1920s,
5½in (14cm) high.
£50–60 *CHe*

A set of London N.W. Railways tins, in the form of luggage, one large and one small trunk, a money box and a suitcase, 1920s, large trunk 6in (15cm) wide.
£25–30 each   *INC*

A William Crawford & Sons Ltd biscuit tin, in the form of scales, 1930s, 8in (20.5cm) wide.
£225–250   *WAB*

A Cachous tin, containing Dubarry perfume, made by Needler's of Hull, c1935, 1¼in (3cm) diam.
£20–25   *INC*

l. A MacFarlane Lang biscuit tin, 1940–50, 8in (20.5cm) wide.
£15–20   *PPe*

A Huntley & Palmers biscuit tin, in the form of the FA cup, 1933, 9in (23cm) high.
£260–280   *WAB*

In 1933, Reading was the hot favourite to win the FA cup, and anticipating their victory Huntley & Palmers modelled this biscuit tin. In the event, Reading were knocked out in the semi-final so this tin never went into full production and only a small number were manufactured, hence its value. There is also a larger edition, of which only 16 were made for presentation to the Directors of Reading Football Club.

An Oxo cubes tin, 1940s, 7in (18cm) wide.
£25–30   *WEE*

FURTHER READING
Robert Opie, *Miller's Advertising Tins: Collector's Guide*, Miller's Publications, 1999

A McVitie & Price biscuit tin, decorated with scenes from Beatrix Potter books, c1938–9, 5½in (14cm) high.
£40–50   *WAB*

A Blue Bird Chocolate Toffee tin, in the form of a chest, c1940, 8½in (21.5m) wide.
£10–12   *UTP*

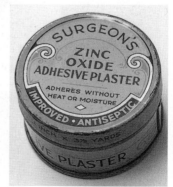

A Surgeon's Zinc Oxide Adhesive Plaster tin, 1940s, 2in (5cm) diam.
£4–5   *FAM*

A Meggezones Throat
Lozenges tin, 1950s,
3in (7.5cm) wide.
£1–2 *MRW*

A Sharp's Toffee tin, 1950s,
8½in (21.5cm) wide.
£10–12 *WEE*

A Marks & Spencer's
Liquorice Allsorts tin, 1990s,
7in (18cm) wide.
50–75p *TRE*

Toothpaste

A Cherry Toothpaste pot lid,
depicting a youthful figure,
c1900, 2¾in (7cm) diam.
£220–250 *SAS*

*The value of pot lids
depends on the rarity
and the visual appeal
of the images. Good
pictorial examples will
command higher prices
than more simple,
inscribed lids.*

A Stone & Son Cherry Tooth Paste
pot lid, c1910, 3in (7.5cm) diam.
£90–100 *BBR*

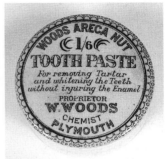

A Woods Areca Nut Tooth Paste
pot lid, c1900, 3in (7.5cm) diam.
£22–26 *HUX*

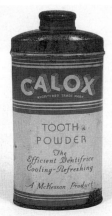

A Calox Tooth Powder
container, 1930s,
4½in (11.5cm) high.
£6–8 *HUX*

A tube of Beauty
Dental Cream,
inscribed 'The Queen
of Tooth Pastes',
1920s, 4in (10cm) long.
£3–4 *HUX*

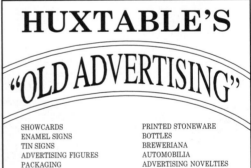

AERONAUTICA

A bronze Hassall aviator mascot, with propeller and ceramic movable head, mounted on a brass cap display base, c1910, 4¾in (12cm) high.
£500–600 *S*

A Brooklands Flying Club member's badge, No. 34, enamelled in red and black, by H. A. Shelley & Co, mounted on a marble display base, 1930s, 4¼in (11cm) high.
£700–800 *S*

A WWII B-type leather flying helmet, by Stag, Australia, c1940.
£100–120 *PC*

A French bronze aviation trophy, depicting man escaping from gravity climbing onto Pegasus, by P. Moreau Veuthier, c1912, 9in (23cm) high.
£2,750–3,000 *PC*

A pair of RAF suede flying boots, with sheepskin linings, 1941.
£100–120 *FAM*

A Longton bone china dish, depicting an RAF Supermarine Spitfire, inscribed 'Never in the field of human conflict was so much owed by so many to so few, Winston Churchill', 1945, 6in (15cm) wide.
£90–100 *BRT*

r. A fibreglass Boeing 747 advertising display model, finished in Aer Lingus livery, 1980s, 74in (188cm) long.
£500–600 *JUN*

Fragments from a Zeppelin, mounted on a mahogany base, with inscription 'Potters Bar, October 1, 1916', 10in (25.5cm) wide.
£100–110 *NC*

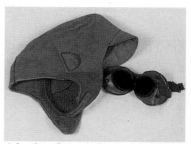

A leather flying helmet and a pair of goggles, 1930s, 7½in (19cm) wide.
£65–85 *WAB*

An RAF wooden exhibition model of a Nimrod plane, late 1950s, mounted on a stainless steel tripod stand, 43½in (110.5cm) high.
£250–300 *COB*

AMUSEMENT & VENDING MACHINES

A Licensed Victuallers Shooting Range, by Haydon Urry Ltd, London, 1900, 21in (53.5cm) high. **£1,800–2,200** *HAK*

A World's Fair Jigsaws pinball machine, 1933, 40in (101.5cm) long. **£400–450** *SAF*

A Jennings 'The Governor' one-armed bandit, with Tic-Tac-Toe reels, 1930s, 15in (38cm) wide. **£300–350** *SAF*

A Mutoscope 'What the Butler Saw' amusement machine, finished in red and blue, with reel of still photographs entitled 'Naughty but Nice', on a metal stand, American, c1900, 74in (188cm) high. **£1,000–1,200** *P(Ba)*

A Mutoscope 'What the Butler Missed' penny-operated, motion picture viewer, American, 1930, 74in (188cm) high. **£1,500–2,000** *HAK*

A C. H. Ahrens patent 'Test Your Strength' machine, with leather punch ball suspended by a chain from a canopy with stained oak column supports, on kidney-shaped cast iron base, 1910, dial 10in (25.5cm) diam. **£1,500–2,000** *P(Ba)*

A British Automatic 'Pussy' shooter coin-operated machine, in painted Art Deco-style case, on cast iron legs, 1926, 60in (152.5cm) high. **£800–1,000** *P(Ba)*

A mechanical pinball
machine, 1930s,
44in (112cm) long.
£350–400 *PING*
*This machine is
unusual in that it has
mechanical counters.*

r. A Groetchen 'Twenty-
One' blackjack counter
game, American, 1934,
12in (30.5cm) high.
£250–300 *TUO*

An Ajax hot nut
vending machine,
American, c1930,
22in (56cm) high.
£200–240 *JUN*

An Archer electrical
pinball machine, 1930s,
38in (96.5cm) long.
£130–150 *PING*
*The backglass on this
machine is in poor
condition. In good
condition and in
working order its value
would be much higher.*

A Slick arcade
machine, 1930s,
28in (71cm) high.
£350–400 *JUN*

An Allwin de Luxe
slot machine, c1930,
27in (68.5cm) high.
£500–600 *SAF*

A Mills Official
counter-top pinball
machine, 1932,
21½in (54.5cm) long.
£275–300 *PING*
*The market for 1930s
machines is select.
Many people buy
amusement games for
nostalgic reasons and
because they played
on them in their youth,
hence the current
popularity of examples
from the 1950s to the
1970s. Pre-WWII
games are in less
demand than later
models, but they are
rare and can
be worth a lot to
specialist collectors.
Amusement machines
should always be
played with their
original currency or
tokens. Using the
wrong coins can
damage the mechanism.*

A Mills silver one-
armed bandit slot
machine, 1940s,
27½in (70cm) high.
£220–250 *SAF*

A Jennings 'Standard Chief' 50 cent slot machine, 1946, 28in (71cm) high.
£900–1,250 *TUO*

A Hawtins All-Win slot machine, c1950, 27in (68.5cm) high.
£400–450 *SAF*

A Playball slot machine, c1955, 31½in (80cm) high.
£350–400 *SAF*

An Orion one-armed bandit, in working order, no keys, German, 1950s, 28in (71cm) high.
£300–350 *SAF*

r. A Bryans 'Tick-Tock' amusement machine, c1960, 30in (76cm) high.
£550–650 *PING*

Bryans machines were sturdy and much loved by collectors. The company ceased trading in the 1970s when they were still making the same games of 25 years earlier!

A Bergmann Jupiter space theme wall machine, with revolving planets, German, 1950s, 38in (96.5cm) high.
£60–80 *SAF*

Cross Reference
Colour Review

A Bryans 'Big Hand on the Red' amusement machine, late 1950s, 23½in (60cm) high.
£500–600 *PING*

A Rotamint amusement machine, German, 1960s, 28in (71cm) high.
£150–200 *PING*

Condition is crucial to the value of amusement machines. A fine example in full working order can be worth at least twice as much as a non-working or poor quality game. This Rotamint in good condition demonstrates the point. In non-working order its value is £75.

A Playball amusement machine, 1960s, 34½in (87.5cm) high.
£450–500 *PING*

A Beromat wall machine, with embossed bells, 1960s, 28½in (72.5cm) high.
£150–200 *SAF*

A change machine for obtaining 10p pieces, c1967, 78in (198cm) high.
£15–25 *SAF*

l. A Roulamint roulette machine, German, 1960s, 28in (71cm) high.
£250–300 *PING*

An Aristocrat Arcadian one-armed bandit, Australian, 1960s, 28½in (72.5cm) high.
£400–500 *PING*

A red gum ball vending machine, 1960s, 16in (40.5cm) high.
£10–15 *SAF*

A Carousel seven-cup wall machine, c1965, 31½in (80cm) high.
£450–500 *SAF*

A Jennings 'Governor' one-armed bandit, 1975, 28in (71cm) high.
£700–800 *JUN*

A Clement & Whales Rondo counter-top betting machine, with spinning disc, c1972, 32in (81.5cm) high.
£80–100 *SAF*

An Allwin Jackpot slot machine, 1970s, 32in (81.5cm) high.
£400–450 *SAF*

ANTIQUITIES

Interest in collecting small antiquities has developed along with the hobby of metal detecting. Metal detectorists are responsible for a considerable number of archaeological finds in Britain, including some of the examples shown here, and increasingly clubs and associations are working together with museums, reporting their findings and sharing their knowledge.

With a metal detector, a bit of experience and a lot of luck, you can build your own collection of small antiquities, but rules and regulations must be strictly followed: do not trespass, and always obtain permission before searching a site. Finders are not necessarily keepers. According to the 1996 Treasure Act coins and objects containing silver or gold over 300 years old are categorized as treasure and must be reported to the local coroner and assessed by an expert. Failure to comply with the rules, could result in a £5,000 fine or three months imprisonment, so watch out! Museums have the right to buy treasure without any commercial competition – items are valued by an official committee – and a reward is paid to the finder.

Would-be metal detectorists should obtain a copy of the 1996 Treasure Act, available free, from the Department of National Heritage, 2–4 Cockspur Street, London SW1Y 5DH. In addition to the many local clubs, there is the National Council for Metal Detecting and two specialist magazines – *The Searcher* and *Treasure Hunting*.

Bronze & Metalware

l. A Luristan bronze boar's head whetstone handle, intact, c1000 BC, 2½in (6.5cm) long.
£200–300 *HEL*

r. An archaic bronze recumbent lion, tail missing, mounted on a wooden plinth with velvet base, excellent condition, 6th century BC, 1½in (4cm) long.
£125–150 *ANG*

A Roman bronze patera handle, with ram's head, 1st century AD, 4¼in (11cm) long.
£500–600 *HEL*

A Byzantine silver buckle, decorated, 7th century AD, 3in (7.5cm) long.
£550–625 *RuC*

A Persian short sword, with flat splayed pommel, flanged hilt and tapering blade, excellent condition, Western Iran, c1000 BC, 15½in (39.5cm) long.
£250–300 *ANG*

l. A zoomorphic bronze sword belt hook, in the form of a serpent, 12th century AD, 1½in (4cm) long. **£20–25** *ANG*

A bronze dagger quillon, excellent condition, 13th/14th century AD, found in Cambridgeshire, 2¼in (6cm) long. **£25–30** *ANG*

A Romanesque bronze belt mount, in the form of a Norman shield, with shaped top, openwork heart terminating in a florid lover's knot with scrolled ends, complete with 4 rivets, found in Cambridgeshire, 12th century AD, 2in (5cm) long. **£25–30** *ANG*

l. A bronze folding balance, excellent condition, 14th/15th century AD, found in Wiltshire, 4in (10cm) wide, when closed. **£85–95** *ANG*

A bronze sword or dagger pommel, scent stopper type, decorated with flutes, late 15th century AD, found in Dorset, ¾in (2cm) diam. **£30–35** *ANG*

A pilgrim's lead ampulla, complete with both handles, found in East Anglia, 14th century AD, 2in (5cm) high. **£25–30** *ANG*

Flint

l. A Swedish Neolithic flint dagger, 2000 BC, 4½in (11.5cm) high. **£200–250** *HEL*

Glass

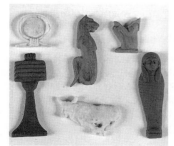

A Mediterranean sand core glass bottle, possibly for oil or perfume, 3rd/2nd century BC, 3¾in (9.5cm) long. **£700–800** *PARS*

This glass vessel was produced by the core technique, which preceded blown glass introduced by the Syrians c100BC. An inner core of mud and straw was coated with molten glass. The surface was then decorated with trails of coloured glass (here black, red and white) and combed with a metal tool to make a festoon pattern. Once the glass had cooled, the inner core was scraped out.

Six Egyptian opaque coloured glass amulets or inlays, *shabti* figure and *djed* pillar in red, figure of Maat and a lion-headed serpent in turquoise, trussed ox and a figure of Shen in white, Ptolemaic, circa 300 BC, tallest 2in (5cm) high. **£600–700** *FW&C*

A Roman square glass flask, with horizontally folded rim and strap handle, 2nd–3rd century AD, 5½in (14cm) high. **£320–360** *FW&C*

A Roman green blown-glass vase, with trailed decoration, Eastern Mediterranean, 4th–5th century AD, 5in (13cm) high.
£1,300–1,500 *PARS*

This vase is pale green in tone, and free-blown with a spiral thread looped around the body.

A Roman glass bottle/vase, with trailed decoration around the top, 7th century AD, 6in (15cm) high.
£175–275 *PARS*

A Roman glass candlestick, from Syria or Jordan, late 2nd–early 3rd century AD, 7in (18cm) high.
£220–250 *PARS*

A Roman green blown glass jug, with handle, from Syria or Jordan, 3rd–5th century AD, 4in (10cm) high.
£180–200 *PARS*

A Roman glass two-handled bottle, Eastern Mediterannean, 4th–5th century AD, 9in (23cm) long.
£800–1,000 *PARS*

This amphora with looped handles is in perfect condition, hence its value.

Jewellery

An Egyptian gold ring, with steatite scarab bezel, intact, 1000–800 BC.
£800–1,000 *HEL*

Steatite is a form of greenish-grey soapstone.

A Greek silver coin, depicting Larissa, 5th century BC, intact, in modern setting as a pendant, ¾in (2cm) diam.
£250–300 *HEL*

A string of Roman and Byzantine agate beads, 1st–8th century AD, 20in (51cm) long.
£160–180 *PARS*

l. A Roman Imperial ruby intaglio, 1st century BC/AD, set in a modern gold ring, .
£2,000–2,500 *HEL*

Sculptures & Figures

A western Asian pottery figure of Astarte, good condition, circa 2000 BC, 7½in (19cm) high.
£150–180 *HEL*

Astarte was the goddess of fertility and reproduction and was also believed to be a moon goddess.

A Mesopotamian stone foundation cone fragment, inscribed in the Cuneiform script for King Gudea of Lagash, circa 2200 BC, 2¾in (7cm) high.
£65–75 *ANG*

An Iron Age Cypriot figure, arm sections and part of lower section missing, 10th–8th century BC, 5½in (14cm) high.
£500–600 *HEL*

An Iron Age Cypriot limestone head of Apollo, 10th–8th century BC, complete, 3½in (9cm) high.
£700–750 *HEL*

A Greek marble head, 5th–4th century BC, 7in (18cm) high.
£1,500–2,000 *HEL*

An Ancient Egyptian part green-glazed *ushabti*, holding a crook and flail, with 6 lines of hieroglyphics, 800–600 BC, 5¾in (14.5cm) high.
£320–350 *Mit*

An Egyptian faïence *ushabti* figure, 800–600 BC, 4½in (11.5cm) high.
£150–200 *HEL*

Ushabti *figures are small statuettes that were left in the tombs of mummies.*

An Etruscan bronze flat-backed figure of a draped priest, wearing a radiate headdress, holding a patera in his left hand, right arm missing, mounted on a wooden block, 3rd century BC, 3¾in (9.5cm) high.
£550–600 *ANG*

This figure originated from the estate of collector Ronald Bullock. An old label on the back reads 'Etruscan, late 4th century BC, excellent'. Many antiquities that appear on the market originally came from 18th or 19th century collections and a good provenance can enhance the value of an item. Old labels should not be removed.

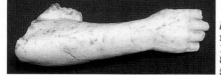

l. A Roman marble arm, reputedly from Pompeii, 1st–2nd century AD, 8½in (21.5cm) long.
£180–220 *HEL*

Vases & Pottery

A Chinese Neolithic jar, circa 3000 BC, excavated in Gansu Province, 4¾in (12cm) high.
£500–550 *INC*

A late Neolithic pale buff coloured 'grooved ware' pottery urn, of waisted form with flat base, decorated with incised lines, old label on base inscribed 'H. Rook's Collection', circa 2000 BC, 4½in (11.5cm) high.
£800–1,000 *FW&C*

Grooved ware (Rinyo-Clacton ware) is found throughout Britain.

A Cypro-Mycenean amphora, decorated with octopus and rodents, restored, circa 1000 BC, 16½in (42cm) high.
£2,500–3,000 *HEL*

An Iron Age Cypriot bichrome redware cup, decorated with a single black ring at the outer rim and concentric black rings on the inner, circa 800 BC, 3½in (8.5cm) diam.
£40–45 *ANG*

A Greek black-glazed dish with foot, southern Italy, 4th century BC, 3½in (9cm) diam.
£65–75 *RuC*

A Roman buff coloured jug, 1st–2nd century AD, 9in (23cm) high.
£135–160 *RuC*

l. A Roman terracotta oil lamp, in the form of a legionnaire's sandalled foot, with relief lion mask spout to the rear of the heel below a circular pierced top with central raised facial mask decoration, label to base reads 'Found Under the Church of St Pierre at Sorrento', 5¼in (13.5cm) long.
£600–700 *Mit*

An Etruscan painted pottery skyphos, good condition, 5th century BC, 4¼in (11cm) high.
£350–400 *HEL*

Three Greek miniature votive vessels, 5th century BC, tallest 2½in (6.5cm) high.
£50–100 each *HEL*

A Greek black-glazed pyxis with lid, 5th–4th century BC, 3in (7.5cm) high.
£60–80 *HEL*

A Greek black-glazed pottery feeder flask, 4th century BC, 3in (7.5cm) high.
£50–60 *HEL*

ARCHITECTURAL SALVAGE

In the 1950s and '60s the fashion was to strip homes of their 'old-fashioned' features. Fireplaces were replaced with radiators, and moulded decorations and panelled doors were ripped out in favour of flush, dust-free surfaces and a smooth contemporary look. In the 1990s trends have reversed and owners are busy trying to put back all the period details.

Architectural reclamation is now a huge and highly sophisticated industry, very different from the traditional image of the *Steptoe & Son* scrapyard. There are some 1,500 well-established salvage yards in the UK, and the business has its own trade association, SALVO, which ensures codes of practice. Clients range from major companies (breweries, hotel chains, leisure and health centres) to private individuals looking to improve their homes. The plethora of TV programmes, books and magazines on interior decoration has stimulated interest in architectural antiques and an awareness of their value. 'People used to think of reclamation items

as a cheap alternative to buying new,' says Steve Tomlin of Reclamation Services Ltd in Painswick. 'Today it is not necessarily cheaper, and what people are looking for is quality and character and also objects that still function.' While some pieces are recycled for purely decorative purposes (chimney pots used as flower planters for example), others (bathroom fittings, door furniture, etc) are expected to work as originally intended. Tomlin points out that salvage companies will now structurally test ancient beams and claims that one of the most significant growth areas is in demand for vintage flooring.

Knowledge is steadily increasing, both in terms of practical restoration and historical research. Many museums house displays of architectural antiques, and the University of Greenwich is home to the Brooking Collection of Architectural Detail, covering everything from windows and doors to fanlights, fire grates and staircase mouldings and provides a fascinating and unique archive of period interior decoration.

A Victorian clay chimney pot,
16in (41cm) high.
£35–40 *ACA*

A limestone garden urn, mid-19thC,
14in (35.5cm) high.
£500–550 *Riv*

A pair of wrought iron gates, c1950,
34in (86.5cm) high.
£75–85 *AL*

MUSEUM

Brooking Collection of Architectural Detail, The University of Greenwich, Oakfield Lane, Dartford, Kent, DA1 2SZ, Tel: 0181 331 9897 – Open to visitors by appointment.

l. A set of 20 turned pine balusters, 1880s, 25in (63.5cm) high.
£50–70 *DOR*

r. A set of 27 barley-twist balusters, c1850, 35in (88cm) high.
£140–160 *DOR*

A selection of textured opaque glass paving bricks, c1940–50,
5¾in (14.5cm) square.
£1–2 each *RECL*

Bathroom Fittings

A pair of copper taps, late
19thC, 6in (15cm) high.
£55–65 *LIB*

A pair of bib taps, early 20thC,
14in (35.5cm) high.
£95–110 *WRe*

r. A pair of brass taps, c1930,
6in (15cm) high.
£30–40 *HEM*

A pair of nickel-plated globe bath
taps, c1910, 6in (15cm) high.
£60–100 *WRe*

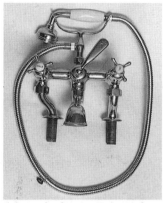

A brass bath mixer tap, early
20thC, 10in (25.5cm) high.
£165–200 *WRe*

A tin bath, c1920, 72in (183cm) long.
£50–60 *AL*

A pair of nickel-plated
butterfly-style bath taps,
c1910, 9in (23cm) high.
£100–150 *WRe*

A brass mixer tap, c1920–30,
10in (25.5cm) high
£175–200 *DRU*

A brass and copper three-rail
towel rail, early 20thC,
37in (94cm) high.
£150–200 *WRe*

Door Bells

A brass bell-push, c1910,
3in (7.5cm) wide.
£20–30 *HEM*

A brass bell-push, c1890,
2½in (6.5cm) diam.
£20–25 *HEM*

A brass bell-push, 1980s,
3in (7.5cm) high.
£55–65 *HEM*

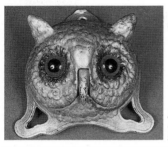

r. A copper bell-push,
c1920, 5½in (14cm) high.
£45–55 *HEM*

l. A cast iron owl bell,
c1890, 4½in (11.5cm) high.
£200–225 *EMC*

Door Furniture

A mahogany and brass door lock, early 19thC,
23in (53cm) wide.
£600–700 *HOK*

l. A rim lock and
keep, by Hobbs,
Hart & Co Ltd,
London, c1880,
6in (15cm) high.
£50–55 *HEM*

A cast iron door knocker,
c1880, 9½in (24cm) high.
£90–110 *HEM*

l. A pair of ebony 'beehive'
door knobs, c1880,
5in (12.5cm) long.
£35–45 *HEM*

A cast iron door knocker,
c1880, 9in (23cm) high.
£35–45 *HEM*

A brass door handle,
c1900, 7in (18cm) high.
£35–40 *DRU*

A brass mortice lock, key and keep, c1910, 6in (15cm) high.
£30–40 *HEM*

r. A brass pull handle, c1930, 10in (25.5cm) high.
£12–15 *HEM*

l. A brass pull handle, c1918, 11¼in (29cm) high.
£12–15 *HEM*

A brass bolt, 1920s, 16in (40.5cm) long.
£35–40 *LIB*

A brass bolt, 1930s, longest 6in (15cm) long.
£18–20 each *LIB*

Finials

A pair of brass pull handles, c1920, 11in (28cm) high.
£55–65 *HEM*

A pair of wood acorn finials, 19thC, 12in (30.5cm) high.
£50–60 *ASM*

A limestone ridge finial, mid-19thC, 25in (63.5cm) high.
£300–350 *RECL*

A terracotta gate post finial, 19thC, 15in (38cm) high.
£500–550 *Riv*

l. A pair of limestone ball finials, 19thC, 24in (61cm) high.
£650–750 *RECL*

Four reconstituted stone solid ball and socle finials, 1930s, 26in (66cm) high.
£250–300 each *RECL*

Stoves & Hobs

A hob grate, with wave pattern, late 18thC, 37in (94cm) wide.
£700–800 *WRe*

Hob Grates

Hob grates became popular during the late 18thC. Set into the fireplace, the grate had a hob on either side, which provided surfaces for keeping kettles hot.

Major manufacturers included Dale of Coalbrookdale and Carron, near Falkirk, who specialised in decorating their cast iron grates with elegant and fanciful neo-classical motifs.

Tiles

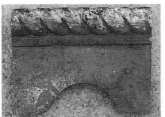

A Victorian rope-twist-top path edging tile, 9in (23cm) long.
£2–3 *RECL*

A Victorian blue clay castellated path edging tile, c1890, 9½ x 10½in (24 x 26.5cm).
£2–3 *RECL*

r. A Cotswold stone ridge tile, 19thC, 30in (76cm) long.
£8–10 per ft *RECL*

A French gas stove, c1890, 31in (79cm) high.
£450–500 *POSH*

A selection of Victorian path edgings, 11 x 8in (28 x 20.5cm).
£1–2 each *RECL*

A selection of terracotta quarry tiles, c1890, 9in (23cm) square.
£35–40 per sq yd *DOR*

A French cast iron wood-burning stove, c1900, 22in (56cm) wide.
£120–140 *RAW*

Four terracotta edging tiles, 19thC, 8½in (21.5cm) high.
£50–60 *Riv*

A ceramic ridge tile, modelled as a cat with a mouse, French, inscribed signature, impressed 'Caen', restored, 19thC, 19in (48cm) high.
£120–140 *L*

Roof tiles with models of cats served as bird scarers.

ART DECO

An Art Deco bone comb, with bone case, 1920s, 4in (10cm) long.
£22–25 *CHU*

l. An American silver-plated cocktail shaker, in the form of a lighthouse, by Meriden S. P. Co, patented 11 Jan 1927, 13¼in (34cm) high.
£1,200–1,400 *RTo*

The cocktail was the ultimate drink of the roaring twenties. The inter-war period gave birth to a huge range of alcoholic concoctions, miniaturised party food (the cocktail sausage and cocktail onions both started appearing in food catalogues in the 1930s), and to a range of handsome, Art Deco drinking accessories. Cocktail shakers come in a wide variety of designs, and rare patented examples are very sought-after today.

A metal toast rack, 1930s, 4½in (11.5cm) high.
£30–40 *WAB*

A pair of Art Deco chrome egg cups, 1920s, 3¾in (9.5cm) high.
£30–35 *WAB*

Ceramics

A Clews Chameleon ware oviform vase, decorated in autumnal tones with geometric panels, c1930, 10⅞in (27.5cm) high.
£130–150 *PrB*

A B. Jones Grafton China hand-painted tea plate, c1930, 6in (15cm) diam.
£10–12 *BKK*

A Fiesta Ware blue water pitcher, c1939, 7½in (19cm) high.
£80–90 *BKK*

Designed by Frederick Hurten Rhead, Fiesta Ware was first produced by the Homer Laughlin China Company, Ohio, in 1936. With its clean and simple Art Deco lines and cool colours, Fiesta Ware is now regarded as one of the classics of modern American design. This moderately priced dinnerware was highly successful, remaining in production throughout the 1950s and '60s. The design was changed in 1969, discontinued in 1972, and reintroduced in 1986.

Furniture

An Art Deco walnut-veneered cocktail cabinet, with Bakelite and steel geometric handles, 1930s, 65in (166cm) wide.
£160–180   *P(B)*

An Art Deco walnut-veneered chest of drawers, the tapering shaped body enclosing 5 graduated drawers each with two drop lozenge-shaped ebony handles, supported on a plinth base, 1930s, 36in (91.5cm) high.
£900–1,100   *P(B)*

A Savoy two-tier trolley, with chrome push handle, the circular chrome frame with 2 shelves supported on 3 casters, 1930s, 30in (77cm) high.
£50–70   *P(B)*

Glass

r. A Czechoslovakian clear glass vase, the fins acid-etched and moulded in relief, c1930, 12in (30.5cm) high.
£20–30   *BKK*

A cut and etched glass vase, supported in a stylistic WMF electro-plated frame, on 4 splayed feet arched and flanked by 2 handles, with matching shallow square cover, 1930s, 8½in (21.5cm) high.
£230–260   *CGC*

An Art Deco silver-plated tantalus, the 2 glass bottles with decorative designs, plated mounts, hinged lids and locking device, c1930, 9½in (24cm) high.
£170–200   *GAK*

A Bagley green pressed glass bamboo-shaped vase, c1933, 8½in (21.5cm) high.
£60–70   *BKK*

A Sowerby amber-coloured pressed glass vase, with textured panels and stylised floral motifs in relief, supported on seperate black glass base, c1938, 8½in (21.5cm) high.
£90–100   *BKK*

Lighting

A porcelain night light, by Becquerel Editions, Etling, Paris, decorated with polychrome enamel, c1920, 8in (20.5cm) high.
£400–500 *MoS*

A pair of Art Deco glass wall lights, c1924, 11in (28cm) high.
£1,000–1,200 *DRU*

A pair of Art Deco vanity lamps, 1930s, 15in (38cm) high.
£220–250 *EKK*

l. An Art Deco alabaster table lamp, with a metal female figure leaning forward with arms outstretched against a spherical shade, on a squared stepped support and rectangular base, 1930s, 10in (25.5cm) high.
£300–350 *Mit*

Statuettes & Decorative Figures

An Art Deco gilt hollow-cast spelter figure, on a white marble base, supporting leg damaged, c1930, 10¼in (26cm) high.
£100–125 *CARS*

r. An Art Deco gilt hollow-cast spelter figure and match striker, with silvered highlights to dress and top, on a black marble base, 1920s, 11in (28cm) high.
£250–300 *CARS*

An Art Deco gilt hollow-cast spelter figure, on a white marble plinth base, c1930, 9in (23cm) high.
£125–150 *CARS*

A French Art Deco spelter model of a swan, on a marble and onyx base, c1930, 15in (38cm) wide.
£325–350 *MiA*

An Art Deco spelter group, modelled as 2 racing gazelles, with incised signature 'Longfils', on sloped green and black onyx base, 26in (66cm) long.
£280–300 *DAC*

ART NOUVEAU

An Art Nouveau oak bookshelf, inlaid with panels of embossed copper, c1900, 35in (89cm) high.
£170–200 *CaC*

A pair of Art Nouveau green and pink iridescent glass vases, with crimped bulbous necks and slender tapering stems, c1900, 13in (33cm) high.
£280–300 *AP*

A Loetz pink opal iridescent glass vase, applied with gold trailed decoration, c1900, 6in (15cm) high.
£300–350 *MoS*

A Byrrh Tonique Hygiénique postcard, depicting a glamour study by Juan Cardona, c1908, 6 x 3½in (16.5 x 9cm).
£50–60 *SpP*

A WMF silver-plated easel mirror, the bevelled plate with figure and floral surround, c1900, 14in (35.5cm) high.
£1,200–1,400 *RBB*

An Art Nouveau mantel timepiece, with cream enamel dial, the hammered and embossed copper case decorated with foliage heightened with enamel, c1900, 13in (33cm) wide.
£600–700 *Bea(E)*

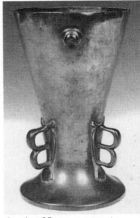

An Art Nouveau pewter three-handled vase, with inset green bosses, by Liberty & Co, No. 038, c1900, 7in (18cm) high.
£240–260 *FHF*

Three Keswick School of Industrial Arts flared copper vases, with repoussé decoration, c1900, tallest 6in (15cm) high.
£80–120 each *MoS*

A Newlyn copper tray, with repoussé decoration of a galleon, c1900, 6in (15cm) square.
£80–120 *MoS*

r. A Scottish School hand-beaten copper frame, probably by Margaret Gilmour, c1910, 10 x 8in (25.5 x 20.5cm).
£200–225 *SUC*

AUTOMOBILIA

An enamel petrol can, c1880, 10in (25.5cm) high.
£90–120 *INC*

In the early days of motoring garages were very few and far between, so drivers had to carry a can of petrol in the backs of their cars.

A Hignett's Mixture pressed tin advertising sign, depicting a blue rear entrance tonneau veteran car at speed in a wooded glade, slight damage, c1900, 13 x 19½in (33 x 49.5cm).
£1,850–2,000 *BKS*

A pair of Helios veteran car oil-powered brass lamps, each with reservoir and duplex burner with gallery, remnants of the glass tube funnel in front of an aluminium focused reflector, with stirrup mountings either side, stylised finial with heat vent and carrying bail, disc feet to the base, cup rims and rear red 'tell-tail' glasses, c1903, 20in (51cm) high.
£600–700 *BKS*

A brass motorists aneroid barometer, retailed by Dunhill of London, the nickled face with rotating bezel ring, c1910, 3¾in (9.5cm) diam.
£1,500–1,700 *S*

A Rolls-Royce 40/50hp instruction book, with blue cloth bound hard covers, January 1914, 10 x 8in (25.5 x 20.5cm).
£500–550 *S*

A Michelin 1,000kg Flirt jack, with brass instruction plate, French text, suitable for Rolls-Royce 20hp, some wear, 1918–1929, 8in (20.5cm) high.
£300–330 *S*

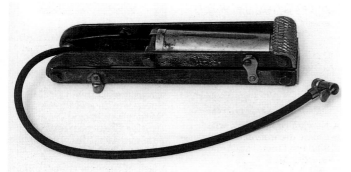

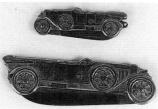

A Nesthill Compact foot pump, with nickel-plated cylinder, suitable for Rolls-Royce 20hp, some wear, 1920s, 14in (35.5cm) long.
£200–240 *S*

r. Two French brass classic car penknives, c1910, largest 3½in (9cm) long.
£15–30 each *WAB*

A Coracle four-person picnic set, the black leather cloth-covered case with running board rubber lid, nickled brightwork, interior fully fitted with kettle, burner, twin milk bottles, sandwich box, food storage, wicker covered bottles, glasses, the lid housing cutlery and saucers, suitable for a Rolls-Royce Silver Ghost, 1920s, 32¼in (82cm) wide.
£3,500–4,000 *S*

A Midland Rolls-Royce Club black and red enamel badge, by Butler of Birmingham, c1930, 3in (7.5cm) diam.
£240–280 *S*

A silver St Christopher dashboard plaque, enamelled in green and white, Birmingham 1936, 2¼in (5.5cm) wide.
£100–120 *S*

A Desmo brass car horn, c1920, 21in (53.5cm) long.
£40–50 *WAB*

r. A pair of Marchal chromium-plated lamps, each with a reeded German silver reflector, rear facing bulb and inscribed starburst glass, c1930, 11in (28cm) diam.
£450–550 *BKS*

A pair of Lucas L76 nickel-plated fork-mounted headlamps, one with original electrical connector, 1920s, lens 8½in (21.5cm) diam.
£700–800 *S*

On early vehicles lighting was not obligatory, and until c1914 there was no legal requirement for cars to have two headlamps. Pairs of vintage lamps are now valued by collectors. Lucas's 'King of the Road' headlamps first appeared in 1905 and lamps by this manufacturer are very prized today.

A Bentley 3½ Litre sales brochure, with printed brown cord-bound card covers, 22 pages with 6 tipped-in monochrome plates, printed by Bradley Press, some wear to cover, February 1935, 9 x 11in (23 x 28cm).
£180–220 *S*

A pair of Lucas STN 44 D-shaped rear lights, each chrome-plated case with correct ruby lenses and electrical connectors, suitable for Rolls-Royce Wraith and Phantom III, Bentley 4¼ Litre, Mk V and Bentley Corniche, restored, patented 1939, 4in (10cm) wide.
£1,000–1,200 *S*

l. A pair of Stephen Grebel pillar-mounted hand spotlamps, each with adjustable mounting bracket, chromed case and etched lens, 1930s, 4in (10cm) diam.
£1,500–1,700 *S*

A signed photograph of Luigi Villoresi in the 8CTF Maserati at Indianapolis, signed in blue ink and with dedication to Oscar Galvez, dated 21st May 1946, 7 x 9in (18 x 23cm).
£500–550 *C*

A KLG Spark Plugs metal advertising clock, 1950s, 14in (35.5cm) high.
£60–70 *JUN*

Stirling Moss at Nürburgring, 1961, oil on canvas, by Roy Nockolds, signed, framed, 22 x 36in (56 x 92cm).
£1,200–1,400 *C*

This was the former property of Stirling Moss, possibly a presentation piece following the accident that ended his career, and highlighting his last Grand Prix win.

l. A Rolls-Royce ceramic advertising dish, 1960s, 5in (12.5cm) diam.
£15–20 *COB*

r. A fully-detailed sectional drawing in ink of a Lotus 18 Grand Prix car, by Dick Ellis, signed and with *Autocar* copyright motif, c1959, framed, 21 x 34in (53.5 x 86.5cm).
£1,400–1,500 *C*

A set of traffic lights, c1970, 31in (79cm) high.
£35–40 *SAF*

A Goodyear Eagle Formula 1 racing tyre, used by Damon Hill driving a Williams FW17 at the French Grand Prix at Magny-Cours in June 1995, with certificate from Goodyear dated 'July 1995', signed by Damon Hill.
£600–700 *BKS*

r. A commemorative silver-plated desk box, by Glyn of London, fascimile signature engraved to lid with applied enamelled badge, mahogany lined, on turned feet, 1997, 8in (20cm) wide.
£1,300–1,500 *C*

Mascots

Early motorists personalized their cars by adding their own individual brass ornaments or statuettes, and manufacturers soon caught on to the idea of identifying and branding their vehicles with a recognized mascot. The first was the Vulcan Motor Company which, in 1903, added the figure of Vulcan the Blacksmith to their cars. In 1910, sculptor Charles Sykes created perhaps the most famous mascot of all time – the Spirit of Ecstasy – which has adorned the Rolls-Royce bonnet ever since.

A huge variety of mascots of every quality, price and design was subsequently made available by mail order. Although most were made of metal, among the most collectable car mascots today are those produced by the great Art Deco glassmaker René Lalique (1860–1940). According to legend, Lalique's involvement in the field began at the famous Paris Exhibition of 1925, where his own pavilions flanked those of André Citroën. The two men forged an instant relationship, which resulted in the creation of Lalique's very first mascot, that was inspired by Citroën's phenomenally successful five-horsepower car and appropriately named 'Cinq Chevaux'.

A French bronze and nickel 'L'oeuf d'Elephant' mascot, an elephant in an egg, base stamped, c1920, 8in (20cm) high, mounted on a radiator cap.
£1,500–1,800 S

A 'Cinq Chevaux' glass mascot, by René Lalique, with strong amethyst tint, moulded 'R. Lalique', inscribed 'France' on base, 1925–39, 6in (15cm) high.
£8,500–9,500 S

This mascot was the first of 30 mascots produced by Lalique and was introduced on 26 August 1925.

l. A Hassall 'Bobby' policeman mascot, with movable ceramic head, registration numbers on base, signed, 1912, 5in (12.5cm) high.
£240–280 S

A nickel-plated bronze Mickey Mouse mascot, 1920s, 3¾in (9.5cm) high, mounted on a wooden base.
£1,000–1,200 S

A 'Tete d'Aigle' grey glass mascot, by René Lalique, moulded 'R. Lalique', etched 'France' to base of neck feathers, 1930s, 4½in (11.5cm) high.
£1,800–2,200 S

First introduced on 14 March 1928, most of these mascots were produced in white glass and the earliest examples in the first two years of production were produced in this darker grey satin finish.

A chrome-plated 'Viking' mascot, 1950s, 4in (10cm) high.
£30–35 DAC

A heavy cast-bronze Rolls-Royce 'Spirit of Ecstasy' showroom display figure, designed by Charles Sykes, on ceramic plinth, 1920–30, 24in (61cm) high.
£900–1,100 C

A chrome-plated Armstrong-Siddeley mascot, late 1920s, 3in (7.5cm) high.
£35–40 DAC

BABY COLLECTABLES

An American pine rocking cradle, c1790, 38in (96.5cm) long.
£180–220 *EON*

A baby walker, early 19thC, 20in (51cm) high.
£145–165 *OCH*

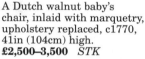

A Dutch walnut baby's chair, inlaid with marquetry, upholstery replaced, c1770, 41in (104cm) high.
£2,500–3,500 *STK*

r. An elm pull-along horse, early 19thC, 24in (61cm) long.
£270–300 *SWN*

Ceramic & Nursery Ware

A Victorian earthenware christening egg, printed in black with figures, the reverse with a boy bird nesting, inscribed 'A Present For A Good Boy', Sunderland or Staffordshire, 2½in (6.5cm) long.
£270–300 *TEN*

A blue and white ceramic feeder, with narrow teat end and filling hole to top, slight rust staining, 19thC, 7¼in (18.5cm) long.
£240–260 *BBR*

r. A child's plate, transfer printed with a blue fish and moulded and painted black rats, c1840, 5½in (14cm) diam.
£60–80 *IW*

A child's mug, transfer printed in blue with a picnic scene, c1880, 2¼in (5.5cm) high.
£40–60 *IW*

A child's porcelain tea service, in original wooden box with glass lid, excellent condition, c1910, box 20in (51cm) wide.
£250–300 *STK*

A Mabel Lucie Attwell plate, with warmer, c1926, 8½in (21.5cm) high.
£70–80 *PC*

A Mabel Lucie Attwell baby's plate, c1926, 8in (20.5cm) diam.
£100–120 *PC*

Warning!

Items illustrated may not comply with EC safety regulations and must not be used for their original purpose!

r. An Art Deco child's bunny tea set, in original box, good condition, c1930, box 12in (30.5cm) long.
£250–300 *STK*

Clothing

An Irish Victorian christening robe, with Irish lace, 44in (112cm) long.
£500–600 *JVa*

A child's silk all-in-one christening gown and cot cover, with holly-point lace, c1780.
£800–1,000 *JPr*

r. A pair of child's canvas button-up booties, c1910.
£40–50 *JPr*

A pair of silk handmade baby's shoes, c1880.
£20–40 *JPr*

A baby's embroidered voile dress, with lace inserts and pin tucks, c1910, 37in (94cm) long.
£55–65 *Ech*

l. An Edwardian baby's lace-trimmed bib, 9in (23cm) long.
£8–10 *MAC*

A baby's cotton appliquéd dress, 1920s, 18in (46cm) long.
£28–32 *Ech*

A handmade lace bonnet, suitable for a newborn baby, c1900.
£15–18 *CCO*

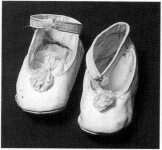

A pair of baby's shoes, with silk rosettes, c1930.
£20–30 *JPr*

A child's satin christening gown, 1950s.
£20–25 *Har*

Plastics

A Bakelite duck potty, by Bex, 1930s, 11¾in (30cm) long.
£30–35 *ORIG*

A baby's hand-painted celluloid powder box, with swan's-down powder puff, 1930s, 3in (7.5cm) high.
£8–10 *CHU*

Silver

A Victorian silver christening mug, by Edward, John and William Barnard, London 1838, 3¼in (8.5cm) high.
£350–400 *BEX*

A Victorian silver christening mug, by Walter and John Barnard, London 1886, 3½in (9cm) high.
£300–330 *BEX*

A Victorian baby's rattle, with whistle and ivory ring, 7in (18cm) long.
£80–90 *EKK*

r. A baby's silver rattle, depicting faces of the moon, c1912, 3in (7.5cm) long.
£100–120 *BaN*

l. A Mappin & Webb silver christening mug, London 1927, 3½in (9cm) high.
£250–300 *BEX*

A Victorian sterling silver and mother-of-pearl rattle, with whistle, 4in (10cm) long.
£70–80 *RRA*

BADGES

Badges are very affordable, with a huge range of material available for well under £5. The majority of the examples shown here date from the 1950s and were predominantly created for children. The most desirable tend to be those, such as the Muffin Club badge, which celebrate a favourite toy or TV character.

With badges made from the 1960s onwards, look out for the rock and pop examples, particularly anything to do with punk rock, which used badges as a cheap and instant art form, and also for protest and political badges, which can provide small but telling insights into social history.

A Bubbly Club badge, 1950s, 1¼in (3cm) diam.
£3–4 *SVB*

A Muffin Club badge, 1950s, 1¼in (3cm) diam.
£6–8 *SVB*

A Matchbox Collector badge, 1950s, 1¼in (3cm) diam.
£3–4 *SVB*

A wooden Noddy badge, 1950s, 3in (7.5cm) high.
£1–2 *TRE*

A Victor Value Supermarkets badge, 1950s, 1¼in (3cm) diam.
£3–4 *SVB*

A Rose Hip Collectors Club badge, 1958, 1in (2.5cm) diam.
£3–4 *SVB*

A badge, inscribed 'Your Tomb or Mine?', 1970–80s, 3in (7.5cm) diam.
20–25p *TRE*

Two Countryside March badges, 1998, 'I'll Be There', 1¾in (4.5cm) diam, and 'I Was There', 1in (2.5cm) diam.
l. **£2–3** *r.* **£10–15** *PC*

BASKETS

A Chinese two-lidded rice straw sewing basket, painted with holly berry design, mid-19thC, 11¾in (30cm) long.
£140–160 *EON*

A grape picker's wooden basket, 19thC, 20in (51cm) wide.
£80–100 *Riv*

A Spanish walnut picker's wooden basket, 19thC, 20in (51cm) wide.
£60–70 *Riv*

A circular wicker basket, with beaded flower decoration around top, 1920–30s, 20in (51cm) diam.
£25–30 *SUS*

A quill basket, the porcupine quills in an ebony frame inlaid with bone, c1860, 10⅜in (27.5cm) long.
£80–90 *SSW*

A fruit picker's basket, 1920s, 18in (45.5cm) wide.
£20–25 *WEE*

A wicker basket, with red double handle, 1930s, 15in (38cm) wide.
£10–15 *UTP*

A wicker basket, 1930s, 15in (38cm) wide.
£12–15 *UTP*

r. A wire basket, c1930, 7in (18cm) high.
£8–10 *AL*

A late Victorian miniature fishing or picnic basket, with 2 opening lids, 3in (7.5cm) high.
£10–15 *MRW*

A wicker basket, 1930s, 12in (30.5cm) wide.
£10–12 *UTP*

A wicker basket, c1930, 16in (40.5cm) wide.
£10–15 *UTP*

BICYCLES

In tandem with growing awareness of pollution, ecology and personal fitness, bicycle sales have doubled in the past ten years and one in three adults now owns a bike.

The expanding interest in cycling has also affected demand for collectable bikes, both old and new. The most expensive model shown here is the Lotus Sport Olympic bicycle, ridden by Chris Boardman at the 1992 Barcelona Olympic Games. This

was the machine on which Boardman broke the 4,000 metre world record twice on two consecutive days, won the gold medal in the final and, one month later, beat the world 5,000 metre record by eight seconds. Sold at auction by Phillips, together with Boardman's distinctive streamlined helmet, this bike shot past its modest £4,000–8,000 estimate to sell for an auction price of £25,000.

An enamelled earthenware plate, depicting a young woman on a hand-lever-driven tricycle, inscribed 'The Lady's Accelerator, Wonders Will Never Cease', c1819, 6½in 16.5cm) diam.
£450–500 *P(NE)*

A Sunbeam cardboard advertising sign, c1910, 20 x 15in (51 x 38cm).
£150–200 *JUN*

A full-colour chromo-litho of the painting 'What Next', by Madame C. Amyot, printed by J. T. Grover, framed and glazed, 1897, 27½ x 19¼in (70 x 49cm).
£200–250 *P(NE)*

A Phillips Bicycles metal advertising sign, 1955, 28 x 20in (71 x 51cm).
£100–120 *JUN*

A Solar gas cycle lamp, American, with original box, c1910, 8in (20.5cm) high.
£125–145 *PC*

l. A Victorian brass cycle rumble bell, 10in (25.5cm) long.
£90–110 *CGC*

A Smiths metal cycle lamp, The Wooton Lantern, paintwork worn and chipped, c1940, 5in (12.5cm) high.
£15–20 *DOM*

A Hedges velocipede, each wheel with 14 eliptical staggered spokes and iron tyres, generally pitted metalwork, overpainted back wheels stripped and varnished, handles, pedals and seat pan possibly replaced, 34in (86.5cm) front wheel and 30in (76cm) rear wheels, c1869.
£2,000–2,200 *P(NE)*

A Belgian child's tandem tricycle, with metal-rimmed wooden-spoked wheels on a metal frame, with upturned handlebars, front wheel with wooden peg pedals on metal arms, saddle back and support recovered, c1870, front wheel 25½in (65cm) diam.
£9,000–10,000 *S*

An Excelsior 'One-Two-Three' tricycle, with single seat and 3 wheels of differing diameters, restored, c1880.
£8,000–9,000 *C*

A child's velocipede, in the form of a 'transitional' machine, the front wheel with 10 staggered eliptical spokes, the rear with 8 plain round spokes both with chamfered rims, diamond section backbone, black overpainted metalwork, some pitting, some parts replaced, 1870s, rear wheel 12in (30.5cm) diam.
£3,300–3,600 *P(NE)*

An Ordinary bicycle, finished in black with later white spray paint marks, with stepped handle bars, simple front wheel brake, red rubber tyres, saddle spring marked 'Anderton Sheffield', leather saddle worn, c1880, front wheel 52in (132cm) diam.
£1,400–1,600 *S*

A velocipede bicycle, with round tapered backbone and D-forks, red wheels with black lines, black frame with white lines, all original components including saddle cover and leather brake thong, c1869, front wheel 36in (91.5cm) diam.
£1,600–2,000 *P(HSS)*

r. A Rudge Light Roadster Ordinary bicycle, No. 34443, with hollow backbone and front forks, open rear forks, hollow rims, tangental butted and soldered spokes, ball bearings to both tubes, cowhorn bars with T-handles, Brooks saddle, white pram tyres, adjustable step, generally good condition, some replacement parts, c1885, front wheel 52in (132cm) diam.
£2,000–2,200 *P(NE)*

An Ordinary bicycle, by
W. Burford of Camden Town,
overpainted in grey, brass
maker's plate on left side of
backbone, simple lever brake,
handle missing, red rubber
tyres missing, saddle worn,
c1880, front wheel
48in (122cm) diam.
£1,700–1,900 *S*

A solid-tyred tandem bicycle, with single drop tube front and cross
frame rear, front frame fitted with removable top bar, rear wheels
with crescent rims and direct spokes, open head steering, front
and rear bars chain linked, good condition, some replacement
parts, 1880s, front wheel 32in (81.5cm) diam.
£3,000–3,500 *P(NE)*

A Crypto geared Facile bicycle,
with direct spokes, crescent
rims, oval backbone, lever drive
to open gear, generally good
condition, some replacement
parts, c1885, front wheel
38in (96.5cm) diam.
£6,500–7,500

A cast iron 'Sirens' cycle stand,
with neo-rococo decoration,
each finial terminating with a
siren resting her chin on her
elbow, late 19th/early 20thC,
28in (71cm) long.
£90–120 *P(NE)*

A child's front-wheel-drive-
tricycle, with direct spokes,
plain bearings, overpainted
black, generally good condition,
most original parts, c1900,
front wheel 26in (66cm) diam.
£250–300 *P(NE)*

A Hartford lady's bicycle,
pattern No. 8, the black frame
with maker's plaque, wooden
handle bars, with cork handles,
brass bell, wooden rimmed
wheels with pneumatic tyres,
wooden rear mudguard, lacking
saddle, some wear, patented
1896, frame 22in (56cm) long.
£250–300 *S*

A Dursley Pedersen gentleman's safety bicycle, with
overpainted green frame,
original saddle, tyres, lacking
pedals, worn condition, c1901.
£1,000–1,200 *S*

A double top tube gentleman's roadster bicycle, built using BSA
fittings, with beaded edge wheels, plunger front brake, upturned
bars, fixed wheel, older restoration, all components seem original,
some parts missing or replaced, c1899, wheels 30in (76cm) diam.
£250–300 *P(NE)*

A child's bicycle, with wooden handle grips and solid tyres, c1912.
£90–120 *JUN*

An Elswick lady's trade cycle, with Dunlop sprung saddle and tool bag, recently restored using original Elswick pedal rubbers, new basket, c1930.
£250–300 *BKS*

A high wheel safety bicycle, of A-frame construction, caliper brake, solid rubber tyres, painted black, home-built from spares, 1930s, front wheel 15in (38cm) diam.
£240–280 *S*

A Gresham Flyer tricycle, repainted in original colours, complete with telescopic pedestrian control bar at rear, 1950s.
£45–55 *PA*

A Raleigh Chopper bicycle, painted in metallic light-blue with chrome brightwork, applied with orange decals, red-handled three-position gear lever and original red line tyres, 1970s, frame 15in (38cm) long.
£120–160 *S*

The Lotus Sport Olympic bicycle, stored since 1992, some corrosion to chain and sprocket, otherwise excellent condition, with original frame bag, travelling crate and streamlined helmet cowl, 1992.
£25,000–30,000 *P(NE)*

This is the actual machine ridden by Chris Boardman at the 1992 Barcelona Olympic Games and stored since then. The prototype of this bicycle was also sold at the same auction and realised £6,200.

A Triang Moulton child's bicycle, complete with all accessories including white pump, back rack and chainguard, with white plastic handlebar grips, Moulton patent suspension system, 1970, 50in (127cm) long.
£100–150 *CARS*

BOOKS

The condition of books is absolutely critical to value. 'I can think of no better example of this than a copy of Arthur Conan Doyle's *Hound of the Baskervilles* that sold recently at auction,' says book dealer Pom Harrington (illustrated on page 71). 'A first edition, in poor condition, might be expected to fetch around £200. In good condition the value shoots up to £1,000–1,200. But this particular *Hound of the Baskervilles* was extremely rare in that it still had its dust jacket. Apart from a copy in the Bodleian Library and one other recorded in America, no other examples with a dust jacket are known, and this book sold for £80,000, an astonishing figure.'

Even Sherlock Holmes himself might have been surprised by such a result, but he is not the only male detective to attract a passionate and high-spending fan club. Although on the one hand the book market is highly academic, it is also subject, like everything else, to fashion and glamour; another figure currently riding high is Ian Fleming's James Bond. 'Every time a new film comes out, Bond attracts a host of new collectors,' explains book specialist Adrian Harrington. 'Prices have doubled and tripled over the last few years, and every time you think they are going to slow down, they come

back like a storm. The James Bond books are well written and very accessible. Also there are only 14 of them, so whilst you can have a great time tracking them down you can also see an end to your collection.'

People collect books for many different reasons. Nostalgia is an important factor, particularly with children's works. Classics such as *Winnie-the-Pooh* and *Alice in Wonderland* will always be in demand, but adults also return to the particular publications that were in vogue when they were children. The boarding school stories of the 1930s and '40s are likely to appeal to those who grew up with them, while today's children, in a few years time, could well be snapping up vintage copies of *Teletubby* annuals. As each generation grows up, certain children's books will fall in and out of fashion and their prices will vary accordingly. Some people concentrate on specific illustrators or authors, others on a particular story (perhaps collecting all the different illustrated versions) or a specific type of book. The children's section this year includes a selection of pop-up books. Given their fragile nature and the fact that they were created for young children, good condition is again crucial to price.

Oscar Wilde, *Lady Windermere's Fan*, first edition, published by Mathews, London, 1893, 8½ x 6⅛in (21.5 x 16.5cm), with original programme of performance staged at St James's Theatre.
£500–550 *CATH*

News from Ireland, the examination and confessions of William Kelso, presented to the Wigan Free public library by Rt Hon Earl of Crawford, June 1901, printed 1679, 11¾ x 7⅞in (30 x 20cm).
£325–375 *CATH*

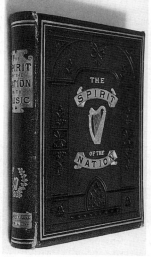

The Spirit of the Nation, Ballads and Songs, second edition, published by James Duffy & Sons, Dublin, 1882, 10½in x 8in (26.5 x 20.5cm).
£140–180 *CATH*

l. Goethe, *Faust*, from the German by John Auster, No. 956 of 1,000 copies, 22 plate illustrations by Harry Clarke, published by Dingwall Rock Ltd, New York, 1925, 10¾ x 8⅛in (27 x 21cm).
£650–750 *CATH*

Children's Books

A bronze hornbook, c1640, 1¼ x 1½in (3 x 4cm).
£240–260 *RuC*

Hornbooks were a form of children's primer used during the 16th–18thC. A sheet of vellum or paper containing the letters of the alphabet and numbers was protected within thin transparent layers of horn and hung from the child's belt. These small letter blocks were also produced in other materials including lead and bronze, with raised letters.

Hans Andersen's Fairy Tales, illustrated by Mabel Lucie Attwell, published by Raphael Tuck & Sons Ltd, c1920, 10 x 7½in (25.5 x 19cm).
£200–250 *AHa*

Bookano Stories, No. 4, published by Strand, with 5 pop-up pictures, 1930s, 8¾ x 6¼in (22 x 16cm).
£60–90 *AHa*

Hans Andersen's Fairy Stories, with pop-up pictures, published by Strand Publications, c1936, 8½ x 6¾in (21.5 x 17cm).
£80–100 *PHa*

Roald Dahl, *Charlie and the Great Glass Elevator*, first edition, illustrated by Joseph Schindelman, published by Alfred A. Knopf, 1972, 9½ x 6¼in (24 x 16cm).
£40–50 *PHa*

Lewis Carroll, *Alice's Adventures Underground*, with 37 illustrations by the author, published by Macmillan & Co, London, 1886, in red bound cover.
£120–140 *HCC*

r. Dell's House, published by Dean, 1940s, 9 x 4½in (23 x 11.5cm).
£12–14 *MRW*

Animal Life, published by Daily Sketch and Sunday Graphic Ltd, with 6 animal pop-up pictures, 1930s, 8¾ x 10in (21 x 25.5cm).
£50–75 *AHa*

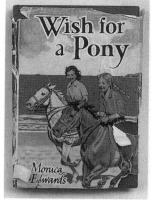

Monica Edwards, *Wish for a Pony*, published by J. Goodchild, 1940s, 7½ x 5in (19 x 12.5cm).
£1–2 *TRE*

A Day in a Child's Life, illustrated by Kate Greenaway, music by Myles B. Foster, first edition, published by George Routledge, 1881, 10 x 8in (25.5 x 20.5cm).
£130–150 *DAC*

Lothar Meggendorfer's International Circus, with pop-up pictures, 1979 reprint, 13 x 9in (33 x 23cm).
£10–12 *DAC*

l. Washington Irving, *Rip Van Winkle*, illustrated by Arthur Rackham, first edition, published by William Heinemann, 1905, 10 x 7½in (25.5 x 19cm).
£250–300 *PHa*

Ali Baba & The Forty Thieves, illustrated by Ionicus, a folding peep-show book, 1950s, 6 x 7in (15 x 18cm).
£30–35 *DAC*

A. A. Milne, *Now We are Six*, with decorations by E. H. Shepard, first edition, 1927, in limp blue leather binding and original card box.
£450–500 *WW*

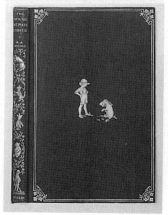

A. A. Milne, *Winnie-the-Pooh*, decorations by E. H. Shepard, first edition, 1926, in limp dark green leather binding.
£200–250 *PHa*

A. A. Milne, *The House at Pooh Corner*, with decorations by E. H. Shepard, first edition, 1928, in limp black leather binding.
£300–350 *WW*

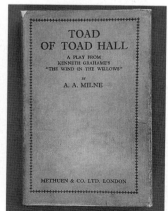

A. A. Milne, *Toad of Toad Hall*, first edition, published by Methuen & Co Ltd, London, in dust jacket, 1929, 7¾ x 5¼in (20 x 13.5cm).
£50–75 *PHa*

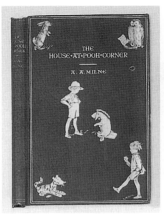

A. A. Milne, *The House at Pooh Corner*, with decorations by E. H. Shepard, first edition, 1928, in limp red leather binding, ink signature on verso of frontispiece.
£500–600 WW

This is a variant binding of The House at Pooh Corner *with gilt blocks of Rabbit, Wol, Tigger and Christopher Robin added at the four corners of the front cover and the central figures enlarged – possibly a publisher's presentation binding.*

The Sleeping Beauty and other Fairy Tales, retold by A. T. Quiller-Couch, illustrated by Edmund Dulac, published by Hodder & Stoughton, 1909, 11¼ x 9in (28.5 x 23cm).
£150–200 PHa

r. I. Henry Wallis, *The Cloud Kingdom*, illustrated by Charles Robinson and signed by the author, first edition, 1910, 8 x 5in (20.5 x 12.5cm).
£100–110 DAC

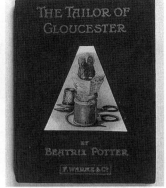

Beatrix Potter, *The Tailor of Gloucester*, published by F. Warne & Co, 1912, 5½ x 4in (14 x 10cm) high.
£20–25 WWY

Beatrix Potter, *The Pie and the Patty Pan*, published by F. Warne & Co, 1905.
£60–70 HCC

Christine Pullein-Thompson, *Phantom Horse*, published by Award Publications, 1968, 7½ x 5in (19 x 12.5cm).
£1–2 TRE

l. The Speaking Picture Book, with pull strings to hear animal noises corresponding to pictures, early 20thC, 12½in (31.5cm) high.
£230–260 JH

Miniature Books

Three miniature books, New Testament, The Bible and *Bryce's English Dictionary*, cased with magnifiers, c1900, largest 2in (5cm) high.
£30–45 each *VB*

A selection of miniature brass and enamelled glass souvenir books, 1890–1935, largest 1in (2.5cm) high.
£5–18 each *VB*

The English Bible, coronation commemorative issue with magnifying glass in back cover, 1911, 1¾ x 1¼in (4.5 x 3cm), with box and leaflet.
£125–135 *CHe*

Modern First Editions

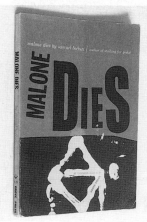

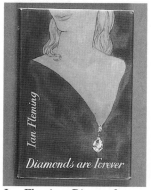

Samuel Beckett, *Malone Dies*, published by Grove Press, New York, inscribed by Beckett, 1956, 8 x 5½in (20.5 x 14cm).
£400–450 *CATH*

Ian Fleming, *Diamonds are Forever*, published by Jonathan Cape, 1956, 7¾ x 5in (19.5 x 12.5cm).
£500–600 *AHa*

Ian Fleming, *For Your Eyes Only*, published by Jonathan Cape, with dust jacket, 1960, 7¾ x 5in (19.5 x 12.5cm).
£200–250 *AHa*

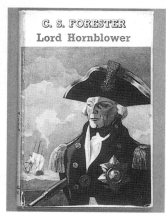

Ian Fleming, *You Only Live Twice*, signed by the author, published by Jonathan Cape, 1964, 7½ x 5¼in (19 x 13.5cm).
£2,000–2,500 *AHa*

Ian Fleming, *The Man With The Golden Gun*, published by Jonathan Cape, 1965, 7½ x 5½in (19 x 14cm).
£30–50 *AHa*

r. C. S. Forester, *Lord Hornblower*, published by Michael Joseph, 1946, 7½ x 5in (19 x 12.5cm).
£20–30 *AHa*

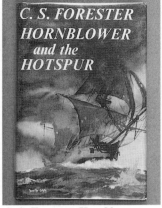

C. S. Forester, *Hornblower and the Hotspur*, published by Michael Joseph, with dust jacket, 1962, 7½ x 5in (19 x 12.5cm).
£20–30 *AHa*

Patrick O'Brian, *The Fortune of War*, published by Collins, 1979, 9 x 5½in (23 x 14cm).
£180–220 *AHa*

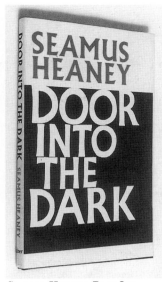

Seamus Heaney, *Door Into The Dark*, published by Faber & Faber, 1969, 9 x 5¾in (23 x 14.5cm).
£300–350 *CATH*

Patrick O'Brian, *Clarissa Oakes*, signed, published by HarperCollins, 1992, 9 x 5½in (23 x 14cm).
£75–120 *AHa*

Cross Reference
Colour Review

l. William Butler Yeats, *The Trembling of the Veil*, No. 820 of 1,000, signed, published by T. Werner Laurie Ltd, privately printed, 1922, 9 x 6in (23 x 15cm).
£725–775 *CATH*

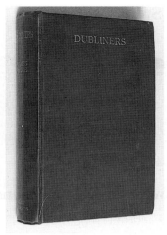

James Joyce, *Dubliners*, published by Grant Richards, 1914, 7 x 5in (18 x 12.5cm).
£2,400–2,700 *CATH*

First editions of the Dubliners *are very scarce.*

FURTHER READING
Catherine Porter, *Miller's Collecting Books*, Miller's Publications, 1995

Sporting Books

Apperley, *Life of John Mytton*, 18 hand-coloured aquatint engravings, published by Rudolph Ackermann, Eclipse Sporting Gallery, 1851, 9½ x 6¼in (24 x 16cm).
£350–400 *HBo*

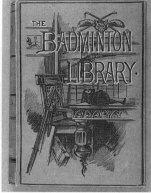

The Badminton Library, J. M. Heathcote, C. G. Heathcote, E. O. P. Bouverie, and A. C. Ainger, *Tennis, Lawn Tennis, Rackets, Fives*, published by Longmans, Green & Co, 1890, 7¾ x 5½in (19.5 x 14cm).
£60–90 *AHa*

l. W. J. A. Davies, *Rugby Football*, published by Websters Publications, c1923, 8¾ x 5¾in (22 x 14.5cm).
£20–25 *AHa*

'APPROACHING THE LAST HOLE'

The Badminton Library, Horace G. Hutchinson, *Golf*, published by Longmans, Green & Co, 1890, 8 x 5¾in (20.5 x 14.5cm).
£75–125 *AHa*

The Badminton Library, *Sea Fishing*, No. 198 of 250, published by Longmans, Green & Co, 1895, 10 x 8in (25.5 x 20.5cm).
£80–90 *PHa*

The Badminton Library, P. E. Warner and others, *Cricket*, edited by His Grace the Duke of Beaufort, published by Longmans, Green & Co, 1920, 7½ x 5½in (19 x 14cm).
£30–45 *AHa*

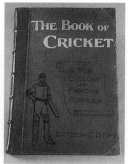

Duncan Fraser, *Angling Sketches from a Wayside Inn*, published by Baxendine, Edinburgh, 1911, 8 x 5½in (20.5 x 14cm).
£15–18 *HBo*

The Book of Cricket

A NEW GALLERY OF FAMOUS PLAYERS

EDITED BY C. B. FRY

The Book of Cricket, edited by C. B. Fry, published by George Newnes, London, c1920, 14¼ x 10in (36 x 25.5cm).
£60–75 *PHa*

l. Hardy's Anglers' Guide, Coronation Number, 55th edition, 1937, 8¼ x 5½in (21 x 14cm).
£35–45 *HBo*

PUGILISTICA

WITH ONE HUNDRED PORTRAITS AND ILLUSTRATIONS

r. Pugilistica, 144 Years of British Boxing, 3 vols, 63 portraits, published by John Grant, Edinburgh, 1906, 9 x 6½in (23 x 16.5cm).
£170–200 *PHa*

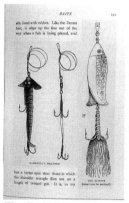

l. Izaak Walton, *The Compleat Angler*, limited edition of 5,000, illustrated by Arthur Rackham, c1931, 10 x 7½in (25.5 x 19cm).
£150–175 *HBo*

First published in 1653, The Compleat Angler *– or the Contemplative Man's Recreation – is among the most famous books about fishing. It takes the form of a dialogue between a fisherman (Piscator), a fowler and a hunter, each one recommending their own sport. The fisherman instructs the hunter in both catching fish and dressing them for the table. There are observations on rivers and ponds as well as directions for the making of artificial flies and lines. Walton himself was an angler rather than a fly fisherman, but the fifth edition, published in 1676, included a continuation by Charles Cotton, with further conversations and a fuller description of the making of artificial flies. 'Fishing is popular across the world and the market for fishing books is international,' says specialist dealer Leo Harrison. 'Collectors are looking for books that are historically important to the sport, and* The Compleat Angler *is a classic in the field. It has appeared in various editions and prices vary depending upon age, rarity and condition.'*

r. Peter Upton, *Desert Heritage*, published by Skilton & Shaw, Burlington Press, 1980, 8½ x 12in (21.5 x 30.5cm).
£20–25 *JAL*

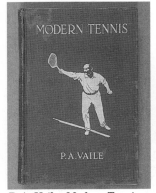

P. A. Vaile, *Modern Tennis*, first edition, published by Funk & Wagnalls Co, 1915, 8¼ x 5⅜in (21 x 14.5cm).
£70–90 *AHa*

Izaak Walton and Charles Cotton, *The Complete Angler*, second edition, published by John Major, London, 1824, 8 x 5¼in (20.5 x 13.5cm).
£170–200 *PHa*

l. Izaak Walton and Charles Cotton, *The Complete Angler*, 16 plates, published by Samuel Bagster, London, full calf Baynton binding, 1808, 8½ x 5¼in (21.5 x 13.5cm).
£450–480 *HBo*

BOTTLES

An olive-green 'shaft and globe' bottle, the long tapering neck with pronounced string rim, base pontil, some pitting, full body sheen, c1670, 9¼in (23.5cm) high.
£1,300–1,500 *BBR*

An olive-green bottle, with seal inscribed 'Prytherect 1819', 10½in (27cm) high.
£200–225 *NWi*

An onion-shaped bottle, with overall body iridescence, base pontil and applied string rim, the seal with a fox surmounted by a coronet, c1700–10, 5¼in (13cm) high.
£1,400–1,600 *BBR*

In the 17thC, wine was not sold in bottles. The client would have his own glass bottles, which he would send to the wine merchant to be filled. Since these were costly items, they would be embossed with the owner's seal. These early onion-shaped bottles are very collectable today, and seals can often be identified to provide an attractive and aristocratic provenance. This particular bottle is believed to be connected to the Pierpont family.

Three beer bottles, 1950s, tallest 3¼in (8.5cm) high.
£3–4 each *MRW*

l. Three green glass chemist's bottles, with glass labels, c1900, tallest 8in (20.5cm) high.
£60–80 *JUN*

A blown 'bladder' form dark green bottle, c1730, 10½in (27cm) high.
£200–250 *NWi*

A green glass seal bottle converted to a Perrier water jug, with silver-plated handle and mount, glass 18thC, top 1890–1910, 10in (25.5cm) high.
£350–375 *INC*

r. A clear glass bottle, embossed 'The Property of O. T. Co, London', 1930s, 11½in (29cm) high.
£3–4 *MAC*

A Victorian oak three-bottle tantalus, 14in (35.5cm) high.
£260–280 *Doc*

A green glass bottle, with a seal commemorating Halley's Comet, paper label inscribed 'Vieux Cognac', c1811, 14in (35.5cm) high.
£110–120 *INC*

The seal on this bottle commemorates Halley's comet and is possibly a mark of quality. 'Comet Wine' was a term given to wine made in years of great comets that were believed to produce grapes of better flavour than other years.

Babies Bottles

A Glaxo baby's feeding bottle, with
rubber teats and original box, 1950s,
8in (20.5cm) long.
£14–18 *MRW*

A glass bottle, inscribed
'Feeding Bottle For
My Baby', c1910,
5½in (14cm) high.
£10–15 *DOL*

> **Cross Reference**
> Baby Collectables

A glass bottle, inscribed
'Mellin's Infant's Food,
London', c1910–20,
7in (18cm) high.
£4–6 *HUX*

r. A Pyrex 8oz feeding
bottle, in original box,
1960s, 6¾in (17cm) high.
£7–8 *HUX*

Bottle Holders

A silver-plated bottle
holder, in the form
of a tricycle, c1880,
10½in (27cm) long.
£275–325 *PC*

r. A silver-plated Codd
bottle stand, c1910,
6in (15cm) high.
£25–30 *WAB*

Ceramic Bottles

A glazed pottery boot flask, c1870, 6½in (16.5cm) high.
£35–40 *WAB*

A salt-glazed porter bottle, with mid-brown top, lower portion impressed 'W. Hooper Rols, 1814', badly cracked, 9in (23cm) high.
£170–200 *BBR*

A salt-glazed bottle, with impressed mark 'Hubaudière Quimper', 1885–90, 12½in (32cm) high.
£100–120 *VH*

A hot water bottle, inscribed 'The Adaptable Hot Water Bottle & Bed Warmer' and 'Old Fulham Pottery', c1910, 8in (20.5cm) diam.
£15–20 *JUN*

A stoneware bottle, with handle to rear, black transfer-printed 'Wicklow Distillery, Old Irish Whiskey', with an owl perched on a branch, some body speckling, 1920–30s, 7¾in (20cm) high.
£80–100 *BBR*

r. A stoneware ginger beer bottle, with pictorial transfer of a bearded man, inscribed 'Brewed Ginger Beer, R. Stothert & Sons, Atherton', c1900–10, 8in (20.5cm) high.
£100–110 *BBR*

Many vintage bottles are recovered by collectors from old bottle dumps, sometimes in vast numbers. In January 1998 two enthusiasts patrolling a field found a likely site. The farmer gave them permission to dig and their first find was a Wadsworth's of Devizes ginger beer bottle. The farmer told them that Wadsworth's had dumped its empties in the field in the 1950s. In four days the two men found 1,236 complete ginger beer bottles together with some 5,000 broken containers, a probable British record for the number of ginger beers found on one site. The value of ginger beer bottles depends on the name of the manufacturer, and the appeal and quality of the transfer-printed image.

Poison Bottles

An aqua glass poison bottle, the flat base with U-bend to the neck, curved end, embossed to one side 'The Martin Poison Bottle', 'Poison' to the other, 'Patented' to curved end, '8oz' under neck and 'S. S. A. Ltd, Manchester' to base, early 20thC, 7in (18cm) long.
£320–350 *BBR*

It is rare to find such a bottle in this large size.

A Gilbertson's wedge clear glass poison bottle, embossed 'Poison' to top, 'H. Gilbertson & Sons' to one side, 'Regd 30th Octr 1861' on the other, original paper labels inscribed 'Laudanum-Poison, E. R. Ing Chemist, Swindon', slight damage, 3½in (9cm) long.
£350–400 *BBR*

A shoemaker's carved wood sign, decorated in black and gilt, with red sole and heel, 19thC, 25in (63.5cm) long.
£550–650 *RBB*

A Shell Motor Oil quart jug, with Customs and Excise seal, c1910, 6½in (16.5cm) high.
£100–120 *INC*

A Kellogg's Wheat Krispies point-of-sale display stand, complete with plates, 1930s, 16in (40.5cm) wide.
£165–185 *EKK*

A Coca-Cola tin tray, c1939, 12 x 10in (30.5 x 25.5cm).
£120–150 *SMAM*

An Ever Ready bicycle lamp battery, filled with pitch, c1950–60, 3in (7.5cm) high.
£1–2 *DOM*

A selection of Brooke Bond ¼lb tea packets, early 1950s–late 1970s, 5in (12.5cm) high.
£10–20 each *FMu*

A Dunlop cycle repair kit tin shop dispenser, 1960s, 12in (30.5cm) high.
£35–50 *COB*

l. A Murraymint badge, 1960s, 1¼in (3cm) diam.
£3–4 *SVB*

A Brooke Bond PG model of Cyril the Cyclist Chimp, with hat and sunglasses, thought to be a trade offer, c1970, 20in (51cm) high.
£130–150 *FMu*

A Gilbert Rae's Aerated
Waters poster, c1880,
28 x 19½in (71 x 49.5cm).
£1,000–1,200   *INC*

A *Chocolat des 3 Frères, Lyon,*
poster, by P. Bonnard, dated
'1901', 25 x 18in (63.5 x 45.5cm).
£80–100   *INC*

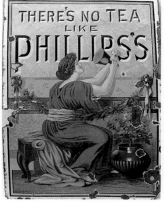

A Phillips's enamel sign, early
20thC, 48 x 36in (122 x 92cm).
£450–500   *P(C)*

A Robin Starch enamel sign,
c1910, 36 x 24in (92 x 61cm).
£400–450   *JUN*

A Morris Trucks enamel sign,
c1930, 22½ x 16in (57 x 40.5cm).
£1,200–1,400   *INC*

A Dinky Toys shop display card,
1950s, 11 x 14in (28 x 35.5cm).
£40–50   *RAR*

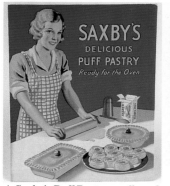

A Saxby's Puff Pastry cardboard
sign, 1950s, 11 x 9in (28 x 23cm).
£8–12   *WAB*

A Craven A framed poster,
1930s, 32 x 22in (81 x 55cm).
£140–180   *P(C)*

A Road Runner metal sign,
1960s, 19in (48cm) high.
£30–40   *SAF*

A Huntley & Palmers biscuit tin, commemorating the Paris Exhibition 1878, 1894, 6½in (16.5cm) wide.
£200–225 *WAB*

A Huntley & Palmers two-handled biscuit tin, depicting *As You Like It* and *A Midsummer Night's Dream*, c1910, 7in (18cm) high.
£130–150 *WAB*

A Crawford's biscuit tin, designed by Mabel Lucie Attwell, c1933, 7in (18cm) high.
£180–200 *HUX*

A Craven A tin, in the form of an ink blotter, 1930s, 6½in (16.5cm) wide.
£30–40 *WAB*

A tin, depicting a cat and a dog, c1880, 2 x 3in (5 x 7.5cm).
£40–50 *INC*

A Huntley & Palmers biscuit tin, in the form of a cannon, c1914, 5in (12.5cm) high.
£400–450 *WAB*

An Art Deco tin, decorated with a cat, 1930s, 5in (12.5cm) high.
£25–30 *BEV*

A Peek Frean's string tin, c1935, 3¾in (9.5cm) high.
£175–200 *INC*

A Victory Linseed liquorice tin, 1890–1920, 9¾in (25cm) high.
£120–150 *INC*

A Huntley & Palmers biscuit tin, in the form of a Japanese screen, c1913, 7in (18cm) high.
£100–120 *WAB*

A Tetley tea tin, 1990s, 5½in (14cm) diam.
£15–20 *WEE*

A Poinsettia one-armed bandit, c1930, 24in (61cm) high.
£500–600 *SAF*

A Prosit counter-top sixpence-operated trade stimulator machine, with drinking theme, by ABT of Chicago, 1940s, 16in (40.5cm) long.
£90–120 *SAF*

A Win-a-KitKat coin-operated machine, 1950s, 31½in (80cm) high.
£500–600 *SAF*

A Mills one-armed bandit, 1950s, 26in (66cm) high.
£250–300 *SAF*

A Little Stockbroker penny-operated machine, 1950–60s, 25in (63.5cm) high.
£550–650 *PING*

A Mills Sega high-top one-armed bandit, 1950–60s, 26in (66cm) high.
£450–500 *PING*

A Football Game amusement machine, early 1960s, 26in (66cm) high.
£150–250 *PING*

A gum ball dispensing machine, c1965, 11½in (29cm) high.
£45–55 *SAF*

l. **A NSM Hit 120 jukebox, 1970s, 41½in (105.5cm) high. £140–180** *SAF*

r. A baseball 10 cent gum and card vending machine, by Oak Manufacturing Company Inc, California, 1960s, 15in (38cm) high.
£200–250 *HALL*

A Gottlieb 4 square pinball machine, 1970s, 52in (132cm) long.
£450–500 *PING*

A Stern electronic Star Gazer pinball machine, c1980, 51in (129.5cm) long.
£500–600 *PING*

A Chinese Neolithic mottled green stone axe, circa 3000 BC, 6in (15cm) long.
£150–200 *HEL*

A Persian dagger or short sword, with flat pommel, open-work hilt, western Iran, circa 1000 BC, 10½in (26.5cm) long.
£150–200 *ANG*

An Egyptian faïence cat, with kittens, one ear missing, circa 800–600 BC, 1½in (4cm) high.
£650–750 *HEL*

A Greek black figure lekythos, minor repair to foot, 6th century BC, 7½in (19cm) high.
£850–950 *HEL*

An Egyptian stuccoed and painted wood osiris figure, plume missing from top of head, circa 600–400 BC, 13in (33cm) high.
£600–700 *HEL*

An Egyptian faïence *ushabti* figure, repaired, 7th century BC, 7½in (19cm) high.
£800–900 *HEL*

An Egyptian faïence bead face, some damage, circa 600–400 BC, 4¼in (11cm) wide.
£350–450 *HEL*

A zoomorphic brooch, in the form of a fly, found in Dorset, pin missing, circa 1st–2nd century BC, ⅜in (1.5cm) long.
£85–95 *ANG*

A Roman glass bowl, 1st–2nd century AD, 6in (15cm) diam.
£775–825 *RuC*

r. An Iranian ceramic bowl, with blue glaze, Iran or Afghanistan, 11th–13th century AD, 6¾in (17cm) diam.
£1,300–1,500 *PARS*

l. A Byzantine Empire bronze cross, incomplete suspension loop, 9th century AD, 3¼in (8cm) long.
£125–145 *ANG*

An Art Deco oak double
photograph frame, c1930,
6½in (16.5cm) high.
£50–70 *BKK*

A Boch Frères smoker's set,
with drip glaze, c1928,
tray 9in (23cm) wide.
£120–150 *BKK*

A Czechoslovakian lustre-
glazed vase, with insert,
c1932, 6½in (16.5cm) high.
£90–100 *BKK*

A Goebel hand-painted wall
mask, No. FX31, c1932,
7in (18cm) high.
£250–280 *BKK*

A Maison Lyons biscuit tin, c1930,
9in (23cm) wide.
£8–10 *AL*

A Roskyl drip-glazed vase,
Shape No. 62A, c1934,
7½in (19cm) high.
£50–70 *BKK*

An Art Deco cocktail set, c1930,
tray 14in (35.5cm) wide.
£100–120 *TWa*

r. A pair of Art Deco mahogany-
veneered children's chairs, 1930s.
£120–150 *P(B)*

A Bagley pressed-glass vase,
with insert, Grantham shape,
c1933, 6in (15cm) high.
£30–35 *BKK*

r. An Art Deco
figure of a boy,
on a variegated
base, 18¼in
(46.5cm) long.
£160–200 *P(B)*

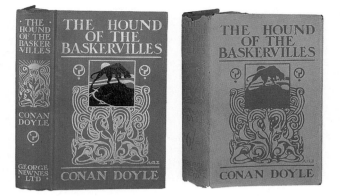

Sir Arthur Conan Doyle, *The Hound of the Baskervilles*, first edition, frontispiece and 16 illustrations by Sidney Paget, early inscription on endpaper, original dust jacket, published by George Newnes, spine of jacket slightly faded, repaired at internal folds with tape, 1902, 7½ x 5¼in (19 x 13cm).
£80,000–90,000 *S*

Apart from the copy in the Bodleian Library, and another formerly known in the Ellery Queen collection (now at Texas), copies of The Hound of the Baskervilles *are unknown in a dust jacket. No copy prior to this copy is recorded as ever having been sold at auction.*

Ian Fleming, *Live and Let Die*, first edition, first issue, published by Jonathan Cape, London, 1954, with dust jacket, 7½ x 5¼in (19 x 13cm).
£1,200–1,500 *PHa*

Surtees, *Plain or Ringlets*, first edition, full polished calf binding by Larkins, published by Bradbury & Evans, illustrated by John Leech, 1860, 8½ x 5¼in (21.5 x 13.5cm).
£200–225 *HBo*

Ian Fleming, *Goldfinger*, first edition, published by Jonathan Cape, London, 1959, 7½ x 5¼in (19 x 13cm).
£250–300 *AHa*

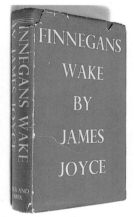

James Joyce, *Finnegans Wake*, first edition, bound in red cloth, published by Faber & Faber, London, 1939, 9¾ x 6½in (25 x 16.5cm).
£450–500 *CATH*

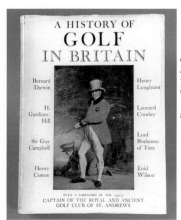

l. *The History of Golf in Britain*, first edition, published by Cassell & Co Ltd, London, 1952, 11 x 8¼in (28 x 21cm).
£140–160 *PHa*

r. *Snow White* pop-up book, published by Bancroft & Co, illustrations by Kubasta, 1961, cover damaged, 10 x 8in (25.5 x 20.5cm).
£60–70 *HBo*

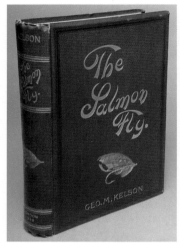

Geo M. Kelson, *The Salmon Fly*, first edition, published by author, 1895, 10 x 8in (25.5 x 20.5cm), with slip case.
£650–700 *HBo*

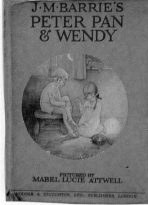

J. M. Barrie, *Peter Pan & Wendy*, illustrated by Mabel Lucie Attwell, published by Hodder & Stoughton Ltd, London, 1921, 8 x 4½in (20.5 x 11.5cm).
£120–150 *GAZE*

Anthony Buckeridge, *According to Jennings*, first edition, published by Collins, 1954, 7½ x 5½in (19 x 14cm).
£12–15 *DAC*

Bookano Stories, No. 14, published by Strand, 1930s, 8¾ x 7in (22 x 18cm).
£60–90 *AHa*

Puss in Boots, published by Dean & Son, c1880, 11¾ x 8¾in (30 x 22cm).
£180–200 *DAC*

A. A. Milne, *Winnie-the-Pooh and the Bees*, pop-up book, published by Methuen & Co Ltd, c1950, 9 x 7in (23 x 18cm).
£80–90 *DAC*

Fairy Tales, published by Thomas Nelson & Son, c1880, 13 x 10in (33 x 25.5cm).
£7–10 *DAC*

Little Dolly and her Friend Golly, 1940s, 5¾in (14.5cm) wide.
£6–8 *CMF*

A Russian brass scribe's box, decorated with mother-of-pearl and coloured stones, c1750, 6in (15cm) long.
£300–350 *MB*

A hand-painted papier mâché table snuff box, c1800, 3½in (9cm) diam.
£150–200 *MB*

An apprentice piece burr elm tea caddy, inlaid with rosewood, harewood, ebony and boxwood, c1880, 4in (10cm) wide.
£350–400 *MB*

A Georgian mahogany travelling box, early 19thC, 12in (30.5cm) wide.
£450–500 *SPU*

A Victorian rosewood box, inlaid with mother-of-pearl, 12in (30.5cm) wide.
£175–200 *SPU*

A walnut tea caddy, with brass fittings, 19thC, 10in (25.5cm) wide.
£300–330 *DAC*

A Victorian shell box, 6¾in (17cm) wide.
£60–70 *BSA*

A Mauchline ware sycamore table snuff box, depicting Canterbury Cathedral, c1870, 2½in (6.5cm) diam.
£50–60 *MB*

A Victorian walnut jewellery box, with mosaic bands and escutcheon, 11in (28cm) wide.
£150–200 *OTT*

A Tartan ware boric powder pot, late 19thC, 3in (7.5cm) diam.
£80–120 *MRW*

A late Victorian novelty tea box, in the form of a tortoise, of shell and wood construction, 11½in (29cm) long.
£375–425 *TMA*

A pottery spirit barrel, inscribed 'Brandy', c1890, 7¾in (20cm) high.
£230–250 *INC*

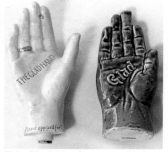

Two Glad Hand pottery flasks, c1900, 6½in (16cm) long.
£30–40 each *EKK*

An Irish Mist advertising figure, 1940s, 19in (48cm) high.
£50–70 *ByI*

A John Dewar & Sons advertising record, c1932, 12in (30.5cm) diam.
£35–40 *DAC*

A Bulmer's Cider tin tray, c1960, 10in (25.5cm) diam.
£3–4 *AL*

A Lone Star Beer advertising sign, 1970s, 14in (35.5cm) diam.
£15–20 *SAF*

A Johnnie Walker jug, by Wade, 1940–45, 5in (12.5cm) high.
£15–20 *UTP*

A Carlton Ware table lamp, 1950s, 9¼in (23cm) high.
£275–325 *P(B)*

A boxed set of 3 Carlton Ware Guinness flying toucans, 1950s, largest 9½in (24.5cm) wide.
£300–350 *P(B)*

Three bottles of Guinness, 1940s–50s, 3¼in (8cm) high.
£4–5 each *MRW*

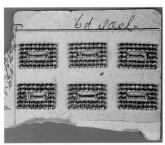

Six gold-plated buckles,
on original card, 1890s,
¾in (2cm) wide.
£2–3 each *MRW*

Two Edwardian stamped
brass buttons, with cold
enamel decoration, c1910,
1in (2.5cm) diam.
£18–20 *BQ*

A set of 6 waistcoat buttons,
lithographed with horses' heads,
c1910, ⅝in (1.5cm) diam.
£18–20 each *SLL*

Six hand-painted wood
buttons, late 1920s,
1in (2.5cm) diam.
£2–3 each *MRW*

A stamped metal and celluloid
clasp, 1920s, 3¼in (8.5cm) long.
£10–12 *BQ*

A selection of French ceramic
novelty buttons, c1920,
largest 1in (2.5cm) diam.
£10–15 each *EBB*

An Art Deco glass dress
clasp, with platinum trim,
2in (5cm) long.
£15–20 *BQ*

A set of 3 crystal
paste buttons, c1950,
⅝in (1.5cm) diam.
£10–12 *SLL*

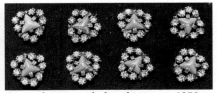

A set of paste and glass buttons, c1950,
¾in (2cm) diam.
£75–85 *EBB*

Two Italian mosaic buttons, c1950s,
⅝in (1.5cm) diam.
£10–12 each *SLL*

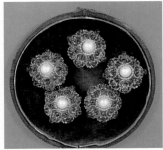

A set of 5 Christian Dior
buttons, 1960s, 1in (2.5cm) diam.
£70–80 *SLL*

r. A selection of French
Studio Pottery buttons,
signed, 1950s, largest
1½in (4cm) diam.
£14–18 each *SLL*

An Arcadian ceramic bowl, enamelled and gilded with a girl in a canoe and floral cartouche, c1915, 6¾in (17cm) diam.
£80–100 *SAS*

An Ault onion-shaped vase, designed by Christopher Dresser, c1893, 9in (23cm) high.
£800–1,000 *NCA*

l. A Belleek shamrock and basketweave pattern biscuit barrel and dish, Second Period, c1892, biscuit barrel 7½in (19cm) high.
Biscuit barrel £235–255
Dish £100–120 *DeA*

A Belleek Tridacna cup and sandwich plate, the plate in the form of a shell, Second Period, 1891–1926, plate 7in (18cm) long.
£300–350 *MLa*

A Beswick peacock, designed by Colin Melbourne, restored, 1950s, 3in (7.5cm) high.
£70–80 *PAC*

A Beswick wall plaque, in the form of a girl's head, No. 380, 1940s, 9in (23cm) high.
£145–165 *PAC*

A Beswick Beatrix Potter model of Appley Dapply, first version, 1971–75, 3in (7.5cm) high.
£80–100 *SAS*

A Beswick model of Mad Hatter, from *Alice in Wonderland* series, 1980, 5in (13cm) high.
£130–160 *PAC*

A Beswick Beatrix Potter model of Simpkin, 1975–83, 4in (10cm) high.
£250–300 *SAS*

l. A blue and white dessert dish, decorated with Grazing Rabbits pattern, c1820, 11in (28cm) wide.
£240–280 *Nor*

r. A pair of blue and white plates, decorated with American historical views of Boston and New York, from the Beauties of America series, c1820, 8in (20.5cm) diam.
£180–200 each *SCO*

ANTIQUES FOR ALL

Antiques & Collectables *magazine*

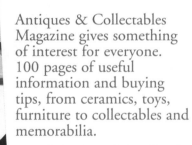

Antiques & Collectables Magazine gives something of interest for everyone. 100 pages of useful information and buying tips, from ceramics, toys, furniture to collectables and memorabilia.

PLUS Antique Price Guide and Auctions and Fairs Diary

IF YOU WOULD LIKE TO RECEIVE A COPY DIRECT OR TAKE OUT A SUBSCRIPTION CALL NOW ON

01225 311077

FAX 01225 334619

PLEASE QUOTE MILL99

the magazine for all collectors

Antiques & Collectables Magazine, 30a Monmouth Street, Bath BA1 2AN

A Clarice Cliff plate, decorated with Castellated Circle pattern, c1930, 10in (25.5cm) diam.
£1,000–1,200 *BKK*

A Clarice Cliff Bizarre vase, shape No. 356, c1930, 7in (18cm) high.
£800–1,000 *BDA*

A Clarice Cliff square step vase, decorated with Autumn pattern, shape No. 369, 1930–34, 7⅞in (20cm) high.
£2,000–2,250 *MAV*

A Clarice Cliff stepped Fern pot, decorated with Liberty pattern, c1931, 5in (13cm) high.
£300–330 *BKK*

A Clarice Cliff beehive jam pot and lid, decorated with Delecia Citrus pattern, c1931, 3in (7.5cm) high.
£300–340 *BKK*

A Clarice Cliff cauldron, decorated with Canterbury Bells pattern, 1932–33, 3in (7.5cm) high.
£380–420 *BKK*

A Clarice Cliff Lynton coffee can and saucer, decorated with Coral Firs pattern, c1933, 3in (7.5cm) high.
£240–280 *BKK*

A Clarice Cliff model of a fox, incised 'F. Ellis, 23/7/37', 1937, 8½in (21.5cm) long.
£1,200–1,400 *BKK*

A Clarice Cliff Inspiration Caprice vase, with 'Bizarre Wilkinson' mark and painted mustard 'Inspiration' mark, 1930s, 24⅛in 62cm) high.
£2,200–2,500 *AH*

r. A Clarice Cliff Bizarre Stamford tea-for-two, decorated with Autumn Crocus pattern, comprising 9 pieces, printed factory marks, 1930s.
£2,000–2,200 *J&L*

A Royal Doulton figure, 'Grace', designed by M. Nicoll, HN2318, 1966–80, 12in (30.5cm) high.
£110–130 *SnA*

A Crown Stafford-shire bone china model of a bird on a tree, decorated with flowers, by J. T. Jones, 1950s, 5in (12.5cm) high.
£100–120 *PAC*

A Royal Doulton Flambé character jug, Confucius, limited edition of 1,750, 1995, 8in (20cm) high.
£175–200 *PAC*

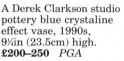

A Derek Clarkson studio pottery blue crystaline effect vase, 1990s, 9¼in (23.5cm) high.
£200–250 *PGA*

r. An Elton Ware jug, with glaze effect applied design, c1900, 7½in (19cm) high.
£160–200 *PGA*

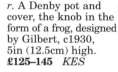

r. A Denby pot and cover, the knob in the form of a frog, designed by Gilbert, c1930, 5in (12.5cm) high.
£125–145 *KES*

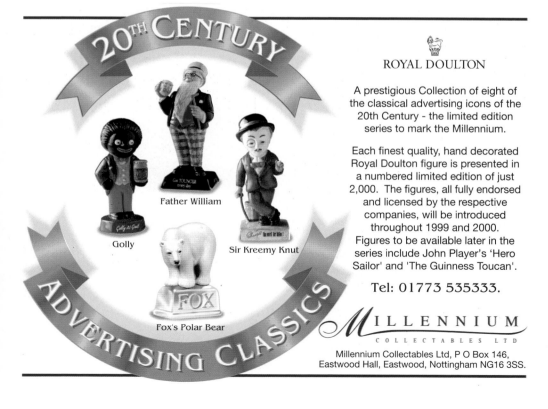

A fairing, entitled 'The Welsh Tea Party', c1895, 4in (10cm) high.
£35–45 *SAS*

A Parian group of a painted haystack, with 3 children, c1870, 6¼in (16cm) high.
£130–150 *SER*

A German porcelain group of a boy and girl, 1880s, 10in (25.5cm) high.
£325–375 *STK*

A T. Forester & Sons flower vase, decorated with Lincrusta pattern, c1930, 8in (20.5cm) high.
£40–50 *BKK*

A set of 6 Fornasetti ceramic coasters, decorated with a musical theme, 1950s, 4in (10cm) high, with a cardboard box.
£125–150 *DSG*

A Goss coloured bust of Shakespeare, c1890, 7in (18cm) high.
£160–180 *CCC*

A Goss ceramic model of Tudor House, Southampton, c1910, 3in (7.5cm) high.
£250–280 *SAS*

A Goss hand-painted cup and saucer, c1925, 3in (7.5cm) high.
£80–100 *CCC*

A Goss bust of Peeping Tom of Coventry, dated '1893', 4½in (11.5cm) high.
£140–160 *PAC*

l. An Arcadian crested model of Mabel Lucie Attwell children on a log, c1925, 3½in (9cm) long.
£150–180 *CCC*

BOXES

A tortoiseshell snuff box, with abalone shell and silver inlay, c1720, 2½in (6.5cm) diam.
£250–300 *MB*

A Dutch Colonial coromandel Bible box, with silver mounts, Colombo, c1780, 9in (23cm) wide.
£2,000–2,500 *CORO*

A type of ebony from the Coromandel coast, coromandel wood became popular in the late 18thC. In The Cabinet Dictionary *(1803), Thomas Sheraton noted that coromandel wood 'is lately introduced into England (from India) and much used by cabinet-makers for banding. Resembles black rosewood, but is intermingled with light stripes'.*

A burr mulberry table snuff box, c1825, 3in (7.5cm) diam.
£75–85 *MB*

A Scandinavian burr maple box, early 18thC, 6½in (16.5cm) diam.
£1,000–1,250 *AEF*

A tulipwood oval snuff box, with mother-of-pearl inlay, c1750, 4in (10cm) wide.
£250–300 *MB*

A partridge wood inlaid lap desk, c1800, 35in (89cm) wide.
£400–450 *MB*

Partridge wood was imported from Brazil and was used for inlay and veneers in the 17th and 18th centuries. Brown and red in tone, the streaked grain is said to resemble a bird's plumage, hence the name of the wood.

A Dutch East Indies burr amboyna document box, with ebony moulding, brass mounts, carrying handles and internal hinges, Ceylon, c1750, 19½in (49.5cm) wide.
£2,000–2,500 *CORO*

A hide-covered box, with metal studs, bandings and carrying handles, 18thC, 6½in (16.5cm) high.
£175–200 *OCH*

A Regency penwork games box, c1820, 11in (28cm) wide.
£275–325 *MB*

Penwork decoration was often applied to japanned furniture and objects in the Regency period. The piece would first be lacquered black and the design painted on in white japan. Details and shadows were then drawn in black Indian ink. As well as being produced professionally, penwork was a popular hobby with young ladies.

l. A Scottish sycamore root snuff box, c1810, 4in (10cm) diam.
£325–375 *MB*

A carved stag's horn silver-inlaid snuff box, c1820, 3in (7.5cm) diam.
£75–100 *MB*

An Anglo-Indian horn and ivory card case, c1840, 4in (10cm) wide.
£120–150 *MB*

A brass-bound mahogany apothecary's chest, containing a collection of glass bottles and stoppers, some with the trade label of Frances Scott, Dundalk, the drawer with sunk brass handle and fitted with containers, scales, weights and other items, mid-19thC, 8in (20.5cm) high.
£700–800 *HOK*

r. A Victorian mahogany inlaid box, 6in (15cm) wide.
£100–150 *SPU*

A William IV mahogany cigar box, inlaid with ebony and pewter, cedar-lined, c1830, 12in (30.5cm) wide.
£325–375 *MB*

An ivory-veneered sandalwood box, Vizagapatam, India, c1840, 8¾in (22cm) wide.
£600–700 *CORO*

A Victorian walnut, mahogany and parquetry inlaid writing/embroidery box, the fall front with inset writing surface, joined to a drawer fitted with pen tray and bottle, the top drawer with fitted interior, 2 further drawers below, on plinth base, 12½in (32cm) high.
£350–400 *GAK*

An Anglo-Indian coromandel and ivory table cabinet, of shaped serrated outline, with fitted interior, c1840, 16½in (42cm) wide.
£1,400–1,600 *HOK*

A pressed horn snuff box, in the form of Napoleon's hat, c1840, 3in (7.5cm) wide.
£300–350 *MB*

A rosewood Tunbridge Ware stamp box, 19thC, 1½in (4cm) square.
£60–70 *OTT*

A Victorian oak miniature safe box, 10in (25.5cm) wide.
£300–350 *SPU*

A pair of brass-bound camphor and teak trunks, 19thC, 41in (104cm) long.
£1,500–1,600 *GBr*

A silver-plated opium holder, base marked, 19thC, 3in (7.5cm) wide.
£350–400 *OTT*

A Victorian olive-wood vaulted stationery box, with brass decoration, 8in (20.5cm) long.
£200–250 *OTT*

An Irish yew-wood jewellery box, marquetry-inlaid with a view of Muckress Abbey and shamrock border, 19thC, 8in (20.5cm) square.
£220–250 *RBB*

A burr ash powder box, the domed top with central silver and enamel plaque, c1860, 2in (5cm) diam.
£75–100 *MB*

A burr cedar card case, c1860, 4in (10cm) wide.
£70–80 *MB*

An Indian sandalwood work box, veneered in reeded and radiating horn, containing a fitted lift-out tray, c1860, 13in (33cm) wide.
£1,800–2,200 *CORO*

A Victorian oak cigar box, lined in cedar, with bevelled glass front and lid, with brass plaque, c1880, 10in (25.5cm) long.
£350–400 *OTT*

Two Shaker miniature wooden boxes, c1880, tallest 2in (5cm) high.
£1,200–1,400 *YAG*

An Indian moulded gesso and gilded jewellery box, 19thC, 18in (46cm) wide.
£350–400 *CORO*

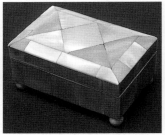

A mother-of-pearl casket, with ivory feet, c1900, 3in (7.5cm) long.
£50–60 *MB*

An Edwardian ivory stud box, 3in (7.5cm) diam.
£100–125 *DRJ*

A French fabric-covered box, 1930s, 12½in (32cm) wide.
£30–40 *WEE*

A Mauchline ware sycamore miniature trunk, decorated with a view of Aberystwith, c1870, 3in (7.5cm) wide.
£70–80 *MB*

A wooden box, the top decorated with sheep in a landscape, 1950s, 5in (12.5cm) long.
£30–40 *CHe*

A Tartan ware powder pot, the top depicting Widow Wadham and Uncle Toby, 1900s, 1½in (4cm) high.
£30–40 *MRW*

l. A Mauchline ware box, decorated with soldiers, c1900, 7in (18cm) wide.
£60–80 *BWA*

Tea Caddies

The word 'caddy' is derived from the term *kati*, a Malay standard of weight, and was first used in England in the late 18th century. Initially imported only from China, tea was an expensive luxury, hence the demand for a locked box. Caddies came in all shapes, sizes and materials, although wooden caskets were the most popular. Since tea was sold unblended, these boxes often contained two separate canisters (one for green and one for black tea), sometimes with a bowl for mixing the leaves or an extra container for sugar. Instead of holding separate canisters, smaller box caddies would have a single compartment, lined with foil known as 'tea pewter'. Caddies are worth more today if they still preserve this original foil, as are chests complete with their containers.

In the late 18th century caddies were often decorated in the rococo manner; the Regency period introduced the fashion for simpler, more architectural styles that showed off the figuring of fine and exotic woods. As the British Empire expanded in the 19th century, so tea was imported from India, Ceylon, Africa and across the world. Prices fell and tea became accessible to everybody. Although it was no longer necessary to keep the leaves under lock and key, the introduction of afternoon tea as a new meal and an important social occasion stimulated the production of many beautiful caddies, and even late Victorian caddies were sometimes fitted with locks, usually of steel rather than brass, in imitation of their Georgian predecessors.

A partridge wood tea caddy, with 2 canisters and a glass mixing bowl, late 18thC, 12in (30.5cm) wide.
£250–300 *OTT*

A Georgian mahogany tea caddy, with ebony stringing and fan inlay, 8in (20.5cm) wide.
£250–300 *MB*

A late Georgian mahogany tea caddy, with compartmented interior, line-inlaid and with star and fan motif, brass lion mask ring handles, on ball feet, 12in (30.5cm) wide.
£300–350 *TMA*

A Regency tortoiseshell tea caddy, with ivory edging and pagoda-shaped lid, 6in (15cm) wide.
£750–850 *RBB*

l. An inlaid pearwood tea caddy, c1790, 4in (10cm) wide.
£300–350 *MB*

A Regency mahogany tea caddy, with compartmented interior, 7in (18cm) wide.
£250–300 *OTT*

Locate the Source

The source of each illustration in Miller's can be found by checking the code letters below each caption with the Key to Illustrations.

A Regency rosewood tea caddy, 7½in (19cm) wide.
£250–300 *SPU*

A Regency tea caddy, with compartmented interior and glass mixing bowl, 13in (33cm) wide.
£250–300 *SPU*

A Regency rosewood tea caddy, edged with satinwood stringing, the 2 lift-out compartments with hinged tops, original etched glass mixing bowl and hallmarked silver caddy spoon, 12in (30.5cm) wide.
£220–260 *DD*

A brass-bound coromandel tea caddy, with compartmented interior, c1840, 8in (20.5cm) wide.
£300–330 *MB*

l. A coromandel tea caddy, with domed lidded canisters, c1850, 9in (23cm) wide.
£250–300 *MB*

l. An Indian ebony tea caddy, with twin compartments and overall carved decoration, late 19thC, 9½in (24cm) wide.
£350–400 *CORO*

A partridge wood tea caddy, with lidded interior, c1810, 12in (30.5cm) wide.
£200–250 *MB*

A Victorian inlaid tea caddy, 8in (20.5cm) wide.
£75–100 *SPU*

A coromandel tea caddy, with mother-of-pearl and brass decoration, c1860, 8in (20.5cm) wide.
£200–250 *MB*

A Russian silver tea caddy, with painted lid, c1900, 4in (10cm) wide.
£250–300 *RdeR*

BREWERIANA

A brewer's brass and steel malt tester, 19thC, 7in (18cm) long.
£60–80 *ET*

This was used for determining the moisture content in the grain.

Two Schweppes Ginger Ale and Devonshire Cider dishes, decorated with blue and white Willow pattern, c1920, 5½in (14cm) diam.
£20–25 each *PrB*

r. A copper and glass brewing scale buoy, with mercury indicator, No. 391865, early 20thC, 24in (61cm) high.
£30–50 *ET*

Cross Reference
Advertising & Packaging
Bottles
Corkscrews

l. An Irish glass soda water syphon, etched 'Mineral Water Distributors Ltd, Dublin', 1930s, 12in (30.5cm) high.
£15–18 *ByI*

The soda water syphon was invented in 1813 by Charles Plinth. Early models had a stopcock attached to a glass tube passing through the top of the bottle. This was later replaced by a spring-operated valve worked by a lever arm.

An Austrian porcelain bottle pourer, in the form of a man's head, 1930s, 3in (7.5cm) high.
£24–28 *JAS*

A blue glass soda water syphon, with plated metal tap, acid-etched 'J. Alexander & Sons, Avenue Works, Kendal', 1920–30s, 2½in (32cm) high.
£35–45 *BBR*

An American bottle opener, in the form of a laughing man's head, c1940, 4in (10cm) high.
£70–80 *SMAM*

A Black & White Whisky bottle opener, 1940–50s, 6¼in (16cm) long.
£4–5 *TRE*

A Johnnie Walker dish, by Wade, 1960s, 10¼in (26cm) wide.
£10–20 *PrB*

A Robinson's beer pine crate, c1950, 18in (45.5cm) wide.
£15–20 *TAN*

A Hey's Gold Cup Ale beer mat, 1950s, 3½in (9cm) square.
50p–£1 *PC*

Advertising Figures & Models

A pair of Gordon's Gin glass advertising display models, in the form of wolves' heads, 1940s, 6in (15cm) high.
£70–100 *DBr*

A Courage metal advertising display model, in the form of a cockerel, 1940s, 13in (33cm) high.
£150–200 *DBr*

A McEwan's Export composition figure, 1950s, 10in (25.5cm) high.
£50–70 *DBr*

A Fremlins Beers plastic elephant advertising model, 1960s, 5in (12.5cm) high.
£40–60 *DBr*

Barrels

A wooden barrel, with metal handle, c1880, 10in (25.5cm) diam.
£55–65 *MLL*

A set of 4 ceramic spirit barrels, decorated with coloured flowers and gilt bands on a white glaze, each fitted with a tap, 19thC, 11½in (29cm) high.
£1,600–1,800 *MCA*

A ceramic spirit barrel, c1890, 7½in (19cm) high.
£230–250 *INC*

This type of barrel was used as travelling salesmen's sample to enable clients to choose from the various label designs available.

l. Eight pottery spirit barrels, 19thC, 13in (33cm) high.
£1,200–1,400 *SWO*

A pair of Royal Doulton ginger wine barrels, c1890, 9½in (24cm) high.
£325–375 *INC*

Guinness

A Guinness plastic-covered cardboard sign, inscribed 'Guinness for Strength', 1950s, 12in (30.5cm) wide.
£35–40 *WaR*

A Guinness ashtray, by Minton, with match holder in the form of a barrel, 1940s, 4in (10cm) high.
£40–50 *PrB*

A fake Carlton Ware Guinness penguin, with blue script mark, 1993–97, 7in (18cm) high.
No commercial value *CCI*

This item is a modern fake. The original model had an oval plaque lithographed on its chest, and the colours are also flat, lacking the depth of true Carlton Ware. For further information see Miller's Collectables 1998–99.

l. An Irish linen tea towel, advertising Guinness, c1960, 28½ x 19in (72.5 x 48.5cm) high.
£15–20 *MED*

r. A Carlton Ware advertising figure, in the form of a zoo-keeper, with baby kangaroo in his apron pocket, inscribed on base 'My Goodness – My Guinness', 1950s, 4in (10cm) high.
£80–100 *BBR*

Jugs

A Barrowfield Pottery stoneware jug, impressed 'A. White, Shirley Arms Hotel, Carrickmacross', signed 'H. Y. Kennedy', late 19thC, 16in (40.5cm) high.
£165–185 *EON*

This jug was made in Scotland for the Irish market.

A Royal Doulton Kingsware whisky jug, c1935, 8in (20.5cm) high.
£250–300 *WaR*

r. A Martell Brandy jug, by Sandland, c1950, 6½in (16.5cm) high.
£45–65 *PrB*

BUCKLES & CLASPS

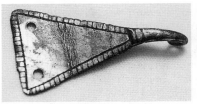

A triangular silver dress fastener, with linear decorated border, circa 9th century, 1¼in (38mm) long.
£30–35 *ANG*

A Regency paste buckle, 2in (5cm) square.
£130–150 *BQ*

A cut-steel buckle, in the form of a wheatsheaf, c1800, 2¼in (5.5cm) high.
£90–100 *BQ*

Cut-steel was first made by blacksmiths from discarded horse-shoe nails.

A silver and diamanté buckle, mid-19thC, 1½in (38mm) wide.
£45–55 *BQ*

A cut-steel buckle, c1890, 4½in (11.5cm) wide.
£45–55 *BQ*

An Edwardian mosaic mother-of-pearl clasp, 2½in (6.5cm) wide.
£12–15 *BQ*

A faceted black glass buckle, 1890s, 1¾in (4.5cm) wide.
£25–30 *BQ*

An etched and stamped brass buckle, c1900, 3¾in (9.5cm) long.
£30–35 *BQ*

A pair of cut-steel and leather shoe buckles/trims, early 20thC, 2½in (6.5cm) wide.
£75–85 *BQ*

A glass and diamanté shoe trim, 1920s, 2¼in (5.5cm) wide.
£20–25 *BQ*

l. A selection of French iridescent tin and plastic buckles, 1920–30s, 1½in (38mm) wide.
£3–4 each *JV*

A stamped metal dress clasp, 1930s, 3¼in (8.5cm) long.
£16–18 *BQ*

BUTTONS

Buttons have been found in Egyptian tombs and the earliest examples shown here are Persian, dating from circa 450 BC. As well as using humble materials such as clay, ancient civilizations also produced fine buttons in semi-precious stones, and throughout history buttons have been used for decorative as well as practical purposes. Henry VIII had one court costume sewn with 15,000 buttons; George II wore buttons made from diamonds, and also in the 18th century elaborate jewelled buttons were worn on breeches, coats and waistcoats. For the less wealthy there were buttons of base metal and other cheaper materials. Main production centres were Birmingham (principal manufacturers of metal and shell buttons) and Shaftesbury, in Dorset, where a largely rural population specialized in hand-stitched flax buttons.

The 19th century saw growing mechanization. Ashton's patent button machine, invented in 1841 for mass-producing fabric buttons, killed off the Dorset 'Butonny', but the Midlands industry flourished, supplying its wares across the Empire. Metal was one of the most popular materials, used on uniforms both military and civilian. Servants wore livery buttons (hence the nickname of the young page in *Cinderella*) decorated with the arms of the house. For the master and mistress there were silver and finely enamelled buttons (very popular during the Edwardian period). Bright and shining cut-steel buttons were worn at court, and when Queen Victoria went into mourning there was a huge demand for black buttons in glass and jet. The elaborate fashions of the Victorian and Edwardian periods stimulated demand for buttons of every style and material. Ivory, tortoiseshell and mother-of-pearl were imported from the colonies, fine ceramic buttons were produced by art potteries such as Pilkington, Ruskin and Brannam, and glass buttons were made in Italy and Eastern Europe as well as by British factories.

The 20th century saw the advent of synthetic buttons. Bakelite (invented by Dr Leo Baekeland in 1907), celluloid and casein (milk plastic) were used for Art Deco buttons of the 1920s and 1930s, and the continued development of plastic technology stimulated the production of affordable buttons in every shape and colour.

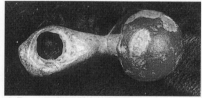

A Bronze Age Celtic button, 1¼in (38mm) long.
£50–60 *SLL*

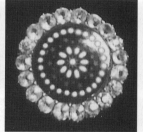

An enamel button, encrusted and set with gold paillons, set in silver with paste, late 18thC, 1¼in (32mm) diam.
£130–150 *BQ*

Paillons are pieces of gold foil set in enamel to provide a flashing effect. Buttons of this type are rare.

A pair of copper buttons, engraved with bees, 18thC, 1½in (38mm) diam.
£150–180 *EBB*

A pair of French cut-steel buttons, late 18thC, 1½in (38mm) diam.
£55–65 *SLL*

l. A manufacturer's sample frame of buttons, made for the Great Exhibition, 1851.
£4,500–5,000 *BQ*

A set of court steel buttons, early 19thC, 1in (25mm) diam.
£150–180 *SLL*

A Victorian carved bone button, ½in (12mm) diam.
£4–5 *SLL*

A set of 6 Victorian dyed horn York Police buttons, by James Grove & Sons, Halesowen, ¾in (19mm) diam.
£8–10 *SLL*

Horn was much used for military buttons. Hoof horn was softened with heat, dyed and then die-stamped with a crest or design. James Grove was a major manufacturer.

A set of late Victorian silver-plated copper livery buttons, by Smith & Kemp, Birmingham, 1in (25mm) diam.
£50–60 *SLL*

r. A cut and mounted cut-steel on etched and lacquered stamped-brass button, 19thC, 1in (25mm) diam.
£65–75 *BQ*

A collection of picture buttons, depicting characters from literature, fables and fairy stories, c1880, largest 2in (50mm) diam.
£15–30 each *BQ*

A set of 6 brass livery buttons, by Armfields, Birmingham, 1890s, 1in (25mm) diam.
£45–55 *SLL*

A set of 6 gilt-brass Kildare Hunt Club buttons, by Gaunt Ltd, London, 19thC, ½in (12mm) diam.
£30–36 *SLL*

A set of 14 Victorian silver-plated copper buttons, in Baron Camoys livery, by Firmin & Sons, London, largest 1in (25mm) diam.
£85–95 *SLL*

l. A Vauxhall glass button, 1870s, 1¼in (32mm) diam.
£15–20 *SLL*

A set of 9 enamel buttons, c1880, largest 1in (25mm) diam.
£30–35 *EBB*

An opaline glass and paste claw-set button, 1890s, 1in (25mm) diam.
£15–20 *BQ*

l. A Ruskin ceramic button, c1890, 1¾in (45mm) diam.
£55–65 *EBB*

A set of 8 papier mâché buttons, 1830–40s, 1in (25mm) diam.
£100–120 *EBB*

A set of 10 late Victorian dyed mother-of-pearl buttons, ¼in (6mm) wide.
£2–3 *MRW*

A set of 6 brass livery buttons, by Firmin & Sons, London, c1900, ½in (12mm) diam.
£18–22 *SLL*

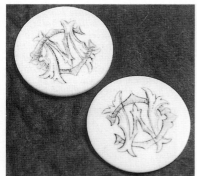

A pair of ivory studs, c1900, 1½in (38mm) diam.
£30–40 *EBB*

A glass paperweight button, ¼in (6mm) diam.
£6–7 *BQ*

An Edwardian stamped-brass button, with moulded design, 1½in (38mm) diam.
£4–5 *BQ*

A pair of shell buttons, with filigree decoration, c1900, 1½in (38mm) diam.
£15–18 *EBB*

A silver-plated shell-shaped button, c1900, 1½in (38mm) long.
£4–5 *SLL*

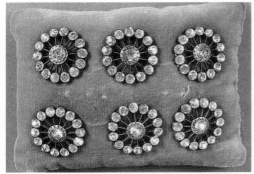

A set of 6 solid silver and paste buttons, c1900, 1¼in (32mm) diam.
£400–450 *SLL*

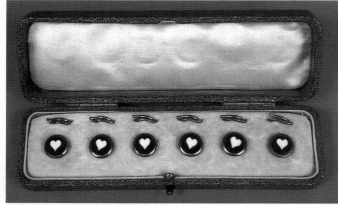

A set of 6 gentleman's black and white glass waistcoat buttons, in original box, c1900, ¼in (6mm) diam.
£90–100 *SLL*

Since buttons were often not washable, they came with detachable clips and could be removed when clothes were cleaned, or transferred to other garments.

A collection of celluloid buttons, c1920, largest 2in (5cm) diam.
£1.50–6 each *BQ*

Celluloid was invented in 1869 by John W. Hyatt of New Jersey. Designed to imitate ivory, it was first used for billiard balls, not altogether successfully, since they were flammable. From the late 19thC onwards celluloid was much used to manufacture buttons, and was suitable both for washing and dry cleaning.

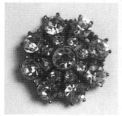

A claw-set paste button, early 20thC, 1in (25mm) diam.
£8–10 *BQ*

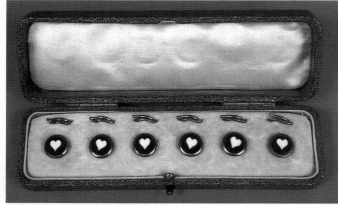

A pair of garter buttons, on original card, 1920s, ½in (12mm) diam.
£35–45 *EBB*

An Art Nouveau *champlevé* enamelled silver button, ¾in (19mm) diam.
£70–80 *SLL*

An embossed-leather button, in a brass surround, 1920s, 1½in (38mm) diam.
£6–8 *BQ*

A set of 6 Italian painted metal buttons, 1930s, 1¾in (4.5cm) diam.
£15–18 *SLL*

A mottled plastic coat button, 1930s, 2½in (6.5cm) long.
£10–12 *MRW*

A set of 4 Art Deco plastic buttons, 1930s, ¾in (19mm) diam.
£4–6 *MRW*

l. A set of 6 Art Deco casein buttons and a buckle, 1930s, buckle 3¼in (8cm) wide.
£35–40 *BQ*

Casein is a protein found in milk and used in the manufacture of plastics and adhesives.

A set of 4 wooden buttons, each
decorated with a dog's head,
1930s–40s, 1¼in (32mm) diam.
£10–12 *EBB*

Two wooden buttons, each
decorated with a dog's head,
c1930, 1in (25mm) diam.
£5–6 *EBB*

A set of 6 Bimini glass buttons,
1940s, 1¼in (32mm) diam.
£30–35 *BQ*

A set of 6 red plastic buttons,
1940s, ¾in (19mm) diam.
£6–8 *MRW*

A selection of leather buttons,
1940s, largest 1¼in (32mm) diam.
40–50p each *SLL*

A sample card of Italian
plastic buttons, 1950s,
1¼in (32mm) diam.
£1.50–2 each *SLL*

A set of 3 Italian glass buttons,
1950s, ½in (12mm) diam.
£12–14 *MRW*

A set of 6 paste buttons, c1950,
½in (12mm) diam.
£50–60 *EBB*

A set of 9 base metal
Tutankamen buttons, 1970s,
largest 1in (25mm) diam.
£15–18 *SLL*

A set of 4 mother-of-pearl
buttons, with plastic surrounds,
c1970, 1½in (38mm) diam.
£6–8 *MRW*

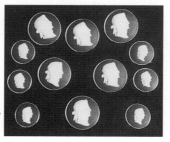

r. A set of 12 Wedgwood buttons,
1990s, largest ¾in (19mm) diam.
£150–170 *BQ*

A set of 6 Danforth pewter
buttons, in the form of pigs,
Rhode Island, USA, c1992,
¾in (19mm) high.
£18–20 *SLL*

CAMERAS

An Asahi Pentax camera,
c1992, 5½in (14cm) wide.
£80–100 *VCL*

An Agfa Record III camera,
c1952, 4½in (11.5cm) wide.
£25–30 *VCL*

A Bencini Comet III camera,
c1953, 4in (10cm) high.
£25–30 *VCL*

A Canon AE-1 Program camera,
c1980, 5½in (14cm) wide.
£80–100 *VCL*

A Dekko standard Model 104
9.5mm cine camera, with Ross
lens, c1937, 5¼in (13cm) high.
£30–50 *CaH*

An Edixa 16-S camera, c1960,
3¼in (8.5cm) wide.
£60–70 *VCL*

l. An Eljy Lumiere
30mm miniature
camera, French,
1937–48, 3in (7.5cm)
wide, in leather case.
£40–50 *TOM*

r. An Ensign Model No. 1
red camera, c1950,
6in (15cm) wide.
£30–35 *JUN*

An Ensign E29 blue camera,
c1930, 5¼in (13.5cm) high.
£25–30 *VCL*

An Ensign Midget camera,
c1936, 3in (7.5cm) wide.
£15–20 *VCL*

A Finetta 88 camera, c1954,
5in (12.5cm) wide.
£15–20 *VCL*

A Kodak Brownie Automatic
camera, c1910, 7in (18cm) wide.
£50–60 *VCL*

*'The dollar camera is at last a
fact,'* announced the Eastman
Kodak Company in February
1900, at the launch of the
Brownie camera. George
Eastman had wanted to create
an inexpensive children's camera
that would stimulate demand
for film. The Brownie was
designed by Frank Brownwell.
It was not named after him, but
after the Brownies, elf-like
creatures, from the stories by the
Canadian writer Pam Cox, who
were chosen for their friendly
and childlike associations.
The first Brownie box camera
retailed in England for
5 shillings. Easy to operate,
they were a huge success with
adults as well as children and
sold in vast numbers. Over the
decades, some 70 different
models were produced until the
1960s when the Brownie was
replaced by another popular
classic, the Instamatic.

A Franka-Werke Super
Frankarette 45mm camera,
with fixed Schneider Xenar
lens, c1958, 5in (13cm) wide.
£50–60 *CaH*

A Kodak Brownie No. 2
Autographic folding
camera, c1917,
8in (20.5cm) high.
£6–8 *VCL*

A Gevabox metal box
camera, German, 1955–59,
9in (23cm) wide.
£5–10 *HEG*

l. A Kodak
No. 1a folding
pocket camera,
116 size film,
Rochester, USA,
c1905, 8in
(20.5cm) wide.
£45–55 *ARP*

A Kodak Model K 16mm
cine camera, with
Anastigmat lens, 1930–46,
9½in (24cm) wide.
£60–70 *CaH*

A Kodak Junior
camera, late 1950s,
8in (20.5cm) high.
£15–18 *Rac*

l. A Kodak Pocket
Instamatic 400
camera, with
110 cartridge,
German, c1972,
5in (12.5cm) wide.
£10–15 *ARP*

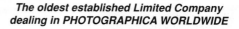

A Konica FS camera, c1961, 5¾in (14.5cm) wide.
£60–70 *VCL*

A Leica R-E camera, c1990, 5in (12.5cm) wide.
£550–600 *VCL*

r. A Leitz Focomat 1C colour drawer and 4.550mm Focatar lens, c1960, 27¼in (69cm) high.
£450–500 *CaH*

A Microflex M.P.P. camera, c1959, 5in (12.5cm) high.
£50–60 *VCL*

A Minolta 16P sub-miniature camera, takes 16mm cassettes, Japanese, c1960, 4in (10cm) wide.
£25–30 *ARP*

A Mamiya C330 Professional interchangeable twin lens reflex camera, c1980, 5in (12.5cm) high.
£400–450 *ARP*

A Minolta Hi-Matic F automatic 35mm camera, c1970, 4½in (11.5cm) wide.
£30–35 *ARP*

An Olympus-Pen half-frame camera, Japanese, c1960, 4in (10cm) wide.
£55–65 *ARP*

This camera is an original model made by a subcontractor for Olympus.

An Olympus OM10 automatic single lens reflex camera, c1979, Japanese, 5½in (14cm) wide.
£65–80 *ARP*

A Praktica MTL3 camera, c1978, 5in (13cm) wide.
£10–15 *VCL*

A Pentacon Six TL camera, c1970, 6in (15cm) wide.
£80–90 *VCL*

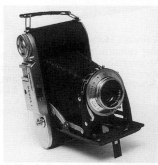

A Voightlander Bessa I 105mm camera, with Vasker lens, c1953. 6½in (16.5cm) high.
£75–110 *CaH*

r. A Zeiss Baby Box camera,
1930s, 3¼in (8.5cm) high.
£25–30 *Rac*

A Voigtländer Vito B 50mm
camera, with Color-Skopar fixed
lens, c1954, 4½in (11.5cm) wide.
£75–90 *CaH*

A Welta Kamera-Werke Penti II
camera, c1962, 5in (13cm) wide.
£30–35 *HEG*

Viewers & Slides

A box of 100 stereoscope cards,
depicting views of Switzerland,
1910–20.
£70–80 *MED*

A tulipwood crossbanded
photograph viewer, c1870,
8in (20.5cm) long.
£150–200 *MB*

A late Victorian magic
lantern and slides,
18in (45.5cm) high.
£250–300 *SPU*

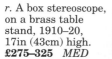

r. A box stereoscope,
on a brass table
stand, 1910–20,
17in (43cm) high.
£275–325 *MED*

A collection of magic lantern slides, late 19thC,
7 x 4in (18 x 10cm).
Hand-painted £15–30 each
Printed   £10–15 each *HEG*

CANDLESTICKS

A pair of brass square-based candlesticks, with side pusher, c1790, 10in (25.5cm) high.
£235–265 *ANT*

A pair of Georgian brass round-based candlesticks, of seamed construction, c1800, 10in (25.5cm) high.
£260–285 *ANT*

A pair of Continental ormolu candlesticks, in the form of anthemia formed from rams' heads, on pierced circular bases, 19thC, 10¼in (26cm) high.
£550–600 *HOK*

A French faïence candlestick, decorated with polychrome colours, 19thC, 8in (20.5cm) high.
£90–100 *SER*

A late Victorian brass chamber stick, designed by Dr Christopher Dresser, with curved turned wood handle and domed base, registration mark and stamp, 5½in (14cm) high.
£100–120 *MCA*

A pair of French brass candlesticks, early 20thC, 10in (25.5cm) high.
£110–120 *DAC*

A Belgian blue and green pottery candlestick, c1900, 9½in (24cm) high.
£18–22 *IW*

l. A blue enamelled chamber stick, with match-box holder, c1900, 4in (10cm) diam.
£10–12 *AL*

An Arnhem pottery chamber candlestick, decorated with batik-style design, c1929, 9in (23cm) high.
£120–150 *PO*

A pair of turquoise pottery candlesticks, by Artus Van Briggle, in the form of tulips, American, 1920s, 6in (15cm) high.
£100–125 *EKK*

r. A Myott hand-painted candlestick, c1934, 3in (7.5cm) high.
£50–70 *BKK*

CERAMICS
Belleek

The Belleek factory was founded in Belleek, Co Fermanagh, Northern Ireland, in 1857, and started porcelain production in 1863. The firm became famous for its paper-thin Parian ware, glazed with 'mother-of-pearl' lustre, with details often highlighted with soft, muted colours. Specialities included featherweight ceramic baskets, applied with finely executed flowerheads, and elaborate tableware often modelled in the form of shells, mermaids and other marine subjects. Irish imagery, including shamrocks and Celtic designs, were popular; the firm also produced Parian statuary. The high prices commanded by the most decorative products, such as openwork baskets and sculptural centrepieces, have stimulated demand both for later ceramics and more functional, domestic items such as cups and saucers.

Early wares were often impressed with the name 'Belleek'. From 1863, pieces carried a transfer-printed mark of a round tower with an Irish harp and Irish wolfhound above the name 'Belleek' in a ribbon with shamrock leaves at each end. Another mark, less frequently used during the same period, was a harp surmounted by a crown. After 1891, the words 'Co Fermanagh, Ireland' were added to the mark. From around 1900 the marks changed again, and in general the more marks there are, the later the piece.

A Belleek cream jug, First Period, 1863–90, 3½in (9cm) high.
£200–220 *MLa*

A Belleek Institute pattern cup and saucer, First Period, 1863–90, saucer 5¾in (14.5cm) diam.
£320–350 *DeA*

A Belleek earthenware crested stand, First Period, 1863–90, 9¼in (23.5cm) diam.
£360–380 *DeA*

This was a special order made for the Fitzgerald family in County Kerry.

A Belleek cauldron, decorated with shamrocks, Second Period, 1891–1926, 5½in (14cm) high.
£100–120 *MLa*

A Belleek Sydney cup and saucer, Second Period, 1891–1926, 3⅓in (8.5cm) diam.
£280–300 *MLa*

r. A Belleek Hexagon demi-tasse cup and saucer, the green tinted cup painted in gold with 'Baby', Second Period, 1891–1926, saucer 4¼in (11cm) diam.
£150–175 *MLa*

A Belleek Beehive honey pot-on-stand, Second Period, 1891–1926, 6½in (16.5cm) high.
£90–100 *DeA*

A Belleek pink sugar dish, decorated with a shell pattern, Second Period, 1891–1926, 3¼in (8.5cm) diam.
£35–45 *MLa*

A Belleek mug, with black transfer print of Blarney Castle, Second Period, 1891–1926, 4in (10cm) high.
£135–155 *DeA*

A Belleek High Lily cup and saucer, Second Period, 1891–1926, cup 3in (7.5cm) high.
£175–195 *MLa*

A Belleek Celtic bowl and cover, Third Period, 1926–46, 3¾in (9.5cm) high.
£170–200 *DeA*

A Belleek Celtic trio, Third Period, 1926–46, cup 3in (7.5cm) high.
£220–245 *MLa*

A Belleek Limpet cup and saucer, decorated in pink with gilding, Third Period, 1926–46, 3¼in (8.5cm) diam.
£65–75 *MLa*

A Belleek hand-painted Celtic saucer, Third Period, 1926–46, 5¼in (13.5cm) diam.
£70–80 *DeA*

A Belleek Newshell cup and saucer, Fifth Period, 1955–65, 2½in (6.5cm) high.
£270–300 *DeA*

A Belleek star-shaped dish, hand-painted with mallard First Green or Fourth Period, 1946–55, 6in (15cm) diam.
£320–350 *DeA*

l. A Belleek Thorn mug, white with gold decoration, Third Green or Sixth Period, 1965–80, 3½in (9cm) high.
£30–40 *MLa*

A Belleek heart-shaped dish, Second Green or Fifth Period, 1955–65, 4½in (11.5cm) long.
£15–20 *MLa*

Beswick

A Beswick model of a man and woman on a donkey, No. 1245, c1950, 5in (12.5cm) high.
£250–300 *PAC*

A Beswick model of a Spaniard pulling a donkey, No. 1223, c1950, 5in (12.5cm) high.
£175–200 *PAC*

A Beswick model of a bull, decorated in orange and black, by Colin Melbourne, 1950s, 5in (12.5cm) high.
£160–190 *PAC*

A Beswick model of a swan, by Colin Melbourne, decorated in black and red, 1950s, 6in (15cm) long.
£100–120 *PAC*

A Beswick model of a British Shorthorn bull, No. 1504, c1957, 5in (12.5cm) high.
£550–600 *PAC*

A Beswick group of partridges, No. 2064, c1966, 5½in (14cm) high.
£200–250 *PC*

A Beswick Bambi plate, 1960s, 4½in (11.5cm) diam.
£15–20 *Rac*

A Beswick figure of the Queen of Hearts, from *Alice in Wonderland*, c1974, 4in (10cm) high.
£40–50 *PAC*

A set of Beswick Top Cat figures, c1998, largest 7in (18cm) high.
£350–400 *PAC*

Beatrix Potter

A Beswick model of Mrs Tittlemouse, carrying a basket, 1948–93, 3in (7.5cm) high.
£20–30 *SAS*

A Beswick model of Timmy Tiptoes, with red jacket, first version, 1948–80, 5½in (14cm) high.
£30–40 *SAS*

A Beswick model of Duchess, from *The Pie and the Patty Pan*, first version, late 1950s, 3¾in (9.5cm) high.
£1,800–2,000 *E*

This is one of the rarest and most sought after of all Beswick figures, taken from The Pie and the Patty Pan. The Duchess figure was introduced in 1955 and withdrawn in 1967.

A Beswick model of Pigling Bland, with deep maroon jacket, first version, 1955–74, 4in (10cm) high.
£70–90 *SAS*

r. A Beswick group of Flopsy, Mopsy and Cottontail, 1954–present, 2½in (6.5cm) high.
£70–80 *WWY*

> **Cross Reference**
> Colour Review

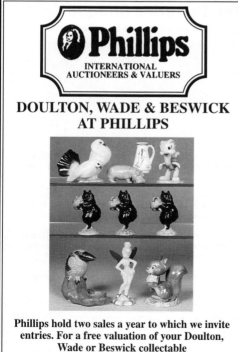

A Beswick model of Tommy Brock, with gold oval back stamp, late 1950s, 3½in (9cm) high.
£230–260 *E*

A Beswick model of Sally Henny Penny, 1974–93, 5in (12.5cm) high.
£20–30 *SAS*

r. A Beswick Ware group of Mrs Rabbit and the four Bunnies, limited edition of 1,997, 1997, 7in (18cm) long.
£450–500 *PAC*

Blue and White

A Thomas Lakin blue and white soup plate, decorated with Classical Ruins pattern, c1810, 9½in (24cm) diam.
£60–80 *GN*

A William Mason blue and white plate, decorated with Furness Abbey pattern, 1811–23, 8in (20.5cm) diam.
£80–120 *GN*

A Spode blue and white plate, decorated with Death of the Bear pattern, c1820, 10in (25.5cm) diam.
£150–180 *GN*

A New Hall blue and white tea bowl and saucer, decorated with Willow pattern, c1815, saucer 5½in (14cm) diam.
£45–55 *BSA*

A blue and white soup plate and dessert plate, from the Durham Ox series, maker unknown, c1820, dessert plate 10in (25.5cm) diam.
£300–350 each *GN*

A Brameld Rockingham plate, decorated with Castle of Rochefort pattern, c1820, 8½in (21.5cm) diam.
£120–150 *GN*

A blue and white drainer, decorated with Grazing Rabbits pattern, maker unknown, c1820, 15in (38cm) wide.
£250–300 *SCO*

A Henshaw & Co blue and white sauce tureen, decorated with Castle and Bridge pattern, hairline crack to base, 1820–30, 5½in (14cm) high.
£100–120 *OCH*

r. A pair of Staffordshire blue and white pearlware strainers, 19thC, 3¾in (9.5cm) diam.
£180–200 *TMA*

l. A blue and white pearlware canted meat dish, decorated with a bridge in a river landscape, Italianate ruins beyond, within a border of hops and leaves, blue printed 'Semi China' mark, c1820–25, 20¾in (52.5cm) wide.
£400–450 *DN*

A blue and white pearlware baluster-shaped jug, with loop handle, printed with a view of Washington, within a broad bands of flowers and leaves, probably J. Tams & Co, c1825, 9½in (24cm) high.
£850–950 *DN*

A Pountney & Allies blue and white soap dish, decorated with The Drama pattern, c1830, 3in (7.5cm) high.
£85–95 *GN*

A blue and white sauce tureen, transfer-printed with Trellis pattern, some damage, mid-19thC, 7½in (19cm) diam.
£30–40 *MEG*

Locate the Source

The source of each illustration in Miller's can be found by checking the code letters below each caption with the Key to Illustrations.

A Minton blue and white candlestick, decorated with Botanical sheet pattern, c1825, 10in (25.5cm) high.
£350–400 *SCO*

A Davenport blue and white child's chamber pot/spittoon, c1830–40, 5in (12.5cm) diam.
£145–165 *OCH*

A blue and white dish, decorated with Wild Rose pattern, 19thC, 16in (40.5cm) long.
£80–100 *AP*

r. A blue and white money box, on raised bun feet, c1880, 6½in (16.5cm) long.
£300–350 *INC*

This was used as an RSPCA charity box.

A Minton invalid feeder, decorated with Butterfly and Flowers pattern, c1830, 6in (15cm) wide.
£220–240 *GN*

A William Ridgway toilet bowl, decorated with Oriental Drama pattern, minor damage and repairs, c1840, 13in (33cm) diam.
£80–100 *MEG*

A Victorian Trent blue and white jug, 5in (12.5cm) high.
£60–70 *LUC*

Bretby

In late 19th-century Britain, a number of small art potteries developed hand-crafted, handsomely glazed earthenware for an educated and design-conscious clientele. William Ault and Henry Tooth, formerly of Linthorpe Pottery, established Bretby Art Pottery in 1883. This Derbyshire-based company won several awards at international exhibitions for their decorative vases and domestic ware. Early pieces are marked with an impressed sunburst motif above the name 'Bretby'; from 1891, the mark incorporated the word 'England' and 20th-century pieces are marked 'Made in England'. Bretby Art Pottery was sold in 1933 to Fred Parker, and manufacture continues today.

A pair of Bretby tall waisted vases, with Islamic-style frieze, decorated in green, yellow, red and blue overlaid with gilt, c1900, 12½in (32cm) high.
£160–200 *P(B)*

A Bretby jug, decorated in shades of brown, red and green, with incised floral decoration and brown handle, 1920–30, 8in (20.5cm) high.
£85–95 *DSG*

> **Cross Reference**
> Colour Review

A Bretby-type majolica umbrella stand, modelled as a green-glazed tree trunk with brown bear support, c1900, 27in (68.5cm) high.
£450–500 *RBB*

A Bretby globular pottery vase, with trumpet-form neck, covered overall with a glaze resembling random splashes of blue, grey-brown and muted yellow, marked, c1930, 5¼in (13.5cm) high.
£40–50 *DSG*

Burmantofts

Burmantofts, near Leeds, was founded by Messrs Wilcox & Co in 1858 to manufacture architectural terracotta such as drainpipes. The company only began producing art pottery in 1880. Their specialities include large and beautifully moulded jardinières, and wares decorated with rich, glowing glazes, ranging from brilliant turquoise to pale yellow to *sang-de-boeuf* red. Pieces are marked on the base with the pottery's name or the monogram 'BF'. Burmantofts' experimental glazework was costly to produce, and owing to economic pressure the art pottery side closed down in 1904, although architectural production continued until the 1950s.

A Burmantofts dimpled blue vase, c1885, 7¾in (19.5cm) high.
£300–330 *NCA*

l. A Burmantofts blue jardinière, c1900, 45in (114.5cm) high.
£700–800 *PAC*

r. A Burmantofts red two-handled vase, c1885, 11in (28cm) high.
£120–140 *NCA*

Burleigh Ware

Burleigh Ware was produced by the firm of Burgess & Leigh, which was established as Hulme & Booth in 1851 and renamed Burgess & Leigh in 1877. Before WWI the company concentrated on toilet wares and it was not until the 1920s and '30s that tea and dinner services became a significant part of their production. Using the trade name Burleigh Ware (a title that united their two names), Burgess & Leigh introduced Art Deco tableware, decorated with hand-painted and enamelled designs in bright fashionable colours. New geometric shapes such as Zenith and Imperial (both launched in the early 1930s) were modelled by Ernest Bailey, while patterns were created by Harold Bennett, art director and chief designer. Bennett was a landscape painter, and many of his designs for Burleigh Ware reflect his personal passion for trees and nature. In addition to tableware, the firm also became celebrated for its novelty relief-moulded jugs with bold, sculptural handles often in the form of animals or birds.

Very sought after today, Burgess & Leigh's colourful Art Deco ceramics were highly successful in the 1930s when the company employed 450 staff, including 100 women painters. Wartime restrictions severely affected the firm's output during the 1940s, and it was not until the 1950s that decorated ware was once again produced for the home market. Traditional styles of hand-painting had become too expensive so lithograph and screen-printed transfers were introduced. Today, Burgess & Leigh still operates from the Middleport factory in Burslem that was first opened in 1889, and the chairman of the factory, Mr Edmund Leigh, is a direct descendant of the original founder.

A Burleigh Ware yellow jug, with moulded Grape pattern, c1930, 7in (18cm) high.
£250–300 *BEV*

A Burleigh Ware jug, decorated with Garden pattern, 1930s, 7½in (19cm) high.
£200–250 *BUR*

A Burleigh Ware jug, with moulded Honeycomb pattern, 1930s, 8½in (21.5cm) high.
£350–400 *BUR*

A Burleigh Ware jug, decorated with Flamingo pattern, c1930, 9in (23cm) high.
£225–250 *BEV*

A Burleigh Ware dish, designed by Charlotte Rhead, pattern No. S606, c1930, 10½in (27cm) diam.
£90–110 *BKK*

A Burleigh Ware pitcher, decorated with a tube-lined design, by Harold Bennett, 1930s, 9½in (24cm) high.
£180–200 *BDA*

A Burleigh Ware hand-painted vase, in the form of a sailing boat, c1932, 6in (15cm) high.
£50–70 *BKK*

A Burleigh Ware dinner service, decorated with Golden Days pattern, comprising 4 tureens, covers and stands, 3 oval dishes, and 3 sets of various sized plates, 1930s.
£350–400 *E*

A Burleigh Ware plate, designed by Harold Bennett, decorated with Dawn pattern, 1930s, 8in (20.5cm) diam.
£22–25 *BDA*

A Burleigh Ware Zenith shape coffee pot, decorated with Meadowland pattern, 1930s, 7in (19cm) high.
£75–90 *BUR*

A Burleigh Ware double vase, hand-painted in green and red on a yellow ground, c1933, 8in (20.5cm) high.
£80–120 *BKK*

A Burleigh Ware sandwich set, decorated with Lakeside pattern, 1930s, large plate 9in (23cm) diam.
£30–40 *BUR*

A Burleigh Ware Zenith shape trio, decorated with Orange Tree pattern, 1930s, cup 3in (7.5cm) high.
£35–45 *BUR*

l. A Burleigh Ware green and yellow jug, the handle in the form of a gnome, 1930s, 7in (18cm) high.
£550–600 *BEV*

A Burleigh Ware cup and
saucer, decorated with Bunny
pattern, 1930s, 3in (7.5cm) high.
£65–70 *BUR*

A Burleigh Ware Zenith
shape coffee cup and saucer,
decorated with Dawn
Breckland pattern, 1930s,
cup 2½in (6.5cm) high.
£35–45 *BUR*

A Burleigh Ware toast rack,
decorated with Meadowland
pattern, 1930s, 6in (15cm) wide.
£40–50 *BUR*

A Burleigh Ware posy holder,
with original label, 1930s,
6in (15cm) diam.
£25–35 *BUR*

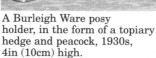

A Burleigh Ware posy
holder, in the form of a topiary
hedge and peacock, 1930s,
4in (10cm) high.
£50–75 *BUR*

A Burleigh Ware Bird
of Paradise jug, 1930s,
10in (25.5cm) high.
£250–275 *BUR*

A Burleigh Ware jug, decorated
with butterflies and flowers,
c1935, 8in (20.5cm) high.
£90–110 *CSA*

A Burleigh Ware green vase,
relief-moulded with flat-
glazed Swan pattern, c1937,
7½in (19cm) high.
£100–120 *BKK*

A Burleigh Ware character jug,
modelled as Winston Churchill
in blue naval uniform, impressed
mark, c1940, 5½in (14cm) high.
£125–145 *W&S*

Miller's is a price GUIDE
not a price LIST

Candle Extinguishers

A candle extinguisher and tray, decorated with lilac blossom and gold trim, unmarked, c1900, 4in (10cm) high.
£250–300 *TH*

A Royal Worcester candle extinguisher, in the form of a beige Japanese lady, c1901, 3in (7.5cm) high.
£200–220 *TH*

l. Two Royal Worcester candle extinguishers, entitled 'Old Woman' and 'Young Girl', reproduced from old factory moulds, 1976–86, 3½in (9cm) high.
£70–110 each *TH*

A Goss candle extinguisher, c1910–20, 2¼in (6cm) high.
£10–12 *TAC*

A Goss candle extinguisher, c1910–20, 2½in (6.5cm) high.
£10–12 *TAC*

A collection of four Royal Worcester candle extinguishers, entitled 'French Cook', 'Mandarin', 'Punch' and 'Owl', all reproduced from old factory moulds, 1976–86, tallest 3½in (9cm) high.
£70–110 each *TH*

Carlton Ware

A Carlton Ware tinted faïence moustache cup and saucer, with ribbon mark, 1890–94, glaze crazed, saucer 6½in (16.5cm) diam.
£20–30 *StC*

A Carlton Ware tinted faïence all-in-one egg cup and stand, with pepper and salt wells, ribbon mark, pattern No. 600, 1890–94, 3¾in (9.5cm) diam.
£30–40 *StC*

A Carlton Ware tinted faïence teapot, with Bain's tea infuser and separator, decorated in Marguerite pattern, No. 604, late 19th/early 20thC, 8in (20.5cm) high.
£80–100 *StC*

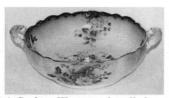

A Carlton Ware two-handled bowl, the blush-ivory ground painted with sprays of flowers, with blue and gilt wavy rim, c1900, 9¾in (25cm) high.
£200–225 *AP*

l. A Carlton Ware model, entitled 'An Irish Cabin', c1920, 3in (7.5cm) high.
£180–200 *MLa*

A Carlton Ware ashtray, decorated in green, red and black with flowers, leaves and seed pods, c1930, 4¼in (11cm) diam.
£25–30 *TAR*

A Carlton Ware dish, brown transfer-printed and hand enamelled on a blush ground, decorated with Poppy pattern, restored, No. 924½, blue crown mark, c1900, 8½in (21.5cm) square.
£40–50 *StC*

A Carlton Ware 15-piece coffee set, decorated with Pagoda pattern, 1930–35, coffee pot 7in (18cm) high.
£500–550 *PAC*

A Carlton Ware blue and green napkin ring, in the form of a clown, enamel chipped, 1930s, 3¾in (9.5cm) high.
£50–60 *StC*

A Carlton Ware coffee pot and cover, painted with red and brown banded decoration, c1935, 8½in (21.5cm) high.
£80–90 *CSA*

A Carlton Ware ashtray, with black transfer-printed hand-enamelled illustration and verse entitled 'Dreamer', shape No. 1755, black script mark, pattern No. 2831, 1930–40s, 3¾in (9.5cm) diam.
£20–30 *StC*

l. Two Carlton Ware toast racks, the outer supports in the form of leaves, decorated with flowers, c1935, 4¼in (11.5cm) long.
£40–50 each *CSA*

A Carlton Ware leaf and lobster bowl, the leaf pattern supported on 3 lobster feet, together with a pair of servers with pincer terminals, c1939, 9½in (24cm) diam.
£50–60 *P(B)*

Cross Reference
Colour Review

A Carlton Ware soap dish, the exterior painted with black stripes on a white ground, late 1940s, 6in (15cm) long.
£12–15 *CHU*

A Carlton Ware preserve pot, in the form of the Queen of Hearts, from *Alice in Wonderland* range, black mark, 1980s, 7in (18cm) high.
£80–100 *StC*

Chintz Ware

A Crown Ducal two-slice toast rack, decorated with Primrose pattern, 1930s, 4in (10cm) wide.
£70–80 *BEV*

A James Kent miniature vase, decorated with Hydrangea pattern, 1930s, 2½in (6.5cm) high.
£40–50 *BEV*

A James Kent jam dish, decorated with Florita pattern, c1940, 4½in (11.5cm) long.
£20–30 *CSA*

A Royal Winton plate and knife, decorated with Somerset pattern, c1936, plate 4in (10cm) square.
£80–100 *BKK*

A Royal Winton dish, decorated with Sunshine pattern, c1935, 5½in (14cm) long.
£20–30 *CSA*

A Royal Winton vase, decorated with Sunshine pattern, 1930s, 3½in (9cm) high.
£75–85 *BEV*

A Royal Winton tea service for two persons, decorated with Orient pattern, 1930s.
£220–250 *HCC*

A Royal Winton tray, decorated with Marguerite pattern, 1930s, 10in (25.5cm) wide.
£60–70 *PAC*

l. A Royal Winton three-bowl dish, decorated with Marguerite pattern, c1950, 8in (20.5cm) diam.
£60–70 *PAC*

r. Three Royal Winton wall pockets, made for Old Chintz Co, decorated with Summertime, Julia and Florence patterns, limited editions of 500 each, c1997, 9in (23cm) high.
£65–75 each *PAC*

Clarice Cliff

The year 1999 is the centenary of the birth of Clarice Cliff, one of Britain's most famous ceramic designers, and probably one of the most collectable names in Art Deco pottery. Christie's biannual sales devoted to Clarice Cliff regularly attract over 1,000 registered bidders. There is a highly active collectors' club, and demand for her work is seemingly insatiable. Recent auction records include £13,800 for an 'Age of Jazz' Bizarre centrepiece, £7,800 for a May Avenue vase and a Bon Jour breakfast set, again decorated with the highly popular May Avenue pattern, exceeded its £5,000–6,000 estimate realizing £13,750.

'I think Clarice herself would have been astonished if she could have seen the money her pottery makes today. She'd have just laughed!' claims Rene Dale, a Clarice Cliff paintress, now in her eighties, who visited the Christie's Clarice Cliff sale with fellow 'Bizarre girl', Alice Andrews, to examine their former handiwork. Both had begun working for Clarice in the 1930s at the Newport Pottery, Stoke-on-Trent. As well as being employed in the factory, they also participated in painting demonstrations, visiting seaside towns, dressed up in artistic smocks to publicize the ware. 'It was lovely to work with, it was so colourful and you never saw anything else like it at the potteries,' remembers Alice.

Bizarre ware was launched in 1927 and was successful throughout the 1930s, but the women painters who produced it were not allowed to purchase crockery from the factory, and even had to bring their own mugs from home for their tea breaks. 'It was pottery for the upper- and middle-classes, you didn't find it at the shops in Stoke-on-Trent,' explains Alice. 'We didn't really think about owning it.'

Fashionable, colourful and artistic, Clarice Cliff ceramics were sold through stores such as Selfridges and Harrods and were popular as wedding gifts and special occasion ware. The best-selling pattern was Crocus. 'We worked in a team at a bench,' recalls Rene. 'Everyone had their own colour and a piece would be passed down the line with each girl painting a different coloured crocus, but we all had to join in to do the green leaves, because there were so many of them.' Though rare shapes and coveted patterns can now fetch hundreds and even thousands of pounds, Crocus pattern cups and saucers can still be found for under £50 apiece, providing an affordable introduction to the work of Clarice Cliff and the Bizarre girls.

A Clarice Cliff figure of Friar Tuck, Newport Pottery printed marks, 1920s, 8¼in (21cm) high.
£220–240 *WL*

A Clarice Cliff Bizarre vase, hairline crack, 1920s, 6½in (16.5cm) high.
£80–100 *MRW*

A Clarice Cliff Chester shape fern pot, decorated with Original Bizarre pattern, c1929, 3½in (9cm) high.
£370–400 *BKK*

A Clarice Cliff plate, decorated with Original Bizarre pattern, c1928, 7in (18cm) diam.
£120–140 *BKK*

r. A Clarice Cliff plate, decorated in the Broth pattern, early gilt mark, c1929, 6¼in (16cm) diam.
£250–280 *BKK*

A Clarice Cliff comport, decorated with Original Bizarre pattern, c1930, 7in (18cm) diam.
£650–750 *MAV*

r. A Clarice Cliff
Lynton shape coffee
set, decorated with
Blue Firs pattern,
1930–37, coffee pot
7½in (19cm) high.
£4,000–4,750 *MAV*

A Clarice Cliff Windsor shape
tea-for-two, decorated with
Gay Day pattern, 1930–34,
plate 6in (15cm) diam.
£2,000–2,300 *MAV*

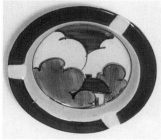

A Clarice Cliff ashtray,
decorated with Umbrellas
and Rain pattern, c1930,
4½in (11.5cm) diam.
£320–360 *BKK*

A Clarice Cliff Newport
Bizarre Fantasque plate,
painted with Chintz pattern,
printed marks, c1932,
9in (23cm) diam.
£300–350 *GAK*

A Clarice Cliff ashtray, decorated
with Pastel Autumn pattern,
c1931, 4½in (11.5cm) high.
£750–850 *BKK*

A Clarice Cliff Fantasque
jug, painted with
brown-roofed cottages
and orange borders,
printed mark and
facsimile signature,
impressed No. '3', early
1930s, 7in (18cm) high.
£300–350 *TEN*

A Clarice Cliff
octagonal Peter Pan
plate, decorated with
Crocus pattern, c1931,
5½in (14cm) diam.
£280–320 *BKK*

r. A Clarice Cliff
smoker's set, decorated
with Gibraltar pattern,
1931–32, tray
7½in (19cm) long.
£5,500–6,000 *MAV*
*The Gibraltar pattern
is very sought after.*

A Clarice Cliff Bizarre candlestick, in the form of a water nymph holding a bowl, 1930s, 6¾in (17.5cm) high.
£400–450 *WL*

A Clarice Cliff oval sugar sifter, decorated with Secrets pattern, printed marks, 1930s, 5in (12.5cm) high.
£320–350 *WL*

A Clarice Cliff Applique toilet jug, with flared rim and moulded loop handle, enamelled in colours with Lugano pattern, black Bizarre mark to base, rim damaged and repaired, 1930s, 9¾in (25cm) high.
£1,200–1,400 *CAG*

A Clarice Cliff Bizarre vase, painted with of stylised sliced fruit, orange and yellow banded, printed marks, 1930s, 7¾in (20cm) high.
£420–460 *WL*

FURTHER READING

Leonard Griffin and Louis & Susan Pear Meisel,
Clarice Cliff – The Bizarre Affair,
Thames and Hudson, 1988

A Clarice Cliff Fantasque dwarf candlestick, 1930s, 3in (7.5cm) high.
£200–250 *P(B)*

A Clarice Cliff candle holder, decorated with Pastel Autumn pattern, c1930, 3½in (9cm) high.
£800–900 *DSG*

A Clarice Cliff Newport Bizarre jardinière, decorated with Latona pattern, painted mark, 1930s, 10in (25.5cm) diam.
£480–520 *GAK*

A Clarice Cliff Bizarre sundae dish, decorated with Nasturtium pattern, shape No. 259, 1930s, 2in (5cm) high.
£180–220 *BDA*

A Clarice Cliff Fantasque Bizarre vase, decorated with Gibraltar pattern, printed factory marks to base, 1930s, 5½in (14cm) high.
£650–750 *CAG*

r. A Clarice Cliff vase, hand-painted with Viscaria pattern, shape 630, c1934, 7½in (19cm) high.
£480–520 *BKK*

A Clarice Cliff Biarritz shape bowl, decorated with Coral Firs pattern, c1934, 6in (15cm) wide.
£200–220 *BKK*

A Clarice Cliff Bizarre cup and saucer, 1930s, cup 3in (7.5cm) high.
£200–225 *DAC*

A Clarice Cliff Biarritz double cake plate, decorated with Pink Pearls pattern, c1935, 9½in (24cm) high.
£450–500 *BKK*

A Clarice Cliff Bizarre Rolls-Royce dinner plate, with yellowed clear glaze, hand-painted 'RR' symbol and silvered lining to bowl, manufacturer's transfer applied to base, crazed, c1934, 14in (35.5cm) wide.
£200–250 *S*

l. A Clarice Cliff six-person dinner service, comprising: soup tureen, 2 vegetable tureens, 5 serving platters, gravy boat and stand, dinner, dessert, soup and side plates, a conical sugar dredger and a similar salt and mustard pot, 1930s.
£750–850 *L&E*

A Clarice Cliff 23-piece part dinner service, decorated with Crocus pattern, Wilkinson Pottery, 1930s.
£1,200–1,400 *AH*

A Clarice Cliff Bizarre jug, 1930s, 3in (7.5cm) high.
£135–155 *DAC*

A Clarice Cliff vase, shape No. 370 decorated with Viscaria pattern, c1936, 5¾in (14.5cm) high.
£750–850 *BKK*

Contemporary Ceramics

Contemporary British studio ceramics are admired and collected across the world. The major auction houses now hold specific auctions devoted to contemporary ceramics, while the works of young artists can be found in galleries and craft shops across Britain.

A pioneer in the field was Bernard Leach (1887–1979), who established his pottery at St Ives, Cornwall, in 1920, and whose ceramics, writings and teachings inspired a whole generation of potters, including Michael Cardew (1901–83) and Japanese potter Shoji Hamada (1894–1979), both of whom worked at St Ives. Leach also founded a personal pottery dynasty, with his wife Janet, sons David and Michael and three grandsons all carrying on the family profession.

Lucie Rie (1902–95) and Hans Coper (1920–81) have been perhaps the most important figures in studio pottery since WWII. Both fled to Britain in the late 1930s, Rie from Austria, Coper from Germany, and together they turned the craft of pottery into high art, wielding tremendous influence on students and fellow potters. Ceramics by Coper and Rie regularly fetch four- and even five-figure sums at auction, and their work is regarded as one of Britain's most significant contributions to the modern movement.

A Gordon Baldwin earthenware bowl-on-stand form, the stand in the form of a drum with a sliced section, applied coil rim, brightly coloured linear decoration, painted 'GB' to base, c1978, 9½in (24cm) high.
£750–850 *Bon*

A Michael Cardew (1901–83) earthenware pitcher, with painted yellow and brown slip decoration, loop handle, impressed 'MC' and Winchcombe seals, 11in (28cm) high.
£500–600 *Bon*

A Cat Pottery crouching black cat, 1990s, 13¾in (35cm) long.
£50–60 *CP*

Two Cat Pottery tabby cats, 1990s, 30in (76cm) long.
£35–45 each *CP*

A Gordon Cooke sculpted flat slab vase, with feather patterning, seal mark, 1990s, 11⅛in (29cm) high.
£225–250 *PGA*

A Joanna Constantinidis 'mushroom' vase, 1990s, 7¾in (20cm) high.
£300–325 *PGA*

l. A Hans Coper Cycladic black bud form, rising from a square grey-green base upwards to a globular body with a fin on each side and an oval opening at the top, impressed 'HC' seal, c1975, 9½in (24cm) high.
£35,000–40,000 *Bon*

Very few examples of this form exist.

An Annie Fourmanoir stoneware hemi-spherical bowl, brick-red with a textured surface and a ball sitting neatly in the well, c1970s, 15½in (39.5cm) diam.
£300–350 *Bon*

l. A Jim Gladwin salt-glazed model of George Ohr, designed by Roger Law and Pablo Bach, c1996, 5in (13cm) high.
£300–350 *RDG*

A Christine Gittins burnished earthenware vessel, 1990s, 7¾in (20cm) high.
£50–75 *ELG*

r. A Gabrielle Koch earthenware rounded vessel, with oval raised pinched rim, incised signature, c1996, 13¼in (34cm) high.
£500–600 *Bon*

A Shoji Hamada stoneware handled jar, ash-glazed, the stem-leaf design brushed in cobalt and brown, 1955, 5¼in (13.5cm) high.
£2,800–3,000 *Bon*

A Bernard Leach (b.1887) stoneware jug, in green ash glaze with vertical combed design, impressed 'BL' and 'St. Ives' seals, 7½in (19cm) high.
£500–600 *Bon*

A David Leach (b.1911) stoneware vase, brown and white with a brown wax-resist motif, impressed 'DL' seal, 9¼in (23.5cm) high.
£160–200 *Bon*

l. An Eileen Lewenstein bowl, decorated with thick drip glaze, supported on a double knop stem and circular base, stamped 'EL' seal, c1950, 10¼in (26cm) high.
£90–120 *P(B)*

A John Maltby
spade vase, 1990s,
8½in (21.5cm) high.
£200–225 *PGA*

An Ursula Marley-Price
pinched stoneware bowl, with
wavy rim covered in oatmeal
slip, 1990s, 12in (30.5cm) diam.
£400–450 *PGA*

A Dame Lucie Rie and Hans Coper
bronze-glazed and sgraffito coffee set,
comprising 4 cups and saucers, a coffee
pot, a milk jug and 4 plates, impressed
'LR' and 'HC' seals, 1950s
£3,000–3,500 *Bon*

A Sue Mundy (b.1965)
stoneware profile vase,
with horizontal
impressed lines inlaid
with porcelain,
impressed 'SJM' seal,
12½in (32cm) high.
£90–120 *Bon*

A Mary Rich studio
vase, with gilded
decoration, red mark,
1980s, 8¼in (21cm) high.
£350–375 *PGA*

A Dame Lucie Rie
stoneware vase, 1960s,
7¾in (20cm) high.
£2,400–2,800 *PLY*

A Sally Tuffin
daffodil jug, Dennis
China Works, c1997,
10in (25.5cm) high.
£145–165 *NP*

A Gotlind Weigel
cylindrical dark
brown stoneware
vase, each side with
black triangular
web pattern, incised
'Weigel 1986', and
seal, 8¼in (21cm) high.
£300–350 *Bon*

A Geoffrey Whiting
(1919–88) stoneware
dish, with impressed 'A'
seal, 8¼in (21cm) long.
£100–120 *Bon*

A John Ward disc-
shaped vessel, the white
ground with green-
blue lines, impressed
'JW' seal, c1990,
16½in (42cm) high.
£700–800 *Bon*

A Ray West pottery
vase, decorated with
burgundy and blue
crystaline effect glaze,
American, c1990,
14¾in (37.5cm) high.
£650–700 *PGA*

r. A Phillip Webb tazza,
decorated with a
cockerel, from a William
Morris tile design,
Dennis China Works,
c1996, 4in (10cm) high.
£85–95 *NP*

Susie Cooper

A Susie Cooper mug, decorated with a golfer in black checked trousers, yellow top and black cap, c1920, 4in (10cm) high.
£300–350 PGA

A Susie Cooper lustre vase, decorated in red with blue, white and gold design, Gray's Pottery, 1920s, 7in (18cm) high.
£500–600 PGA

A Susie Cooper lustre vase, decorated in blue with orange, red and gold design, Gray's Pottery, 1920s, 9in (23cm) high.
£450–500 PGA

A Susie Cooper lustre vase, decorated with gold stag on a white ground, Gray's Pottery, 1920s, 12in (30.5cm) high.
£600–650 PGA

A Susie Cooper Kestrel coffee pot, decorated with apple-green polka dots, restored, unsigned, 1930s, 8in (20.5cm) high.
£30–35 DAC

A Susie Cooper dinner service, comprising 30 pieces, hand-painted with goose-berries and black-berries and banding to rims, 1960s.
£170–200 P(B)

Cottage Ware

A Burlington 'Devon Cob' biscuit box, 1920s, 6in (15cm) wide.
£30–40 PC

A Burlington 'Thatched Roofs' three-piece cruet set-on-stand, 1920s, 7in (18cm) wide.
£30–40 PC

A Continental sugar sifter, in the form of a water tower, 1920s, 6½in (16.5cm) high.
£20–30 LA

Crown Staffordshire

A Crown Staffordshire child's cup and saucer, decorated with golfing figures and gold rim, c1920, 2¼in (6cm) high.
£150–175 *PGA*

A Crown Staffordshire model of a shrike, decorated in black and yellow, by J. T. Jones, 1960s, 6in (15cm) high.
£135–155 *PAC*

A Crown Staffordshire figure of a Chinaman, hand-painted with green jacket and red trousers, 1920s, 4¾in (12cm) high.
£60–80 *MRW*

Cups & Saucers

r. A Böttger porcelain tea bowl, painted in polychrome with a scene in the manner of J. G. Horoldt, the rim with scrolls and flowerheads in gilt, slight damage, c1725, 3in (7.5cm) high.
£300–350 *Bon(C)*

A Coalport trio, hand-painted in gilt, mid-19thC, 3in (7.5cm) high.
£120–140 *MRW*

l. A Benjamin E. Goodwin cup and saucer, decorated in black with a peacock pattern, marked, 1834–41, saucer 4½in (11.5cm) diam.
£16–18 *OCH*

A Hammersley coffee cup and saucer, decorated with violets, 1920s, saucer 4¾in (12cm) diam.
£16–18 *TAC*

r. A Dresden hand-painted cup, with ivy leaf handle and base, 1930s, 4in (10cm) wide.
£20–30 *MRW*

A Continental two-person tea set, c1920, unmarked, saucer 4¾in (12cm) diam.
£30–40 *OD*

l. A set of 4 Paragon hand-painted cups and saucers, with stylised tree decoration on a cream ground, 1960s, saucer 4½in (11cm) diam.
£50–60 *P(B)*

A Paragon china cup and saucer, 1940s–50, 5½in (14cm) diam.
£150–175 *PAC*

Moustache Cups

Moustache cups were a 19th-century innovation. In Queen Victoria's reign, long drooping moustaches became fashionable for men, particularly after the Crimean War. This new passion for facial hair created considerable problems when drinking tea – moustaches looked far less elegant when they were soggy – so Harvey Adams & Co of Longton, Staffordshire, introduced the first moustache cup c1855. It looked like an ordinary cup except that inside the rim on one side was a little pierced shelf on which the moustache could rest dry and protected, while the gentleman sipped his tea through the hole.

Moustache cups remained in use for the next half century and were produced by many factories and also imported from Germany. They were often sold as gifts and souvenirs and were a popular Christmas present for the men in the family.

An English porcelain cup and saucer, decorated with a green cornucopia of flowers and gilded deep crimson border, the white bridge gilded with scrolls, c1880, saucer 6½in (16.5cm) diam.
£65–75 *SAS*

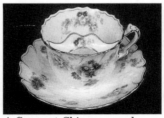

A Crescent China cup and saucer, the spirally fluted bodies decorated with flowers and gilded, puce printed mark, c1890, saucer 6in (15cm) diam.
£55–65 *SAS*

r. A Foley cup and saucer, enamelled with heraldic shields flanked by a lion and unicorn on an inscribed ribbon for the 1897 Jubilee, gilded bridge and rims, 6¼in (16cm) diam.
£25–30 *SAS*

A Belleek Tridacna moustache cup and saucer, decorated in green with gilded rim, 1891–1926, saucer 6in (15cm) diam.
£500–550 *MLa*

Miller's is a price GUIDE not a price LIST

Denby

A Denby buff-coloured preserve pot, with 2 birds forming the finial, c1930, 4in (10cm) high.
£120–130 *KES*

A Denby giraffe, with green markings, original South African store sticker, c1930, 10in (25.5cm) high.
£320–375 *KES*

l. A Denby seagull bird bath, c1930, 16in (40.5cm) wide.
£350–375 *KES*

A Denby green, brown and blue tube-lined tobacco jar, with golf ball finial, c1925, 6in (15cm) high.
£450–500 *KES*

r. A Denby blue/green mottled vase, with orange fish design, c1930, 9in (23cm) high.
£125–145 *DSG*

A Denby hand-painted dish, Glyn Colledge painted signature, c1950, 9½in (24cm) diam.
£125–150 *PGA*

A Denby hand-painted vase, with Glyn Colledge back stamp, c1960, 9in (23cm) high.
£100–125 *PGA*

l. A Denby Tigo ware retek (sugar shaker), and mug, designed by Tibor Reich, c1954, retek 7½in (19cm), mug 4in (10cm) high.
£60–65 each *KES*

Doulton

A Doulton Lambeth blue and cream salad bowl and servers, by Florence E. Barlow, with silver rim, c1880, 12in (30.5cm) diam.
£1,400–1,600 *POW*

A Doulton Holbein green vase, decorated with yellow rabbits, c1880–90, 5½in (14cm) high.
£180–200 *PGA*

l. A pair of Doulton Lambeth stoneware baluster-shaped vases, by Hannah Barlow, incised with a wide band of donkeys and calves, within green and brown leaf pattern borders, impressed date '1884' and Nos. '631' and '656', 9½in (24cm) high.
£900–1,000 *CAG*

A Doulton ewer, by Emily Stormer, with looped handle, moulded and decorated in colours with stylised rosettes and foliage, impressed marks, dated '1881', 12in (30.5cm) high.
£250–280 *GAK*

A pair of Doulton Lambeth candlesticks, incised and moulded with strapwork decoration in blue and gold, c1890, 8in (20.5cm) high.
£350–400 *BWA*

A pair of Doulton baluster vases, with everted rims, on a blue and treacle reserve, impressed marks, c1900, 13½in (34.5cm) high.
£320–360 *GAK*

A Royal Doulton Sung vase, designed by Charles Noke, painted with a peacock in green, blue and red on a red flambé ground, by A. Eaton, c1900, 11½in (29cm) high.
£1,400–1,600 *AH*

A Doulton Lambeth black vase, with blue and gold central band, c1900, 13½in (34.5cm) high.
£175–200 *PAC*

A pair of Doulton Slater's patent vases, with pink floral tube-lined decoration on a buff ground, c1920, 8¾in (22cm) high.
£180–220 *P(B)*

l. A Doulton Lambeth Toby jug, The Standing Man Variation Two, wearing a slate-blue jacket, olive green waistcoat and olive green breeches, No. 8572, produced 1925 onwards, 7in (18cm) high.
£120–150 *P(B)*

A Doulton Rembrandt vase, decorated with the 'Wife of Charles II', by Walter Munn, signed, c1900, 9in (23cm) high.
£680–720 *POW*

A Royal Doulton double-gourd shaped vase, with striations and flambé glaze, 1920s, 6in (15cm) high.
£200–250 *PGA*

A Royal Doulton Pip, Squeak and Wilfred mug, 1930s, 9in (23cm) diam.
£85–95 *SnA*

Pip, Squeak and Wilfred was a children's cartoon strip appearing in The Daily Mirror *1919–46. The characters were a penguin, a dog and a rabbit, and the series also featured Popski, a bearded anarchist. The Daily Mirror started a children's fan club, members of which were known as 'The Gugnuncs'. Pip, Squeak and Wilfred also became army slang for three medals of WWI: the 1914–15 Star, the British War medal and the Victory medal.*

A Royal Doulton Series Ware 'George and the Dragon' plate, decorated in orange and brown on a blue ground, c1931, 10½in (27cm) diam.
£80–100 *BKK*

l. A pair of Royal Doulton stoneware vases, each with narrow neck and splayed rim, with a frieze of floral swags and blue lower band, c1900–10, 10¼in (26cm) high.
£160–200 *P(B)*

A Royal Doulton stoneware vase, the body decorated with heart-shaped cartouches filled with flowers and leaves on a dark blue ground, neck and foot in mottled green, c1910–20, 16in (41cm) high.
£80–100 *P(B)*

A Royal Doulton lamp base, designed by A. Hoy, signed, c1950, 12½in (32cm) high.
£160–200 *DSG*

A Royal Doulton model, entitled 'Piggy Back', 1981–94, 6½in (16.5cm) long.
£30–40 *TAC*

A Royal Doulton flambé Aladdin's genie, by David Biggs, limited edition of 1,500, 1994, 7in (18cm) high.
£175–200 *PAC*

A Royal Doulton flambé group, Images of Fire series, 'Motherhood', 1995–97, 11in (28cm) high.
£500–550 *PAC*

Bunnykins

A Royal Doulton Billy Bunnykins, the brown bunny with red trousers, blue jacket, white bow tie with blue spots, designed by Charles Noke, issued c1940, 4½in (11.5cm) high.
£850–950 *PFK*

A Royal Doulton Daisie Bunnykins, with blue dress, 1972–83, 3in (7.5cm) high.
£165–185 *PAC*

A Royal Doulton Policeman Bunnykins, 1988–present, 4in (10cm) high.
£25–30 *TAC*

A Royal Doulton Boy Skater Bunnykins, 1995–present, 4in (10cm) high.
£24–28 *TAC*

A Sweetheart Bunnykins, 1997 special limited edition of 2,500, 3¾in (9.5cm) high.
£145–165 *PAC*

l. A Royal Doulton Nurse Bunnykins, second variation Green Cross, 1989–present, 4in (10cm) high.
£25–30 *TAC*

Two Royal Doulton Bunnykins figures, c1990, 3½in (9cm) high.
l. Harry the Herald, *r.* Prince Frederick.
£85–95 each *PAC*

Figures

A pair of Royal Doulton figures, 'The Mask', HN733, 1925–38, and 'Pierrette', HN644, 1924–38, 7in (18cm) high.
l. **£750–800**
r. **£300–350** *P*

A Royal Doulton figure, 'The Proposal', slight chip, HN1209, 1929–1938, 4⅛in (11.5cm) high.
£700–800 *LT*

A Royal Doulton figure, 'Nadine', HN1885, slight chip, 1938–1949, 7½in (19cm) high.
£340–380 *LT*

A Royal Doulton figure, 'The Jester', HN2016, 1949–present, 10in (25.5cm) high.
£90–110 *SAS*

A Royal Doulton figure, 'Wig-maker of Williamsburg', HN2239, 1960–1983, 7½in (19cm) high.
£120–130 *SnA*

l. A Royal Doulton figure, 'A Good Catch', HN2258, 1966–86, 7½in (19cm) high.
£90–110 *SAS*

A Royal Doulton figure, 'The Seafarer', HN2455, 1972–76, 9in (23cm) high.
£70–80 *SAS*

A Royal Doulton figure, 'The Helmsman', HN2499, 1974–86, 9½in (24cm) high.
£80–100 *SAS*

A Royal Doulton figure, 'Maxine', HN3199, 1989–90, 9in (23cm) high.
£100–120 *SnA*

l. A Royal Doulton figure, 'Amy', HN3316, Figure of the Year 1991, 8½in (22cm) high.
£450–500 *PAC*

Royal Doulton Figures

All Doulton figures carry the Royal Doulton lion and crown backstamp on their base. In addition to this most, but not all, figures carry a registration number, an HN number and the figure's name on their base. The style of these extra marks provides useful hints for the precise dating of figures.

Earthenware & Slipware

A redware tripod pipkin, with pouring lip and single lug handle, inscribed in white slip under an orange-brown glaze, 'Anno 1657', probably Low Countries, 4¼in (11cm) high.
£550–600 *FW&C*

A North Devon slipware water jug, the amber glazed baluster body decorated with a stag between giant flowering stems, the back with a panel of verse above the words 'Made for Mrs Felix, Aberayon 1807', 10¼in (26cm) high.
£2,000–2,200 *P(G)*

r. A Staffordshire slipware foot warmer, early 19thC, 8in (20.5cm) high.
£235–265 *TVM*

A terracotta jar and cover, early 19thC, 16in (40.5cm) high.
£65–85 *CPA*

l. A green-glazed moulded earthenware jug, c1810, 4½in (11.5cm) high.
£75–90 *IW*

A Yorkshire yellow spongeware miniature cradle, c1820, 4in (10cm) long.
£120–150 *IW*

r. A Derbyshire salt-glazed top hat, c1830, 3¼in (8.5cm) high.
£55–70 *IW*

A Derbyshire salt-glazed pipkin, c1840, 4in (10cm) high.
£40–60 *IW*

A Halifax brown slipware miniature lambing chair, initialled and dated 'EC 1863', 8in (20.5cm) high.
£85–95 *ANV*

A Scottish brown slipware bread crock, the handle and edges in the form of bamboo, c1880, 17in (43cm) wide.
£425–475 *B&R*

An Alsace jug, with blue splashes, c1880, 18in (45.5cm) high.
£140–160 *MLL*

A tavern salt-glazed water jug, with pewter lid, moulded in relief, c1880, 5in (12.5cm) high.
£25–35 *CPA*

A miniature brown pottery rustic chair, Cumbria or north east England, c1890, 8¼in (21cm) high.
£120–140 *IW*

A slip-decorated brown pottery pub jug, probably Halifax, inscribed 'Parr Sept 1906', 3¼in (8.5cm) high.
£65–80 *IW*

A Cornish earthenware jug, Lakes Pottery, Truro, c1900, 7½in (19cm) high.
£20–30 *IW*

l. A Buckley brown pottery dish, c1900, 13¾in (35cm) wide.
£150–180 *IW*

An earthenware jug, south Wales or West Country, late 19thC, 8¼in (21cm) high.
£35–45 *IW*

Elton Ware

Sir Edmund Elton (1846–1920) was an English baronet who devoted the latter part of his life to making art pottery. His under-gardener, George F. Masters, became his chief assistant, and Elton set up a studio on his estate at Clevedon in Somerset in 1880, trading initially as Sunflower Pottery, but from 1881–1920 using the name Elton Ware.

Ceramics were predominantly decorative and Elton's particular interest lay in experimenting with new, often challenging shapes. His pots were decorated with incised patterns and naturalistic motifs, and marbled and streaked with layers of coloured slip. From c1902 he began to use lustre and crackled glazes and his gold and silver iridescent wares are among the most collectable of all Elton's products. Pieces are inscribed either with the monogram 'E' or the name 'Elton' on the base. After Sir Edmund's death, his son Ambrose briefly took over the pottery, and a painted 'X' was added to the name Elton on the mark.

An Elton Ware eight-handled vase, with white, black and brown flowing glaze, c1885, 7½in (19cm) high.
£180–200 *NCA*

An Elton Ware tyg, the green slip glaze with burgundy decoration of flower and birds in flight, c1900, 8¼in (21cm) high.
£270–300 *WAC*

An Elton Ware ewer, decorated with butter-flies and flowers, with brown and green glaze, c1885, 10in (25.5cm) high.
£300–330 *NCA*

An Elton Ware jug, with applied dot design, marked, c1890, 13¼in (34cm) high.
£280–300 *PGA*

Egg Cups

A yellow egg cup, Savill & Co retailer's mark, c1880, 2¼in (5.5cm) high.
£35–40 *AMH*

A Crown Derby egg cup, decorated with roses, 1876–90, 2in (5cm) high.
£50–55 *AMH*

A Snoopy egg cup, 1960s, 2¾in (7cm) high.
£4–6 *PPe*

A Wedgwood creamware egg cup, with moulded body, internally decorated with a red rosebud and green leaves, c1940, 2in (5cm) high.
£8–10 *AnS*

l. A majolica egg holder set, with central chick in an eggshell, c1900, 3in (7.5cm) high.
£130–150 *MLL*

Miller's is a price GUIDE not a price LIST

Fairings

A fairing, entitled 'Cancan', c1875, 4in (10cm) wide.
£300–350 *SAS*

A fairing, entitled 'Please Sir, what would you charge to christen my doll?', c1875, 4in (10cm) wide.
£230–260 *SAS*

l. A fairing, entitled 'Our sisters of charity', c1870, 4in (10cm) wide.
£500–550 *SAS*

r. A fairing, entitled 'Our soldiers', c1870, 4in (10cm) wide.
£500–550 *SAS*

A Victorian fairing, entitled 'Tea Party', German, 4in (10cm) high.
£140–160 *LeB*

A fairing, entitled 'Come along these flowers don't smell very good', c1875, 4in (10cm) wide.
£100–120 *SAS*

A fairing, entitled 'Dangerous', restored, c1880, 4in (10cm) wide.
£450–500 *SAS*

A fairing, entitled 'Morning Prayer', German, c1900–20, 4in (10cm) high.
£200–220 *LeB*

A fairing, modelled as a dressing table, c1890, 4½in (11.5cm) high.
£35–45 *OD*

Figures

A pair of Derby groups, each of a young boy and girl dancing arm-in-arm, painted in coloured enamels, on green-glazed mound bases, some damage and repair, c1775, 5½in (14cm) high.
£850–950 *DN*

This design is taken from the Falconet model 'La Danse Allemande', produced at Sèvres c1765.

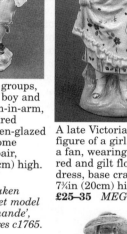

A late Victorian figure of a girl with a fan, wearing a red and gilt floral dress, base crack, 7¾in (20cm) high.
£25–35 *MEG*

A pair of Continental figures of musicians, the girl holding a lute, the man holding a violin, possibly Sarreguemines, raised on shaped circular bases, late 19thC, 19¼in (49cm) high.
£300–350 *TRL*

A terracotta figure, depicting Venus de Milo, 1920s, 24½in (62cm) high.
£70–80 *SER*

A Ridgway semi-porcelain head of a Native American Indian, 1930s, 5in (13cm) high.
£40–45 *GIN*

A Goldscheider figure of a woman, her apron filled with flowers, wearing a red dress sprigged with flowers, 1930s, 12in (30.5cm) high.
£175–195 *PAC*

A pair of Chinese ceramic figures of children playing instruments, 1950s, 1½in (4cm) high.
£10–12 each *MRW*

l. A Coalport figure, entitled 'The Ball', from the Ladies of Fashion series, modelled and decorated by hand, 1977–87, 7in (18cm) high.
£145–165 *TP*

A Coalport figure, entitled 'An Enchanted Evening', from the When Dreams Come True series, Danbury Mint, c1995, 9¼in (23.5cm) high.
£130–150 *TP*

A Coalport Craft series figure, entitled 'The Saddler', No. 236 of 1,000, 1974–80, 7in (18cm) high.
£125–145 *TP*

Goss & Crested China

William Henry Goss (1833–1906) of Stoke-on-Trent began producing porcelain decorated with heraldic crests for schools and colleges in the 1870s. In 1887, Goss received permission from the towns and cities of Britain to reproduce their coats-of-arms on his wares, and thus began a craze for collecting crested china that was to sweep Britain.

With the development of the railway system in the 19th century the tourist industry had flourished. All Victorian and Edwardian holiday-makers visiting seaside towns and beauty spots wanted to bring back a memento of their trip, and a piece of miniature heraldic china, affordable, portable and decorative, was the perfect souvenir. W. H. Goss led the way. Over 7,000 different heraldic devices have been recorded on Goss ceramics, and the firm produced a huge variety of wares, with agents in every town.

Goss was predominantly aimed at the middle classes; pieces were high in quality, often sober in style, and frequently academic in subject matter, reproducing ancient works of art from British museums as well as covering lighter-hearted topics. A host of other potteries, such as Arcadian, Carlton, Shelley and Willow Art, also cashed in on the demand for crested china, and while they could not match Goss in terms of technical standards, they catered for the cheaper end of the market with a wide range of novelty designs. Most factories marked their wares on the base, making them easy to identify. The collecting of Goss and crested china peaked during the Edwardian period, when it is estimated that an astonishing 90 per cent of British homes had at least one piece. Demand declined after WWI. The Goss family sold their business in 1929, and the depression in the 1930s marked the end of the crested china craze.

A Goss & Peake terracotta vase, the waisted neck printed in black with classical equestrian subjects, the squat body with a repeated design, c1870, 5½in (14cm) high.
£110–130 *SAS*

A Goss oval vase, with coloured flower in high relief, c1880, 6½in (16.5cm) high.
£140–160 *CCC*

A Winchester flagon, with the arms of St. Cross Hospital, c1890, 4½in (11.5cm) high.
£50–60 *SAS*

A Goss vase, decorated with forget-me-nots, c1880, 4½in (11.5cm) high.
£80–100 *CCC*

A Goss cylindrical box and cover, with flower knop, c1890, 3in (7.5cm) high.
£225–275 *CCC*

A Goss teapot stand, printed with a verse and multiple crests, c1900, 5in (12.5cm) square.
£40–50 *CCC*

A Goss three-handled loving cup, with portrait of W. H. Goss in high relief, c1900, 4in (10cm) high.
£160–180 *CCC*

A Goss flask, with
knurled handles and
multiple crests, c1900,
8in (20.5cm) high.
£100–120 *CCC*

A Goss Pompeiian
centrepiece, c1900,
5in (13cm) high.
£90–110 *CCC*

A Goss cream jug, in the
form of a Welsh lady,
c1920, 4in (10cm) high.
£50–60 *CCC*

A Goss sugar shaker,
1920s, 5in (12.5cm) high.
£60–80 *MRW*

Animals and Birds

An Arcadian Shetland pony,
1910–25, 4¼in (11cm) long.
£35–40 *G&CC*

An Arcadian
peacock, bearing
Harrogate crest,
c1910, 5in
(12.5cm) high.
£40–50 *CCC*

r. An Arcadian
model of Bill
Sykes' dog,
inscribed 'My
word if you're
not off', c1920,
2½in (6.5cm) long.
£25–30 *G&CC*

A Willow Art lion, bearing
Great Yarmouth crest,
1910–1925, 6in (15cm) long.
£20–25 *G&CC*

A Saxony eagle
perched on a
rock, c1910,
5½in (14cm) high.
£60–80 *CCC*

l. A posy vase, in
the form of a turkey,
bearing Whitley Bay
crest, foreign, c1930,
4in (10cm) high.
£45–55 *CCC*

Architectural

A Goss 'Window in Thrums' night light, c1898, 4in (10cm) high.
£350–400   *CCC*

A Willow Art model of Canterbury Cathedral, West front, c1910, 5in (12.5cm) high.
£60–70   *CCC*

l. A Goss model of Wordsworth's birthplace, c1912, 2in (5cm) high.
£210–250   *CCC*

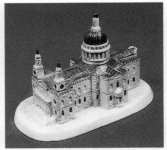

A Willow Art model of St Paul's Cathedral, coloured beige, c1910, 3½in (9cm) high.
£250–300   *CCC*

A Goss model of Ellen Terry's farmhouse, near Tenterden, Kent, with red roof, chimneys restored, 1900, 2in (5cm) high.
£60–70   *SAS*

A Goss model of Beachy Head lighthouse, c1912, 5in (12.5cm) high.
£80–100   *CCC*

A Goss model of Samuel Johnson's house, Lichfield, 1900, 3in (7.5cm) high.
£120–140   *SAS*

Goss Buildings

W. H. Goss began producing models of buildings in 1893, starting with Shakespeare's and Anne Hathaway's cottages in Stratford-upon-Avon, which are still the most commonly found of all Goss houses today. The company manufactuered many edifices, ranging from castles to cottages to the homes of famous personalities. Values depend on rarity and condition is very important.

Figures

An Arcadian statue of St Winifred, c1910, 6in (15cm) high.
£90–110 *CCC*

A Carlton Ware figure of a boy, blowing bubbles, with blue collar, c1914, 4in (10cm) high.
£90–110 *CCC*

A Grafton bust, depicting Admiral Jellicoe, c1915, 6in (15cm) high.
£60–80 *CCC*

A Willow Art statue, with St Alban's crest, 1910–25, 5½in (14cm) high.
£65–75 *G&CC*

A Carlton Ware figure of a drunk leaning against a lamp post, entitled 'Show me the way to go home', 1920–30, 4¼in (11cm) high.
£65–75 *G&CC*

A Willow Art dish, depicting an Irish colleen on a shamrock, c1920, 4in (10cm) wide.
£100–125 *CCC*

l. A Carlton Ware figure of a child riding a donkey, c1920, 4in (10cm) high.
£150–180 *CCC*

An Arcadian Welsh tea party group, bearing British Empire Exhibition decoration, 1924–25, 3¾in (9.5cm) high.
£60–70 *G&CC*

A Carlton Ware figure of an Irish colleen, bearing Dublin crest, c1925, 5in (12.5cm) high.
£100–120 *MLa*

Non Heraldic Figures

A Goss Parian figure of Shakespeare, leaning on books, c1880, 7½in (19cm) high.
£280–320 *CCC*

A Goss Parian bust of Southey, c1880, 7½in (19cm) high.
£170–200 *CCC*

A Goss figure, The Bridesmaid, c1920, 4in (10cm) high.
£250–275 *PAC*

A Goss figure, The Mother-in-Law, c1920, 4in (10cm) high.
£250–275 *PAC*

Transport

A Limoges car, French, c1910, 4in (10cm) long.
£70–100 *CCC*

A Shelley charabanc, c1910, 5in (12.5cm) long.
£60–80 *CCC*

A Carlton Ware model of HMS *Lion*, c1915, 6½in (16.5cm) long.
£125–150 *CCC*

A Willow Art monoplane, c1918, 6in (15cm) long.
£90–100 *CCC*

A Carlton Ware two-seater car, c1925, 4in (10cm) long.
£45–55 *CCC*

A Shelley steam roller, c1920, 6in (15cm) long.
£700–800 *CCC*

A Carlton Ware model, entitled 'Luggage in Advance', c1920, 3¼in (8cm) long.
£35–45 *G&CC*

Hummels

A Hummel figure, Apple Tree Girl, No. 141, marked 'TMK2', 1950s, 4in (10cm) high.
£95–115 *ATH*

A Hummel figure, entitled Retreat to Safety, No. 201, marked 'TMK3', 1955-68, 4in (10cm) high.
£85–105 *ATH*

A Hummel figure, Band Leader, No. 129, marked 'TMK3', 1955–68, 5in (12.5cm) high.
£95–115 *ATH*

A Hummel figure, For Father, No. 87, marked 'TMK3', 1955–68, 5½in (14cm) high.
£110–130 *ATH*

A Hummel wall plaque, Child in Bed, No. 137/B, marked 'TMK3', 1955–68, 3in (7.5cm) diam.
£40–50 *ATH*

A Hummel figure, The Photographer, with doughnut ring shaped base, No. 178, marked 'TMK4', 1960s, 5in (12.5cm) high.
£135–155 *ATH*

A Hummel annual plate, Heavenly Angel, first edition of first annual plate, mint condition, dated '1971', 7½in (19cm) diam, with box and certificate.
£750–850 *ATH*

A Hummel figure, Be Patient, 1964–72, 5in (12.5cm) high.
£120–140 *TAC*

A Hummel figure, The Lost Sheep, 1964 onwards, 5in (12.5cm) high.
£80–100 *TAC*

A Hummel figure, School Girl, 1972 onwards, 5in (12.5cm) high.
£80–100 *TAC*

A Hummel figure, Serenade, 1972 onwards, 5in (13cm) high.
£85–95 *TAC*

Jugs

A Cologne ware jug, decorated and incised with stylised foliage, on a cobalt ground, early 17thC, 15in (38cm) high.
£260–280 EH

This jug was a gift from the 19thC artist Dante Gabriel Rossetti to his friend Alice Boyd.

A New Hall fluted baluster-shaped cream jug, with C-scroll handle, the blue bands painted in gilt with pendant leaves, the handle, spout and rim picked out in blue, slight damage, 1782–85, 4½in (11.5cm) high.
£600–700 DN

l. A Staffordshire Pratt ware mask jug, decorated in yellow, red, and green, c1830, 4½in (11.5cm) high.
£165–185 SER

A Liverpool blue and white sauce boat, with scroll and gadroon moulded body, decorated with rococo cartouches of chinoiserie landscapes, slight damage, 18thC, 7in (18cm) high.
£220–250 RBB

A Liverpool jug, with sparrow beak and scroll handle, the green ground painted with a gilt sailing ship to the front, Masonic Emblem beneath the spout and gilt rose and foliage to the reverse, late 18thC, 11in (28cm) high.
£1,800–2,000 Mit

This jug was until recently on loan to Whitehaven Museum and formed part of a collection of items associated with Andrew Green who was Master of the Whitehaven vessel, John and Bella, in 1763. The jug was exhibited along with various documents, glassware and a painting and it is believed that this jug may carry the portrait of the afore-mentioned ship, the John and Bella.

A Bristol baluster-shaped sparrow beak jug, with reeded loop handle, painted in *famille rose* palette with flowers and leaves, with a brown line rim, c1770, 3¼in (8.5cm) high.
£240–260 DN(H)

A pearlware ovoid jug, with angular loop handle, decorated in coloured enamels, with a toper and trees, painted in black with verse 'Come My Lads Lets Drink About, and Sing a Merry Song ...', beneath a green ground leaf scroll band, the reeded neck picked out in green and black, 1815–25, 7½in (19cm) high.
£450–500 DN

A stoneware bellarmine, the oval reserve enclosing a crowned shield with double chevron beneath a typical bearded mask, possibly 18thC, 8½in (21.5cm) high.
£200–220 Bon(C)

A buff jug, with pewter lid, decorated with Tam-o'-Shanter and Souter Johnnie design, c1830, 9½in (24cm) high.
£180–220 P(B)

Tam-o'-Shanter was the hero of an eponymous poem by Robert Burns (1759–96). The character also gave his name to the Scottish cap. In the same poem Burns also popularised another figure who was to be turned into a jug: Sir John Barleycorn, a personification of malt liquor.

l. A Mason's Ironstone grey jug, decorated with Falstaff pattern, c1830, 10¼in (26cm) high.
£180–220 P(B)

A Charles Meigh & Sons buff-coloured jug, decorated with Julius Caesar pattern, c1839, 8in (20cm) high.
£120–140 *P(B)*

An Edward Walley buff jug, decorated with the Cup Tosser design, c1841, 9in (23cm) high.
£120–140 *P(B)*

A Derbyshire salt-glazed jug, c1840, 5⅝in (14.5cm) high.
£100–120 *IW*

A Staffordshire gravy boat, decorated in grey with a deer pattern, possibly by J. Meir or J. Maddock, with moulded sectional handle, star crack, late 19thC, 5in (13cm) high.
£18–25 *MEG*

A pottery frog jug, decorated in brown and green, impressed 'Steel', c1875, 8in (20.5cm) high.
£250–300 *BRT*

A Staffordshire cottage jug, c1860, 5½in (14cm) high.
£40–60 *OD*

A Savoie jug, with yellow rim, c1880, 5in (12.5cm) high.
£40–45 *MLL*

A Campbellfield Pottery jug, decorated in blue, 1870–80, 6½in (16.5cm) high.
£30–40 *CSA*

A Mason's Ironstone jug, decorated in blue and orange, c1880, 7½in (19cm) high.
£150–175 *SPU*

Miller's is a price GUIDE not a price LIST

r. A china jug, depicting cockfighting scenes, c1880, 8in (20.5cm) high.
£320–350 *PAC*

A barrel-shaped jug, decorated with blue bands, c1890, 7in (18cm) high.
£50–70 *IW*

A Tams patent measure one pint jug, blue with cream handle and spout, c1902, 4½in (11.5cm) high.
£40–60 *IW*

A French pottery wine jug, painted with grapevines and a verse, c1900, 7in (18cm) high.
£40–50 *MLL*

A Kirklands jug, painted with flowers, c1935, 11in (28cm) high.
£50–60 *CSA*

A Shorter jug, decorated with Iris design, c1935, 11in (28cm) high.
£60–70 *CSA*

A Radford Jug, decorated with flowers, c1935, 8½in (21.5cm) high.
£50–60 *CSA*

A Monaco painted and gilded jug, c1950, 9in (23cm) high.
£75–85 *MLL*

Character & Toby Jugs

A Pratt ware Toby jug, Gin Woman, her dress decorated with floral sprigs in underglaze blue, green and brown, yellow ochre collar, with brown hat and highlights, slight damage, c1790, 10in (25.5cm) high.
£550–600 *DD*

A pearlware character jug and cover, Mr Punch, seated in an armchair and picked out in blue, green, yellow, black and puce, on green-glazed base, some restoration, 1870–80, 12¼in (31cm) high.
£550–600 *DN*

A pottery Toby jug, with ochre coat, brown breeches, wavy brown and white stockings and brown boots, early 19thC, 9in (23cm) high.
£110–130 *AP*

A Kevin Francis Toby Jug, depicting David Winter, limited edition, No. 742 of 950, 1991, 9½in (24cm) high.
£250–275 *ANP*

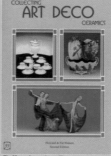

A Gouda Princess pattern plate, decorated with floral designs resembling batik, c1935, 10in (25.5cm) diam.
£120–140 *DSG*

A Gray's dish, painted with pink sprays of flowers, on a green ground, c1935, 9in (23cm) diam.
£30–40 *CSA*

A Hancock's Corona Ware hand-painted shallow dish, decorated with flowers, c1930, 7¾in (20cm) diam.
£40–50 *BKK*

A La Rochelle tray, depicting 2 strolling figures, c1880, 12in (30.5cm) wide.
£75–90 *SER*

A Pilkington's Royal Lancastrian vase, with feathered and striated glaze effect, c1911, 9in (23cm) high.
£450–500 *PGA*

l. A Goss chamberstick, in yellow lustre and lined in gilt, c1920, 4in (10cm) long.
£40–50 *SAS*

A Longwy crackle-glazed cat, c1900, 14¼in (36cm) high.
£200–235 *DSG*

A Zsolnay brown pottery lustre figure, Hungarian, 1930s, 10in (25.5cm) high.
£340–380 *SLL*

l. A Minton Secessionist jardinière-on-stand, c1910, 48in (122cm) high.
£700–800 *PAC*

r. A Bernard Moore rouge flambé studio vase, with Chang-like glaze, painted by R. Tomlinson, c1908, 6in (15cm) high.
£475–525 *PGA*

An Irish spongeware mug, 19thC, 4¼in (11cm) high.
£90–100 *ByI*

A Moorcroft vase, decorated with Clematis design, c1950, 8in (20.5cm) high.
£550–600 *DAC*

A Moorcroft vase, decorated with Hibiscus design, 1950s, 15in (38cm) high.
£400–450 *PAC*

A Moorcroft Florian vase, decorated with Roses and Poppy design, c1902, in (20.5cm) high.
£2,300–2,500 *RUM*

r. A Myott hand-painted diamond-shaped flower vase, with insert, c1933, 6in (15cm) high.
£80–100 *BKK*

A Myott hand-painted flower jug, hairline crack, c1933, 8in (20.5cm) high.
£100–120 *BKK*

A Pilkington vase, compressed collared shape with coral glaze effect, shape No. 2818, c1911, 8½in (21.5cm) high.
£400–450 *PGA*

A Gien green leaf plate, c1880, 8in (20.5cm) diam.
£35–40 *MLL*

An Austrian baby's plate, decorated with bear cricketing scene, c1920, 7in (18cm) diam.
£30–40 *WaR*

A Carter, Stabler & Adams vase, decorated by Ruth Pavely with Persian Deer pattern, 1938–42, 11in (28cm) high.
£450–500 *ADE*

A Carter, Stabler & Adams free-form bowl, decorated by Gwen Haskins, 1955–59, 17in (43cm) wide.
£250–300 *ADE*

A Staffordshire pot lid, The Village Wakes, No. 232, c1855, 3in (7.5cm) diam.
£550–650 *SAS*
A rare pot lid without a title. Two figures which were originally in the background have been deleted.

A Staffordshire pot lid, A Pretty Kettle of Fish, No.48, first issue, 1850–90, 4in (10cm) diam.
£200–220 *SAS*

A Poole Pottery Delphis plant pot, orange with black and blue decoration, 1960–70s, 5in (12.5cm) high.
£50–60 *HarC*

r. A Radford jug, decorated with floral design, 1930s, 4in (10cm) high.
£40–50 *DAC*

A Price Bros Maltona Ware hand-painted bowl, c1930, 9in (23cm) diam.
£70–80 *BKK*

A Charlotte Rhead wall plaque, designed for Crown Ducal, pattern No. 4926, c1937, 14in (35.5cm) diam.
£325–375 *PC*

A Rosenthal umbrella vase, designed by Raymond Peynet, good condition, 1950–60s, 4¾in (12cm) high.
£80–100 *RDG*

A Frederick Rhead vase, designed for Bursley Ware, decorated with Baghdad pattern, 1920s, 8½in (21.5cm) high.
£90–120 *BDA*

A Royal Copenhagen figure group, c1897, 18¼in (46.5cm) high.
£1,200–1,400 *FrG*

A pair of Royal Dux figures, c1910, 10½in (27cm) high.
£800–875 *DKH*

A Rye Pottery pig, decorated with green glaze, c1900, 5in (12.5cm) wide.
£100–120 *NCA*

A Royal Copenhagen model of a deer, c1952, 7in (18cm) high.
£75–85 *DAC*

A Salopian pottery vase, incised with lappets and stylised foliage beneath a streaked green and orange glaze, c1880, 11¼in (28.5cm) high.
£300–350 *DSG*

A Ruskin high-fired vase, c1908, 8in (20.5cm) high.
£1,400–1,800 *DSG*

A Shelley Harmony Ware hand-painted jug and bowl, c1936, jug 3½in (9cm) high.
£70–80 *BKK*

A Staffordshire figure group, entitled 'Departure', c1815–30, 9½in (24cm) high.
£300–350 *SER*

A Staffordshire figure, Little Red Riding Hood, c1860, 9in (23cm) high.
£80–100 *JO*

A SylvaC jug, the handle in the form of a squirrel, c1930, 9in (23cm) high.
£34–38 *TAC*

Two Wade models of Tom and Jerry, boxed, c1973, Tom 3in (7.5cm) high.
£85–95 *PAC*

A Wedgwood terracotta jug, enamelled with Chinese flowers, c1805, 6in (15cm) high.
£380–400 *PGA*

A Thoune plate, c1890, 10⅝in (27cm) diam.
£125–140 *DSG*

A Vallauris fish platter, c1950, 17in (43cm) long.
£250–275 *MLL*

A Wedgwood majolica shell, 1930s, 8½in (21.5cm) long.
£70–80 *BRU*

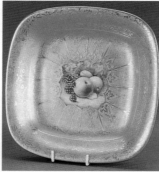

A Royal Worcester bowl, painted with a central still life of fruit, with gilt tooled surround, signed 'T. Nutt', c1955, 9in (23cm) square.
£400–450 *RBB*

A pair of Wedgwood lustre vases, decorated with green dragons, 1920s, 8in (20.5cm) high.
£500–600 *PC*

A German bisque cake decoration, c1925, 4¾in (12cm) high.
£15–20   YC

A German Christmas tree cake decoration, 1920–30s, 4in (10cm) high.
£8–10   PC

A light bulb in the form of Father Christmas, c1940, 9in (23cm) high.
£100–120   SMAM

r. A selection of Christmas tree decorations, c1950s, baubles 2½in (6.5cm) diam.
£4–6 each   PC

A Christmas card, depicting Father Christmas delivering parcels, c1905–10, 5½ x 3½in (14 x 9cm) high.
£4–5   TAC

Three Christmas decorations, 1930s: gnome, 1¼in (3cm) high. **£10–12** small Father Christmas. **£16–20** Father Christmas with tree, 2¼in (6cm) high. **£24–28   PSA**

A set of Noma bubble Christmas tree lights, 1950s, box 16in (40.5cm) wide.
£55–65   SMAM

A cardboard Christmas decoration, c1926, 10in (25.5cm) high.
£70–80   SMAM

A set of Pifco Christmas fairy lights, decorated with a nursery rhyme on each shade, 1930s, box 12½in (32cm) wide.
£20–25   WAB

A Christmas tree angel, 1990s, 11½in (29cm) high.
£20–25   SWN

A lustre pottery jug, commemorating the death of George IV, the lobed body printed in black with portrait, the reverse with inscription including dates, 1830, 6¼in (16cm) high.
£300–350 *SAS*

A Doulton jug, commemorating the death of Queen Victoria, moulded with circular portrait medallions, 1901, 8in (20.5cm) high.
£300–350 *W&S*

A Crown Staffordshire box and cover, commemorating the coronation of George VI, the interior inscribed and dated, 1937, 3½in (9cm) high.
£100–120 *SAS*

A boxed set of 3 medals, commemorating Crystal Palace, 2 bronze and one metal, depicting Victoria and Albert, a portrait of Paxton and Crystal Palace, 1854.
£120–140 *SAS*

A Shelley WWI jug and basin, enamelled with the crossed flags of Britain, Belgium, France and Russia, surmounted by the ribboned inscription 'For Freedom', gilt rims, jug 3in (7.5cm) high.
£40–50 *SAS*

A Paragon loving cup, commemorating the marriage of the Duke of Windsor, with twin gilt lion handles and enamelled in colours with a heraldic shield supported by a lion and a unicorn, the reverse with flags, 1937, 4¼in (11cm) high.
£200–220 *SAS*

An English majolica jardinière, by George Skey, commemorating Queen Victoria's Jubilee, inscribed and dated 'Jubilee 1887' with bacchanalian scenes and vine leaves, the interior impressed 'George Skey, Wilnecote Works, Tamworth', 1887, 8¼in (21cm) high.
£750–850 *SAS*

A biscuit tin, inscribed 'British Empire Exhibition 1924', 8in (20.5cm) wide.
£18–24 *COB*

A ceramic plate, by Homer Laughlin, commemorating the New York World's Fair, 1939, 10in (25.5cm) diam.
£250–300 *YAN*

l. An Aynsley ware mug, commemorating the 10th birthday of Prince William, 21 June 1992, produced for Peter Jones China, Wakefield, limited edition of 1,500, 3½in (9cm) high.
£30–35 *TAC*

Lustre Ware

Lustre ware became popular in Britain from the first part of the 19th century. The lustrous finish was obtained by painting the ceramic vessel with a liquid containing metallic oxides and then firing it. Gold was used for gold lustre and, when combined with tin, also produced pink or purple lustre. Platinum was employed for silver lustre, since silver metal itself tarnished, and in the latter part of the 19th century there was a revival in copper lustre.

Lustre ware was produced by many 19th-century manufacturers, and although some stamped their work, the vast majority of pieces tend to be unmarked. The Sunderland potteries became famous for their pink lustre ware: commemorative pieces, jugs, plaques inscribed with religious mottoes, and works decorated with nautical themes. A black and white transfer print was often framed or highlighted with splashes of coloured lustre. The same print could be used many times and current values depend not only on the quality of the lustre but also the rarity of the print or inscribed verse. Although much pink lustre is referred to as Sunderland ware, it was also produced in other areas including Staffordshire, Liverpool and Bristol. In the 20th century such factories as Carlton, Maling, Wedgwood and Wilton all produced lustre ware.

A pink lustre double-handled pot and lid, slight damage, c1820, 4¼in (11cm) high.
£40–50 *TAC*

A pearlware jug, painted in purple lustre, c1820, 6¼in (16cm) high.
£110–125 *OCH*

A lustre harvest pearlware jug, with loop handle, printed in black with a view of the Iron Bridge, the reverse with agricultural emblems in a shield with motto, within purple lustre borders, printed marks in black 'J. Phillips, Hylton Pottery' and 'Dixon, Austin & Co, Sunderland', c1825, 9in (23cm) high.
£650–700 *DN*

A Sunderland pearlware ovoid jug, with straight neck and loop handle, printed and painted with a view of the Iron Bridge, the Sailor's Farewell and a verse, within purple lustre borders, 1830–40, 7¼in (18.5cm) high.
£250–300 *DN*

A lustre wall plaque, with pink rim and decorated in green, impressed 'C. C. & Co', North Shields Pottery, c1830, 6½in (16.5cm) high.
£150–175 *IS*

r. A lustre pottery jug, decorated with 'The Great Australia Clipper-Ship', 'True Love from Hull' and verse, with orange lustre surround, 19thC, 9in (23cm) high.
£380–420 *RBB*

Miller's is a price GUIDE not a price LIST

A pink lustre pottery jug, monochrome printed with 'Iron Bridge at Sunderland' and verses with coloured surrounds, 19thC, 8½in (21.5cm) high.
£250–300 *RBB*

A lustre wall plaque, with pink surround, attributed to Dixon & Co, Sunderland Pottery, c1839, 6½in (16.5cm) diam.
£160–180 *IS*

A Sunderland pink lustre jug with loop handle, colour printed with 'West View of the Castle on Bridge over the River Wear ... open'd 9 Augt 1796' to one side and 'Sailor's Farewell' to the other, with floral printed upper border, 19thC, 7½in (19cm) high.
£380–420 *P(C)*

A Tyneside/Wearside pink lustre wall plaque, with unnamed sailing ship, c1850, 8in (20.5cm) wide.
£120–140 *IS*

Ship plaques are more sought after if the ship is named.

A Tyneside/Wearside orange lustre wall plaque, c1850, 8in (20.5cm) square.
£110–130 *IS*

Orange lustre is generally not as popular as pink lustre.

A pink lustre pottery jug, printed with 'A West View of Iron Bridge over the Wear', slight damage, dated '1853', 9in (23cm) high.
£350–400 *RBB*

l. A Victorian lustre cup and saucer, decorated in pink and green, slight damage, saucer 5½in (14cm) diam.
£10–15 *TAC*

A Sunderland lustre plaque, with pink and gold border, decorated with 'Sailor's Farewell', c1880, 9¼in (23.5cm) wide.
£120–150 *SER*

A lustre dish, with pink design depicting the zodiac sign Gemini, c1880, 7½in (19cm) diam.
£70–80 *SLL*

A copper lustre mug, with central blue stripe, c1860, 2¾in (7cm) high.
£25–30 *OCH*

A Royal Winton Grimwades green lustre vase, c1910, 7in (17.5cm) high.
£40–45 *DSG*

A Wedgwood octagonal bowl, the orange lustre interior decorated with gold butterflies around a central medallion, the green mother-of-pearl lustre exterior printed in gold with a *papillon* border, pattern No. Z4832, early 20thC, 9¾in (24.5cm) diam.
£480–550 *Bea(E)*

A Royal Winton orange lustre vase, c1930, 6in (15cm) high.
£50–60 *CSA*

A Moorcroft copper lustre three-handled pot, c1916, 6½in (16.5cm) wide.
£270–300 *CEX*

A Maling lustre bowl, with blue band and decorated with flowers, 1940s, 6¼in (16cm) wide.
£100–120 *SLL*

A Gray's Pottery lustre bowl, with gold rim, 1930s, 9in (23cm) diam.
£130–150 *SLL*

A Wedgwood lustre plate, hand-painted in brown and green, c1920, 10½in (26.5cm) diam.
£60–70 *PGA*

A Wilton orange lustre vase, with geisha girl design and lustre inside, c1920, 10in (25.5cm) high.
£250–275 *PGA*

A lustre model of a yacht on waves, decorated in orange and green, 1920–30s, 4½in (11.5cm) high.
£10–12 *JMC*

l. A lustre model of a peacock, with yellow neck and head, pink breast and silver tail, 1930s, 4¼in (11.5cm) high.
£8–10 *JMC*

Midwinter

A Midwinter pint jug, decorated with yellow, green and brown Yang design, 1930s.
£18–20 *AND*

A Midwinter trio, decorated in Red Domino pattern, c1953, cup 3½in (9cm) high.
£15–20 *RAT*

A Midwinter black cat, designed by Colin Melbourne, c1956, 7in (17.5cm) high.
£180–200 *AND*

A Midwinter cruet set on a tray, decorated with Riviera pattern, designed by Sir Hugh Casson, c1954, tray 5½in (14cm) wide.
£65–75 *GIN*

A Midwinter Stylecraft cup, saucer and side plate, decorated with Nature Study pattern in black and white, designed by Sir Terence Conran, c1955, plate 6½in (16.5cm) diam.
£40–50 *P(B)*

A selection of Midwinter Saladware, decorated in yellow, green and red, designed by Sir Terence Conran, c1956, largest plate 9½in (24cm) diam.
£65–80 each *AND*

A Midwinter 22-piece tea set, decorated with Hollywood pattern in yellow and grey, designed by Jessie Tait, c1956, teapot 6½in (16.5cm) high.
£300–350 *AND*

A Midwinter tureen, decorated in Zambesi pattern in black, white and red, designed by Jessie Tait, c1956, 9in (23cm) wide, on original stand.
£75–90 *AND*

A Midwinter Modern pattern black and white tube-lined vase, designed by Jessie Tait, c1956, 9in (23cm) high.
£250–300 *BDA*

A Midwinter 15-piece coffee set, decorated in Zambesi pattern in black, white and red, designed by Jessie Tait, c1956, coffee pot 8in (20.5cm) high.
£200–220 *AND*

A Midwinter turquoise gravy boat, saucer and ladle, decorated with Quite Contrary pattern, designed by Jessie Tait, c1957, gravy boat 8½in (21.5cm) long.
£45–55 *AND*

A Midwinter gravy boat, saucer and ladle, decorated with Cherokee pattern in orange, blue and yellow, designed by Jessie Tait, c1957, gravy boat 8½in (21.5cm) long.
£75–85 *AND*

A Midwinter 15-piece coffee set, decorated with Cherry Tree pattern in red, green and blue, designed by Nigel Wilde, c1966, coffee pot 8in (20.5cm) high.
£120–140 *AND*

Miniatures

A Spode miniature blue and white tureen, marked, 1820–30, tureen 3½in (9cm) high.
£125–145 *OCH*

A Harding miniature tureen, transfer-printed in brown and white, c1840, 4in (10cm) high.
£70–80 *OCH*

Miniatures
Ceramic miniatures were produced both as decorative objects in their own right and were also used by travelling salesmen as samples.

A Minton De Gaunt Castle miniature, transfer-printed in brown and white, marked, c1870, 2¾in (7cm) diam.
£30–40 *OCH*

l. A Limoges miniature tea set, with gilt edges, early 20thC, 2¾in (7cm) wide.
£40–45 *TAC*

A Mason's Ironstone miniature wash jug, with blue neck, gilt handle and design, late 19thC, 1¾in (4.5cm) high.
£30–40 *MRW*

r. A Booth's sample tureen and 2 plates, decorated with blue and gilt Willow pattern, 1930s, tureen ¾in (2cm) high.
£30–40 *MRW*

l. Two Royal Worcester miniature plates, decorated by Roberts, black mark, c1930, largest 3¼in (8.5cm) diam.
£85–95 *DKH*

Minton

A Minton tile, decorated with a lady and white blossom, c1865, 9in (23cm) square.
£110–140 *DSG*

A Minton majolica two-handled game dish, the cover moulded with a hare and game birds, the basket-weave body moulded and decorated in green on a brown ground with foliage and acorns, damage to cover, impressed marks and date cypher for 1871, 12in (30.5cm) wide.
£500–550 *GAK*

A Minton plate, decorated with a bird sitting on blossom branch, on a brown ground, c1875, 11½in (29cm) diam.
£120–140 *DSG*

A Minton & Hollins tile, corner chip, 1880s, 6in (15cm) square.
£6–7 *GIN*

A Minton Celladine ware jug, with white decoration on a green ground, c1890, 8in (20cm) high.
£800–875 *PAC*

A Minton Celladine ware jug, with white decoration on a green ground, c1890, 6½in (16.5cm) high.
£145–165 *PAC*

A Minton three-tile Secessionist style panel, 1901–1909, 18in (45.5cm) high.
£90–95 *DAC*

A pair of Minton vases, with gilt rims, painted with lilac blossom on a pale green ground, by J. Hackley, signed, puce printed marks, 1891–1902, 9¾in (25cm) high.
£500–600 *WL*

A Minton majolica green-glazed jardinière, with ribbon banding, c1900, 12¼in (31cm) high.
£200–240 *AH*

r. A Minton Secessionist style jardinière and stand, decorated in purple and green on a mottled blue ground, slight damage, printed and impressed marks and shape No. 3472/1, 1901–1909, 35½in (90cm) high.
£400–450 *DN*

Moorcroft

A Moorcroft Florian Ware jardinière, decorated with Poppy pattern, c1902, 2in (30.5cm) high.
£3,500–4,000 *RUM*

A Moorcroft Florian Ware vase, decorated with stylised poppies in blue and green on a pale silicon reserve, slight rim restoration, the base signed 'W. M. Des' in green, c1900, 8½in (21.5cm) high.
£850–950 *GAK*

A Moorcroft vase, decorated with floral and leafage moulded decoration in greens and blues in William Morris style, slight repair, c1902, 13in (33cm) high.
£450–500 *RBB*

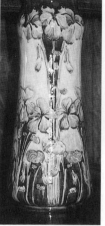

A Moorcroft Florian Ware vase, decorated with Heartsease pattern in blue, yellow and green, c1902, 12in (30.5cm) high.
£2,200–2,600 *RUM*

l. A Moorcroft Florian Ware cup and saucer, c1902, saucer 4in (10cm) diam.
£500–600 *RUM*

A Moorcroft globular vase, decorated with Claremont pattern, with red and yellow toadstools against a green ground, c1905, 11in (28cm) high.
£2,500–3,000 *DSG*

l. A Moorcroft vase, decorated with vine leaves and grapes in cream, fawn and black on a mottled green and brown ground, early 20thC, 9¾in (25cm) high.
£550–650 *DDM*

A Moorcroft bowl, decorated with Pomegranate pattern, on a dark blue ground, on a Tudric pewter base, c1912, 10¼in (26cm) diam.
£750–850 *P(B)*

A Moorcroft preserve jar and cover, decorated with Wisteria pattern, in shades of yellow, green and pink on a blue ground, c1920, 4in (10cm) high.
£250–300 *RUM*

A Moorcroft lamp base, decorated with leaves and berries, in blue, orange and green on a green ground, 1920s, 15in (38cm) high.
£600–700 *PAC*

A Moorcroft pale blue glazed vase, c1930, 6in (15cm) high.
£180–210 *DAC*

A Moorcroft jar and cover, decorated with Clematis pattern, in shades of blue and pink on a pale green ground, 1930s, 7in (18cm) diam.
£400–450 *PGA*

A Moorcroft vase, decorated with leaves and berries in yellow, red and green, full signature and inscribed 'Potter to the Queen', c1930, 7in (18cm) high.
£450–500 *PGA*

A Moorcroft vase, decorated with Hibiscus pattern, in white and yellow on a blue ground, c1949, 11in (28cm) high.
£425–475 *DAC*

A Moorcroft jug, decorated with a green Art Deco peacock feather pattern, impressed factory mark with facsimile signature and painted signature to base, c1938, 9in (23cm) high.
£300–350 *RTo*

A Moorcroft tazza, decorated with Pansy Nouveau pattern, in blue and yellow on a natural ground, c1970, 7in (18cm) diam.
£200–220 *NP*

> **Miller's is a price GUIDE not a price LIST**

A Moorcroft Thaxted Morris Men mug, c1987, 3½in (9cm) high.
£80–100 *NP*

A Moorcroft year plate, decorated with Columbine pattern, in shades of brown and orange on a green ground, c1984, 8in (20.5cm) diam.
£260–280 *NP*

A Moorcroft clock and 2 vases, decorated with Blue Finch pattern, designed by Sally Tuffin, 1988–96, 6in (15cm) high.
£150–200 *NP*

Moss Ware

A pair of moss ware candlesticks, c1860, 4½in (11.5cm) high.
£30–36 *OCH*

A pair of moss ware vases, late 19thC, 3¾in (9.5cm) high.
£12–18 *JMC*

A pair of moss ware vases, late 19thC, 4¼in (11cm) high.
£12–18 *JMC*

A moss ware egg-shaped box, late 19thC, 3in (7.5cm) wide.
£10–12 *JMC*

Mugs

A pair of moss ware square pots, late 19thC, 2½in (6.5cm) high.
£12–18 *JMC*

A moss ware six-sided spill vase, late 19thC, 3in (7.5cm) high.
£10–12 *JMC*

A pearlware frog mug, with leaf moulded scroll handle, flower scrolls, fluted and basketwork bands, inscribed 'Winchester Measure, Warranted', and picked out in black, green, yellow and iron-red, the interior modelled with a frog, c1825–30, 4¼in (10.5cm) high.
£270–300 *DN*

A pottery mug, printed in black with portraits centred by a crown and the inscription 'Victoria & Albert, married Feb 10th 1840', flanked by flowers of the union, 3½in (9cm) high.
£350–400 *SAS*

A Staffordshire mug, with black transfer print depicting Battle Church, c1850, 3in (7.5cm) high.
£10–15 *VSt*

A Victorian Staffordshire mug, with black transfer print depicting the Residence of Shakespeare, 3¼in (8.5cm) high.
£20–25 *VSt*

An Irish mug, with brown transfer print of a rural scene, 19thC, 4¼in (11cm) high.
£90–110 *ByI*

An Irish mug, with brown transfer print, inscribed 'Cattle D L & S' on the base, 19thC, 4¼in (11cm) high.
£90–110 *ByI*

A Scottish pearlware frog mug, with 2 leaf scroll handles, the exterior modelled with monkeys in Turkish costume, picked out in puce, blue, green and brown, inscribed 'Thomas Parkes', the interior modelled with 2 frogs and 2 lizards, picked out in brown, c1840, 6¼in (16cm) high.
£600–700 *DN*

A lustre frog mug, commemorating the Crimean War, c1854, 5in (12.5cm) high.
£235–255 *OCH*

Also known as surprise mugs, frog mugs were produced in Staffordshire and Sunderland. A realistically modelled frog or toad was placed inside the mug, only to be seen by drinkers once they had finished their beverage. Larger mugs can contain up to 3 frogs, on the base and climbing the sides, and frogs were also produced with hollow bodies and open mouths, so that they could spurt the drinker with liquid.

An Irish spongeware mug, decorated with brown, red and green flowers, 19thC, 4¼in (11cm) high.
£90–110 *ByI*

An Adams mug, transfer printed with a scene from *David Copperfield*, c1910, 6in (15cm) high.
£40–50 *Rac*

An Irish mug, with cockerel design, 19thC, 3¼in (8cm) high.
£80–90 *ByI*

A Clee Pottery tankard, the handle modelled as an oarsman, inscribed 'Britannia', the blue tapering body moulded with circular cartouche entitled 'Floreat Etona and Henry VI Founder 1440' with views of the College and river with rowing scene, stamped 'Clee Pottery, Eton, Windsor', c1962, 7¼in (18.5cm) high.
£300–350 *SAS*

Old Bill

Old Bill, a walrus-moustached, disillusioned, Cockney soldier from WWI, was created by artist and journalist Captain Bruce Bairnsfather (1888–1959). The latter served in France during the 1914–18 war and became famous for his cartoons starring Old Bill, who featured in books, periodicals and was even translated into ceramics.

During WWII Bairnsfather was appointed official war cartoonist and attached to the US Army in Europe. Old Bill, however, remained his most successful cartoon, a popular hero and a symbol of resilient trench humour. Old Bill's sidekick was his pal Bert, gormless and grousing and with a cigarette dangling perpetually from his lip. Bairnsfather's most famous cartoon showed the pair of them stuck in a shell hole, with the caption: 'Well if you knows of a better 'ole, go to it', thus creating with the words 'better 'ole' one of the catch phrases of WWI.

A pottery bowl, printed in sepia, inscribed 'Well if you knows of a better 'ole, go to it', with wavy black and gilt-lined border, c1918, 9¾in (25cm) diam.
£50–60 *SAS*

A bellied pot and cover, printed in sepia, the reverse and cover with heraldic shields on a buff ground, with gilt and black lining, c1918, 4½in (11.5cm) high.
£100–110 *SAS*

A Grimwades mug, transfer printed in brown, inscribed 'Gott Straff, This barbed wire', c1917, 3in (7.5cm) high.
£130–145 *LeB*

l. A pottery mug, modelled as Old Bill, decorated in brown on a buff ground, c1918, 4½in (11.5cm) high.
£50–60 *SAS*

More Fragments from France, by Capt Bruce Bairnsfather, 1914–18, 12 x 8in (30.5 x 20.5cm).
£18–20 *HUX*

r. A pottery bowl, printed in sepia, inscribed 'Here with a loaf of bread ...', c1918, 10in (25.5cm) diam.
£60–70 *SAS*

An oviform vase, printed in sepia, inscribed 'Well if you knows ...', c1918, 6in (15cm) high.
£100–110 *SAS*

164 CERAMICS • Pendelfins • Plates

Pendelfins

A Pendelfin model rabbit, 'Poppet', 1966, 3½in (9cm) long.
£8–10 *PC*

A Pendelfin model cobble cottage, c1990, 8in (20.5cm) high.
£24–28 *PAC*

A Pendelfin model shop, 1980s, 10in (25.5cm) high.
£40–50 *PAC*

r. Two Pendelfin model rabbits, one dressed as a bellringer, the other with a baby in her arms, 1990s, 8in (20.5cm) high.
£28–30 each *PAC*

l. Three Pendelfin model rabbits, 1980s, 3in (7.5cm) high.
£14–18 each *PAC*

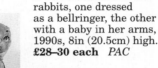

PENDELFIN SPECIALISTS

Please phone for our free newsletter giving up to date information on the latest releases and retirements

**Arch House
St George Street, Tenby
Pembrokeshire SA70 7JB
Telephone 01834 843246**

VISA   **MAIL ORDER WELCOME**   MasterCard

Plates

A Dutch Delft charger, painted in blue with chinoiserie figures in a garden within a border of similar scenes, interspersed with cell diaper panels, 18thC, 15¼in (38.5cm) diam.
£300–350 *Bon(C)*

A Bristol delft plate, painted in yellow, blue and iron-red, with a cockerel and manganese trees within a blue line rim, slight damage, c1730, 8¾in (22cm) diam.
£2,200–2,400 *DN*

r. A Lambeth polychrome plate, with green, blue, yellow and red chinoiserie decoration, 18thC, 9in (23cm) diam.
£170–200 *E*

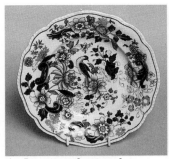

An Ironstone dessert plate, with moulded edge, decorated with birds and flowers, impressed 'Ironstone China', c1830, 8¼in (21cm) diam.
£100–120 *JP*

A child's plate, transfer-printed with a view of Windsor Castle, possibly Davenport, c1840, 6¾in (17cm) diam.
£70–90 *IW*

A Fell & Co nursery plate, printed with a scene of Chinese figures dancing, entitled 'Polka' within a moulded and enamelled border of animals, impressed mark, c1845, 6¼in (16cm) diam.
£90–110 *SAS*

Said to have been invented by a Bohemian servant girl, the Polka took its name from the Czechoslovakian word pulka *meaning 'half step'. The lively dance was introduced in Paris in 1843 and took Europe by storm, coming to England in 1844, where it was commemorated in prints and the decorative arts. The oriental illustration decorating this plate may also have been inspired by the ending of the first Opium War between China and Britain with the Treaty of Nanking in 1842. In the 19thC, children's plates and nursery wares were often decorated with what today we might regard as comparatively adult subjects.*

A gilt-decorated plate, entitled 'The Truant', with oak leaf and acorn border, c1860, 9½in (24cm) diam.
£130–150 *SAS*

A plate, depicting Chatsworth, with reclining classical female border in green, blue and gilt, c1870, 9in (23cm) diam.
£220–240 *SAS*

l. An Ashworth charger, decorated in brown with a woman's head, c1885, 14in (35.5cm) diam.
£250–300 *DSG*

A set of 6 plates, decorated with asparagus and artichokes, c1880, 9in (23cm) diam.
£325–365 *MLL*

r. A Royal Venton cake plate on stand, decorated with the The Star Inn, Alfriston, in brown, red, green and yellow, c1940, 9in (23cm) diam.
£16–18 *UTP*

A ribbon plate, inscribed 'A Present from Eastbourne', decorated with flowers, 1920–30s, 8¾in (22cm) diam.
£10–15 *JMC*

Poole Pottery

A Carter & Co pottery vase, decorated in underglaze blue in Seccessionist style with figures in panels, signed 'Carter & Co, Poole', c1915, 8in (20.5cm) high.
£400–450 *P(B)*

A Carter, Stabler & Adams pottery vase, designed by Truda Carter, decorated by Marjorie Batt, 1928–34, 8¾in (22cm) high.
£350–400 *ADE*

A Carter, Stabler & Adams pottery vase, designed by Truda Carter, decorated by Ann Hatchard, 1928–34, 8¾in (22cm) high.
£450–500 *ADE*

A Carter, Stabler & Adams pottery vase, with geometric pattern designed by Truda Carter, decorated by Ann Hatchard, 1928–34, 7½in (19cm) high.
£450–500 *ADE*

r. A Carter, Stabler & Adams slip cast white earthenware three-branch candelabra, designed by John Adams, 1930s, 8½in (21.5cm) high.
£120–150 *ADE*

A Carter, Stabler & Adams twin-handled pottery vase, designed by Truda Carter, c1930, 7in (18cm) high.
£275–300 *RDG*

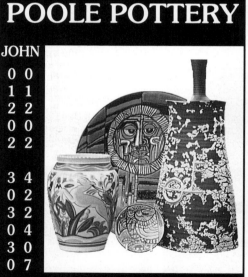

A Carter, Stabler & Adams pottery vase, with Blue Bird pattern, designed by Truda Carter, decorated by Vera Bridle, 1928–33, 8¾in (22cm) high.
£250–300 *ADE*

A Carter, Stabler & Adams baluster jug, decorated with panels of stylised flowers in puce, green and blue, on a crackle glaze off-white ground, by Ruth Pavely, repaired, impressed No. 623, inscribed 'ZG', 1950s, 11½in (29cm) high.
£200–220 *GAK*

A Carter, Stabler & Adams freeform pottery vase, decorated by Betty Gooby, 1955–59, 7½in (19cm) high.
£200–250 *ADE*

A Carter, Stabler & Adams pottery vase, with contemporary pattern designed by Alfred Read, decorated by Gwen Haskins, 1952–55, 9¾in (25cm) high.
£200–250 *ADE*

A Carter, Stabler & Adams freeform pottery vase, designed by Alfred Read and Guy Sydenham, 1955–59, 7½in (19cm) high.
£250–300 *ADE*

A Carter, Stabler & Adams freeform vase, designed by Alfred Read and Guy Sydenham, decorated by Diane Holloway, marked, 1955–59, 10in (25.5cm) high.
£450–500 *ADE*

A Poole Pottery Delphis vase, designed by Guy Sydenham, decorated with semi-circles of mottled green, stamped 'Poole, England', with maker's mark 'G.S.', 1960s, 5¾in (14.5cm) high.
£150–170 *P(B)*

A Poole Pottery Atlantis paperweight/ vase, designed and thrown by Guy Sydenham, 1960–70s, 4½in (11.5cm) diam.
£90–100 *HarC*

l. A Poole Pottery Delphis bowl, painted in shades of blue, orange and black, 1960–70s, 13½in (34.5cm) diam.
£75–100 *HarC*

l. A Poole Pottery ship plate, painted by Gwen Haskins after a 1930s design by Arthur Bradbury, c1974, 15½in (39.5cm) diam.
£450–600 *HarC*

Two Poole Pottery calendar plates, designed by Tony Morris, painted by Susan Pottinger, 1972–79, 12½in (32cm) diam.
£100–120 each *HarC*

Pot Lids

Pot lids are the decorative covers for food jars containing such products as potted meat and fish paste and the pomade pots that were a stalwart of the Victorian gentleman's dressing table. Wigs and hair powder had been the ultimate in male fashion during the 18th century, but when the government taxed dusting powder, and wigs fell from fashion, demand grew for oils and ointments that would enhance the condition both of a gentleman's hair and the luxuriant beards and moustaches that came into vogue in the 19th century.

A favourite preparation was bear's grease, often obtained from Russian bears and manufactured by a number of British firms including J. & E. Atkinson. Initially pots for bear's grease and other products were either plain or had fairly simple monochrome decoration. In the 1840s, however, coloured pot lids were introduced.

Jesse Austin, an engraver employed by F. R. Pratt of Fenton, Staffordshire, developed the process of transfer printing in polychrome, and the firm produced millions of colourful pot lids for cosmetic preparations and foodstuffs.

Numerous other firms also manufactured these decorative covers. Many pots were illustrated with scenes containing bears and other popular subjects, as well as landscapes, buildings, portraits of prominent personalities and reproductions of paintings. Some covers are signed on the reverse and many of Jesse Austin's engravings bear his signature.

Multi-coloured lids tend to be more desirable than monochrome examples, although rare black and white pieces will command high prices. While collectors are primarily interested in covers, pots retaining their original bases can fetch a premium.

'Bear Hunting', No. 4,
1850–90, 3in (7.5cm) diam.
£230–250 *SAS*

'Otto of Rose Cold Cream,
prepared by W. Charles Baker
Chemist, Edinburgh',
1890–1900, 2¾in (7cm) diam.
£18–20 *BBR*

'The Wolf and the Lamb',
No. 361, by F. & R. Pratt,
c1860, 4¼in (11cm) diam.
£40–50 *BBR*

'New Houses of Parliament',
No. 195, 1850–90,
4½in (11.5cm) diam.
£550–600 *SAS*

'Buckingham Palace', No. 176,
1850–90, 5in (12.5cm) diam.
£320–360 *SAS*

'Autumn', No 342b, 1850–90,
4in (10cm) diam.
£90–100 *SAS*

'Old Jack', No. 215, 1850–90,
3in (7.5cm) diam.
£130–150 *SAS*

'The Shrimpers', No. 63, by
F. & R. Pratt, minor damage,
c1850, 4in (10cm) diam.
£24–28 *BBR*

'The Outs', No. 16, 1850–90,
4in (10cm) diam.
£190–220 *SAS*

'Napirima, Trinidad', No. 225,
1850–90, 5in (13cm) diam.
£220–250 *SAS*

'The Ins', No. 15, 1850–90,
3in (7.5cm) diam.
£750–800 *SAS*

*This pot lid is a rare example,
thus commanding a premium.*

'Westminster Abbey', No. 189,
1850–90, 4½in (11.5cm) diam.
£320–350 *SAS*

'Tam-o'-Shanter and Souter
Johnny', No. 346, 1850–90,
4in (10cm) diam.
£100–120 *SAS*

'Tam-o'-Shanter', No. 347,
1850–90, 4in (10cm) diam.
£130–150 *SAS*

A pot lid, inscribed 'Genuine
Bears Grease', by Patey & Co,
c1880, 3in (7.5cm) diam.
£220–250 *SAS*

l. 'Rose Lip Salve, Savory &
Moore, London', 1890–1900,
1½in (3cm) diam.
£60–70 *BBR*

r. 'Shakespeare's Birthplace',
No. 227, by Messrs Cauldon Ltd,
'Made in England' backstamp,
1860–70s, 4¼in (11cm) diam.
£24–26 *BBR*

Frederick & Charlotte Rhead

A Foley Intarsio Toby jug, designed by Frederick Rhead, decorated in shades of brown, green, yellow and red, c1890–1900, 7¼in (18.5cm) high.
£450–500 *PGA*

A Foley Intarsio vase, designed by Frederick Rhead, decorated with Watermill and Asparagus Trees pattern, in shades of blue, green and red, c1890–1900, 9in (23cm) high.
£450–500 *PGA*

l. A pair of Wood & Sons spill vases, designed by Frederick Rhead, decorated with Sheraton pattern in shades of pink, mauve, blue and green on a black ground, c1918, 6in (15cm) high.
£50–65 *PC*

A Wood & Sons Korea ware vase, designed by Frederick Rhead, decorated with flowers and peacocks in yellow and white on a black ground, c1910, 6in (15cm) high.
£40–50 *DSG*

A Wood & Sons ovoid vase, designed by Frederick Rhead, decorated with Chung pattern in shades of blue on a red ground, c1918, 8in (20.5cm) high.
£85–120 *PC*

A Royal Cauldon vase, designed by Frederick Rhead, minor rim damage, c1930, 10in (25.5cm) high.
£50–60 *DSG*

A Wood & Sons blue and white waisted vase, designed by Frederick Rhead, decorated with Prunus pattern, c1916, 8½in (22cm) high.
£65–85 *PC*

A Bursley Ware dish, designed by Frederick Rhead, decorated with Amstel pattern in shades of blue, red and black, 1920s, 4½in (11.5cm) diam.
£30–50 *BDA*

l. A Wood & Sons plate, designed by Frederick Rhead, decorated with Benaris pattern in shades of red, blue and orange, c1918, 10in (25.5cm) diam.
£65–85 *PC*

A Crown Ducal wall plate, designed by Charlotte Rhead, decorated in green, yellow, blue and turquoise, pattern No. 3052, made by A. G. Richardson, 1930s, 12in (30.5cm) diam.
£220–260 *PC*

A Bursley Ware charger, designed by Charlotte Rhead, tube-lined and painted in pale green, lemon, pink and blue, printed marks, 1930s, 14¼in (36cm) diam.
£230–250 *WL*

A Crown Ducal pottery plaque, designed by Charlotte Rhead, with Autumn Leaf pattern in orange and green on a caramel ground, printed mark, No. 4921, signed, 1930s, 14¼in (36cm) diam.
£200–240 *Mit*

A Crown Ducal twin-handled vase, designed by Charlotte Rhead, painted in orange, blue, yellow and green, made by A. G. Richardson, 1930s, 6in (15cm) high.
£140–165 *PC*

A Crown Ducal charger, designed by Charlotte Rhead, decorated with Hydrangea pattern, No. 3797, c1935, 14½in (37cm) diam.
£320–350 *BDA*

A Crown Ducal charger, designed by Charlotte Rhead, in shades of blue and mauve on a mottled grey ground within a blue border, printed mark, signed, c1935, 14½in (37cm) diam.
£280–320 *GAK*

A Crown Ducal wall plaque, designed by Charlotte Rhead, decorated in shades of pink, blue and brown, pattern No. 5803, c1938, 14in (36cm) diam.
£250–300 *PC*

A Crown Ducal planter, designed by Charlotte Rhead, decorated in shades of pink and cream, pattern No. 6778, shape No. 279, c1940, 10½in (27cm) diam.
£150–180 *PC*

r. A Bursley Ware tray, designed by Charlotte Rhead, decorated in shades of green, orange and blue, pattern No. TL5, 1940s, 8¾in (22cm) long.
£100–125 *PC*

A Bursley Ware pitcher, designed by Charlotte Rhead, decorated in shades of orange, green and blue, pattern No. TL5, 1940s, 9in (23cm) high.
£230–250 *BDA*

Rosenthal/Raymond Peynet

The French artist and designer Raymond Peynet was born in 1908. He achieved great success with his romantic and whimsical drawings in the 1950s and 1960s. Peynet's Lovers, an idealized portrayal of a Parisian couple, became an institution in France; illustrations of them appeared in books, newspapers and magazines, they were transformed into postcards and dolls and appeared as decorative motifs on everything from scarves to handkerchiefs. Ceramics were another important medium, and Peynet worked with the German company Rosenthal (est. 1879) to produce a range of figurines and decorative tableware inspired by his lovers. There is currently a revival of interest in Raymond Peynet. His designs have become collectors' items, and two museums devoted to his work have been founded in France and Japan.

A Rosenthal large triangular dish, designed by Raymond Peynet, painted with a veteran car, c1950–60, 8in (20.5cm) wide.
£70–80   *RDG*

A pair of Rosenthal vases, designed by Raymond Peynet, each painted with a figure, c1950–60, 7in (17.5cm) high.
£90–100   *RDG*

A Rosenthal coffee set for 4, designed by Raymond Peynet, c1950–60, coffee pot 7¾in (19.5cm) high.
£300–350   *RDG*

A Rosenthal dish, designed by Raymond Peynet, decorated with Nymolte pattern, slight damage, 1950s–60s, 5½in (14cm) wide.
£10–15   *RDG*

l. A Rosenthal pin tray, designed by Raymond Peynet, decorated with Poet and The Lady pattern, 1950s, 5in (12.5cm) wide.
£10–15   *PC*

A pair of Rosenthal lovers with hearts, designed by Raymond Peynet, c1950–60, man 11in (28cm) high.
£500–550   *RDG*

l. A Rosenthal flowerpot holder, designed by Raymond Peynet, c1950–60, 5½in (14cm) high.
£130–150   *RDG*

A Rosenthal model of a centaur, designed by Raymond Peynet, 1950s–60s, 10in (25.5cm) high.
£700–800   *RDG*

Royal Copenhagen

Royal Copenhagen, the Danish pottery, has enjoyed a long if disrupted history. Founded in 1755 under the patronage of Frederick V, the first Copenhagen factory specialized in soft-paste porcelain, producing wares influenced by the French firm of Sèvres. After Frederick's death, the factory closed down in 1766. It was reopened on a new site in 1775, destroyed by Nelson's ships during the bombardment of Copenhagen in 1807, and was then rebuilt and eventually moved to a new location in Smallegarde.

In the late 19th century Royal Copenhagen won many international awards and developed the underglaze decoration in softly muted blues, greys and pinks that was to become the company's trademark. The firm also began to specialize in the figures, animals and decorative pieces, for which they are perhaps best known today. 'Every Scandinavian home had its collection of Royal Copenhagen figures, and we tend to buy most of our vintage pieces from Scandinavia today,' says dealer Michel Bach. 'The nice thing about Royal Copenhagen was that not only were works high in quality, but they were also very reasonably priced, which explains the huge success of the pottery.'

From the early 20th century onwards, vast numbers of models were produced, particularly between 1920 and 1940. Popular subjects include animals, (especially dogs), birds and children, as well as Christmas and commemorative plates, vases and decorative tableware. 'Some models have been used for 70 years,' explains Bach, 'but although the figure itself might not change in design, the standard of workmanship is less good on the more recent models. Also new models can be twice as expensive – or more – than the same figure produced in the 1930s and purchased second-hand.'

Unlike collectors in other areas of the ceramics market, such as Beswick and Royal Doulton, Royal Copenhagen aficionados tend not to be looking for withdrawn models, or very specific rarities. 'Collectors are generally attracted by the subject matter. Dog enthusiasts will look at the dogs for example, and models of children are another great favourite,' says Bach. For him, however, perhaps the greatest appeal of Royal Copenhagen is its quality. 'Pieces have a very restrained beauty, they don't shout at you. They are finely painted, meticulously modelled and every detail is exact.'

A Royal Copenhagen vase, with gold top and base, decorated with fish and lilies, experimental version, c1895, 9in (23cm) high.
£1,000–1,200 *FrG*

This rare trial piece did not go into full production.

A Royal Copenhagen vase, decorated with grey butterflies, c1900, 6in (15cm) high.
£250–300 *FrG*

r. A Royal Copenhagen blue and white Christmas plate, decorated with The Virgin and Child, 1920, 3¼in (8cm) diam.
£55–65 *GSW*

A Royal Copenhagen vase, decorated with a pink tulip, 1895–99, 6½in (16.5cm) high.
£160–180 *SUC*

A Royal Copenhagen bird bath, c1920, 9in (23cm) wide.
£200–250 *FrG*

A Royal Copenhagen model of a rabbit, c1923, 6in (15cm) high.
£135–155 *GSW*

A Royal Copenhagen model of a fly catcher, c1923, 3in (7.5cm) high.
£110–130 *GSW*

A Royal Copenhagen model of a pheasant, 1923–30, 8in (20.5cm) high.
£360–400 *GSW*

A Royal Copenhagen model of a moose, c1930, 10in (25.5cm) long.
£140–160 *FrG*

A Royal Copenhagen crab dish, decorated with fish, c1930, 9¾in (25cm) wide.
£100–120 *FrG*

A Royal Copenhagen figure of a milkmaid and cow, c1930, 6¼in (16cm) high.
£100–120 *FrG*

A Royal Copenhagen figure of Pan and his pipes, c1930, 5½in (14cm) high.
£200–220 *FrG*

A Royal Copenhagen figure of a Scandinavian child knitting, c1950, 5¾in (14.5cm) high.
£80–100 *FrG*

l. A Royal Copenhagen model of a brown and white bull, c1944, 15in (38cm) long.
£550–600 *GSW*

r. A Royal Copenhagen model of a puppy, white with brown markings, c1952, 6in (15cm) long.
£80–100 *DAC*

A Royal Copenhagen model of geese on grass, c1961, 8in (20.5cm) wide.
£300–350 *GSW*

A Royal Copenhagen blue and white Christmas plate, Little Mermaid, dated '1962', 3¼in (8cm) diam.
£125–135 *GSW*

A Royal Copenhagen model of a German Boxer, c1962, 4in (10cm) high.
£120–140 *GSW*

l. A Royal Copenhagen model of a fox and cubs, c1963, 5in (12.5cm) wide.
£250–280 *GSW*

A Royal Copenhagen figure of a herdsman with pig, c1966, 7in (18cm) high.
£200–220 *GSW*

A Royal Copenhagen model of an owl, c1963, 5½in (14cm) high.
£150–170 *GSW*

A Royal Copenhagen figure of a boy with calves, c1968, 9in (23cm) high.
£350–400 *GSW*

r. A Royal Copenhagen model of a pointer, c1975, 9in (23cm) wide.
£250–280 *GSW*

A Royal Copenhagen model of a penguin, c1980, 4in (10cm) high.
£60–70 *GSW*

Royal Dux

r. A Royal Dux figure of a girl, semi-draped and seated on a rock, on a square base, 1910–20, 12in (30.5cm) high.
£1,000–1,200 *HCC*

Royal Dux figures and busts are highly sought after today.

l. A Royal Dux bust of a lady, dressed in a lace-trimmed décolleté dress and ribboned hat, impressed tablet mark '454' and painted 'No. 15', applied pink triangle mark, c1900, 22in (56cm) high.
£1,700–2,000 *WL*

A Royal Dux figure of a cockatiel, impressed 'No. 1240', painted 'No. 37', applied pink triangle, c1900, 15¼in (39cm) high.
£350–400 *WL*

Rye Pottery

A Rye Pottery carpenter's bag, c1890, 8in (20cm) wide.
£120–150 *NCA*

A Rye Pottery green basket, c1900, 8⅝in (22cm) diam.
£100–120 *NCA*

A Rye Pottery dish, decorated with hops on a brown glaze, c1920, 4in (10cm) wide.
£100–120 *NCA*

A Rye Pottery vase, decorated with blue, pink and black bands, 1950s, 5⅝in (14.5cm) high.
£35–45 *PrB*

l. A Rye Pottery candle holder, by Walter Cole, decorated with green leaf pattern, c1968, 10in (25.5cm) diam.
£85–95 *PrB*

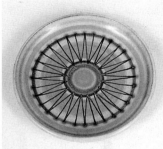

A Rye Pottery butter dish, decorated in yellow, red and grey bands and blue zig zag pattern, c1950, 5in (12.5cm) diam.
£22–26 *NCA*

These dishes were made to hold the individual post-war butter ration.

Two Rye Pottery ducks, with black markings, c1950, largest 7in (18cm) wide.
£25–45 each *DSG*

Shelley

A Shelley trio and plate, decorated with blue irises, 1920–30, large plate 9½in (24cm) diam.
£100–120 *SLL*

A Shelley Harmony ware vase, hand-painted with yellow and blue bands, c1936, 7½in (19cm) high.
£60–70 *BKK*

A Shelley Melody jug, decorated with flowers on a green ground, c1935, 6½in (16.5cm) high.
£50–60 *CSA*

l. A Shelley tea service for 12 persons, decorated in pink and green diamond pattern, 1930s.
£2,000–2,600 *Doc*

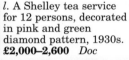

A Shelley nursery tea set, designed by Mabel Lucie Attwell, decorated in red, green and white, c1938, 6in (15cm) high.
£500–575 *PAC*

Staffordshire

A Staffordshire pearlware group of a shepherd and shepherdess, a hound and 2 lambs at their feet, decorated in coloured enamels, on square bordered mound base, entitled 'Shepherd' in black, 1790–1800, 12½in (32cm) high.
£700–800 *DN*

FURTHER READING

P. D. Gordon Pugh, *Staffordshire Portrait Figures,* Barrie & Jenkins Ltd, 1970

A Staffordshire reclining figure, decorated in green, yellow and pink, slight damage, c1800, 3½in (9cm) high.
£130–150 *SER*

A Staffordshire figure of Charity, slight damage, 1800–15, 7½in (19cm) high.
£230–250 *SER*

A pair of Staffordshire models of lions, with curly white manes, each with a lamb nestling before them on a shaped and gilded base, early 19thC, 4¼in (11cm) high.
£3,300–3,600 *DA*

A Staffordshire figure of a lady, wearing a white dress with red pattern and yellow and red shawl, slight damage, 1800–15, 8in (20.5cm) high.
£250–280 *SER*

A Staffordshire Walton figure of a lady gardener, dressed in pink, on green base, slight damage, 1815–25, 5½in (14cm) high.
£180–200 *SER*

A Staffordshire group, entitled 'Return', the sailor wearing a blue jacket and trousers and black hat, his companion wearing a white dress and white hat with black band, restored, 1815–30, 9in (23cm) high.
£300–350 *SER*

A Staffordshire figure, entitled 'Fire', holding a magnifying glass and burning branch, wearing green trousers, a white jacket with brown edging and a black hat with yellow flower, c1825, 6in (15cm) high.
£170–190 *SER*

A Staffordshire musician group, modelled as a male flautist and his female companion, seated beside a waterfall with lambs and swans, with a bocage background, painted in overglaze enamel colours, on a rustic sprigged base, early 19thC, 8½in (21.5cm) high.
£280–330 *HYD*

A Staffordshire group of an egg vendor, clutching a basket of eggs, painted in colours with naturalistic faces, 19thC, 13in (33cm) high.
£160–180 *GAK*

A Staffordshire spill vase, depicting a Guardian Angel watching over 2 sleeping children, c1840, 9in (23cm) high.
£145–160 *SER*

A Staffordshire character jug, modelled as a standing figure of Nelson, 19thC, 11½in (29cm) high.
£140–160 *GAK*

A Staffordshire figure of Nelson, in blue jacket with yellow sash, blue hat and green trousers, 1840s, 8in (20.5cm) high.
£380–420 *TVM*

A Staffordshire figure of a sailor, wearing a black wide-brimmed hat and yellow trousers, on a gilt-lined base, c1850, 9in (23cm) high.
£240–280 *CGC*

A Staffordshire figure of a Turkish soldier, with a plumed hat and holding a flag, 1850–60, 15in (38cm) high.
£270–300 *SER*

l. A Staffordshire group, entitled 'Queen & King of Sardinia', both wearing black spotted robes, the Queen's dress in white painted with flowers, c1855, 13¾in (35cm) high.
£225–250 *SER*

A Staffordshire spill vase, depicting a group of gypsies sitting around a fire with a cooking pot, with branch behind, c1855, 9½in (24cm) high.
£160–180 *JO*

A Staffordshire figure of Napoleon, dressed blue jacket, white trousers and black boots, holding his plumed black hat, c1854, 16in (40.5cm) high.
£310–330 *SER*

A Staffordshire model of Jessica and Lorenzo, from *The Merchant of Venice*, with green bocage, c1860, 10in (25.5cm) high.
£160–175 *JO*

A Staffordshire figure of a jockey, wearing pink jacket with black polka dots, yellow stockings and green hat, c1860, 9in (23cm) high.
£165–185 *RWB*

l. A Staffordshire figure, entitled 'Uncle Tom's Cabin, c1861, 9in (23cm) high.
£220–240 *JO*

r. A Staffordshire figure of Reverend John Wesley, wearing white robes, c1870, 6in (15cm) high.
£165–185 *JO*

A Staffordshire figure entitled 'Prince of Wales', by Sampson Smith, white with blue sash, pink belt and red robe, c1870, 18in (45.5cm) high.
£300–330 *SER*

A Staffordshire figure, depicting Queen Victoria's daughter dressed in black, and a goat with brown marking, c1860, 4⅓in (11.5cm) high.
£130–145 *JO*

A Staffordshire figure entitled 'Queen of England', by Sampson Smith, in white and gilt dress with ermine-edged cloak and blue sash, c1870, 17⅓in (44.5cm) high.
£300–330 *SER*

r. A Victorian Staffordshire figure of Shakespeare, leaning on a pillar, 18⅓in (47cm) high.
£220–240 *WilP*

SylvaC

A SylvaC lustre vase, decorated with a parrot, in shades of green, blue, pink and yellow, 1930s, 11in (28cm) high.
£90–100 *PAC*

A SylvaC pale blue vase, with a white lamb, No. 2656, c1934, 4in (10cm) high.
£32–36 *TAC*

l. A SylvaC yellow bowl, decorated with a harvest mouse, No. 5250, c1934, 4in (10cm) high.
£25–30 *TAC*

A SylvaC chipmunk, white with black eyes, No. 5105, c1930, 6½in (16.5cm) high.
£35–40 *TAC*

A SylvaC Puss in Boot, coloured in yellow with green cats, No. 4977, c1934, 5in (12.5cm) high.
£28–33 *TAC*

A SylvaC brown camel, No. 5230, c1934, 5in (12.5cm) wide.
£40–45 *TAC*

A SylvaC bowl, decorated with an elf and a rabbit, in orange, green and pink, No. 1614, c1930, 7½in (19cm) wide.
£50–60 *TAC*

A SylvaC pink rabbit, No. 1027, 1930s, 9in (23cm) high.
£275–300 *TAC*

A SylvaC yellow giraffe, No. 5234, c1934, 6in (15cm) high.
£38–43 *TAC*

Torquay Pottery

Torquay pottery is best known for its motto wares, created for tourists visiting the Devon coast, and which reached its peak of popularity during the 1920s and 1930s.

The first Torquay pottery was Watcombe, established circa 1867, which produced unglazed terracotta wares in a classical style, using the local red clay. In 1881 an art pottery opened at Aller Vale, near Newton Abbot, Devon, which used traditional methods, and produced hand-thrown wares on a wheel decorated with slip and sgrafitto. Designs reflected an interest in Turkish and Persian patterns and Renaissance ceramics. Aller Vale looked back to a more local, rural past and, inspired by traditional country pottery, produced vases and simple tablewares

inscribed with mottoes and moral sayings. In 1901 Aller Vale and Watcome merged, and a host of other potteries sprang up both in the South Devon area and even further afield to meet demand for motto wares and Torquay-style pottery. Production boomed between the two World Wars, and while new potteries such as Dartmouth manufactured motto wares in the 1950s, by the 1960s most companies had either switched to mass production or ceased trading.

Torquay pottery is becoming increasingly collectable, although the more common pieces can still be very inexpensive, with prices at under £20. Beware of condition, however, since the pottery chips very easily, revealing the red Devon body beneath.

An Aller Vale udder vase, decorated with cream and blue scrolls, minor damage, 1891–1902, 4in (10cm) high.
£10–15 *PC*

An Aller Vale tyg vase, decorated with Scandy pattern, inscribed 'Never say die', c1900, 4¼in (11cm) high.
£20–25 *ATQ*

A Watcombe pottery jardinière, decorated with yellow daffodils on a green ground, c1900, 42in (106.5cm) high.
£1,200–1,300 *PLY*

A Watcombe pottery udder vase, decorated in shades of blue and brown with Sandringham pattern, slight damage, 1901–20, 4in (10cm) high.
£20–30 *PC*

This design was known as Sandringham, apparently in honour of Queen Alexandra, who liked the design so much that she commissioned a special order for her own use.

A Watcombe pinch vase, decorated with Wild Rose pattern in shades of pink and green on a white ground, 1901–20, 3¼in (8.5cm) high.
£20–30 *BEV*

A Longpark two-handled vase, with fluted rim, decorated with yellow daffodils on a green and brown ground, 1903–09, 5½in (14cm) high.
£60–70 *PC*

r. A Longpark plate, decorated in shades of orange, brown and green, inscribed 'Du zummat, Du gude ef you ken, But du zummat', 1903–09, 5in (13cm) diam.
£15–20 *ATQ*

A Longpark tyg vase, decorated with Scandy pattern No. 27NI, inscribed 'Tak care 'o me', 1904–18, 3¼in (8.5cm) high.
£10–15 *TPCS*

A Longpark plate, decorated with Scandy pattern, inscribed 'From Margate, may the hinges of friendship never grow rusty', 1910–24, 9in (23cm) diam.
£20–30 *ATQ*

A Longpark tyg vase, decorated with pattern No. NI, inscribed 'Gude things be scarce', 1910–20, 4¼in (11cm) high.
£20–25 *ATQ*

A Hele Cross vase, decorated with a parrot and trees, 1905–18, 5¼in (13.5cm) high.
£25–30 *PC*

The Scandy pattern was devised by Aller Vale and much used by other West Country firms. Inspired by Oriental pottery, the design was said to be based on the tail of a peacock.

l. A Torquay pottery coffee pot, decorated with white flowers, 1908–15, 6½in (16.5cm) high.
£30–35 *DSG*

r. A Torquay candle holder, decorated with a cockerel, inscribed 'From Kirkby Lonsdale', 1915–28, 4in (10cm) wide.
£35–45 *BEV*

l. A Dorset sugar bowl, inscribed 'elp theezel to the sugar', c1915, 3in (7.5cm) high.
£20–30 *PC*

A Dorset tooth mug, decorated with a landscape scene, c1915, 3½in (9cm) high.
£20–30 *TPCS*

A Longpark udder vase, decorated with yellow daffodils, black rubber stamp mark, 1918–25, 6in (15cm) high.
£40–50 *PC*

A Watcombe bowl, decorated with yellow bearded irises on a green ground, c1920, 3½in (9cm) diam.
£15–20 *TPCS*

A Torquay bowl, decorated with a kingfisher in shades of blue, orange and green on a blue ground, c1920, 6½in (16.5cm) diam.
£40–45 *DSG*

A Longpark cream jug, decorated with Crocus pattern in shades of red, yellow, green, mauve and blue, 1930–40, 2½in (6.5cm) high.
£15–20 *PC*

Potters often 'borrowed' fashionable designs from other factories and this pattern is clearly based on Clarice Cliff's famous crocus pattern.

A Watcombe pin/ashtray, depicting Shakespeare's house, 1920–45, 3½in (9cm) wide.
£10–15 *PC*

A Barton sugar bowl, decorated with a sailing boat in black on a blue ground, inscribed 'Ryde', 1922–38, 3½in (9cm) wide.
£10–15 *PC*

l. A Lemon & Crute posy vase, decorated with heather in shades of blue, green and mauve, c1925, 3in (7.5cm) high.
£10–15 *TPCS*

A Daison Art Pottery bowl, decorated with a pixie on a mushroom in shades of green and blue, 1928–32, 5in (13cm) diam.
£25–30 *PC*

r. A Dartmouth pin tray, decorated with a group of figures riding a horse, inscribed 'Widecombe Fair', 1950s, 5¼in (13.5cm) high.
£10–15 *PC*

An Aller Vale vase, decorated in shades of blue and brown on an off-white ground, inscribed 'All's well that ends well', c1920, 4in (10cm) high.
£45–50 *BEV*

A Barton milk jug, decorated with a flower in pink, white and green within black lines on a blue ground, 1922–37, 2½in (6.5cm) high.
£15–20 *PC*

A Torquay jug, decorated in blue and brown on a cream ground, inscribed 'Say little but think much', 1920–30s, 4in (10cm) high.
£35–45 *BEV*

Trusty Servant

The Trusty Servant was an ancient and emblematic figure painted on the wall adjoining the kitchen of Winchester College. He was accompanied by the following verse explaining the significance of his curious appearance:

'A Trusty Servant's portrait would
    you see,
This Emblematic Figure well survey;
The Porker's Snout – not nice in
    diet shews;
The Padlock Shut – no Secrets
    He'll disclose;
Patient the Ass – his Master's wrath
    will bear;
Swiftness in Errand the Staggs
    Feet declare;
Loaded his Left Hand – apt to
    labour Saith;

The Vest – his Neatness; Open hand –
    his Faith;
Girt with his Sword, his Shield upon
    his Arm,
Himself and Master He'll protect
    from harm.'

In 1839, William Savage opened a shop in Winchester selling fancy needlework. As the tourist trade blossomed thanks to cheap railway travel, Savage helped to develop and sold a whole range of souvenir Winchester china, modelled on local antiquities and including a figure of the Trusty Servant, who appeared both as a free-standing model and a decoration on china. Savage's designs were produced by Copeland and W. H. Goss, and the Trusty Servant became a well-known character in Goss and Crested China ware.

l. A Winchester porcelain flagon, enamelled with the Trusty Servant, inscribed in brown and lined in gilt, c1890, 6in (15cm) high.
£80–90 *SAS*

A porcelain morning cup and oval-shaped shell-moulded saucer, enamelled in colours with the Trusty Servant and Wykham crest within a gilt oval cartouche on a deep crimson ground, the rims lined in gilt, the underside inscribed, c1890, cup 3in (7.5cm) high.
£70–80 *SAS*

An Arcadian figure of the Trusty Servant, the base inscribed in black, c1890, 5½in (14cm) high.
£140–160 *SAS*

l. A Winchester Goss model of the Trusty Servant, with blue jacket, decorated with red and gilt, on a pedestal inscribed with verse in black, inscribed on base, c1900, 8in (20.5cm) high.
£1,800–2,000 *G&CC*

A Goss tapering jug, enamelled and gilded with the Trusty Servant and inscribed in black, gilt-lined rim, c1890, 5in (12.5cm) high.
£85–95 *SAS*

A Continental pottery figure of the Trusty Servant, c1890, 7½in (19cm) high.
£55–65 *SAS*

Vases

A Sicilian albarello, painted with yellow and pale green stylised foliage on a blue ground, the central cartouche with a temple and trees, 18thC, 9¼in (23.5cm) high. **£320–350** *BIG*

A Delft vase, of waisted cylindrical form, with everted rim, painted in underglaze blue with scenes of figures, houses and rosettes, minor damage, 18thC, 8½in (21.5cm) high. **£160–180** *GAK*

A pair of oviform vases, printed with a Chinese river scene and junks, gilt-lined foot and rims, minor restoration, c1865, 5¼in (13.5cm) high, together with a pair of carved wood stands. **£850–950** *SAS*

A Pratt ware vase, with trumpet-shaped neck, shoulders set with twin-loop handles, the black ground enamelled with a classical chariot scene and angels above a Greek key pattern in red, Pratt/Prince Albert stamp, rim restored, c1860, 17in (43cm) high. **£210–230** *SAS*

A French faïence vase, decorated with flowers and butterflies on a white ground, 19thC, 9¾in (25cm) high. **£130–140** *SER*

A Linthorpe moon flask, designed by Christopher Dresser, marked, c1880, 6in (15cm) high. **£650–750** *NCA*

A stoneware vase, decorated with yellow flowers on a light green ground, marked to base 'DCS 1025', c1900, 19¼in (49cm) high. **£160–180** *P(B)*

A Pilkington vase, with feathered blue, green and brown crystaline glaze effect, incised mark, c1903, 8in (20.5cm) high. **£550–600** *PGA*

r. A Lancastrian vase, with striated blue glaze effect, c1913, 11in (28cm) high. **£400–450** *PGA*

r. An A. J. Wilkinson Royal Staffordshire hand-painted Oriflamme vase, signed 'Butler', minor chips to rim, c1927, 5½in (14cm) high. **£140–160** *BKK*

A Hancock & Sons pottery vase, designed by Mollie Hancock, decorated with Waterlily pattern in shades of red, yellow, green and pink, c1930, 9in (23cm) high.
£120–130 *CSA*

A Royal Stanley ware cylindrical vase, decorated with clematis in various colours, c1930, 12in (30.5cm) high.
£135–160 *DSG*

A Reid & Co Roslyn hand-painted lustre vase, c1930, 10in (25.5cm) high.
£70–80 *BKK*

A Crown Devon wall vase, hand-decorated in green and blue, pattern No. H422, c1934, 7½in (19cm) high.
£70–80 *BKK*

Wade

Two Wade figures of Sam and Sarah, designed by Mabel Lucie Attwell, 1930s, 3¼in (8.5cm) high.
£375–425 *PGA*

> **WHY NOT JOIN THE MILLER'S CLUB?**
>
> For details of this free club, available to Miller's readers Tel: 0171 225 9244

A Wade cellulose figure, 'Barbara', decorated with black and pink bonnet, green ribbons and pink and yellow dress, 1930s, 9in (23cm) high.
£180–200 *PAC*

A Wade cellulose figure, 'Sunshine', decorated in orange and yellow, 1930s, 8in (20.5cm) high.
£150–165 *PAC*

A Wadeheath musical jug, moulded with 3 Little Pigs and Big Bad Wolf handle, 1930s, 10in (25.5cm) high.
£750–850 *SWO*

Two Wade cottages, from Whimsey-on-Why collection, 1981–83, largest 1¾in (4.5cm) high.
£6–8 each *MAC*

Two Wade nursery rhyme character models, 1970–71, tallest 1½in (4cm) high.
l. **£6–8** *r.* **£8–10** *HEI*

Wedgwood

A Wedgwood tureen and cover, with gilt handles and rim, c1820, 11in (28cm) diam.
£500–550 *AMH*

A Wedgwood Rosso Antico jug, with applied basalt decoration on a terracotta coloured ground, c1800, 5¾in (14.5cm) high.
£380–400 *PGA*

A Wedgwood scent bottle, depicting 'Night Shedding Poppies' in white on a pale blue ground, with silver-gilt top and inner stopper, c1780, 4½in (11.5cm) high.
£1,600–1,800 *BHa*

A Victorian Wedgwood game pie dish, with liner and cover, the unglazed oval body moulded and decorated with a rabbit finial, dead birds and fruiting vine decoration, 11½in (29cm) long.
£200–220 *DDM*

A Wedgwood blue and white footbath, with scenes of the Tower of London, Balmoral Castle and Windsor Castle, the base with a scene after Claude Lorraine from a series of prints In and Around Rome, c1825, 14in (35.5cm) high.
£1,500–2,500 *GN*

l. A Wedgwood pottery vase, designed by Keith Murray, with decorated horizontal banding beneath a straw-coloured glaze, c1935, 11¼in (28.5cm) high.
£400–450 *ADE*

A Wedgwood pottery vase, designed by Keith Murray, decorated with horizontal ribbing beneath a cream-coloured glaze, c1930, 6½in (16.5cm) high.
£400–450 *PGA*

A Wedgwood white model of a monkey and baby, 1980s, 8in (20.5cm) high.
£140–150 *Rac*

A Wedgwood pottery vase, designed by Keith Murray, with horizontal ribbing beneath a grey glaze, full signature on base, 1930s, 6½in (16.5cm) high.
£700–800 *PGA*

A Wedgwood jasper bowl, decorated with Dancing Hours pattern, c1975, 10in (25.5cm) diam.
£200–250 *PAC*

Wemyss

A Wemyss honey pot with lid, decorated with beehive pattern, c1890, 5in (13cm) high.
£200–250 *RdeR*

A Wemyss plate, decorated with deep purple plums on a white ground with green line rim, c1895, 6in (15cm) diam.
£150–180 *RdeR*

A Wemyss vase, decorated with deep purple plums on a white ground with green line rim, c1900, 6in (15cm) high.
£150–200 *RdeR*

A Wemyss covered slop bucket, of tapering cylindrical form, decorated in colours with roses, within green borders, wicker handle, unmarked, hairline crack, c1900, 11in (28cm) high.
£250–300 *GAK*

A Wemyss bowl, decorated with black cockerels and hens on shaded green bands, with a puce line rim, impressed 'Wemyss', printed retailer's mark, minor chip, c1900, 15½in (39.5cm) high.
£600–650 *WW*

A Wemyss model of a pig, with black markings on a white ground, impressed mark, 'T. Goode' retailer's mark, early 20thC, 6¼in (16cm) high.
£1,000–1,200 *TEN*

Wemyss pigs in good condition are very sought after.

A Wemyss basin and ewer, decorated with bands of black cockerels and hens on a green shaded grass band, with puce line rims, impressed marks, the basin with hairline crack, the ewer with small rim chip, c1900, basin 11in (28cm) diam.
£450–500 *WW*

A Wemyss trumpet-shaped vase, painted with pink roses and green leaves on a white ground, early 20thC, 11¾in (30cm) high.
£160–180 *RTo*

A Wemyss cat, by Plichta, painted with a red clover decoration, c1930, 3¼in (8.5cm) high.
£35–50 *RdeR*

Worcester

A Worcester bowl, painted with 2 polychrome floral reserves within gilt scrollwork on flow-blue ground, with gilt dentil rim and central internal floral sprig, 1751–74, 6½in (16.5cm) high.
£320–350 *RBB*

l. A Royal Worcester figure of Sir Walter Raleigh, with mauve jacket and pink hat, c1880, 6½in (16.5cm) high.
£350–400 *TH*

r. A Royal Worcester model of a seated fox, early 20thC, 7in (18cm) high.
£220–250 *BIG*

A pair of Royal Worcester figures of Egyptian musicians, c1911, 12¾in (32.5cm) high.
£1,200–1,400 *TH*

A Royal Worcester pot, the lower section moulded in the form of a basket, painted in shades of pale blue, green and beige, with gilt line rim, dated '1912', 4in (10cm) high.
£100–120 *MiA*

Two Royal Worcester figures, Harlequin and Pierrot, painted in shades of blue, green orange and red, c1931, 6½in (16.5cm) high.
£600–700 *TH*

A Royal Worcester figure, Thursday's Child, in light blue tunic, c1940, 8in (20.5cm) high.
£150–170 *VSt*

A Royal Worcester ovoid vase, painted in coloured enamels with blackberries, leaves and blossom on a cream ground, within gilt line borders, by Kitty Blake, shape No. 2491, signed, printed mark in black for 1950, 3¼in (8.5cm) high.
£260–300 *DN*

A Royal Worcester figure, Serena, with flowing pale green dress and hat, 1980–90s, 9in (23cm) high.
£100–125 *HEI*

CHRISTMAS COLLECTABLES

Elaborate Christmas decorations came into vogue with the Victorians. Christmas trees were a German custom and Prince Albert is credited with introducing the first one to Britain in 1840. When *The Illustrated London News* (a popular journal of the day) printed an engraving of the Royal family gathered around their candle-lit tree, the fashion was set.

Initially tree decorations were home-made, and included strings of glass beads, gilded walnuts, shaped biscuits and paper ornaments. It was not until the last quarter of the 19th century that commercially manufactured ornaments became available, and the fashion for delicate glass baubles, many imported from Germany, developed in the 1890s.

Other Christmas fashions were born in Britain. The cracker was invented in 1846 by the British confectioner Tom Smith who, in a stroke of marketing genius, decided that his sweets would sell better if they were contained in a brightly decorated exploding package. Similarly, firms such as Huntley & Palmers also sought to capture the Christmas market by housing their biscuits in decorative novelty tins. The first Christmas card was commissioned in 1843 by Sir Henry Cole, instigator of the Great Exhibition of 1851 and founder of the Victoria and Albert Museum. He asked the artist J. C. Horsley to produce a Christmas card, which he could send to friends rather than visiting them all in person. The idea took off, and publishers began to print Christmas cards. They were often extremely elaborate – embossed, pierced, gilded, pop-up – and expensive, but postcards, which first appeared in 1870, provided a cheaper Christmas alternative. Christmas cake decorations, made from bisque or tin, also became popular from the Victorian period, although as with other Christmas decorations, most of the examples found today date from the 1930s to the 1950s.

A Buckley slipware Christmas dish, with yellow trailing, cracked, c1900, 14in (35.5cm) wide.
£250–300 *IW*

Two Christmas table decorations, wicker cones with red and green ribbons and flowers, c1920, 12½in (31.5cm) high.
£40–50 *LB*

A Maison Lyons toffee tin, in the shape of a Christmas lantern, c1911, 6½in (16.5cm) high.
£145–175 *WAB*

r. A Christmas tree stand, c1920, 7½in (19cm) square.
£30–35 *AL*

A Dresden Christmas decoration, of silver-coloured pressed cardboard, c1900, 3in (7.5cm) long.
£300–350 *SMAM*

A pressed cardboard Santa Claus, c1930, 10in (25.5cm) high.
£45–55 *SMAM*

A Santa Claus Christmas cake tin, 1950s, 3in (7.5cm) diam.
£18–20 *JUN*

Mr and Mrs Santa Claus cloth dolls, dressed in red, c1950, 15in (38cm) high.
£40–50 *EKK*

A Carlton Ware Christmas pudding bowl, painted in orange, yellow and green, Cooper black mark, 1986, 6¼in (16cm) diam.
£20–30 *StC*

A Royal Copenhagen blue and white Christmas plate, entitled 'Christmas Night', 1959, 3¼in (8cm) diam.
£55–65 *GSW*

A Belleek Parian bear, decorated in red and green and inscribed '1997 Baby's First Christmas', 3in (7.5cm) high.
£12–15 *EDC*

r. A Father Christmas figure, made from old textiles, cloak edged with fur, 1990s, 24in (61cm) high.
£65–75 *SWN*

Cake Decorations

A bisque snow baby cake decoration, c1890, 1in (2.5cm) high.
£15–20 *WAB*

Cross Reference
Colour Review

A Japanese bisque baby riding a polar bear cake decoration, c1920, 2¼in (5.5cm) long.
£40–45 *PC*

r. A German bisque snow baby cake decoration, 1920–30, 1½in (3.5cm) high.
£35–40 *PC*

l. A Japanese bisque snow bear cake decoration, wearing a green hat, 1920–30, 1¼in (3cm) high.
£25–30 *PC*

An American cast iron Santa cake decoration, 1930s, 1½in (3.5cm) high.
£40–50 *SMAM*

A German bisque bear on
a sledge cake decoration,
1920–30, 2½in (6.5cm) long.
£50–55 *PC*

A Japanese bisque baby cake
decoration, on an orange sledge,
1920–30, 2¼in (5.5cm) long.
£45–50 *PC*

A German bisque monkey
cake decoration, wearing
a red coat and yellow hat,
c1925, 4¾in (12cm) high.
£15–20 *YC*

A Japanese bisque
Father Christmas
cake decoration, with
original price sticker
for 3s 9d, 1920–30,
2¼in (5.5cm) high.
£30–35 *PC*

A German bisque
windmill cake
decoration, in red,
yellow and blue, c1925,
4¾in (12cm) high.
£15–20 *YC*

A German Christmas
tree cake decoration,
with red barrel
base, 1920–30,
3¼in (8.5cm) high.
£8–10 *PC*

A German bisque dog
cake decoration, playing
the double bass, dressed
in red jacket, c1925,
5½in (14cm) high.
£25–30 *YC*

A German bisque
gold elf cake
decoration, c1925,
4in (10cm) long.
£15–20 *YC*

r. A German
bisque snow
baby cake
decoration, c1925,
5½in (14cm) long.
£30–40 *YC*

A German bisque Mickey
and Minnie Mouse
Christmas cake decoration,
1930s, 2in (5cm) high.
£120–150 *CWo*

*The Disney subject matter
and the early date make
this rare cake decoration
very desirable.*

A German bisque
Father Christmas
cake decoration,
c1925, 4¾in
(12cm) high.
£15–20 *YC*

Ephemera

Sheet music, Christmas Carols, published by Alf Harrison & Sons Ltd, Leeds, c1930, 14 x 9in (35.5 x 23cm).
£3–4 *SVB*

Sheet music for 'Rudolph The Red-Nosed Reindeer', by Johnny Marks, Chappell & Co Ltd, c1940, 11 x 8in (28 x 20.5cm).
£2–3 *SVB*

Sheet music for 'I Saw Mommy Kissing Santa Claus', by Edwin H. Morris & Co Ltd, c1952, 11 x 8½in (28 x 21cm).
£2–3 *RAD*

A Coca-Cola advertisement, dated '1960', 9½in (24cm) high.
£6–8 *SAF*

r. A Charles M. Schulz 'Peanuts' pen and ink cartoon strip, signed, 1998, 21in (53.5cm) wide.
£550–600 *VS*

Lights

A set of Walt Disney brightly coloured Christmas tree lights, c1938.
£35–40 *AL*

An orange milk glass cat Christmas tree light bulb, 1940s, 3in (7.5cm) high.
£45–55 *SMAM*

l. A set of 'Bon Bon' Christmas lights, c1935, box 10in (25.5in) wide.
£120–150 *JUN*

Three milk glass Christmas tree light bulbs, 1940s, 3in (7.5cm) high.
£10–12 each *SMAM*

A yellow milk glass owl Christmas tree light bulb, 1940s, 3in (7.5cm) high.
£60–70 *SMAM*

A Royal Santa Claus, with bubble light, 1950s, 10in (25.5cm) high.
£100–110 *SMAM*

Postcards

A German Christmas postcard, 1899, 3½ x 5½in (9 x 14cm).
£2–3 *JMC*

A chromolithograph Christmas postcard, 1905–10, 3½ x 5½in (9 x 14cm).
£2–3 *JMC*

A Christmas pop-up postcard, 1905–10, 3½in (9cm) square.
£1–2 *JMC*

A Christmas greetings postcard, by Harry Payne, depicting the 3rd London Rifle Volunteers, with embossed ivy and gun, 1900–10, 5½ x 4in (14 x 10cm).
£2–3 *JMC*

A Christmas greetings postcard, depicting a girl in a red coat and hat with a reindeer, c1910, 3½ x 5½in (9 x 14cm).
£3–4 *JMC*

l. A Christmas greetings postcard, 'Yule' decorated in shades of greens, c1908, 3½ x 5½in (9 x 14cm).
£1–2 *JMC*

A Christmas greetings postcard, dated '1903', 3½ x 5½in (9 x 14cm).
£1–2 *JMC*

A Christmas greetings postcard, by Harry Payne, 1900–10, 3½ x 5½in (9 x 14cm).
£100–120 *VS*

l. A Christmas greetings postcard, 1905–10, 3½ x 5½in (9 x 14cm).
£4–5 *JMC*

A Christmas greetings postcard, with gold lettering, c1906, 3½ x 5½in (9 x 14cm).
£1–2 *JMC*

CLOCKS & WATCHES

A German spelter novelty clock, by Junghans, the case in the form of a chimpanzee with moving eyes and jaw, late 19thC, 9½in (24cm) high.
£450–500 *P(G)*

A Ferranti electric alarm clock, with brown and cream Bakelite case, c1929, 5in (12.5cm) high.
£45–55 *TIH*

l. A Brooke Bond PG Tips perspex and cardboard battery clock, 1970–80s, 17¾in (45cm) high.
£15–20 *FMu*

An oak-cased factory time recorder, 1910, 36in (91.5cm) high.
£500–600 *JUN*

A Smith's MkI painted brass novelty alarm clock, with pecking chickens, c1930, 4in (10cm) high.
£85–95 *TIH*

A Wesco Wallace & Gromit plastic talking alarm clock, c1996, 8½in (21.5cm) high.
£25–30 *PC*

A mahogany 24-hour Pullman clock, by Williamson Ltd, London, 1920s, 12in (30.5cm) diam.
£300–350 *HAX*

A Smith's cream and gold-coloured wall clock, c1960, 8½in (21.5cm) diam.
£30–35 *UTP*

A hand-painted bone china clock, commemorating the closure of Dinnington Colliery, South Yorkshire, No. 30 of limited edition of 250, c1991, 11in (28cm) diam.
£45–50 *DOM*

r. A Waltham 14ct gold half-hunter fob watch, with 15 jewels, c1914, 2in (5cm) diam.
£380–420 *DQ*

A Swiss silver fob watch, with key wind and key set, late 19thC, 1½in (4cm) diam.
£120–150 *DQ*

An 18ct gold half-hunter fob watch, with Swiss cylinder movement, c1915, 1½in (4cm) diam.
£300–350 *PSA*

l. A Railway Time-keeper fob watch, inscribed 'Shock-Proof, Specially Examined', Austrian, mid-20thC, 2in (5cm) diam.
£30–35 *BGA*

A lady's finely engraved silver fob watch, with silver chain, acorn and twist bar, Swiss cylinder jewelled movement, signed 'Kendall, Blackheath', c1900, 1¼in (3cm) diam.
£220–240 *PC*

An Addison gold open-faced pocket watch, movement fitted with Duplex escapement, American, c1910, 1½in (4cm) diam.
£280–320 *DQ*

A chrome wristwatch, with leather strap, c1918, 1in (2.5cm) diam.
£150–175 *MANS*

A silver-cased wrist-watch, with gold button, red numeral '12', Swiss lever movement by S. S. & Co, original strap with hallmarked buckle, c1911, 1½in (4cm) diam.
£220–240 *DQ*

r. A lady's platinum and diamond wristwatch, the cord strap with diamond-set platinum loops, c1920, 1¾in (4.5cm) long.
£500–600 *PSA*

A Rotary gentleman's 9ct
gold wristwatch, 1930s,
1in (25mm) diam.
£120–140 *BWC*

A lady's 9ct gold
wristwatch, 1950s,
1¼in (3cm) diam.
£140–160 *MANS*

l. An Omega
Constellation rose gold-
plated wristwatch, with
day and date display,
c1967, 1¼in (3cm) diam.
£350–400 *BWC*

A lady's platinum and
diamond-set cocktail
wristwatch, with
tonneau-shape case,
c1930, ¾in (2cm) wide.
£750–800 *HofB*

A Rolex Tudor gold-
plated wristwatch,
manual wind, Swiss,
1950s, 1¼in (3cm) diam.
£170–200 *BWC*

FURTHER READING

*Miller's Watches:
A Collector's Guide*
Miller's Publications,
1999

An Elco 9ct gold wrist-
watch, with Swiss lever
movement, curved back
and cambered front,
c1936, 1in (2.5cm) wide.
£200–220 *DQ*

A Rotary gentleman's
9ct gold dress watch,
c1977, 1in (2.5cm) diam.
£130–150 *BWC*

A Sicura lady's gold-
coloured wristwatch,
with 17 jewels, 1940s,
1½in (4cm) long.
£180–200 *MANS*

l. An Oris Super
chrome wristwatch,
the Swiss movement
with 17 jewels, 1960s,
1¼in (3cm) diam.
£85–95 *TIH*

A Star Trek Deep
Space Nine Space
Station quartz watch,
c1995, 7in (18cm) long,
on original card.
£12–15 *ALI*

COMICS

The most collectable comics tend to be first issues, special issues (for commemorative or holiday numbers), and those that mark the introduction of a famous character. Most enthusiasts buy for nostalgic reasons, returning to the comics that they read in their childhood, and, as such, values change as new generations grow up and enter the collectors' market.

Journals such as *Chips* or *Comic Cuts*, popular in the first half of the century, tend to be less desirable than many comics from the 1950s and 1960s, which people actually remember reading, and have dropped in value over the last 20 years. While some comics go out of fashion, classics such as the *The Beano* and *The Dandy*, launched in the 1930s and

still published after more than half a century, are increasingly sought after. The market is predominantly male orientated, and prices for such girls' vintage comics as *Girl* and *Bunty* tend to be comparatively low. Similarly, comics published for the nursery market are generally less desirable than those published for older children who are more likely to remember their favourite journals.

If a comic still retains an original free gift, its value is considerably enhanced. Collectors usually prefer to keep their comics in original condition, but if repairs do become necessary use a specific document repairing tape rather than clear adhesive tape, which will discolour and damage the paper. Store comics in specialist plastic bags, away from sunlight.

Adventure comic, published by D. C. Thompson, June 1947. **£4–8** *DPO*

Amazing Fantasy comic, No 15, origin and first appearance of Spider Man, worn, August 1962. **£175–200** *P*

Batman Annual 1, published by Atlas, 1959–60. **£60–70** *CBP*

Big Budget, published by Pearson, February 1907. **£5–12** *DPO*

Bonanza comic, first issue, c1960. **£70–80** *CBP*

The Champion comic, April 1947. **£4–8** *DPO*

Chips, published by
Harmsworth, April 1923.
£3–6   *DPO*

Comic Cuts comic, published by
Harmsworth, September 1936.
£3–6   *DPO*

Dandy comic, No. 3, worn, 1937.
£260–280   *CBP*

Detective Comics, No 102, with
Joker cover and story, 1945.
£700–800   *CBP*

Eagle comic, June 1957.
£1–2   *DPO*

Fantastic Four comic, No. 1,
origin and first appearance of
The Fantastic Four and Mole
Man, slight damage, 1961.
£350–400   *P*

Hotspur comic, July 1951.
£3–5   *DPO*

Green Lantern comic, No. 1,
July/August 1960.
£330–360   *P*

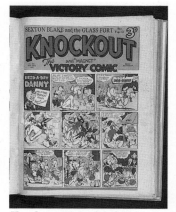

Knockout comic, April 1944.
£35–70   *DPO*

The Magic comic, No 27, with Koko The Pup and Sooty Snowball, slightly worn, c1940.
£170–190 *CBP*

r. *Lion* comic, Nos. 1–72, with No. 1 free gift 'Sports Stars In Action', slightly worn, 1952–3.
£190–220 *CBP*

The *Magnet* comic, April 1917.
£3–6 *DPO*

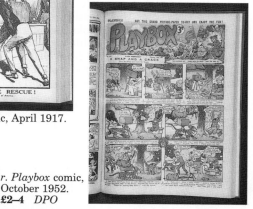

r. *Playbox* comic, October 1952.
£2–4 *DPO*

Rawhide comic No. 1097, 1960.
£40–45 *CBP*

Cross Reference
Newspapers & Magazines

Two copies of The *Rover* comic, December 1947 and April 1958.
£2.50–5 each *DPO*

Star Trek comic, No. 1, Gold Key, c1967.
£160–180 *CBP*

Wanted: Dead or Alive, comic No. 1,102, with Steve McQueen photocover, c1960.
£25–30 *CBP*

COMMEMORATIVE WARE

In Britain, the tradition of major exhibitions began with the Great Exhibition of 1851, proposed by Prince Albert and orchestrated by Sir Henry Cole. Celebrating art and industry across the Empire, the exhibition in Hyde Park attracted millions of visitors, and Joseph Paxton's glass and iron building, nicknamed the Crystal Palace, became world famous. London was also home to the 1862 International Exhibition, but the next major event was not until 1924 when the British Empire Exhibition was held at Wembley. Among the most popular exhibits was a life-size model of the Prince of Wales carved from New Zealand butter. Glasgow hosted the 1938 Empire Exhibition just before the outbreak

of WWII, while for many the ending of wartime austerity and the dawning of the new Elizabethan age was heralded by the 1951 Festival of Britain on the South Bank in London. Although, sadly, few of the exhibition buildings have survived (most notably the Royal Festival Hall), many of the commemorative items produced for visitors are still collected today.

The proposed millennium celebrations will no doubt stimulate a wealth of commemorative items, from exhibition guides to models of the Millennium Dome itself. Could these memorabilia items become the collectables of the 21st century? Looking at this evidence from the past, the answer would seem to be yes.

Exhibitions

A pottery plate, printed in brown with a dog and child, within a daisy moulded border, entitled 'The Deliverer' and inscribed '1851 Exhibition', 7¾in (19.5cm) diam.
£40–50 *SAS*

A Cremona tin, decorated in browns and greens with a portrait of Edward, Prince of Wales, commemorating the 1929 Newcastle Exhibition, c1929, 7in (17.5cm) wide.
£20–25 *HUX*

A Victor Vaissier Paris tin, painted in red, yellow and blue, inscribed 'Souvenir de l'Exposition', c1900, 3½in (9cm) wide.
£10–15 *HUX*

A Huntley & Palmers biscuit tin, decorated with a lady dressed in white and red and a boy in blue robes, commemorating the British Empire Exhibition, Wembley, 1924, 4 x 6½in (10 x 16.5cm).
£80–90 *HUX*

l. A tin, decorated in orange, blue and green, inscribed 'Souvenir de l'Exposition Coloniale Inter'le, Paris 1931', 10½in (26.5cm) wide.
£22–25 *HUX*

r. A faded yellow and red souvenir tin, commemorating the Empire Exhibition, Scotland, 1938, 6in (15cm) high.
£25–30 *HUX*

A pictorial tin, decorated in grey, black and green commemorating the Empire Exhibition, Scotland, 1938, 6¼in (16cm) wide.
£15–20 *HUX*

A Paragon plate, decorated in bright colours, commemorating the Empire Exhibition, Scotland, 1938, inscribed on reverse, gilt rim, 10⅝in (27cm) diam.
£200–220 *SAS*

A Tiffany brown and white plate, commemorating the New York World's Fair, 1939, 10in (25.5cm) diam.
£200–240 *YAN*

A J. & G. Meakin blue and white plate, commemorating the New York World's Fair, 1939, 10in (25.5cm) diam.
£150–170 *YAN*

A plate, commemorating the 1939 San Francisco World's Fair, the blue border decorated with yellow sun and buff buildings, by Homer Laughlin China Co, 10in (25.5cm) diam.
£145–165 *YAN*

A gold-coloured metal brooch, commemorating the Festival of Britain, 1951, 1¼in (3cm) wide.
£12–14 *HUX*

A crown, commemorating the Festival of Britain 1951, with green drawer-type case.
£7–8 each *PC*

Crowns were struck and sold on site in the Royal Mint's pavilion in the Homes and Gardens section of the Festival of Britain exhibition, London, as well as at the Royal Mint itself, near the Tower of London. Boxes should be in good condition and contain their original slips of printed paper. Two types of boxes were produced (drawer-type and lid-type) in two colours, maroon and green. The lid-type boxes are the rarest.

A Festival of Britain guide, in yellow with black, red and blue design, c1951, 9½ x 7¼in (24 x 18.5cm).
£10–12 *GIN*

r. A gentleman's brown tie, commemorating the Festival of Britain, 1951, 50in (127cm) long.
£12–15 *RAD*

Royalty
Queen Victoria

A pottery plate, commemorating the wedding of Queen Victoria and Prince Albert, with floral and scroll moulded border, brown portraits and black rim, inscribed and dated '1840', 5½in (14cm) diam.
£230–250 *SAS*

A pottery mug, commemorating the wedding of the Princess Royal, transfer-printed in black with portraits, lined in pink lustre, c1858, 2½in (6.5cm) high.
£160–180 *SAS*

A pottery mug, commemorating the Diamond Jubilee of Queen Victoria, hand-printed in sepia and enamelled in red, yellow and blue, slight damage, 1897, 4½in (11.5cm) high.
£40–45 *SAS*

A pottery plate, commemorating the birth of Edward VII, printed in green, inscribed 'Albert Edward Prince of Wales, Born Nov 9 1841', 7¾in (19.5cm) diam.
£170–200 *SAS*

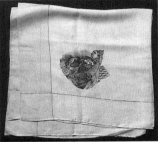

A sepia-coloured silk handkerchief, commemorating the Diamond Jubilee of Queen Victoria, 1897, 16in (40.5cm) square.
£25–35 *VS*

A set of 3 Doulton Lambeth globular jugs, commemorating the Diamond Jubilee of Queen Victoria, each with young and old portrait medallions in green on a blue ground, inscribed and dated, the neck and foot rim coloured brown, 1897, largest 9½in (24cm) high.
£440–480 *SAS*

A pair of hardwood plaques, moulded as heads in profile, entitled 'Victoria Queen of England' and 'Prince Albert', in turned wood frames, slight damage, mid-19thC, 6¼in (16cm) diam.
£220–250 *SAS*

A pottery cup and saucer, by William Lowe, commemorating the Diamond Jubilee of Queen Victoria, printed in sepia with inscribed cartouche flanked by brightly coloured flags and flowers, gilt rims, 1897, saucer 8in (20.5cm) diam.
£70–80 *SAS*

A Stevengraph, commemorating the death of Queen Victoria, woven in pure silk in black, yellow and blue, inscribed 'Her Majesty, The Late Queen Victoria', c1902, 7 x 5in (17.5 x 12.5cm) high.
£140–160 *VINE*

Edward VII

A pottery mug, by WC & Co, commemorating the wedding of Edward VII to Princess Alexandra in 1863, printed in purple with an oval portrait panel depicting the Prince and Princess, inscribed and dated, printed mark, c1863, 3¼in (8.3cm) high.
£130–150 *SAS*

A Parian bust of Edward VII, by H & L, on a socle base, late 19thC, 8¼in (21cm) high.
£55–65 *SAS*

A pair of spoons, commemorating the Coronation of Edward VII, in original silk-lined box, c1902, 10in (25.5cm) wide.
£180–190 *DAC*

r. A silver commemorative vesta case, with a portrait of Edward VII, maker J. & C., c1901, 2in (5cm) high.
£120–140 *GH*

George V

A Paragon loving cup, commemorating the Silver Jubilee of George V and Queen Mary, with floral handles, inscribed and lined in silver, 1935, 3½in (9cm) high.
£90–100 *SAS*

A Hammersley mug, commemorating the Silver Jubilee of George V and Queen Mary, enamelled in red and green with a silver rim, c1935, 3½in (9cm) high.
£65–75 *W&S*

A Royal Doulton buff-coloured loving cup, commemorating the death of George V, printed with a sepia portrait within green foliate branches, inscribed and lined in silver, 1936, 4¾in (12cm) high.
£150–170 *SAS*

Edward VIII

A pottery mug, commemorating the Prince of Wales' visit to Egremont, printed in black, inscribed for June 29th 1927, gilt rim, 2¾in (7cm) high.
£90–110 *SAS*

A Paragon plate, decorated with a coat-of-arms in red, yellow and blue enamels and inscribed in sepia, with wide gold banding, dated '1937', 10½in (26.5cm) diam.
£90–110 *SAS*

A CWS Windsor china mug, commemorating the Coronation of Edward VIII, with red and blue 'ER' handle, c1936, 3in (7.5cm) high.
£60–70 *W&S*

l. A cream-coloured mug, commemorating the accession of Edward VIII, moulded with monogram and inscription, c1936, 5in (12.5cm) high.
£65–75 *SAS*

r. A porcelain globe, commemorating the accession of Edward VIII, picked out in red and green, the gilt foot inscribed in black, c1936, 3½in (9cm) high.
£130–150 *SAS*

George VI

An Adderley Ware pottery twin-handled vase, commemorating the Coronation of George VI, printed in sepia and enamelled in colours with a cartouche of St George slaying the dragon, on an apple-green ground, the reverse and inner rim inscribed and dated, gilt handles and lining, 1937, 7in (17.5cm) high.
£380–420 *SAS*

A black pottery Coronation mug, with green mouldings, by Giles Rumney Pottery, Cardiff, c1937, 5¾in (14.5cm) high.
£20–30 *IW*

r. A Gray's pottery plate, commemorating King George VI and Queen Elizabeth's visit to South Africa, printed in black and enamelled in red, green and yellow, inscribed and dated, gilt rim, 1947, 10¼in (26cm) diam.
£50–60 *SAS*

A Grafton porcelain Coronation mug, designed by Dame Laura Knight, decorated in red, gold and blue, 1937, 3½in (9cm) high, with certificate.
£140–160 *SAS*

Elizabeth II

A Paragon cup, saucer and octagonal plate, commemorating the birth of Princess Elizabeth, printed in sepia with a portrait by Marcus Adams, inscribed and dated with red and gilt rims, 1926, cup 3in (7.5cm) high.
£120–140 *SAS*

A Wedgwood mug, commemorating the Coronation of Queen Elizabeth II, decorated in sepia, pink and gilt, with a lion and unicorn supporting the crown, by Guyatt, 1953, 4in (10cm) high.
£50–60 *SAS*

A Royal Crown Derby dish, commemorating the Coronation of Queen Elizabeth II, with a portrait within a gadrooned and gilded border, 1953, 4in (10cm) long.
£20–25 *SAS*

A pottery plate, commemorating the Coronation of Queen Elizabeth II, with a crowned portrait after Frank Reynolds, within a gilded blue border, the reverse inscribed and dated, 1953, 10½in (26.5cm) diam.
£50–60 *SAS*

A pottery bowl and cover, commemorating the Coronation of Queen Elizabeth II, modelled as an orb and decorated in red and gilt, 1953, 5in (12.5cm) high.
£55–65 *SAS*

l. A ruby red and gilt Royal Albert loving cup, commemorating the Coronation of Queen Elizabeth II, with sepia portrait, 1953, 4in (10cm) high.
£160–190 *W&S*

A Paragon plate, commemorating the Coronation of Queen Elizabeth II, decorated with heraldic shield supported by a yellow lion and unicorn, inscribed in sepia around the pale blue border, lined in gilt, 1953, 10¾in (27.5cm) diam.
£90–110 *SAS*

A pottery mug, commemorating the Coronation of Queen Elizabeth II, 1953, 4in (10cm) high.
£15–20 *PC*

A Churchill pottery mug, commemorating the Silver Jubilee of Queen Elizabeth II, 1977, 3½in (9cm) high.
£10–15 *PC*

CORKSCREWS

A George II combined nutmeg grater and corkscrew, with inverted acorn-shaped top and small acorn finial, screw-on cap and detachable cylindrical base containing a steel tubular grater fitting over the corkscrew, by David Field, c1745, 3¼in (8.5cm) long.
£5,300–6,000 *P*

This corkscrew is early in date, extremely rare and has a maker's mark.

Two steel travelling pocket corkscrews:.
l. A bright steel picnic pocket corkscrew, c1780, 4½in (11.5cm) long.
£50–60
r. A peg and worm corkscrew, with facet-cut decoration, 18thC, 4in (10cm) long.
£35–45 *CS*

r. A patent corkscrew, with the royal coat-of-arms, turned wood handle and steel side wind to ribbed brass case, early 19thC, 5in (12.5cm) long.
£220–250 *TMA*

A pocket corkscrew, with a barrel-shaped mother-of-pearl handle applied with reeded silver bands, by Samuel Pemberton of Birmingham, maker's mark on the base, c1800, 2¾in (7cm) long.
£500–550 *P*

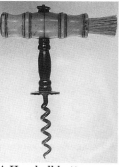

A Henshall button corkscrew, with turned bone handle and steel shank and button, c1830, 5½in (14cm) long.
£35–45 *CS*

A Victorian champagne tap, with turned rosewood handle, steel shank with large finger hole and hollow shaft through which the champagne is drawn and poured through tap, marked 'Holborn Champagne Screw', c1880, 6½in (16.5cm) long.
£55–65 *CS*

An all-steel two-part lever corkscrew, the triangular hinge marked 'The Patent Lever' with Gothic style initial 'H' in the centre, c1880, 8¼in (21cm) long.
£35–45 *CS*

l. A steel lever corkscrew, marked on the handle 'James Heeley & Sons, 6006 Patent Double Lever', c1880, 6¾in (17cm) long.
£30–40 *CS*

A Clough finger band corkscrew, advertising Panopepton patent medicine, c1884, 2in (5cm) long.
£25–30 *DHA*

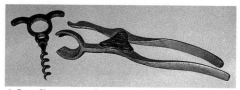

A Lund's tangent lever corkscrew, 19thC, 8½in (21.5cm) long.
£70–80 *TAC*

A wooden handled two-prong cork extractor, marked 'Patented May 9th 99', complete with protective sheath, 1899, 4in (10cm) long.
£45–55
A Cork extractor, patented by Greely, the ebonised handle with steel shaft and hook, marked 'Pat. Mar. 6. 88', 1888, 3½in (9cm) long.
£50–60   *CS*

A novelty corkscrew, the handle formed from a nut carved with a grotesque face with glass eyes, iron worm, 19thC, 6½in (16.5cm) long.
£230–260   *FW&C*

l. A Scandinavian silver corkscrew, made by Georg Jensen, hallmarked, c1920, 4¼in (10.5cm) long.
£120–150   *CS*

A corkscrew combined Codd bottle marble ejector and pourer, made by W. Vaughan, with registration number for 1890, 6in (15cm) long.
£65–75   *CS*

r. A nickel-plated champagne tap, in original cardboard box, complete with instructions for use, c1890, box 4in (10cm) wide.
£20–30   *CS*

An all-steel corkscrew, marked 'Magic Lever Cork Drawer, Pat Appd For', c1890, 6½in (16.5cm) long.
£20–30   *CS*

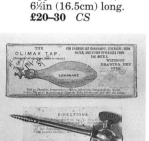

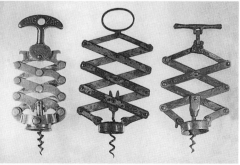

Three all-steel concertina type corkscrews:
l. French Zig Zag, c1920, 6in (15cm) long.
£25–35
c. Weir's patent of 1884, by James Heeley & Sons, 5½in (14cm) long.
£45–55
r. French Ideal Breveté, c1890, 5in (12.5cm) long.
£15–20   *CS*

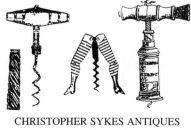

DISNEYANA

A Britains No. 1645 Mickey Mouse set, containing Disney figures, some damage, in original box, c1938.
£5,000–5,500 *DN*

Disney material from the 1930s is the most sought-after, and rare items such as this Britains set, complete with box, can command very high prices, especially when in good condition.

A Schuco tinplate Donald Duck toy, with yellow beak and feet, c1936, 6in (15cm) high.
£160–180 *RAR*

Two Mickey and Minnie Mouse figures, in black, white and red, by Dean's Rag Book Co Ltd, c1935, 8in (20.5cm) high.
£130–150 *PrB*

A set of Snow White and the Seven Dwarfs metal figures, marked 'Walt Disney Prod', 1980s, Snow White 3½in (9cm) high.
£100–120 *MED*

A gouache animation cel of Snow White, on patterned paper, with 'Walt Disney Enterprises' label on the back, c1937, 7½in (19cm) square.
£5,000–5,500 *S(NY)*

A Snow White and the Seven Dwarfs paper ruffle for a cake, 1960s, 36in (91.5cm) long.
£4–5 *HUX*

A plastic and litho tinplate Donald's Acroball Game, by Louis Marx (GB), c1950, 6in (15cm) wide, in printed coloured box.
£40–45 *CDC*

A Donald Duck ceramic money box, in red, yellow and blue, 1960s, 6in (15cm) high.
£20–25 *HUX*

A Mickey Mouse plastic musical toy, c1971, 5in (12.5cm) high.
£20–25 *DUD*

DOGS

From the earliest times the dog has been regarded as man's best friend, used for hunting, protection and companionship. Dogs were celebrated both in Classical and Christian mythology: Cerberus, a three-headed hound, guarded the entrance to Hades; a dog was the symbol of Saint Roch (patron of the plague-stricken); and in the Old Testament a dog accompanied Tobias and the Archangel Raphael on their perilous journey – Toby, the dog in Punch and Judy, was named after this legend.

From King Charles spaniels to corgis, dogs have always been associated with royalty, and it was Queen Victoria – a passionate animal enthusiast – who popularized the trend for keeping dogs as pets rather than just working animals.

Dog ownership flourished during her reign, a period that saw the rise of the great painters of dogs, notably Sir Edwin Landseer, the opening of Battersea Dogs' Home in 1860, and the launch in 1886 of the most famous dog show in the world, by dog biscuit manufacturer Charles Cruft.

As dogs became regarded as members of the family, so they were increasingly portrayed in the fine and decorative arts. The canine collectables featured here date from the 19th century to the present day. Only cats can rival dogs in terms of collectable popularity, but there is a difference: cat enthusiasts will often collect any feline image, whereas dog collectors tend to be more faithful to their favourite breed.

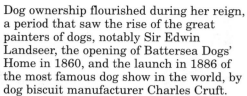

A cast iron dog nut cracker, 19thC, 9in (23cm) long.
£20–25 *DAC*

A painted spelter model of a reclining greyhound, c1880, 7in (17.5cm) long.
£125–145 *WeH*

A plaster model of a German shepherd dog, c1900, 18in (45.5cm) high.
£40–50 *PAC*

A gold dog bar brooch, 1930s, 3in (7.5cm) long.
£80–100 *DAC*

A silver vesta case, with a standing hound, maker RW, Birmingham 1906, 1½in (3.5cm) diam.
£400–450 *GH*

A collection of hand-carved bone animals, c1930, 3in (7.5cm) high.
£85–95 *HOB*

A Gerry metal brooch, in the form of a poodle dog, painted grey with red collar and bow, c1980, 2in (5cm) high.
£35–40 *PKT*

r. A brass dog corkscrew, 1930s, 3in (7.5cm) high.
£20–25 *DAC*

l. Two glass buttons, each decorated with a brown dog, 1940s, 1in (2.5cm) diam.
£4–5 *MRW*

Ceramic

A black and white Staffordshire setter, on a green, red and brown base, c1820, 7½in (19cm) high.
£1,000–1,200 *JHo*

A life-sized pottery figure of a pug dog, mid-19thC.
£700–800 *AAV*

A pair of Staffordshire brown and white King Charles spaniels, late 19thC, 11in (28cm) high.
£200–250 *SER*

l. Two German white bisque dogs, with red collars, by Gebrüder Heubach, impressed on the base with a sunburst, c1920, 7in (18cm) high.
£200–250 *YC*

A pair of Staffordshire porcelain poodles, c1840, 3½in (9cm) wide.
£300–350 *DAN*

A Worcester white pug dog, c1899, 3½in (9cm) high.
£400–440 *TH*

A lustre ware white dog with a puppy, with brown markings, c1920, 3¼in (8cm) high.
£15–20 *JMC*

A brown stoneware dog tobacco jar, 1840–60, 5in (12.5cm) high.
£275–300 *INC*

l. A Staffordshire greyhound pen holder, mustard yellow on a blue base, 19thC, 6in (15cm) long.
£120–150 *DAC*

An Austrian terracotta dog, with black head and ears, unmarked, 1890–1910, 5½in (14cm) high.
£220–250 *INC*

An Austrian terracotta figure of a terrier, painted in off-white and dark brown, c1900, 18½in (47cm) high.
£1,700–2,000 *P(G)*

A Royal Doulton dark brown spaniel, model No. 755, K9, 1930s, 2½in (6.5cm) high.
£300–350 *PGA*

A Crown Devon biscuit barrel, Patch, c1930, 11in (28cm) high.
£150–200 *BEV*

A SylvaC beige drop-eared dog, No. 2951, c1930, 7½in (19cm) high.
£40–50 *TAC*

A Royal Doulton white bull-terrier, HN 1133, Model No. 959B, 1930s, 7in (18cm) wide.
£800–900 *PGA*

A Bing & Grøndahl brown dachshund, c1948, 7in (18cm) high.
£150–170 *GSW*

A Royal Doulton Alsatian, HN 1116, 'Champion Benign of Picardy', c1948, 12in (30.5cm) long.
£200–250 *PAC*

A Royal Worcester Pekinese dog, painted in reddish-brown, c1939, 2in (5cm) high.
£165–195 *TH*

A Royal Doulton black labrador, HN 2667, Model No. 1946, c1970, 5in (12.5cm) high.
£55-65 *PAC*

A brown and white King Charles spaniel and puppy, by Cat Pottery, 1990s, dog 20in (53.5cm) high.
Dog £70–80
Puppy £25–30 *CP*

A Beswick dog, light brown with white tip to the tail, c1950, 4in (10cm) high.
£45–55 *PAC*

Famous Dogs

A plaster model of
Nipper, His Master's
Voice dog, 1920s,
14in (35.5cm) high.
£250–275 PAC

A Bonzo lavender
bottle, by Potter
& Moore, c1930,
3in (7.5cm) high.
£90–120 LBr

A Japanese orange
ceramic Bonzo jar,
c1930, 4¾in (12cm) high.
£150–175 ARo

Squeak from *Pip, Squeak
and Wilfred*, in brown
and white painted wood,
c1920, 4in (10cm) high.
£65–75 CWo

Pip, Squeak and Wilfred
*was a children's comic
strip about a penguin,
a dog and a rabbit that
appeared in* The Daily
Mirror *1919–46. The
newspaper also ran
a children's club
surrounding the comic
strip, members of which
were called 'Gugnunks'.*

*The gramophone
company HMV, His
Master's Voice, took its
name from the title of a
painting by François
Barraud (1856–1924)
showing the artist's
terrier-cross, Nipper,
staring at a phono-
graph horn from which
'his master's voice' was
sounding. The company
purchased the picture in
1899. Nipper appeared
in his first advertisement
in 1900 and on record
labels from 1902,
subsequently becoming
the most frequently
reproduced dog of
all time.*

*Created by illustrator
George Studdy, Bonzo
first appeared in the
Daily Sketch news-
paper in 1922 and
rapidly became
Britain's most popular
cartoon character.
The little dog was
ruthlessly merchan-
dised appearing in
every medium from
soft toys to scent
bottles and is very
sought after by
collectors today.*

A rubber squeaking
model of Tramp, from
Lady and the Tramp,
c1960, 8¾in (22cm) high.
£50–60 CWo

Lady and The Tramp,
*based on a story by
Ward Greene, was
released in 1955.*

A Snoopy soft toy,
1960s, 8in (20cm) high.
£25–35 CWo

*Created by Charles
Schultz, the Peanuts
cartoon strip first
appeared in the US in
1950. The main stars
were Charlie Brown
and his beagle Snoopy.
Merchandising began
in the 1950s, boomed in
the 1960s and Snoopy
became one of the world's
favourite cartoon dogs.*

A Rosebud rubber
figure of PC 49, c1950,
10in (25.5cm) high.
£40–50 CWo

l. A Snoopy egg
cup, stamped
'United Feature
Syndicate Peanuts
Characters', 1958–65,
3in (7.5cm) high.
£5–6 PC

r. A composition model of Perdita,
from *101 Dalmations*, Taiwan,
c1961, 6in (15cm) wide.
£125–145 CWo

101 Dalmations, *written by Dodie
Smith in 1956, was made into a
Disney cartoon feature in 1961.*

A ceramic Snoopy, lying on a slice of water melon, limited edition, 1960s, 6in (15cm) wide.
£15–20 *PPe*

A Corgi Toys *Magic Roundabout* yellow car, with Dougal, c1972, 4½in (11.5cm) long.
£55–65 *SpM*

One of the most famous dogs from the 1960s was Dougal, from the cult series Magic Roundabout. *Created by Frenchman Serge Danot, the* Magic Roundabout *was first shown on British TV in 1965, and was narrated by writer Eric Thompson, father of actress Emma.*

A rubber Bendy Rolf dog from *The Muppets*, brown with buff-coloured bib, cuffs and hat and green bow tie, c1977, 7½in (19cm) high.
£25–30 *CWo*

A Wade Heath model of Pluto, yellow with black ears, chipped base, 1960s, 7in (17.5cm) long.
£300–350 *CWo*

The character of Pluto first appeared in Disney films in 1930, although it was not until the following year he was named Pluto. 1930s Pluto toys can appear in many colours and it was not until 1938–9, when all cartoons featuring Mickey Mouse and Pluto were made in colour, that his familiar yellow coat became standard.

A plastic model of a grey and white dog, sitting in a green spaceship, from *The Jetsons*, by Hanna Barbara, c1989, 3in (7.5cm) high.
£10–15 *CWo*

A Royal Doulton group, entitled 'Patch, Rolly and Freckles' from *101 Dalmations*, limited edition, with certificate, c1997, 7in (17.5cm) wide.
£155–185 *PAC*

Toys

A green pâpier maché growling French bulldog, with a chain to operate the mouth and bark, studded leather collar and hair ruff, coat texture worn, c1910, 21¼in (54cm) long.
£600–700 *HAM*

A Steiff brown and black terrier, 'Fellow', with black boot button eyes and vertically stitched nose, with button to ear and label to chest, German, 1930s, 8in (20.5cm) high.
£250–300 *Bon(C)*

r. A light brown stuffed dog, with moving head, 1950s, 6in (15cm) long.
£15–20 *DAC*

A Steiff orange dachshund, no button, 1950s, 11in (28cm) long.
£50–60 *DAC*

The Windsor Pugs

Pugs were the Duke and Duchess of Windsor's favourite dogs, and at the recent auction of their effects in New York, pug lovers were out in force competing for pug pictures, silver dog bowls and porcelain figures. In addition to the items shown here, 11 pillows for pugs sold for a total of £22,800 ($37,375) against a high estimate of £1,037 ($1,700) and a group of 10 dog collars sold for £7,012 ($11,500) estimated at £300–500 ($500–800). The combination of royalty, romance and pugs proved irresistible, and virtually every canine lot went astonishingly over estimate.

A Derby porcelain figure of a pug, seated on a turquoise oval mound base with rose enamel and gilding, chips to ears, 1790–1800, 2½in (6.5cm) high.
£1,600–1,800 *S(NY)*

A Meissen porcelain miniature figure of a pug, with dark brown muzzle, tail tip and paws, 19thC, 2in (5cm) high.
£3,000–3,500 *S(NY)*

A Continental porcelain figure of a seated pug, covered in a thick peacock-blue glaze with black facial details, wearing an iron-red and gilt collar with gilt-heightened bells, restored, incised mark, late 19thC, 6½in (16.5cm) high.
£4,000–4,500 *S(NY)*

A Rockingham porcelain figure of a pug, with tan coat and black muzzle, slight restoration, c1830, 2¾in (7cm) high.
£1,500–1,800 *S(NY)*

An American silver bowl, on a stepped circular spreading foot, the body inscribed 'The Manhattan Savings Bank, Institutional Exhibition of Champion Dogs Ch. Pugville's Imperial Imp II, February 1960,' reproduction of an original by Paul Revere, 8in (20.5cm) diam.
£1,300–1,500 *S(NY)*

This bowl was awarded to the Duke and Duchess of Windsor's pug 'Ch Pugville's Imperial Imp II' in the Manhattan Savings Bank Institutional Exhibition of Champion Dogs, February 1960.

l. A pair of French gilt plaster pug's head paperweights, slight damage, 20thC, 4in (10cm) wide.
£3,000–3,500 *S(NY)*

A Dorothy Wilding portrait of the Duke of Windsor with Dizzy, inscribed by the Duke to the Duchess, 'With Love From David and Dizzy, 1955', photographer's credit label on reverse with reference No. 3531, in a silver frame by Cartier, Paris, 9¼ x 7½in (23.5 x 19cm).
£12,000–13,000 *S(NY)*

A *Mickey Mouse Weekly* comic, published by Odhams, October 31, 1950, 13¾in (34cm) high.
£5–10 *DPO*

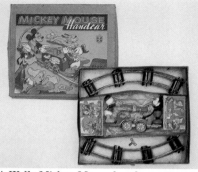

A Wells Mickey Mouse handcar set, comprising a four-wheel clockwork-powered handcar, with Mickey Mouse and Donald Duck composition figures, complete with track, No.99, 1930s, box 12in (30.5cm) wide.
£400–450 *WAL*

A Mickey Mouse tin umbrella stand, 1950s, 20in (51cm) high.
£160–170 *JUN*

A gouache on celluloid promotional cel, of Jiminy Cricket perched on Pinocchio's toe, with 'to Erik O. Hansson, Best Wishes, Walt Disney' on mat at lower right in studio artist Manuel Gonzales' hand, and a Walt Disney Productions label on back, c1940, 7in (17.5cm) high.
£4,700–5,200 *S(NY)*

A Walt Disney cubed picture and box, West German, c1955, 7in (18cm) wide.
£15–18 *DAC*

A Walt Disney Hissing Sid soft toy, made in Japan under licence to Disney, 1960s, 6in (15cm) high.
£25–35 *GrD*

A stainless steel kettle with wire handle in the shape of Mickey Mouse's ears, designed by Michael Graves for Disney Stores, 1970s–80s, 9½in (24cm) high.
£60–70 *MED*

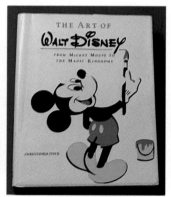

A Walt Disney hardback edition of *The Art of Walt Disney*, by Christopher Finch, 1983 edition, 13in (33cm) high.
£30–40 *VS*

A Walt Disney promotional Pelham puppet, from *Snow White and the Seven Dwarfs*, c1977, 18in (45.5cm) high.
£110–130 *RAR*

A pair of Staffordshire
dog spill vases, c1880,
13in (33cm) high.
£380–425 *JO*

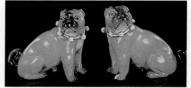

A pair of German porcelain models
of pugs, after Meissen originals,
one slightly damaged, impressed
numerals '1560', '45' and 'III',
late 19thC, largest 4in (10cm) high.
£3,700–4,000 *S(NY)*

*These models were the property of
the Duke and Duchess of Windsor.*

A Bonzo print, entitled 'Bonzo
Gives Tongue', published by
the Sketch, from original
print, c1922, 15½ x 13in
(39.5 x 33cm).
£20–25 *JER*

A vinyl and Perspex bag,
decorated with a poodle
made from jewels and
gilded shells, 1950s,
11in (28cm) high.
£230–260 *SpM*

Two Royal Doulton models of
bulldogs, draped in the Union Jack,
designed by Charles Noke, c1941,
largest 4½in (11.5cm) high.
l. **£150–175**
r. **£650–675** *PGA*

A SylvaC dog, No. 1379,
c1930, 7½in (19cm) high.
£70–80 *TAC*

A Walt Disney Productions
Lady and the Tramp hot
water bottle, inscribed
'Duanny, made in Spain',
c1965, 12½in (32cm) high.
£75–85 *CWo*

A Beswick fireside dachshund,
1950s, 15in (38cm) long.
£100–125 *PAC*

A Beanie Baby, Weenie,
1995, 8in (20.5cm) long.
£5–6 *BeG*

A Snoopy pop-up music box, by
Mattel, c1960, 11in (28cm) high.
£75–85 *CWo*

A German papier mâché-headed doll, on kid and wood body, with unusual hairstyle, c1840, 15in (38cm) high.
£1,200–1,400 *YC*

A German Parian-headed boy doll, in Scottish dress, c1870, 13in (33cm) high.
£300–350 *STK*

A Jumeau bisque-headed doll, with blue paperweight eyes, original clothes, labelled 'Au Nain Bleu', c1890, 18in (45cm) high.
£2,000–2,200 *STK*

A Belgian bisque-headed doll, by De Fuisseaux, with well matched body, brown paperweight eyes, original and replacement dress, 1890–1900, 14in (35.5cm) high.
£350–400 *STK*

A Kämmer & Reinhardt bisque-headed doll, on jointed composition body, all original including box, incised 'K ☆ R', c1900, 20½in (52cm) high.
£900–1,000 *YC*

A Simon & Halbig bisque-headed lady doll, on jointed composition body, with moulded breasts and waist, incised 'S & H 1199', c1900, 19½in (50cm) high.
£800–900 *YC*

A Simon & Halbig bisque-headed doll, on jointed composition body, dressed as a boy, incised 'S & H 1078' c1905, 19in (48cm) high.
£500–550 *YC*

An S. F. B. J. bisque-headed character doll, on jointed composition body, incised 'S.F.B.J. 236 Paris 8', c1910, 17½in (44cm) high.
£750–850 *YC*

l. An Armand Marseille bisque dome-headed baby doll, on 'frog'-shaped cloth body, closed pouty mouth and celluloid hands, antique outfit, 'Dream baby' type, mould No. 341, 1915–25, 14in (35.5cm) high.
£250–300 *STK*

r. An Armand Marseille 'Ellar' type Oriental baby doll, c1915, 15in (38cm) high.
£800–1,100 *STK*

Two character dolls, dressed in crêpe paper with paper heads, c1900, 5in (12.5cm) high.
£30–35 *CHU*

An Armand Marseille 'Dream Baby', with brown weighted glass eyes, open mouth with 2 lower teeth, on a five-piece composition baby body, wearing pink dress, bonnet, shoes and socks, incised 'A.M.', c1920, 10in (25.5cm) high.
£180–220 *Bon(C)*

A William Goebel all-bisque piano baby, c1920, 9½in (24cm) high.
£100–120 *YC*

A pair of Dean's rag dolls, brightly printed young boy and girl holding a doll, 1920s, 16in (40.5cm) high.
£50–60 *Bon(C)*

A Dean's Hygienic rag doll, complete with manufacturer's button on her bottom, c1925, 14in (35.5cm) high.
£70–90 *DOL*

A pair of Lenci series 1500 bride and groom dolls, with jointed arms, legs and neck, on stiffened bodies, painted eyes and mouths, the bride wearing a layered white organza wedding dress with train and pink underclothes, yellow felt gloves, holding a felt bouquet of flowers, shoes and socks, the groom wearing top hat and tails made of felt, with white felt flower buttonhole, holding white gloves, c1930, 17½in (44.5cm) high.
£2,800–3,000 *Bon(C)*

A doll, with flirty eyes and original clothes, c1930, 16½in (42cm) high.
£55–65 *DOL*

r. A Chad Valley Snow White and the Seven Dwarfs, in original boxes with names and original price tags, late 1930s, Snow White 16in (40cm), Dwarfs 6in (15cm) high.
£1,600–2,000 *Bon(C)*

A Vivienne Westwood Pirate sash, with weighted tassels, World's End label, c1981, 84in (213.5cm) long.
£100–120 *ID*

A Crawford's shortbread tin, with a photograph of Lady Diana Spencer and Prince Charles, c1981, 6in (15cm) diam.
£8–10 *HUX*

A Spitting Image Game of Scandal, Spitting Image Productions Ltd, c1984, 13 x 18in (33 x 45.5cm).
£10–15 *PC*

A South Atlantic medal, with rosette, Awarded to ALS(R) S. A. McKeown, HMS *Minerva*, c1982.
£160–180 *RMC*

A glass tumbler, transfer-printed with a Cummings cartoon of Margaret Thatcher, 1980s, 4¼in (11cm) high.
£10–15 *PC*

A Kevin Francis Toby jug, depicting Margaret Thatcher, 1979–90, 9in (23cm) high.
£160–200 *BRT*

A diamanté Mickey Mouse brooch, by Butler & Wilson, marked Disney, 1980s, 3½in (9cm) high.
£100–120 *CRIS*

A Roland Rat soft toy, c1983, 16in (40.5cm) high.
£10–12 *CMF*

A Rubik's Revenge cube, by Ideal, with original packaging, 1980s, 3½in (9cm) high.
£15–20 *CWo*

A signed colour photograph of Madonna, 1980s, 10 x 8in (25.5 x 20.5cm).
£350–400 *FRa*

r. A McDonald's toy car, c1989, 2½in (6.5cm) long.
£3–4 *CMF*

Gallagher Ltd, The Reason Why, complete set of 100 cigarette cards in original album, average condition, 1924.
£10–12 *MED*

W. A. & A. C. Churchman, 'In Town Tonight', set of 50 cigarette cards, 1938.
£8–10 per set *LCC*

CHANCE, CHICAGO NAT'L

Sweet Caporal Cigarettes, Frank Chance baseball card, excellent condition, 1910.
£100–125 *HALL*

W. D. & H. O. Wills, Garden Flowers, New Varieties, 2nd series of 40 cigarette cards, 1939.
£18–22 *LCC*

W. D. & H. O. Wills, Cricketers 2nd series, set of 50 cigarette cards in album, 1929.
£50–60 *MAC*

An educational poster entitled 'The Greengrocer's Shop', designed for schools, 1930s, 21in (53.5cm) high.
£4–6 *HUX*

A Billy Smart's Circus brochure, 1950s, 7in (18cm) high.
£6–8 *MRW*

A Raymond Peynet limited edition print, 'Don't walk about', original lithograph, signed in pencil, 1950s, 20in (51cm) high.
£200–220 *RDG*

l. A Paul McCartney CD, 'This One', disc still present, signed to plastic casing, good condition, 1997.
£170–200 *VS*

'*Shirley Temple through the day*', booklet published by Saalfield No. 1716, 1930s.
£40–45 *VS*

A blonde gilded tortoiseshell fan, with hand painted silk and sequins, signed, 1830–40, 13in (33cm) wide.
£350–380 *JPr*

An ivory fan, hand-painted on vellum, c1850, 11in (28cm) wide.
£200–250 *JPr*

A Chinese lacquer fan, hand-painted with inset ivory faces, 1860–80, 13in (33cm) wide, boxed.
£200–250 *JPr*

A feather fan, with bone sticks, c1870, 11in (28cm) wide.
£25–40 *JPr*

A painted wood and paper fan, decorated with a Spanish scene, c1910, 13in (33cm) wide.
£35–40 *DAC*

A collection of bone, ivory and paper doll's fans, 19thC, largest 4in (10cm) wide.
£10–50 each *VB*

Two fan brooches, decorated with paste stones, c1910, 2in (5cm) wide.
£10–20 each *VB*

A sandalwood and paper fan, with printed country scene, 1930s, 14in (35.5cm) wide.
£10–15 *JPr*

r. A feather fan, with plastic handle, c1930, 23in (58.5cm) long.
£40–50 *PC*

An Indian peacock feather fan, c1990, 15in (38cm) long.
£10–12 *PC*

A Crown Devon hand-painted plate, 1950s, 9¼in (24cm) diam.
£80–100 *PGA*

A hand-painted sugar jar, 1950s, 6¼in (16cm) high.
£30–35 *PGA*

A Tala aluminium doughnut maker, 1950s, 8in (20.5cm) high.
£5–6 *AL*

An American tapestry hand-bag, with plastic handle and brass fittings, 1950s, 8in (20.5cm) wide.
£110–120 *LBr*

A crystal five-strand necklace, 1950s, 16in (40.5cm) long.
£25–30 *CHU*

A tin tray, 1950s, 15in (38cm) wide.
£5–7 *UTP*

A glass-topped coffee table, painted with pink flamingos, after a painting by Bernard Russell, 1950s, 35in (89cm) wide.
£40–45 *RAT*

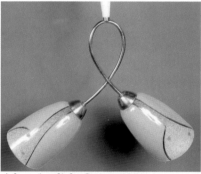

A hanging light fitting, 1950s, 20in (51cm) high.
£30–40 *TWa*

A Japanese plastic apple-shaped ice bucket, with glass liner, by Eagle, 1950s, 8in (20cm) high.
£40–50 *RAT*

l. A two-tone Formica sideboard and cocktail cabinet, late 1950s, 72in (183cm) wide.
£150–180 *RAT*

An Indian ivory chess set, c1750, king 3½in (9cm) high.
£650–750 *TMi*

A Cantonese carved ivory chess set, c1850, king 4in (10cm) high.
£225–275 *MB*

An ivory travelling chess set, c1820, 7in (18cm) square.
£150–200 *TMi*

A satin walnut counter box, decorated with transfer scenes of the life and times of Napoleon, containing 4 lift-out boxes, each with a sliding cover and containing stained ivory counters, mid-19thC, 9in (23cm) wide.
£275–325 *TMA*

A wooden architectural game, in original box, c1880, 20in (51cm) wide.
£125–145 *MLL*

A Ping-Pong table tennis set, by J. Jacques, with vellum-covered bats, brass uprights, original net, balls and rules, in original box, excellent condition, c1901, 21in (53.5cm) wide.
£150–200 *STK*

A Bussey's table croquet set, in maker's original box, lid loose, complete with internal instructions, minus one ball and one peg, c1860.
£20–25 *MUL*

A Chad Valley wooden 'Bruin Boys' bagatelle, with printed paper pop-up figures, in original box, 1920s, 21in (53cm) long.
£35–45 *CDC*

A game of 'Toupe Royale', the gilt-brass gallery with leaf finials enclosing playing surface with 5 figures of a Jester and 4 other attendants, within outer gallery and on turned legs, 1950s, 35in (89cm) high.
£1,800–2,200 *CAG*

l. A pack of playing cards, designed by Raymond Peynet, mint condition, 1950s–1960s.
£30–35 *RDG*

A tulip-shaped wine glass, with plain foot, c1780–1820, 5¼in (13.5cm) high.
£45–60 *JHa*

A set of 6 wine glasses, with conical bowls, plain drawn stems and plain conical feet, c1790, 5¼in (13.5cm) high.
£400–480 *Som*

A pair of Bristol blue glass chemists' bottles, with blown stoppers, c1800, 9in (23cm) high.
£120–140 *FD*

A roemer-type wine glass, with hollow strawberry prunted stem, the domed foot with trailed decoration, c1825, 6in (15cm) high.
£130–150 *Som*

A glass decanter, with slice-cut neck and pillar-cut body, c1840, 11½in (29cm) high.
£400–450 *MJW*

A glass decanter, with step-cut neck and arch-cut body, c1840, 12¾in (32.5cm) high.
£575–625 *MJW*

l. A yellow glass decanter, c1850, 14in (35.5cm) high.
£600–700 *MJW*

A red glass carafe, with dimpled pattern, c1850, 9½in (24cm) high.
£325–375 *MJW*

A green cut-glass covered dish, c1840, 7½in (19cm) high.
£500–550 *MJW*

Three 'shaft and globe' glass decanters, mid-19thC, tallest 11in (28cm) high.
£150–250 each *BELL*

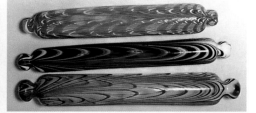

Three 'Nailsea' glass rolling pins, with pulled loop decoration, c1860, longest 15¾in (40cm).
£150–170 each *Som*

A Victorian glass bird feeder, 6in (15cm) high.
£30–40 *MRW*

l. A Victorian white opaque and ruby glass edged épergne, the 4 trumpet-shaped vases with clear trailed and crimped decoration, rims and base, 21½in (54.5cm) high.
£200–250 *CAG*

A cranberry glass smoke bell, c1860–70, 12½in (32cm) diam.
£100–125 *WAB*

An Antonio Salviati glass cup and saucer, c1880, 2in (5cm) high.
£600–680 *MJW*

l. A Victorian cranberry glass bowl, with moulded swags and applied Vaseline glass pinched feet, c1880, 6in (15cm) wide.
£90–100 *BELL*

A cranberry glass vase, c1880, 8in (20.5cm) high.
£180–200 *AMH*

An amethyst glass hyacinth vase, c1890, 6in (15cm) high.
£40–50 *CB*

A Victorian Bristol blue enamelled and gilt goblet, 5¼in (13.5cm) high.
£45–55 *TAC*

A ruby glass decanter, with engraving and cut neck, c1880, 9in (23cm) high.
£600–700 *MJW*

A pair of pressed glass lions,
c1890, 5in (12.5cm) high.
£200–250   *ARE*

l. A Victorian splashed and spiralled
vase, 10¾in (27.5cm) high.
£250–300   *PGA*

A Stevens & Williams plate,
c1900, 8in (20.5cm) diam.
£600–700   *MJW*

A Continental glass jug and 2 tumblers, with
enamel decoration, c1890, jug 5½in (14cm) high.
£85–100   *DKH*

A James Couper Clutha
vase, Liberty and
Dresser marks on base,
c1890, 7in (18cm) high.
£2,000–2,250   *NCA*

A Sowerby Daisy Block rowboat, on pale amethyst
base glass, made from an 1880s mould, c1925–35,
12in (30.5cm) long.
£120–150   *ASe*

A Stevens & Williams
decanter, c1890,
16¼in (41.5cm) high.
£2,000–2,200   *MJW*

l. An Imperial Lustre Rose
Carnival glass footed bowl,
on purple base glass, c1910,
7½in (19cm) diam.
£55–75   *ASe*

r. A Fenton Carnival
glass Diamond and
Rib vase, c1908–25,
11in (28cm) high.
£15–20   *ASe*

JOHN DITCHFIELD – GLASFORM
Telephone: +44 (0)1253 626410 Email: glasform@btinternet.com

Iridescent glass bowl with coral fritt, signed and numbered, 3¼in high, 7in diam. **£250-280** *GLA*

Unique piece signed by J. Ditchfield, Glasform No. 4489.

Glass paperweight with hearts, pearl with gold trails and red hearts, signed, 31/2in diam. **£100-120** *GLA*

Unique piece signed by J. Ditchfield, Glasform No. 5918.

Iridescent glass bowl with red waves, signed and numbered, 4in high, 6½in diam. **£160-200** *GLA*

Unique piece signed by J. Ditchfield, Glasform No. 4442.

Coral scale pattern glass bowl, signed and numbered, 6½in high, 14½in diam. **£750-800** *GLA*

Unique piece signed by J. Ditchfield, Glasform No. 4497.

Volcanic glass vase, pearl with dark iridescent, signed and numbered, 6in high, 6in diam. **£300-350** *GLA*

Unique piece signed by J. Ditchfield, Glasform No. 4421.

Iridescent volcanic glass vase, signed and numbered, 7¼in high, 5in diam. **£300-350** *GLA*

Unique piece signed by J. Ditchfield, Glasform No. 4498.

Iridescent glass vase with gold feathering, signed and numbered, 9¾in high. **£275-300** *GLA*

Unique piece signed by J. Ditchfield, Glasform No. 4470.

Clear gold glass vase with opaque green lily trail and pads, signed and numbered, 7½ high. **£120-150** *GLA*

Unique piece signed by J. Ditchfield, Glasform No. 4001.

Cranberry glass vase with black lily trail and pads signed, 10in high, 6¼in diam. **£300-350** *GLA*

Unique piece signed by J. Ditchfield, Glasform No. 5919.

Iridescent peacock-eye glass vase, signed and numbered, 10in high. **£520-600** *GLA*

Unique piece signed by J. Ditchfield, Glasform No. 4441.

ADVERTISEMENT FEATURE

A Sowerby Carnival glass chicken and cover, with iridescent purple colouring, c1900, 4½in (11.5cm) high.
£40–50 *MRW*

A Sowerby Carnival glass swan butter dish, with marigold iridescence, re-use of an 1880s mould, c1925–35, 6in (15cm) high.
£100–120 *ASe*

A Rosenthal studio glass vase, c1925, 9¼in (23.5cm) high.
£125–140 *DSG*

A Bohemian hand-blown Flames glass vase, c1928, 17in (43cm) high.
£340–380 *BKK*

Two Sabino opalescent glass models, c1930, 4½in (11.5cm) high.
£40–50 each *P(B)*

Three bulb vases, 1950s, 7½in (19cm) high.
£6–8 each *AL*

A Davidson's glass vase, of globular shape with flared neck and broadly-ribbed lower body, c1930, 8in (20.5cm) high.
£70–80 *JHa*

A Gray-Stan vase, with red swirls, fully marked, c1930, 10in (25.5cm) high.
£350–400 *JHa*

r. A Karlin Rushbrooke 'hand-in-hand' jug, 1997, 5¾in (14.5cm) high.
£40–50 *JHa*

A Siddy Langley Narajo vase, 1997, 10½in (27cm) high.
£120–140 *NP*

A Clichy paperweight, with
pink daisy on a spiral filigree
cushion, c1850, 3in (7.5cm) diam.
£6,000–7,000 *DLP*

A Wedgwood dolphin paperweight,
1970s, 8¼in (21cm) long.
£30–40 *SWB*

A Whitefriars paperweight,
c1977, 2¾in (7cm) diam.
£250–275 *SWB*

A Perthshire floral overlay
paperweight, signed
'P', c1980, 2¾in (7cm) diam.
£250–300 *STG*

l. A Strathearn Glass paperweight,
with millefiori design, c1980,
3in (7.5cm) diam.
£40–60 *STG*

A William Manson Secret
Garden paperweight, 1997,
3¼in (8.5cm) diam.
£175–195 *SWB*

A silver-framed purse, embroidered in silver thread and mother-of-pearl, marked, c1790, 8in (20.5cm) wide.
£220–250 *JPr*

A beaded bag, embroidered with roses, the silver handle encrusted with roses, c1840, 6in (15cm) wide.
£220–240 *JPr*

An Irish chainwork purse, with landscape design and gold-coloured metal clasp, c1850, 8in (20.5cm) long.
£150–180 *JVa*

A beaded draw-string purse, with original lining, c1870, 5in (12.5cm) wide.
£100–120 *JPr*

A gold lamé clutch bag, embroidered in gold, blue and red with an Art Deco design, with matching mirror inside, 1920s, 8in (20.5cm) wide.
£30–35 *PC*

An enamel mesh evening bag, c1900, 6in (15cm) long.
£35–40 *CHU*

An embroidered and enamelled handbag, c1920, 6in (15cm) wide.
£130–150 *JPr*

A black plastic handbag, decorated with goldfish, with brass fittings, 1950s, 10in (25.5cm) wide.
£140–160 *LBr*

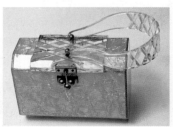

A Wilardy hard plastic tortoiseshell handbag, American, c1950, 8in (20.5cm) wide.
£230–260 *LBr*

An American plastic handbag with brass fittings, 1950s, 8in (20.5cm) wide.
£180–200 *LBr*

An American yellow plastic handbag, with brass fittings, 1950s, 7in (18cm) wide.
£180–200 *LBr*

DOLLS

A wooden doll, the head with inset black enamelled eyes, dotted lashes and eyebrows, rouged cheeks and nailed brown wig, in original pantaloons, petticoats and brown striped dress, restored, c1780, 15¾in (40cm) high.
£450–500 *S(S)*

A German papier mâché shoulder-headed doll, on a kid body, wearing original pink dress and hat, c1850, 13½in (34cm) high.
£350–400 *YC*

A collection of eight Victorian Frozen Charlottes, 1–1½in (2.5–3.5cm) high.
£5–15 each *VB*

'Frozen Charlottes' was the name given to glazed china dolls. Though larger figures were also produced (sometimes referred to as Bath dolls), the most commonly found Frozen Charlottes are miniature. Like silver sixpences and good luck charms, these were often hidden in Christmas puddings and they are also known as pudding dolls.

r. A Motschmann papier mâché and cloth baby doll, wearing white dress, German, c1860, 24½in (62cm) high.
£650–750 *YC*

A porcelain pedlar doll, wearing a cream dress with red pattern and a black hat, with a collection of artefacts including dolls, gavel, penknife, monocular and scent bottle, c1880, 16½in (42cm) high, under glass dome.
£1,000–1,200 *GSP*

An Oriental boy doll, with gofun head, black hair wig and freckles to face, wearing original brown patterned kimono, c1890–1900, 16in (40.5cm) high.
£120–150 *STK*

Gofun is a Japanese material made from crushed oyster shells, creating a pearl-like finish.

A German baby doll, with composition head on a sewn stockinette body, dressed in white knitted dress and hat, with extra clothes, c1920, 16in (40.5cm) high.
£120–150 *STK*

A half doll, with arms folded, wearing a pink top, 1920s, 1¾in (4.5cm) high.
£20–30 *MRW*

l. A pair of French cloth dolls, modelled as an old lady and gentleman in peasant clothes, with wooden clogs, by Rauca, c1935, 19in (48cm) high.
£275–375 *GrD*

A black doll string dispenser, made from card and light brown patterned cloth, with green hat, 1920s, 8in (20.5cm) high.
£10–15 *SMAM*

A composition pot-headed black doll, wearing yellow checked dress with red sash, small repairs to neck and one wrist, c1940, 11in (28cm) high.
£60–70 *STK*

A German porcelain doll, in two parts, with pink and yellow hair, 1920s, 3½in (9cm) high.
£30–35 *DOL*

A Pedigree hard plastic walking doll, with brown hair, pink bow, blue and red patterned dress and pale blue shoes, c1950, 21in (53cm) high.
£75–85 *CMF*

A Mabel Lucie Attwell green felt pyjama case, with green hat and brown checked bow, c1930, 22in (56cm) high.
£200–250 *DOL*

Bisque

A Steiner Series C pressed bisque-headed *bébé*, with blue paperweight eyes, on fully-jointed wood and composition body, French, c1855, 28in (71cm) high.
£5,500–6,000 *Bon(C)*

An Armand Marseille bisque-headed doll, with weighted brown glass eyes, open mouth, strawberry blonde wig, fully jointed wood and composition body, wearing a beige sailor outfit with beret, mould No. 390, German, c1900, 22in (56cm) high.
£250–280 *Bon(C)*

An E.D. *bébé*, wearing blue sailor suit, by Emile Douillet, French, 1890s, 16in (40.5cm) high.
£1,150–1,350 *GrD*

E.D. dolls were produced by Emile Douillet when he was the director of the Jumeau factory from 1892 to 1899.

A Gebrüder Krauss bisque-headed mulatto doll, with jointed body, with a red and white striped dress, incised 'G.K.', c1905, 11in (28cm) high.
£200–250 *YC*

A Schoenau and Hoffmeister bisque-headed doll, with mohair wig, sleeping eyes and jointed body, c1900, 15in (38cm) high.
£300–350 *STK*

A J. D. Kestner bisque-headed girl doll, with jointed composition body, wearing a pale blue and white net dress, incised 'J.D.K. 168', German, c1900, 19in (48cm) high.
£600–700 *YC*

l. A Simon & Halbig doll, with weighted blue glass eyes, pierced ears, original hair wig, fully jointed wood and composition body, incised, 'K☆R 43', c1905, 17in (43cm) high.
£300–350 *Bon(C)*

A Catterfelder Puppen-fabrik bisque-headed toddler doll, with composition body, dressed in beige sailor suit, incised 'C. P. 208', c1914, 15¾in (40cm) high.
£350–400 *YC*

A Franz Schmitt character baby doll, dressed in blue checked outfit, c1915, 16in (40.5cm) high.
£600–700 *GrD*

An S. F. B. J. bisque-headed character baby, with five-piece body, 'jewel' eyes and mohair wig, wearing a knitted costume, small restoration, mould No. 236, c1915, 18in (45.5cm) high.
£700–800 *STK*

A pair of Gebrüder Heubach bisque dome-headed character boy and girl dolls, in original costumes contained in a green quilted hamper, c1915, dolls 12in (30.5cm) high.
£1,200–1,500 *STK*

A Heubach Kopplesdorf 399 bisque-headed doll, with composition five-piece body, dressed in black and white checked outfit, 1920s, 15in (38cm) high.
£400–450 *GrD*

l. A Rose O'Neill Kewpie doll, signed under feet, c1925, 8½in (21.5cm) high.
£600–700 *GrD*

Kewpie dolls became extremely popular in the 1920s. They were based on the work of American illustrator Rose O'Neill, whose cupid-like figures (hence the doll's name) appeared in the Ladies' Home Journal *from 1909. Modelled by Joseph Kallus under O'Neill's supervision, the first bisque Kewpie dolls were made by Kestner in 1913. Demand was huge, and Kewpies were soon being produced by many other companies in Germany and the USA. Kewpies were made in every medium from cloth to celluloid, but the most sought after examples today are bisque models. Dolls are often marked on the foot with O'Neill's signature and may have a circular or heart-shaped label on their bodies. Beware, however, since some unauthorised Japanese Kewpies have faked labels. Kewpies were made in various sizes, including miniature versions.*

Miller's is a price GUIDE not a price LIST

A German all-bisque piano baby, c1925, 10¾in (27cm) long.
£220–250 *YC*

l. A German bisque-headed googly-eyed doll, wearing white crochet dress, by Demalcol, 1920s, 10in (25.5cm) high.
£600–700 *BaN*

Three bisque-headed miniature character dolls, dressed in bright costumes, 1920s, 5in (12.5cm) high.
£30–35 each *CHU*

Wax Dolls

A poured wax fashion doll, with glass eyes, wearing silk mourning gown and underclothes, possibly French, c1880, 18in (46cm) high.
£600–650 *Bon(C)*

r. Two French wax-over-composition fashion shoulder doll's heads, with painted eyes and mouths, blonde mohair wigs, slight damage, late 19thC, 6¼in (16cm) high.
£350–400 *S(S)*

A Mad Alice-type wax-over-composition doll, with blue glass eyes, brown real hair wig, kid leather arms, original white dress and underclothes, c1880, 19in (48cm) high.
£150–200 *Bon (C)*

'Mad Alice' or 'Crazy Alice' dolls were manufactured from c1830. They were so-called because of the slit in their heads, into which the hair was inserted.

Wax-over-composition Dolls

Wax-over-composition dolls were made from a moulded core of composition (a mixture of wood pulp, plaster of Paris, glue and other products), which was then painted or dipped in wax. This provided a cheaper alternative to poured wax dolls, built up from several layers of molten wax, and far more time-consuming to produce. Another main type of wax-over-composition doll was the pumpkin head, popular from c1860, with large, hollow, rounded faces. Heads conforming to neither of these distinctive models are simply known as 'wax-overs'.

r. A poured wax baby doll, possibly by Pierotti, with brown glass eyes, inserted blonde hair on a shoulder plate to cloth body, with wax lower arms and legs, wearing a white christening gown, underclothes and lace bonnet, c1880, 21in (53cm) high.
£240–280 *Bon(C)*

A German wax-headed doll, with a cloth body, composition arms, in original pale blue dress, cream bonnet and bow, c1890, 20½in (52cm) high.
£250–300 *YC*

A German wax-over-composition doll, with opening and closing eyes, in original beige dress with brown bows and edging, c1890, 23in (58.5cm) high.
£150–200 *GrD*

Dolls' Clothes

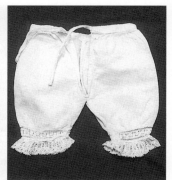

A French *bébé* doll's dress, in fine cream wool overlaid with lace, some moth damage to wool, c1885.
£300–350 *STK*

A Jumeau-style cream cotton dress, with lace trim, c1890.
£250–300 *STK*

A pair of doll's white cotton pantaloons, with lace trim, early 20thC.
£4–6 *CHU*

Dolls' House Furniture

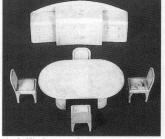

A whatnot and desk, made by Napoleonic prisoners of war, early 19thC, desk 3in (7.5cm) high.
£200–220 each *HOB*

A doll's house dining room set, comprising a Bakelite table, chairs and sideboard, c1930, sideboard 5½in (14cm) wide.
£25–30 *ARo*

l. A doll's library table, with drawers, c1970, 4in (10cm) diam.
£50–60 *HOB*

A pink plastic dressing table, c1960, 4in (10cm) high.
£8–10 *ARo*

Dolls' Houses

l. A late Victorian doll's house, the hinged front opening to reveal 3 floors with central staircase and opening doors to 6 rooms containing filigree metal and wooden furniture, dolls and accessories, 44in (112cm) high.
£2,500–3,000 *RTo*

A Christian Hacker wooden doll's house, in 4 detachable sections, damaged and restored, and a small quantity of furniture, c1900, 31in (79cm) high.
£700–800 *S(S)*

A doll's house, the front with white pebble-dash effect and green wooden door, grey paper printed tiled roof, 1930s, 26in (66cm) high.
£90–110 *Bon(C)*

EIGHTIES

The market for collectables moves extremely swiftly and collectors are already beginning to 'lay down' objects from the 1980s. In British politics the dominant figure of the decade was Margaret Thatcher, the most famous prime minister since Winston Churchill and WWII. Thatcher memorabilia is already sought after. The powerful, often negative emotions she inspired are vividly expressed in some of the more humorous commemoratives.

Spitting Image, the TV programme launched in 1984, led the field in satirizing contemporary celebrities, and the associated merchandise, particularly the Carlton Ware ceramics, captures the mood of the period and is becoming increasingly collectable. Royalty was a favourite *Spitting Image* target, and 1981 provided such material as the Royal Wedding and the emergence of

that other great female icon of the decade, Diana, Princess of Wales.

The eighties saw the creation of the male 'Yuppie', in red braces, with mobile phone in one hand and Filofax in the other. His female equivalent was the power-dressed, shoulder-padded executive, scented with Christian Dior's Poison and sipping designer mineral water.

Design was the buzz word of the decade in which favourite household items included black ash furniture, chromium or polished steel accessories, and ruched blinds in shiny glazed chintz. Included here is a small selection of items celebrating events and personalities of the period. Eighties material can be found elsewhere in the book, including our new sections on Vivienne Westwood (page 444) and computer games (page 446).

A one pound note, from the last issue, 1978–1981.
£15–20   *WP*

A skit note, with a portrait of Margaret Thatcher, issued in London by the Bank of Greenland, printed 'For the Avarice and Self-Indulgence of the Comp[a] of Brewer Jones Knowles', c1985, 6in (15cm) wide.
£4–5   *WP*

A mug, commemorating the 1979 General Election, impressed 'England', 3½in (9cm) high.
£30–40   *BRT*

A plastic figure of Mrs Thatcher, dressed in blue, made in Taiwan, 6in (15cm) high.
£15–20   *CWo*

When squeezed the figure breaks wind.

A South Atlantic medal, with rosette and Naval Long Service medal awarded to Petty Officer (EW) I. J. Stevens, Royal Navy, 1980s.
£200–225   *RMC*

Falklands medals and memorabilia are attracting an increasing number of collectors.

A badge, commemorating the Royal Wedding Day, 29 July 1981, 2in (5cm) diam.
£6–7   *LEG*

l. A Christmas card, sent by Prince Charles and Princess Diana to a Mrs Laurence, December 1984, 6in (15cm) high.
£3,750–4,000 *FRa*

A Wedgwood pint-size mug, commemorating the birth of Prince Henry, 15 September 1984, printed in blue, limited edition of 1,000, 4in (10cm) high.
£40–60 *W&S*

An Alessi stainless steel and plastic kettle, designed by Michael Graves, 1984–85, 10in (25.5cm) high, with box.
£60–70 *PC*

A green and gold perfume bottle, in the form of a bracelet, containing Christian Dior's Poison perfume, 1980s, 4in (10cm) diam.
£60–80 *LBr*

A Butler & Wilson Christmas tree brooch, made from multi-coloured rhinestones, 1980s, 4in (10cm) high.
£85–95 *CRIS*

A signed colour photograph of Michael Jackson, 1980s, 10 x 8in (25.5 x 20.5cm).
£350–400 *FRa*

A Kylie and Jason record, 'Especially for You', c1988, 7¼in (18.5cm) square.
50p–£1.00 *TRE*

A colour photograph of George Michael and Hot 100 singles chart list, showing his 'Father Figure' at No. 1, signed in bold red ink, 1980s, chart list 13in (33cm) high.
£125–150 *FRa*

A black cotton jacket, from *The Tube*, a Tyne Tees TV show, 1980s.
£30–35 *DOM*

l. A colour photograph of Tom Cruise, as he appeared in *Top Gun*, signed in black ink, 1980s, 10 x 8in (25.5 x 20.5cm).
£150–175 *FRa*

EPHEMERA

A *Brear's Monthly Diary and District Time Table*, October 1888, 3 x 2in (7.5 x 5cm).
£4–5 *BAf*

An Official Guide to Stratford-upon-Avon, early 1900s, 6½in (16.5cm) high.
£7–8 *MRW*

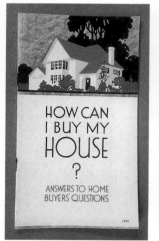

A buyer's guide to house purchase, c1936, 8in (20.5cm) high.
£5–6 *MRW*

A collection of theatre programmes from the Gaiety Theatre, 1860s–80s, 10 x 8in (25.5 x 20.5cm).
£45–55 *VS*

The Spotter's Book of Car Crests, in presentation album, c1956, 5 x 8in (12.5 x 20.5cm).
£20–25 *VS*

> **Cross Reference**
> Books

British Birds, a Worthington booklet, with caricature sketches and verse, 1960s, 10 x 7in (25.5 x 17.5cm).
£20–25 *VS*

A collection of theatre programmes from the Comedy Theatre, 1880s–90s, 10 x 6in (25.5 x 15cm).
£25–30 *VS*

Four theatre programmes for Royal Command Performances at the London Palladium, slight damage, 1932–34 and 1937, 12 x 8in (30.5 x 20.5cm).
£120–140 *VS*

A political promotional leaflet, for Chris Patten, Conservative MP for Bath, 1970s, 8 x 12in (20.5 x 30.5cm).
£2–3 *SVB*

A Glyndebourne programme, signed by the cast and conductor, c1978, 12 x 9½in (30.5 x 24cm).
£20–25 *AHa*

Autographs

'Autograph collecting is a personality cult,' says Poppy Collinson, at Fraser's Autograph Gallery in London. 'The more interesting and attractive the person, the more desirable their signature.' The market, however, is influenced by fashion, and values fluctuate along with the popularity of the individual concerned. 'A Michael Jackson signature, for example, is far less sought after today than in the 1980s,' explains Collinson. 'On the other hand, interest in Diana, Princess of Wales, was waning before her death, but now, as you might expect, demand is huge.'

Prices are not only affected by the subjects themselves, but also by the medium on which the autograph is inscribed. The most desirable objects tend to be signed photographs. Next in line are letters with important content or good quality signed contracts, followed by signed programmes (the more significant the event the higher the value), and, finally, pages from autograph books. Timing matters too, and it is generally better to have signatures from subjects at the height of their fame rather than those from later in their lives.

Autographs can be purchased from dealers and auction houses, but for fans and autograph hunters who track down the celebrities in person, Collinson offers the following advice: 'Get a signature on a photograph or something more interesting and personal than just an autograph book. Try to get non-dedicated signatures, and if you can persuade the subject to do a little drawing or add a quote or a comment, all the better.' As with all works on paper, autographs should be kept out of direct sunlight and preserved in acid-free mounts.

l. Ronnie Biggs, a signed card inscribed 'The Brain of the Great Train Robbery', 1963, 3 x 5in (7.5 x 12.5cm).
£65–75 *FRa*

r. Marlene Dietrich, a framed black and white photograph, signed in later years, c1940, 9 x 7in (23 x 18cm).
£160–170 *DOM*

A copy of the sports weekly *The Game*, signed by all 11 of England's cup winning team for the 1966 World Cup championships, 1970, 11¾ x 8¾in (29.5 x 22cm).
£775–875 *FRa*

Stan Laurel and Oliver Hardy, a signed page with a large photograph, mounted, framed and glazed, 1930s, 18 x 16in (45.5 x 40.5cm).
£100–120 *HAM*

Pope John Paul II, a signed colour photograph, 19th October 1996, 6 x 4in (15 x 10cm).
£220–250 *VS*

Martin Luther King, a first day cover issued to honour the United Nations, 10th December, 1953, 6¼ x 4in (16 x 10cm) and photograph.
£2,500–2,750 *FRa*

Grace Kelly, a signed colour postcard, as Princess of Monaco, creased, late 1970s, 6 x 4in (15 x 10cm).
£130–150 *VS*

l. Madonna, a signed black and white photograph, 1995–6, 8 x 10in (20.5 x 25.5cm).
£170–200 *VS*

The Magpies, by Hagg, a black
and white caricature poster
of the Collingwood American
Football team mascot, signed
by members of the team,
1973, 28 x 23½in (71 x 59cm),
framed and glazed.
£40–50 *P(M)*

Robert Mitchum, a signed black
and white photograph, 1980s–90s,
10 x 8in (25.5 x 20.5cm).
£70–80 *DOM*

*r. Odette: The Story of a British
Agent*, by Jerrard Tickell, signed
by Odette and her husband Peter
Churchill, presented at a POW
reunion in 1950, 4th edition,
9 x 5½in (23 x 14cm).
£15–20 *MED*

Richard Milhous Nixon, a signed
and dedicated colour photograph,
c1974, 14 x 11in (35 x 28cm).
£1,000–1,250 *FRa*

Jodie Foster, Anthony
Hopkins and Scott
Glenn, in *Silence of
the Lambs*, a signed
black and white
photograph, 1990s,
10 x 8in (25.5 x 20.5cm).
£170–200 *VS*

Ellen Terry, a signed
and inscribed hardback
souvenir programme
for the Ellen Terry
Jubilee Commemoration
1856–1906, slight
damage, 12 x 10in
(30.5 x 25.5cm).
£40–50 *VS*

l. W. H. Thompson,
a signed hardback
edition of *Sixty Minutes
With Winston Churchill*,
sun discolouration to
spine, 1956, 8 x 6in
(20.5 x 15cm).
£25–30 *VS*

Cigarette & Trade Cards

W. D. & H. O. Wills, Soldiers of the
World, set of 52, 1895.
£950–1,150 *LCC*

Ogden's Cigarettes,
Henry Vardon, 1902.
£40–50 *HALL*

Smith's Tobacco, Medals,
set of 50, 1902.
£400–450 *LCC*

Lambert & Butler, Birds and
Eggs, set of 50, 1906.
£120–140 *MAr*

W. D. & H. O. Wills, Vanity
Fair, 2nd Series, 1902.
£120–140 *VS*

Lambert & Butler, Motors,
set of 25, 1908.
£575–625 *LCC*

John Player & Sons, Arms and
Armour, set of 50, 1909.
£90–110 *MAr*

John Player & Sons, Historic
Ships, set of 10, 1910.
£40–45 *MAr*

Muratti, Sons & Co, Crowned
Heads, set of 35, 1912.
£400–450 *LCC*

John Player & Sons,
Regimental Uniforms,
set of 25, 1912.
£70–85 *MAr*

r. Taddy & Co, Honours &
Ribbons, set of 25, 1915.
£350–400 *MAr*

Thompson & Porteous,
V. C. Heroes, set of 41, 1915.
£400–450 *LCC*

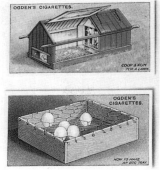

Ogden's Ltd, Poultry
Rearing and Management,
set of 25, 1923.
£35–40 *VS*

J. Sainsbury Ltd, Foreign Birds,
set of 12 tea cards, 1924.
£60–65 *LCC*

A. Boguslavsky, Sports
Records, set of 50, 1925.
£65–75 *LCC*

Ogden's Ltd,
Modern British
Pottery, set of
50, 1925.
£35–45 *MAr*

J. Sinclair, British Sea Dogs,
set of 50, 1926.
£80–100 *VS*

John Player &
Sons, Straight
Line Caricatures,
set of 50, 1926.
£15–20 *MAr*

John Player & Sons,
Ship Models,
set of 20, 1926.
£40–45 *MAr*

r. John Player &
Sons, Game Birds
and Wild Fowl,
set of 50, 1927.
£55–65 *MAr*

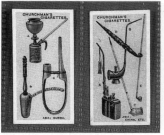

W. A. & A. C. Churchman,
Pipes of the World,
set of 25, 1927.
£50–60 *MAr*

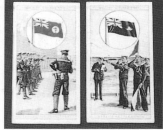

W. D. & H. O. Wills, Flags of
the Empire, set of 25, 1929.
£20–25 *LCC*

W. A. & A. C. Churchman,
Prominent Golfers, Gene
Sarazen, 1931.
£45–50 *HALL*

Ardath Tobacco Co Ltd,
Famous Film Stars,
set of 50, 1934.
£35–40 *MAr*

John Player & Sons,
Cricketers, set of 50, 1934.
£35–40 *MAr*

r. W. D. & H. O. Wills,
The Reign of H. M.
King George V,
set of 50, 1935.
£20–25 *LCC*

John Player & Sons,
Kings & Queens
of England,
set of 50, 1935.
£50–60 *MAr*

r. Lambert & Butler,
Dance Band Leaders,
set of 25, c1936.
£80–90 *MAr*

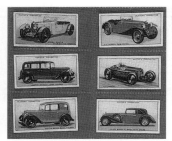

Lambert & Butler, Empire Air
Routes, set of 50, 1936.
£70–80 *MAr*

John Player & Sons, Motor
Cars, set of 50, 1936.
£50–60 *MAr*

W. D. & H. O. Wills, Household
Hints, set of 50, 1936.
£8–9 *LCC*

Typhoo Tea, Interesting
Events in British History,
set of 25, 1938.
£10–12 *LCC*

Senior Service Cigarettes,
British Railways,
set of 48, 1938.
£25–30 *LCC*

W. D. & H. O. Wills, The King's
Art Treasures, set of 40, 1938.
£10–12 *LCC*

l. Ogden's Ltd, British
Birds & Their Eggs,
set of 50, 1939.
£50–60 *VS*

W. D. & H. O. Wills,
Garden Flowers,
set of 50, 1939.
£12–15 *LCC*

l. R. & J. Hill, Famous
Ships, set of 40, 1940.
£35–40 *LCC*

An album for 1st series of Brooke Bond cards, British Birds, set of 20, 1954, 7¼ x 5in (18.5 x 12.5cm).
£100–120 *FMu*

Carreras Ltd, Famous British Flyers, 2 missing from set of 50, 1956.
£30–35 *VS*

John Barker's bubble gum, Famous People, set of 24, 1961.
£16–18 *LCC*

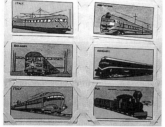

Clevedon Cigarette Card Album, with complete set of Trains of the World, 1962, 5in (12.5cm) square.
£40–45 *VS*

Kellogg Co, Famous Firsts, set of 12, 1963.
£1–2 *LCC*

Primrose Confectionery, Dad's Army, set of 25, 1973.
£1–2 *LCC*

Carreras Ltd, British Birds, set of 50, 1976.
£3–4 *LCC*

Golden Era, Land Rover, set of 7, 1996.
£2–3 *LCC*

l. Kellogg Co, Gardens to Visit, set of 20, 1987.
£3–4 *LCC*

Prints & Posters

A Baxter print, entitled
'Puss Napping', No. 266, signed,
overmounted and framed,
1830s, 4 x 5in (10 x 12.5cm).
£80–90 *SAS*

*George Baxter (1804–67) began
his career as a wood engraver
of book illustrations before
developing his own process of
printing in oil colours using
metal and wooden blocks. He
patented his invention in 1835,
subsequently licensing it to
other publishers including
Abraham Le Blond (1819–94),
who copied many of his works.
Baxter covered a wide range
of popular subjects, from
sentimental genre pictures to
great personalities of the day.
Colour prints, however, are prone
to fading and values today
depend very much on condition.*

A Baxter print, entitled 'His
Royal Highness Prince of Wales',
No. 211, overmounted and framed,
1840s, 3 x 2in (7.5 x 5cm).
£60–70 *SAS*

> **Cross Reference**
> Advertising & Packaging

A Baxter print of Sir Robert
Peel and Admiral Lord Nelson,
c1860, 6 x 7¾in (15 x 19.5cm).
£140–160 *TVM*

A Baxter print, entitled 'The
First Lesson', No. 262, over-
mounted and framed, 1840s,
8 x 7in (20 x 17.5cm).
£70–80 *SAS*

A Shell advertising poster,
depicting Dinton Castle near
Aylesbury, inscribed 'You Can
Be Sure of Shell', Landmark
Series No. 450, c1930,
30 x 45in (76 x 114cm).
£175–225 *ONS*

A Le Blond print, entitled
'Returning from Prayer', No. 161,
the reverse with blue printed Le
Blond label, over-mounted and
framed, c1850, 6 x 4in (15 x 10cm).
£35–40 *SAS*

r. A poster, inscribed 'ARP,
Where's yours?', c1938,
15 x 10ins (38 x 25.5cm).
£45–50 *PC*

A Raymond Peynet lithograph,
limited edition of 35, signed in
pencil, 1950s–60s, 20 x 15in
(51 x 38cm).
£220–250 *RDG*

FANS

An ivory-inlaid fan, hand-painted in pale blue, pink and green on vellum, 1830–40, 10in (25.5cm) wide.
£300–350 *JPr*

Two dance cards/fans: *l.* carved ivory painted in pink and red, *r.* carved mother-of-pearl and ivory, pencils missing, 1840–50, 4½in (11.5cm) wide.
£50–60 each *VB*

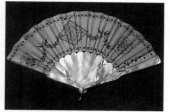

A silk fan, decorated in blue, purple and pink on a buff ground, with mother-of-pearl sticks, c1850, 13in (33cm) wide.
£150–180 *JPr*

A Victorian Brussels lace fan, with mother-of-pearl sticks, 18in (45.5cm) wide.
£80–90 *VB*

A blue and white silk leaf fan, with fine worked net panels and gilded bone sticks, c1870, 16in (40.5cm) wide.
£100–120 *VB*

A black and white ostrich feather fan, with tortoise-shell sticks, c1890, 18in (45.5cm) wide.
£30–40 *JPr*

Seven miniature brooches, earrings and charms, in the form of fans, 1900–30, ½–1¾in (1–4.5cm) wide.
£5–15 each *VB*

A black machine lace fan, with wooden sticks, hand-painted with a Dutch scene, 1920s, 13in (33cm) wide.
£20–30 *JPr*

A tortoiseshell fan, 1910–20, 6in (15cm) wide.
£80–100 *JPr*

A Chinese embroidered silk and ivory fan, in hand-painted box, c1920, 15in (38cm) wide.
£150–180 *JPr*

A Japanese hand-painted paper and lacquered bamboo fan, decorated in black and red on a yellow ground, 1930s, 7in (17.5cm) wide.
£15–20 *DAC*

Two wooden handled fans, one painted with a temple within a decorative ring, the other with a mountain landscape, by Bernard Leach, both signed 'BL' and dated '53', 10¼in (26cm) diam.
£3,300–3,600 *Bon*

FIFTIES
Ceramics

A Beswick fruit bowl, painted in black and white with red interior, influenced by Zambezi pattern, designed by Jim Hayward, c1956, 14in (35.5cm) wide.
£45–55 *RAT*

A Ridgway Pottery Homemaker pattern cup and saucer, decorated in black and white, made for Woolworth's, c1955, cup 3¼in (8.5cm) high.
£10–15 *RAT*

A Burleigh ware vase, hand-painted in grey and black with a turquoise interior, 1950s, 8in (20.5cm) high.
£40–50 *RAT*

A Villeroy & Boch jug, c1950, 6in (15cm) high.
£12–14 *UTP*

l. A Washington Pottery trio, with pale blue polka dot border, c1954, cup 3½in (9cm) high.
£10–15 *RAT*

A 'Cow Jumped Over the Moon' cookie jar, by Robbinson Ransbottom Pottery, 1950s, 9in (23cm) high.
£95–115 *EKK*

Cookie jars are a favourite American collectable. The subject received huge publicity when Andy Warhol's famous cookie jar collection was sold after his death in 1987; however, the high prices paid for containers belonging to the pop artist bear little relation to the values of similar pieces without such a glamorous provenance. Cookie jars were made in a huge range of styles, often in novelty, figural shapes. Different manufacturers sometimes used identical moulds, so the same design could be produced by several factories. Cookie jars were created as fun, affordable objects (not as fine china) and, given the nature of their contents, were handled by children; hence lids were damaged or broken, and collectors should also check for chips and flaking paint.

Fashion

A basket-weave handbag, with brass fittings, 1950s, 10in (25.5cm) wide.
£70–80 *LBr*

l. A cream satin evening dress, embroidered with gold and silver beads, by John Cavanagh, 1950s.
£120–150 *TT*

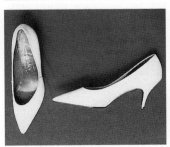

A pair of Clarks white stiletto heeled shoes, unworn, c1955.
£8–10 *CHU*

An American gold hard plastic
handbag, with clear lucite
lid and handle, c1950,
8in (20.5cm) long.
£180–200 *LBr*

A white hard plastic handbag,
with clear lucite lid, 1950s,
10in (25.5cm) long.
£160–180 *LBr*

l. A 'Waspie' or waist nipper,
by Corsets Charmereine, Paris,
1950s, 26in (66cm) long.
£4–5 *PER*

*Fifties fashions required a small
waist, and the 'waspie' served as
a mini corset.*

A pair of Bluebird 15 denier
nylons, size 9½, including a
card with a picture of Robert
Wagner, inscribed 'The
stockings sponsored by the
stars', 1950s, pack 10 x 7in
(25.5 x 18cm).
£9–10 *RAD*

Furnishings

A black metal magazine
rack, with yellow feet
and handle, 1950s,
15in (38cm) high.
£15–20 *TWa*

A black and gold painted
iron fire screen, 1950s,
28in (71cm) high.
£40–50 *RAT*

r. A ceiling light,
with 3 orange
misted glass
shades, 1950s,
18in (45.5cm) wide.
£65–80 *TWa*

l. A two-tone
Formica side-
board, early
1950s, 60in
(152.5cm) wide.
£120–150 *RAT*

FIREPLACE FURNITURE

A wrought iron log fork, c1550,
36in (31.5cm) long.
£650–800 *PC*

A set of mechanical fire bellows,
c1880, 21in (53.5cm) long.
£175–200 *JUN*

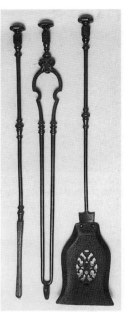

A set of steel fire
irons, early 19thC,
29½in (75cm) long.
£750–850 *PC*

A pair of lazy tongs, c1880,
24in (61cm) long.
£40–50 *ET*

A copper helmet-shaped coal scuttle,
19thC, 20in (51cm) long.
£175–200 *SPa*

A brass coal scuttle and shovel,
with black turned handles,
restored and repolished,
c1890, 13in (33cm) high.
£175–200 *LCA*

A Patent Portable Fire Escape, c1890,
15in (38cm) long.
£40–45 *WAB*

r. A pair of steel and brass fire tongs
and shovel, c1890, 36in (91.5cm) long.
£175–200 *DAC*

A brass and copper fire screen,
c1890, 29in (73.5cm) high.
£120–135 *GBr*

An Edwardian cast silver toasting fork, with rosewood handle,
19in (48cm) long.
£120–150 *PSA*

GAMES

GAMES

A Chinese carved ivory
intaglio puzzle box, c1840,
2in (5cm) square.
£100–120 *MB*

A Victorian coromandel games
compendium, by H. Rodrigues,
Piccadilly, London, with hinged
lid containing draughts/
backgammon board opening
to reveal 3 removable red
leather fitted trays, split
hinged front opening to
reveal ivory chess pieces,
14in (35.5cm) wide.
£1,600–1,800 *AH*

r. A Staunton club size
ebony and boxwood
weighted chess set,
kings stamped 'Jacques,
London', c1900, king
4⅛in (11.5cm) high.
£1,600–1,800 *TMi*

A selection of various wood and
bone spinning tops, 1880–1930,
1–1¾in (2.5–4.5cm) high.
£8–25 each *VB*

A Chinese export ivory chess set,
c1840, king 8¼in (21cm) high.
£3,500–4,000 *TMi*

*These chess pieces are ususual as
they are exceptionally large.*

An ivory Lund-type chess set,
c1860, king 3in (7.5cm) high.
£500–600 *TMi*

A set of playing cards and a
miniature dominoes set,
1890–1910, 2in (5cm) wide.
£15–45 each *VB*

Locate the Source

**The source of each
illustration in Miller's can
be found by checking the
code letters below each
caption with the Key
to Illustrations.**

r. A brass whist marker,
c1920, 4in (10cm) diam.
£15–20 *WAB*

A Burmese ivory chess set,
c1850, king 3½in (9cm) high.
£450–500 *TMi*

A mahogany, coromandel
and birch, chess/
backgammon board, c1870,
11½ x 20in (29 x 51cm).
£400–450 *GeM*

A mahjong set, with bone tiles,
in a brass-mounted wooden
box, c1920, 9in (23cm) wide.
£200–225 *MB*

A Put and Take celluloid spinning top, c1920, 1½in (3.5cm) high.
£14–16 *VB*

Put and Take, very popular in the early 1920s, was a game of chance derived from an earlier game called Teetotum. It was played by spinning a faceted top, each side inscribed with letters, numbers or symbols and signifying a different course of action. Once the top had come to rest, players followed the instructions on the uppermost side.

A dice thrower, with a brass and beech base and glass dome top, c1920, 5¾in (14.5cm) high.
£1,600–1,800 *INC*

A pack of Gibbs Happy Families playing cards, 1940s–50s, 3in (7.5cm) wide.
£4–5 *TRE*

A travelling draughts and noughts and crosses set, c1930, 5¼in (13cm) square.
£40–50 *GeM*

A game of Owzthat, c1950, 1in (2.5cm) wide.
£14–16 *VB*

r. A hand-carved king, from a garden chess set, 1960s, 24in (61cm) high.
£450–500 *FB*

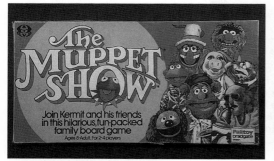

A Palitoy *Muppet Show* board game, c1977, 20in (50.5cm) wide.
£35–40 *ARo*

r. A 3D money jigsaw, with specs for 3D viewing, c1990.
£4–5 *WP*

GARDEN COLLECTABLES

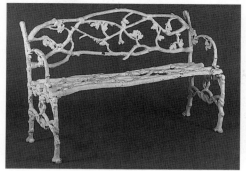

An elm wheelbarrow, painted light green, 19thC, 58in (147.5cm) long.
£250–300 *SWN*

A Victorian Coalbrookdale white painted cast iron garden seat, with naturalistic fruiting vine design, 51¼in (130cm) long.
£500–600 *WL*

l. An earthenware garden gnome, wearing a purple hat, red jacket and green trousers, seated under a red toadstool, c1900, 25in (63.5cm) high.
£450–500 *GNR*

A fruit picker's wooden carrier, c1900, 20in (50.5cm) high.
£75–85 *WEE*

A Shanks Arbroath Brivisher lawn mower, 1920s.
£60–75 *JUN*

r. A hard plastic gnome, wearing red hat and blue jacket, 1950–60, 13in (33cm) high.
£5–10 *TWa*

Three turfing irons, c1900, largest 55in (139.5cm) long.
£25–30 each *AL*

A reconstituted stone gnome, with red hat and green boots, 1930s, 36in (91.5cm) high.
£200–240 *DRU*

A French wooden trug, c1920, 12in (30.5cm) wide.
£15–20 *AL*

A 2½ gallon galvanized watering can, with copper rose, early 1930s, 17in (43cm) high.
£30–40 *SMI*

GLASS

A sweetmeat glass, with
notched rim, centre knop
stem and domed foot,
c1755, 7in (17.5cm) high.
£300–350 *GS*

A Bristol blue egg cup,
with opaline rim, c1790,
3in (7.5cm) high.
£120–140 *FD*

A pillar-cut wine glass rinser,
c1820, 4in (10cm) high.
£40–50 *JHa*

A sweetmeat glass, the
double ogee bowl with
moulded panels and a
dentated rim, supported on
a multi-spiral opaque twist
stem and radially grooved
foot, c1760, 4in (10cm) high.
£300–350 *GS*

A pair of bonnet glasses, with
serrated rims and segmented bowls,
on square lemon squeezer feet,
c1800, 3¾in (9.5cm) high.
£140–170 *GS*

*Bonnet glasses were used for
sweetmeats. A lemon squeezer foot is
dome-shaped with moulded ribs,
usually on a solid square base.*

An oval cut-glass butter dish,
cover and stand, all cut with
bands of diamonds and prisms,
with crenellated rim and ball
finial, c1800, 6¼in 16cm) high.
£500–550 *Som*

l. An amethyst glass cream jug, with
overall honeycomb moulding, foot ring and
loop handle, c1700, 3¼in (8.5cm) high.
£380–420
r. A blue wrythen glass sugar basin,
with folded rim, c1800, 2½in (6.5cm) high.
£100–120 *Som*

A blue wrythen-moulded
glass sugar basin, with hollow
conical, folded foot, c1800,
3¼in (8.5cm) high.
£150–175 *Som*

FURTHER READING
*Miller's Glass of the '20s &
'30s: A Collector's Guide*
Miller's Publications, 1999

A free-blown glass fly trap,
on 3 blob feet, early 19thC,
7in (18cm) high.
£55–65 *FD*

A glass cream jug, engraved with roses, thistles and shamrocks, c1820, 4½in (11.5cm) high.
£100–120 *JHa*

A glass comport and cover, cut with stylised leaves between diamond panels, on a radial cut foot, c1820–30, 6¼in (16cm) high.
£150–180 *JHa*

A glass tazza, the rimmed flat platform on a stem with pedestal moulded stalk and 3 neck rings below, on a domed folded foot, c1740, 10¼in (26cm) diam.
£250–300

A set of 6 jelly glasses with flared trumpet bowls, on plain conical feet, c1830, 4¼in (10.5cm) high.
£150–170 *Som*

A Scottish cut-glass bowl, c1830, 8in (20.5cm) high.
£220–250 *BWA*

A cranberry glass jug, slight flaw in handle, 19thC, 9in (23cm) high.
£100–125 *DQ*

A pink glass hanging basket, with clear glass handle, on a clear glass support in the form of a serpent, c1880, 9in (23cm) high.
£345–385 *MJW*

A Fenton Carnival glass Orange Tree hatpin holder, in blue base glass, 1908–25, 5½in (14cm) high.
£250–300 *ASe*

A Millersburg Carnival glass Peacock and Urn fruit bowl, with satin finished iridescence on amethyst base glass, 1909–11, 6in (15cm) diam.
£150–175 *ASe*

An Imperial Carnival glass Pansy sugar bowl and milk jug, in amber base glass, 1910–25, 3½in (9cm) high.
£120–135 *ASe*

An American cut-glass bowl,
by Libbey Glass Co, marked,
1919–30, 8¾in (22.5cm) diam.
£300–330 *BrW*

A Bagley frosted glass Tulip light
and vase, c1936, 9½in (24cm) high.
Lamp £60–70
Vase £75–85 *PC*

A cut-glass powder
bowl and cover, c1930,
5½in (14cm) diam.
£40–50 *TAC*

A Gray-Stan yellow marbled
effect glass candlestick,
c1930, 5in (12.5cm) high.
£100–120 *TCG*

A Gray-Stan glass candlestick,
with a green, lilac and
white spiral pattern, c1930,
3in (7.5cm) high.
£55–65 *TCG*

A Lalique glass dish, decorated
with dandelion leaf pattern,
1930–40, 12in (30.5cm) diam.
£200–220 *DAC*

r. A Powell pink glass bowl,
1930s, 13in (33cm) diam.
£100–120 *TCG*

A Murano glass
figure, with lilac
and clear glass
body, 1950s,
14in (35.5cm) high.
£250–300 *TCG*

A clear glass swan, with
yellow wings and beak,
1960s, 7⅞in (20cm) high.
£10–12 *GIN*

A Powell yellow and amber
glass powder box and cover,
c1930, 3½in (9cm) high.
£80–100 *TCG*

r. A Wedgwood green glass
candleholder, with hollow
stem, labelled and engraved,
1960–70s, 11in (28cm) high.
£25–30 *TCG*

Decanters

An Irish ovoid glass decanter, the lower half fluted and moulded and engraved with fruiting vine, a rose spray and a thistle, 2 milled neck rings, moulded grid patterned disc stopper, c1810, 9in (23cm) high.
£340–380 *Som*

A glass toddy lifter, with flute- and printy-cut bowl, facet-cut neck and diamond-cut neck ring and lip, c1820, 6¼in (16cm) high.
£140–160 *Som*

Toddy lifters were used for decanting punch from the bowl to the glass.

A pair of glass claret jugs, with ovoid flute-cut bodies, strap handles, marked 'Sherry' and 'Claret', c1830, 6¾in (17cm) high.
£350–400 *Som*

An amber flashed glass decanter, etched with fruiting vine, c1840, 13in (33cm) high.
£180–200 *BELL*

A shaft-and-globe glass decanter, the neck cut with facets, the body and stopper with cut printies, 1880–1910, 10in (25.5cm) high.
£35–45 *JHa*

Two green glass onion-shaped carafes, each engraved with a band of thistles and roses, c1840, largest 9in (23cm) high.
£200–230 each *Som*

l. A blue glass jug decanter, with clear glass stopper and handle, c1880, 9½in (24cm) high.
£220–250 *MJW*

r. A wrythen dimpled glass decanter, with stopper, c1900, 12in (30.5cm) high.
£100–120 *JHa*

Although the original wrythen dimpled service was designed by Harry Powell for James Powell, (Whitefriars), c1880, it became so popular that many factories, including Walsh, Birmingham, Webb's, and Webb Corbett made their own variations.

Drinking Glasses

A wine and water glass, engraved with fruiting vine, c1740, 3¼in (8cm) high.
£275–300 *BrW*

A firing glass, with engraved ogee bowl, single series opaque-twist stem, on a terraced foot, c1765, 4in (10cm) high.
£350–400 *FD*

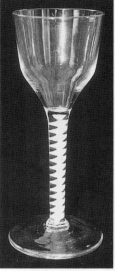

A wine glass, the ogee bowl supported on a single series opaque-twist stem, c1760, 6¼in (16cm) high.
£225–250 *GS*

A wine glass, the round funnel bowl with double knopped multiple spiral air-twist stem and plain conical foot, c1750, 6¾in (17cm) high.
£300–350 *Som*

l. A Sunderland Bridge glass rummer, with bucket bowl, on a blade knop stem, c1800, 6in (15cm) high.
£350–380 *FD*

r. A glass rummer, with engraved bowl c1810, 5¾in (14.5cm) high.
£200–220 *Som*

A bell bowl wine glass, on a double series opaque-twist stem, c1765, 6¼in (16cm) high.
£180–200 *JHa*

Drinking Glasses – Glossary of Terms

Cordial: small drinking glass for liqueurs.

Firing glass (bumping glass): short, sturdy drinking glass with a thick foot, used for toasting and rapping on the table.

Folded foot: the foot of a glass with its rim turned slightly under to provide a more solid, stable base.

Jacobite glass: 18th-century glass celebrating Bonnie Prince Charlie and his descendants and decorated with Jacobite symbols, motifs and mottoes.

Knop: bulge or raised ring in the stem of a drinking glass.

Ogee bowl: cylindrical bowl with a concave curve where it joins the stem.

Printies: a shallow-cut circular pattern on glass produced by using a slightly convex cutting wheel.

Prunts: blobs of glass applied to the stem of a drinking vessel both as decoration and to stop the glass from slipping in the hand.

Roemer (Römer): German drinking glass with a spherical bowl and wide hollow stem with prunts and a flared foot, often decorated with trailing.

Rummer: English goblet-shaped drinking glass with a stemmed foot.

Tear: air bubble, in the shape of a tear, encased in a glass stem.

Twists: decorations in drinking glass stems produced by twisting one or several rods of glass. There are said to be over 150 varieties of twists, ranging from air-twists, using embedded columns of air, to opaque-twists, decorated with threads of opaque glass.

Four turquoise wine glasses, c1825, largest 5¼in (13.5cm) high.
£70–90 each *Som*

An amber wine glass, the conical bowl with milled collar, hollow stem with raspberry prunts and trailed foot, c1830, 4in (10cm) high.
£120–140 *Som*

A bell-mouth glass, engraved with a horse and rider, c1830, 7in (18cm) high.
£200–240 *BWA*

A set of 8 green wine glasses, with panel-cut tulip bowls, c1830, 5in (13cm) high.
£350–400 *FD*

l. A glass goblet, the bowl engraved with stylised acanthus, on a hollow-cut pedestal stem, mid-19thC, 6¼in (16cm) high.
£65–75 *JHa*

A Bohemian green hock glass, with engraved bowl, on a clear glass stem, c1950, 8¼in (21cm) high.
£120–135 *MON*

An American champagne glass, made for the Shriner Convention, Pittsburgh, the bowl inscribed 'Syria', the stem in the form of tobacco leaves, 1909, 4½in (11.5cm) high.
£80–90 *ASe*

A Powell glass goblet, designed by G. T. Jackson for William Morris, c1870, 5¾in (14.5cm) high.
£100–120 *JHa*

l. A Bohemian amber hock glass, with engraved bowl and clear glass stem, c1965, 7¼in (18.5cm) high.
£30–40 *MON*

r. A glass tumbler, with smiley face, c1970, 4½in (11.5cm) high.
£5–6 *RCh*

A Roman gold ring, with a flat section band and an applied sheet gold bezel, stamped with a clasped hands motif, eastern European.
£300–350 *ANG*

A gilt-metal chatelaine, c1760, 6½in (16.5cm) long.
£1,750–2,000 *BEX*

A *pietra dura* brooch, set with shaded hardstones with a rose and other foliage, the glazed gold mount in the Etruscan revivalist manner, c1860, 2 x 1½in (5 x 3.5cm).
£900–1,000 *HofB*

l. A silver and agate brooch, in the form of a key, c1850, 3½in (9cm) long.
£500–600 *BWA*

A gold brooch, set with central amethyst, turquoises and pearls, 19thC, 1½in (3.5cm) long.
£140–155 *DAC*

l. A Victorian pinchbeck and amethyst cross pendant, 3in (7.5cm) long.
£50–60 *DAC*

A 9ct gold Albert chain, c1880, 17in (43cm) long.
£800–900 *GEM*

A selection of five metal and paste jewelled hat pins, 1900–15, largest 11in (28cm) long.
£30–45 each *VB*

A gold arrow brooch, set with a pearl, c1890, 2½in (6.5cm) long, in original case.
£60–80 *HofB*

l. A reverse intaglio bar brooch, decorated with the head of a dog, in a plain gold surround on 9ct gold bar, c1910, 3in (7.5cm) long.
£200–250 *HofB*

A Sibyl Dunlop necklace,
set with citrines, peridots
and tourmalines among
leaves, tendrils
and berries, 1920s,
18in (45.5cm) long,
and matching brooch.
£2,500–3,000   *P*

A French glass and gilt-
plated metal 'flapper'
necklace, 1930s.
£70–80   *GLT*

A Marcel Boucher pink
and green enamel and
paste orchid pin, c1940,
3¼in (8.5cm) high.
£400–450   *MAU*

A pair of cherub
earrings, by Joseff of
Hollywood, c1940.
£150–180   *GLT*

An Eisenberg brooch, set
with red and pink round
and baguette-shaped
diamanté with white
stone overlays, signed,
c1950, 2in (5cm) wide.
£300–350   *PKT*

A Warner insect brooch,
yellow metal with white
and green painted wings,
green painted bead body
and green diamanté
eyes, signed, c1955,
1½in (3.5cm) long.
£70–80   *PKT*

An American brooch,
set with aquamarine
rhinestones on a gold-
plated setting, 1940s,
2½in (6.5cm) high.
£70–80   *BaH*

A glass crystal and gilt bracelet and earrings
set, unsigned, probably by Schiaparelli, 1950s.
£230–260   *GLT*

A Hollycraft bracelet,
set with multi-coloured
paste stones, c1950,
7in (17.5cm) long.
£550–600   *MAU*

l. A Miriam Haskell gilt-metal
bangle, set with baroque pearls,
garnet and turquoise coloured
beads, 1950s, 2in (5cm) diam.
£400–450   *MAU*

r. A pair of Kenneth J. Lane
earrings, each body in the
shape of lions' heads, with
interchangeable plastic disc
drops, c1970, 2in (5cm) long.
£75–85   *PKT*

A bell metal skillet, inscribed on handle 'Warner', late 17thC, 8½in (21.5cm) diam.
£200–230 *ANV*

A hardwood and sycamore chopping block, c1890, 39in (99cm) long.
£475–525 *MTa*

A knife polisher, inscribed 'Harrods Limited London', early 20thC, 17in (43cm) high.
£250–280 *SMI*

A wooden flour barrel, early 20thC, 11in (28cm) high.
£85–95 *SMI*

A pair of copper flat-back kettles, suitable for use on a range, 19thC, 6in (15cm) high.
£240–265 *ANV*

r. A copper chestnut roaster, early 19thC, 28in (71cm) long.
£135–150 *SMI*

An Edwardian copper one gallon jug, marked 'ER/186', 10½in (26.5cm) high.
£80–100 *MEG*

r. A sycamore bread plate, with blue and white Willow pattern liner, early 20thC, 11in (28cm) diam.
£70–80 *SMI*

An American ice-cream scoop, c1908, 10in (25.5cm) long.
£80–100 *EKK*

An oak brass-bound butter churn, 19thC, 20¼in (51.5cm) high.
£150–185 *ANV*

Cox's Manual of Gelatine Cookery,
1930s, 7½in (19cm) high.
£10–12 *MRW*

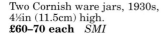

Two Cornish ware jars, 1930s,
4½in (11.5cm) high.
£60–70 each *SMI*

A Tala aluminium cook's
measure, and a glass measure
and egg tester, c1950,
5¾in (14.5cm) high.
£6–8 each *AL*

l. A set of Spillers
Homepride spice
jars and rack,
c1978, 14in
(35.5cm) wide.
£25–30 *AL*

An orange enamel bread bin,
c1930, 11½in (29cm) high.
£40–45 *B&R*

A Prestige stainless steel and
plastic egg beater, c1950,
11in (28cm) long.
£6–8 *AL*

A Hygene glass pourer jug,
c1950, 8in (20.5cm) high.
£6–8 *AL*

A handmade raffia tea cosy,
1930s, 12½in (32cm) wide.
£30–40 *SUS*

A Skyline whisk and slice,
1950s, 12in (30.5cm) long.
£2–3 each *AL*

A set of Nutbrown aluminium
cookie cutters, 1950s,
7in (18cm) long.
£6–8 *AL*

An *Alice in Wonderland* tea
tin, 1970s, 4½in (11.5cm) high.
£24–28 *HUX*

A Continental ceramic nightlight, in the form of a sailor boy, wired for electricity, c1928, 10½in (26.5cm) high.
£200–220 *BKK*

A French gilt-brass and crystal chandelier, 1920s, 35in (89cm) high.
£1,200–1,500 *JPr*

An oil lamp with iron base, the glass font with floral decoration, c1890, 23in (58.5cm) high.
£100–120 *TWa*

A brass oil lamp, with green glass shade and wooden base, c1920, 24½in (62cm) high.
£125–140 *TWa*

r. A moulded amber-coloured table lamp, in 2 sections, wired for electricity, c1930, 9in (23cm) high.
£120–140 *BKK*

A painted and marbled glass ceiling bowl hanging light, 1930s, 12½in (32cm) diam.
£30–40 *TWa*

A Bursley ware lamp, with original hand-painted shade, designed by Charlotte Rhead, pattern No. T. L. 76, 1940s, 15½in (39.5cm) high.
£280–320 *BDA*

A Pink Panther table light, 1970s, 20½in (52cm) high.
£15–20 *DUD*

A wood and celluloid galleon lamp, 1950s, 12in (30.5cm) high.
£18–25 *TWa*

l. A chrome triple ceiling lamp, 1960–70, 17in (43cm) wide.
£60–70 *TWa*

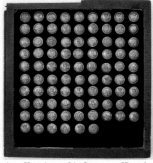

A collection of infantry officer's gilt numbered buttons, mounted on black velvet in an old wooden frame, c1860, frame 14in (35.5cm) high.
£1,300–1,500 *WAL*

r. A silver nail buffer, c1810, 4½in (11.5cm) wide.
£20–25 *VB*

A 21-piece silver dressing table set, made for a 21st birthday, hallmarked, complete in original silk-lined box, 1896, 21 x 15in (53 x 38cm).
£4,000–4,500 *PC*

l. A silver photograph frame, by J. & W. Deakin, Chester, c1902, 8½in (21.5cm) high.
£550–600 *THOM*

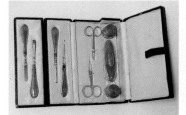

A French fireman's brass helmet, late 19thC.
£200–250 *ET*

A lady's travelling manicure set, with blue enamelled silver-gilt accessories, catch repaired, hallmarked Birmingham, c1926, case 8¾in (22cm) wide.
£300–350 *S*

A painted manhole cover, by Clark, Hunt & Co, Shoreditch, c1860, 12in (30.5cm) diam.
£30–40 *WAB*

A copper and brass water jug, c1900, 20in (50.5cm) high.
£85–95 *DQ*

l. Eight Edwardian silver and enamelled spoons, with decorative tops and crests celebrating various towns, events and views, 4¾in (12cm) long.
£10–15 each *VB*

A Hurtley cast iron Mammy door stop, 1900s, 12in (30.5cm) high.
£450–500 *SMAM*

A set of 4 silver salts and
spoons, Birmingham 1908,
box 17in (43cm) square.
£200–225 *WAC*

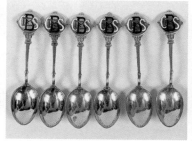

A set of 6 silver with enamel
teaspoons, Birmingham 1924,
4¼in (10.5cm) long.
£110–130 *CoHA*

A Continental silver singing
bird box, in the form of a
book, each corner set with
a cabochon amethyst,
opening to reveal a singing
bird and winding screw,
with sliding spine key
compartment, importation
mark for 1926, 4¼in x 3½in
(10.5 x 9cm) high.
£3,000–3,500 *DD*

A silver-plated condiment set,
in the neo-classical style, 1930s,
3in (7.5cm) high, in moulded box.
£90–110 *TAC*

l. A pair of French
brass okapi, 1940s,
18in (45.5cm) high.
£165–170 *DAC*

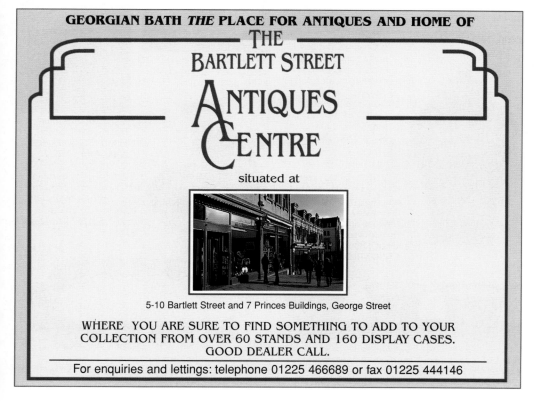

A Chinese pottery camel, Tang Dynasty, AD 618–907, 13in (33cm) high.
£1,000–1,250 *ORI*

A Chinese blue and white tankard, slight damage, c1640, 10½in (26.5cm) high.
£650–750 *ORI*

A Chinese blue and white baluster vase and domed cover, from the 'Vung Tau cargo', c1690, 4½in (11.5cm) high.
£450–500 *RBA*

A Chinese blue and white porcelain vase and cover, Kangxi period, 16962–1722, 12in (30.5cm) high.
£1,200–1,400 *ORI*

A Chinese Imari jar and cover, early 18thC, 5½in (14cm) high.
£650–750 *GeW*

A Chinese tea bowl and saucer, decorated with a pagoda river-scape in underglaze blue and white, from the 'Nanking cargo', c1750, bowl 3in (7.5cm) diam.
£200–250 *RBA*

A Chinese Imari plate, early 18thC, 9in (23cm) diam.
£150–200 *GeW*

A pair of Japanese Imari vases, c1880, 13½in (34cm) high.
£600–700 *MCN*

l. A Chinese terracotta floor vase, with painted and lacquered decoration, moulded handles and matching turned wood cover, 18thC, 30in (76cm) high.
£1,300–1,500 *DD*

l. A Chinese chamber stick, exported in blue and white, repainted possibly in Holland, c1830, 5in (12.5cm) high.
£150–175 *DKH*

A set of 5 Japanese Kutani sake cups, signed, c1880, 4in (10cm) diam.
£80–100 *MCN*

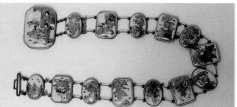

A Japanese Satsuma belt, with 14 links, Meiji period, 1868–1911, 28in (71cm) long.
£850–950 *MER*

r. A Japanese Noritake plate, decorated with a lake scene, c1918, 8½in (21.5cm) diam. **£35–40** *DgC*

A Japanese porcelain blue and white stick stand, c1880, 24in (61cm) high. **£220–250** *Ber*

A Japanese Noritake vase, c1908, 9¼in (23.5cm) high. **£150–200** *DgC*

A Chinese mask badge, for 7th civil rank, decorated with a Mandarin duck, mid-19thC, 12in (30.5cm) square. **£250–300** *PBr*

An Indo-Persian bazu band, chiselled with battle scenes, c1830, 14½in (37cm) long. **£300–350** *GV*

A silver and enamel cigarette
case, decorated with reclining
nude with a fan, c1900,
3¼in (8.5cm) wide.
£90–100 *SFL*

l. A 'Thinking of
You' stationery kit,
made for US
servicemen, 1940s,
22½in (57cm) open.
£44–48 *SpM*

A pack of Glamour Girls
plastic-coated playing cards,
depicting 55 different girls,
1950s, 3¾ x 2⅛in (9.5 x 5.5cm).
£50–60 *SpM*

A watercolour drawing,
artwork for a calendar, by
Dickens, slight damage, 1950s,
20 x 29in (51 x 73.5cm).
£280–320 *VS*

l. A Varga
calender, 1948,
12 x 8½in (30.5 x
21.5cm) high.
£150–170 *SpM*

A cigarette lighter,
decorated with a lady,
c1950, 2in (5cm) high.
£34–38 *SpM*

*Flash, The Photograhic
Magazine,* No. 1, 1956,
9½ x 6¾in (24 x 17cm).
£8–10 *RAD*

A ceramic salt and pepper set, in the form of a
pin-up girl, with diamanté nipples and navel,
1950–60, 7in (18cm) long.
£20–25 *PB*

A Biba poster, 1970s,
20 x 34in (51 x 86.5cm).
£100–125 *PB*

A Playboy Play-
mate centrefold
puzzle, 1960–70,
6in (15cm) high.
£20–25 *PB*

A signed photo of pin-up
girl Traci Lords, 1990s
10in (25.5cm) high.
£20–30 *VS*

An autograph book, with original postcard drawings by L. Wood, Tom Browne and other postcard artists, c1900, 7 x 4in (18 x 10cm).
£450–500 *MRW*

A postcard, Sunrays, depicting a girl with flowers, by Raphael Kirchner, Dell'Aquila, c1903.
£45–55 *VS*

A postcard, with a picture of RMS *Lusitania* woven in silk, c1905.
£35–40 *VS*

A Louis Wain postcard, 'Auf den Bummel', German edition, c1908.
£35–40 *VS*

A postcard, 'Hearty Greetings', decorated with violets, c1913.
£2–3 *THA*

A Louis Wain tennis postcard, 'We're all in the finals', postally used, c1900.
£35–40 *SpP*

A woven silk postcard, dated '1917'.
£35–40 *VS*

A silk embroidered postcard, sent from France during WWI, entitled 'To my dear Father', c1915.
£3–4 *MAC*

A French glamour postcard, by Xavier Sager, entitled 'Porte-lui mon souvenir', c1916.
£7–8 *JMC*

An album containing approximately 94 post-cards of Kentish subjects, including Gravesend Airport and Flying School, early 20thC.
£25–35 *MED*

An Edison Diamond Disc
mahogany table gramophone,
with a selection of discs, c1918,
22in (56cm) high.
£350–450   *ET*

A portable gramophone in a black
case, c1920, 11in (28cm) wide.
£80–100   *DAC*

A Coca-Cola radio, American,
c1949, 10in (25.5cm) high.
£550–600   *EKK*

An RCA radio, American,
c1934, 19in (48cm) high.
£200–250   *OTA*

A Marconiphone walnut
radio, model T26A, c1949,
16in (40.5cm) high.
£50–60   *DAC*

A Fada yellow plastic bullet
radio, c1945, 10in (25.5cm) wide.
£650–750   *EKK*

A Roberts radio, c1961,
9in (23cm) wide.
£30–35   *UTP*

A Tomy 'Mr D. J.' plastic radio,
in the form of a robot,
1970–80, 7in (17.5cm) high.
£30–40   *PB*

l. A Roberts portable transistor
radio, on swivel base, the
wooden body covered in vinyl,
with wooden veneered sides
and metal speaker grille and
controls, slight damage,
1970–80, 10in (25.5cm) wide.
£25–30   *DOM*

A Pepsi plastic radio/alarm
clock, battery or mains powered,
c1990, 5in (12.5cm) high.
£18–20   *DOM*

A Stevengraph picture woven in silk, entitled 'The First Train', No. 192, by Thomas Stevens, c1880, 5 x 8in (12.5 x 20.5cm).
£400–450 *VINE*

Sheet music for 'The Railway Whistle Galop', composed by G. Richardson, cover by Alfred Concanen, c1860, 14 x 10in (36 x 25.5cm).
£100–120 *SRA*

A Stevengraph portrait of George Stephenson, No. 79, 1893, 7 x 5in (18 x 12.5cm).
£200–230 *VINE*

A ceramic mug, depicting an early coloured 2–2–2 locomotive express and 5 carriages, c1850, 5in (12.5cm) high.
£130–150 *SRA*

Father Tuck's Book of Trains, illustrated by A. H. Browne, and *Our Train ABC*, published by Raphael Tuck & Sons Ltd, early 20thC, 8½ x 10⅞in (21.5 x 27.5cm).
£20–25 *SRA*

An LNER type signal box block instrument, with brass mounts, 1940s, 18in (45.5cm) high.
£50–60 *HAX*

An Edwardian North Eastern Railway guard's three-aspect hand lamp, 12½in (32cm) high.
£50–60 *SRA*

A Southern Railway cast iron sign, 1920s, 26in (66cm) wide.
£55–65 *RAR*

r. A Lyme Regis nameplate, with crest, 'West Country Class' scroll and smokebox numberplate 34009, on a green painted wooden display board, 1960s, 64in (162.5cm) long.
£20,000–25,000 *SRA*

A Beatles diary, 1960s,
4in (10cm) high.
£20–30   *BTC*

A Corgi Toys Beatles Yellow
Submarine toy, boxed with
insert, 1960s, 7in (18cm) wide.
£220–250   *SAF*

A *Movie Life* magazine,
including a Beatles article,
1960s, 11in (28cm) high.
£4–5   *BTC*

A white enamelled tray, with
colour pictures and 'signatures'
of the Beatles, 1960s,
13in (33cm) square.
£45–55   *SAF*

An American Beatles bubble-
gum wrapper, 1960s,
5½in (14cm) wide.
£40–50   *SAF*

A *Beatles Around the World*
magazine, 1960s, 11 x 9in
(28 x 23cm).
£4–5   *BTC*

A Beatles cushion, made from
Dutch curtain material, 1960s,
12½in (32cm) square.
£20–25   *BTC*

A Beatles jigsaw puzzle,
damaged, 1960s, 11 x 8in
(28 x 20.5cm).
£40–50   *PC*

A colour postcard of Paul
McCartney, signed, 1980s,
6 x 4in (15 x 10cm).
£80–100   *BTC*

l. A brick, one of 5,000 salvaged
from the Cavern Club by Royal
Life and sold for charity in 1983,
9in (23cm) long.
£80–100   *BTC*

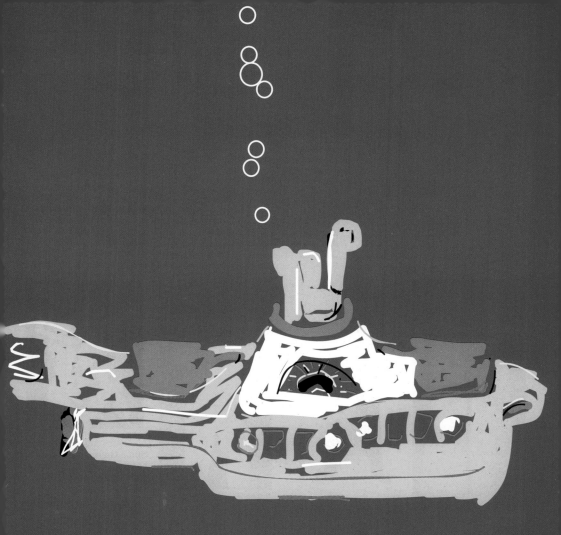

A pair of Marks & Spencer's cream knickers, signed 'All Saints Love Natalie' in black pen on the waistband, size 10, 1990s, and a letter of authenticity.
£220–250   *Bon*

Fashions, a book of David Bowie 7in (17.5cm) picture discs, 1969–79, 8in (20cm) square.
£45–55   *SAF*

r. An original Elvis in Concert souvenir scarf, from the Imperial Palace, Las Vegas, c1970, 20in (51cm) square.
£30–35   *SAF*

A pair of Mick Jagger's velvet trousers, the waist with star and heart-shaped bead fasteners, flared bottoms with buttons and multi-coloured braid strips to the inside, c1970.
£1,800–2,000   *S*

Elton John's matador stage costume, together with a signed Ret Turner costume design in ink, watercolour and pencil with several fabric swatches, 1980s.
£8,500–9,500   *S*

Elton John's suit, with designer's logo, labelled 'Gianni Versace', with a colour picture of the star wearing the suit, 1990s.
£2,000–2,500   *S*

A colour photograph of the Spice Girls, in bikinis and basque, signed by all 5, first names only, 1997.
£280–300   *VS*

l. A brocaded satin cheung-sam dress, worn by Ginger Spice, Geri Halliwell, for her meeting with President Mandela in 1997, with similar evening bag and a pair of red suede platform shoes with gold dragons inscribed 'Terry de Havilland 97', and a signed photograph.
£3,800–4,200   *S*

The Stars and Stripes outfit worn by Ginger Spice, Geri Halliwell, for the MTV awards ceremony, 1997, with signed photograph.
£3,500–4,000   *S*

The Union Jack costume, worn for the Brit Awards, 1997, by Ginger Spice, Geri Halliwell, made by Karen Davis, with signed photograph.
£42,000–45,000   *S*

Paperweights

Paperweight manufacture began in the mid-19th century. Although the Venetian glassmaker Pietro Bigaglia is credited with introducing the first recorded examples, the finest paperweights were made in France. Production began at Baccarat in 1846. Many weights were millefiori, sometimes dated and marked with the letter 'B' on one of the canes, often with star-cut bases. Clichy made paperweights between 1846 and 1870 and Saint Louis between 1845 and 1860. Other European manufacturers include the Val-Saint-Lambert Glassworks in Belgium,

Whitefriars in England, and many weights were made in the USA by firms such as the glass companies of New England and the Mount Washington.

Production tailed off in the last quarter of the 19th century but was revived early in the 20th century and paperweights are once more made by Baccarat and Saint Louis. Major modern British manufacturers include Whitefriars, Wedgwood and the Caithness and Perthshire glass factories in Scotland. Weights by individual designers, both European and American, are also eagerly collected.

A Baccarat paperweight, with flower and silhouette canes, on white ribbon latticinio, with 'B' signature, dated '1847', 3in (7.5cm) diam.
£3,000–3,500 *STG*

A Baccarat faceted red paperweight, with silhouette of Queen Victoria, inscribed, 1845–60, 3¼in (8.5cm) diam.
£1,150–1,350 *SWB*

A Baccarat close-pack paperweight, with 9 silhouettes, c1850, 2¾in (7cm) diam.
£2,000–2,200 *SWB*

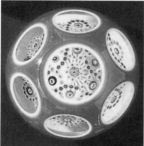

r. A Baccarat paperweight, with double overlay millefiori garlands and silhouettes, c1850, 3¼in (8.5cm) diam.
£4,500–5,000 *DLP*

l. A Baccarat pansy paperweight, Type III, c1850, 2in (5cm) diam.
£450–500 *SWB*

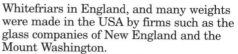

A Baccarat paperweight, with red and white flower in a garland surround, c1850, 2½in (6.5cm) diam.
£2,200–2,400 *SWB*

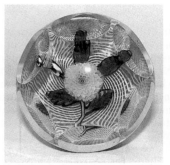

A St Louis faceted paperweight, with a white flower on latticinio, c1850, 3in (7.5cm) diam.
£1,800–2,000 *SWB*

A Clichy paperweight, with a turquoise and white swirl pattern, c1850, 3in (7.5cm) diam.
£1,200–1,500 *DLP*

A Clichy paperweight, with spaced concentric garlands and a central pink rose, 1845–60, 2½in (6.5cm) diam.
£600–675 *SWB*

r. A Clichy paperweight, with close-scattered millefiori flower pattern on turquoise ground, c1850, 3in (7.5cm) diam.
£2,400–2,700 *STG*

A Clichy paperweight, with a purple, black and white spoke design, c1850, 3¼in (8.5cm) diam.
£6,500–7,500 *DLP*

A Clichy paperweight, with Sodden Snow spaced concentric design, c1850, 3in (7.5cm) diam.
£950–1,150 *SWB*

A Saint Louis paperweight, with a single golden pear in clear glass, c1850, 3in (7.5cm) diam.
£1,700–2,000 *DLP*

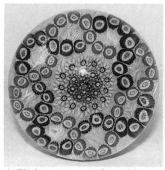

A Clichy paperweight, with interlaced quatrefoils on a muslin ground, c1850, 3in (7.5cm) diam.
£1,350–1,550 *SWB*

l. A Saint Louis paperweight, with a pink chrysanthemum in clear glass, c1850, 3¼in (8.5cm) diam.
£1,500–1,800 *DLP*

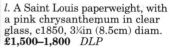

A Saint Louis paperweight, the pattern in the form of an upright bouquet of red flowers, with blue torsade, c1850, 3in (7.5cm) diam.
£3,000–3,300 *SWB*

A New England Glass Co paperweight, with violet-coloured poinsettia on a spiral filigree cushion, c1860, 3in (7.5cm) diam.
£875–1,150 *DLP*

A Pantin paperweight, with a pink rose on a white ground, c1878, 3in (7.5cm) diam.
£7,000–8,000 *DLP*

l. A Paul Ysart paperweight, with a bouquet on a red and white cushion, 1960–70, 2¾in (7cm) diam.
£450–500 *SWB*

r. A Baccarat paperweight, with red, white and blue millefiori pattern, c1974, 3in (7.5cm) diam.
£400–450 *SWB*

r. Two Glasform frog paperweights, with green and purple lustre effect, c1995, tallest 4¼in (11cm) high.
£45–60 each *GLA*

l. A William Manson paperweight, with a snake and ladybird, c1995, 2¾in (7cm) diam.
£250–300 *SWB*

r. A Correia paperweight, decorated in relief with a snake, c1998, 3¼in (8.5cm) diam.
£125–155 *SWB*

Vases

A pair of Victorian vaseline glass *solifleur* vases, c1890, 6in (15cm) high.
£130–160 *BELL*

A pair of opaline glass vases, with ruby fold-over tops, c1890, 6in (15cm) high.
£200–245 *ARE*

A Stevens & Williams (Brierley), green glass globular vase, designed by Keith Murray, with a cylindrical neck, applied with 2 fluted handles and supported on a spreading circular foot, signed 'S & W', 1930s, 9in (23cm) high.
£500–600 *ADE*

r. A pair of George Bacchus glass vases, c1890, 12in (30.5cm) high.
£325–375 *ARE*

Based in Birmingham, George Bacchus & Sons was one of the first firms to use transfer printing on glass.

A satin glass lustre vase, with decorative metal top, c1900, 9½in (24cm) high.
£35–45 *DKH*

A Graal glass vase, by Edward Hald for Orrefors, with seaweed and fish decoration, etched to base 'Orrefors Graal No. 403K', signed 'E. D. W. Hald', c1930, 4½in (11.5cm) high.
£330–360 *Mit*

r. A Walsh & Co green glass vase, with iridescent finish and thrown top, c1920, 7¾in (20cm) high.
£150–200 *JHa*

A Webb glass vase, with brown and white looped trailing decoration, c1910, 10in (25.5cm) high.
£100–120 *TCG*

A Stuart & Co green lily vase, with thrown top and domed and folded foot, c1890, 6½in (16.5cm) high.
£50–60 *JHa*

A Gray-Stan brown glass vase, 1920–30s, 7½in (19cm) high.
£100–120 *TCG*

A Monart green and blue glass vase, with bubble inclusions, 1930s, 7½in (19cm) high.
£100–120 *TCG*

A Powell white glass
vase, with combed
herringbone pattern,
1930s, 7½in (19cm) high.
£130–150 *TCG*

A Webb pseudo cameo
glass vase, c1930,
9in (23cm) high.
£200–240 *TCG*

A Whitefriars smoky
amber glass vase,
optic moulded, 1930s,
9¾in (24.5cm) high.
£40–50 *P(B)*

A Vasart Harlequin
glass vase, 1956–63,
7½in (19cm) high.
£60–70 *TCG*

A Vicke Lindstrand clear
glass vase, inscribed
mark on base, 1950–60s,
6in (15cm) high.
£75–95 *TCG*

An Orrefors clear glass
vase, designed by Sven
Palmqvist, of tapering
oval section, the thick
walled glass engraved
with geese in flight,
engraved factory
marks and monogram,
No. 3724, c1950,
7¼in (18.5cm) high.
£120–150 *WeH*

A Orrefors smoky
grey glass vase, by
Nils Landberg, c1960,
9in (23cm) high.
£75–100 *TCG*

A Dartington glass
vase, 1960s,
5½in (14cm) high.
£10–15 *TCG*

l. A Whitefriars green
glass vase, by Geoffrey
Baxter, c1974,
9in (23cm) high.
£125–150 *TCG*

r. A Whitefriars
kingfisher blue glass
vase, by Geoffrey
Baxter, with green
spots, 1969–71,
6in (15cm) high.
£50–60 *TCG*

A Glasform gold glass
vase, with black
iridescent trails,
signed, No. 4496,
c1995, 7in (18cm) high.
£220–250 *GLA*

HAIRDRESSING & SHAVING

A set of Victorian seven-day open razors, labelled 'Monday' to 'Sunday', by Ibbotson, Sheffield, in a velvet-lined mahogany box, 7in (18cm) long.
£80–100 *ET*

A celluloid painted butterfly comb, 1920s, 3¾in (9.5cm) long.
£25–30 *CHU*

An electric hairdryer, in a Bakelite box, 1930s, 8 x 10in (20.5 x 25.5cm).
£40–50 *GIN*

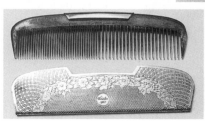

An Oriental bamboo and bone comb, early 20thC, 4½in (11.5cm) long.
£20–25 *CHU*

r. A Wilkinson Sword safety razor, with blades and sharpener, in a painted pine box, early 20thC, box 4in (10cm) square.
£50–60 *ET*

A five-piece silver-backed dressing table set, comprising hand mirror, 2 clothes brushes and 2 hair brushes, Birmingham 1928/9, in original case, 15in (38cm) wide.
£130–150 *GAK*

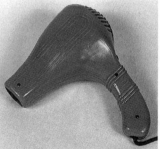

A Pifco green plastic hairdryer, c1950, 9in (23cm) long.
£8–10 *UTP*

l. A brown plastic comb, resembling tortoiseshell, with brass cover, c1961, 5in (13cm) long.
£18–20 *CHU*

A celluloid comb and case, late 1920s, 4in (10cm) long.
£18–20 *CHU*

A Derbac metal dust/nit comb, 1940–50, 2½in (6.5cm) long.
£4–6 *CHU*

A brown plastic folding comb, with handle cover, 1940s, 4in (10cm) long.
£16–18 *CHU*

HANDBAGS & PURSES

A brown velvet sovereign purse, couched in silver and gold thread, c1660, 13in (33cm) long.
£140–180 *JPr*

A multi-coloured beaded purse, with gilt frame, c1810, 4in (10cm) high.
£100–120 *JPr*

A burgundy velvet gaming purse, embroidered in silver and gold thread, c1680, 10in (25.5cm) long.
£350–450 *JPr*

A silver-gilt purse, with plaques depicting dead game, c1820, 3in (7.5cm) wide.
£325–375 *MB*

A red and black metal beaded purse, with silver-gilt frame, c1790, 7in (18cm) high.
£65–80 *JPr*

A beaded purse, with silver frame and original silk lining, c1860, 9in (23cm) long.
£240–260 *JPr*

A Victorian black velvet purse, with silver hallmark, c1880, 7in (18cm) high.
£80–100 *JPr*

A silver purse, Birmingham 1915, 3in (7.5cm) wide.
£130–140 *PSA*

A mother-of-pearl sovereign purse, c1880, 1¼in (3cm) wide.
£30–35 *VB*

A beaded purse, with suede interior, c1920, 3in (7.5cm) wide.
£40–50 *JPr*

A white and silver beaded evening bag, 1920s, 7in (18cm) wide.
£15–18 *CHU*

A snakeskin handbag, 1920s, 11in (28cm) long.
£110–125 *MLL*

A Turkish prisoner-of-war opaque glass beaded bag, decorated with blue and red beads, c1918, 6in (15cm) wide.
£24–28 *CCO*

l. A red and black chain mail bag, with metal clasp, 1920s, 6in (15cm) high.
£20–25 *PC*

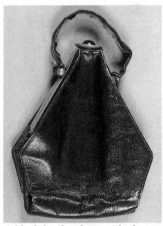

A black leather bag, with chrome clasp, some wear and clasp damaged, 1930s, 9in (23cm) high.
£8–10 *PC*

A black striped fabric handbag, with chrome and enamel clasp, 1930s, 9½in (24cm) wide.
£40–50 *PC*

A gold lamé bag, with gold-plated clasp, c1930, 9in (23cm) wide.
£28–33 *CCO*

A black leather bag, with chrome and Bakelite clasp, 1930s, 9in (23cm) wide.
£6–8 *PC*

A beaded white satin evening bag, 1930s, 8in (20.5cm) wide.
£8–10 *CHU*

l. A black cloth bag, with black and white Bakelite clasp, 1930s, 6in (15cm) wide.
£15–17 *PC*

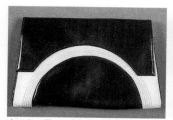

An Art Deco brown and cream leather bag, with matching mirror, 1930s, 9½in (24cm) wide.
£35–40 *PC*

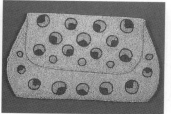

A red and white beaded handbag, c1930, 9in (23cm) wide.
£35–40 *PC*

A navy diamond-patterned printed cloth clutch bag, with chrome clasp, c1930, 11½in (29cm) wide.
£14–16 *PC*

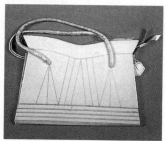

A cream Bakelite handbag, with leather handles, c1940, 8in (20.5cm) wide.
£6–8 *PC*

An Evans gold mesh purse, with an enamelled compact top, 1940s, 4in (10cm) high.
£140–160 *LBr*

A brown mock crocodile skin handbag, 1940s, 10in (25.5cm) high.
£14–16 *PC*

An American white hard plastic box bag, with brass fittings and simulated pearls, c1950, 5in (12.5cm) square.
£160–180 *LBr*

An American grey hard plastic handbag, with plastic fittings, 1950s, 6in (15cm) diam.
£150–180 *LBr*

A tapestry bag, with blue and white porcelain clasp, c1960, 7in (18cm) wide.
£18–22 *CCO*

r. A white beaded bag, with beaded clasp, c1960, 8in (20.5cm) wide.
£18–22 *CCO*

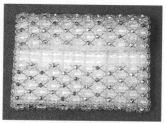

An Italian white beaded bag, with silver beads incorporated, 1960s, 7in (18cm) wide.
£10–12 *CCO*

JEWELLERY

A paste bead necklace,
3rd century BC–Roman,
28in (71cm) long.
£1,800–2,000 *PARS*

A metal one-piece brooch, with re-curved
foot, complete with catchplate and most of
spring, pin missing, 4th–3rd century BC,
2in (5cm) long.
£65–75 *ANG*

A 15ct gold bracelet, c1880, 7½in (19cm) long.
£2,750–3,000 *WIM*

An 18ct gold fob seal,
with open foliate
scrollwork and vacant
table, Birmingham
1911, 1in (2.5cm) high.
£150–200 *HofB*

A fob seal, with carved
shells and foliage and a
vacant cornelian table,
c1825, 1in (2.5cm) high.
£225–275 *HofB*

A pair of 9ct rose gold cuff
links, c1851.
£50–60 *TAC*

r. A pair of 9ct gold
cufflinks, Chester 1876.
£45–55 *TAC*

A silver and steel
teddy tie pin, by
Adie & Lovekin Ltd,
Birmingham 1909,
3in (7.5cm) long.
£145–165 *BEX*

A silver chatelaine, with
penknife, corkscrew, pencil
and *aide memoire*, by
Sampson Mordan, London,
1879–82, 15¼in (39cm) long.
£900–1,100 *AMH*

Abbatucci Cargo

On 7th May 1869, the steam packet
General Abbatucci sank in a
collision off the coast of Corsica.
Fifty-four lives were lost but
interest in the tragedy was further
stimulated by the fact that the
vessel, bound for Italy, was
rumoured to be carrying several
million French francs, destined for
the coffers of the Vatican. In 1996
the wreck was excavated, and
while the papal millions were not
discovered, the cargo recovery team
did rescue a considerable amount of
jewellery, probably the stock of a
jeweller travelling aboard ship. The
principle value of the pieces
illustrated here from the *Abbatucci*
cargo lies in their provenance.

A gold locket, from the
Abbatucci cargo, c1869,
1½in (4cm) high.
£200–225 *RBA*

A gold ring, from the
Abbatucci cargo, c1869.
£175–200 *RBA*

Brooches & Pins

A Scottish silver double heart brooch, early 19thC, 3in (7.5cm) high.
£120–150 *BWA*

A 15ct gold long-eared owl brooch, perched on a branch, with diamond eyes, c1890, 2in (5cm) long.
£350–400 *HofB*

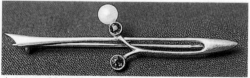

A 15ct gold bar brooch, set with a sapphires and a pearl, c1890, 2in (5cm) long.
£250–300 *HofB*

A gilt-metal bird-shaped shawl pin, c1900, 6¾in (17cm) long.
£40–50 *VB*

r. An 18ct gold stickpin, set with Essex crystal, c1870, 3½in (9cm) long.
£1,500–1,750 *SHa*

Essex crystal is a term used to describe a reverse intaglio crystal – a crystal cut in the form of a cabochon and carved in intaglio on its flat back and then painted in minute detail, giving a three-dimensional, trompe l'oeil effect. The technique was invented by the jeweller Emile Marius Pradier c1860. Worn by both men and women these crystals were mounted in pins, brooches and cuff links, and were extremely popular during the Victorian period. The term Essex crystal derives from the belief that these objects were painted by the enamel miniaturist William Essex.

A gold horseshoe and arrow brooch, c1870, 2in (5cm) long.
£170–200 *HofB*

r. A gold bar brooch, in the Etruscan revivalist manner, set with a single diamond, c1880, 2in (5cm) long.
£150–200 *HofB*

l. Two Victorian name brooches, 1¾in (4.5cm) long.
£35–40 each *SPE*

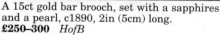

Cameo Brooches

A Regency scroll gilt-mounted cameo brooch, with classical figure, 2in (5cm) high.
£350–400 *DAC*

Scottish Hardstone Brooches

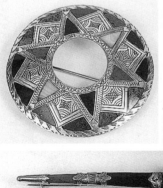

A Scottish grey agate strap brooch, c1860, 2½in (6.5cm) diam.
£300–350 *BWA*

A Scottish silver dagger pin, 1860–80, 3¼in (8.5cm) long.
£170–200 *WIM*

l. A gold-mounted cameo brooch, with female bust in profile, 19thC, 2in (5cm) high.
£170–190 *DAC*

A pinchbeck-mounted cameo brooch, depicting a Greek philosopher, 19thC, ¾in (2cm) high.
£20–30 *DAC*

l. A gilt-metal mounted cameo brooch, depicting Hebe and Zeus, 19thC, 2in (5cm) high.
£45–55 *DAC*

A Scottish silver, agate and citrine penannular brooch, c1860, 2½in (6.5cm) long.
£250–300 *BWA*

l. A Scottish silver and agate ring brooch, c1870, 2in (5cm) diam.
£250–300 *BWA*

A Scottish silver, agate with citrine brooch, c1870, 1½in (4cm) diam.
£100–150 *BWA*

A Scottish silver and agate brooch, c1850, 3in (7.5cm) long.
£500–600 *BWA*

Costume Jewellery

A collection of butterfly, bird and insect brooches, 1900–40, 1–2in (2.5–5cm) wide.
£10–25 each *VB*

A metal filigree brooch, with coloured paste stones, 1920s, 3in (7.5cm) long.
£12–15 *CHU*

A green plastic and paste clasp, 1930s, 4in (10cm) long.
£8–10 *CHU*

l. A yellow plastic and brass clasp, 1920s, 2½in (6.5cm) wide.
£10–12 *CHU*

A baroque-style pearl choker, with front clasp, by Miriam Haskell, 1940s, 14in (35.5cm) long.
£300–350 *GLT*

An Art Deco Bakelite bracelet, with pewter decoration, c1930s, 3in (7.5cm) wide.
£25–30 *MRW*

Miriam Haskell

Miriam Haskell is one of the most collectable names in costume jewellery. She began her career in 1924, when she opened a small costume jewellery shop in New York's McAlpine Hotel, moving some ten years later to Fifth Avenue, where the workshop remained until the 1960s. Haskell was particularly famous for her lustrous, baroque-style pearls, often combined with tiny seed pearls and arranged in both abstract and naturalistic patterns. A distinctive motif found on many of her necklaces is a flower-shaped fastener. Whether using pearls or other materials quality tends to be very high.

Haskell metalwork has a warm matte finish known as 'antique Russian gold,' an alloy made by fusing gold and silver onto a copper base. Its subtlety made Haskell's jewellery perfect for 'day into evening' wear. Early pieces tend to be unmarked. The 1940s saw the introduction of a horseshoe-shaped plate bearing Haskell's name, soon to be replaced by the oval metal tag still used on Haskell jewellery made today.

Miller's is a price GUIDE not a price LIST

A Miriam Haskell silver-coloured metal leaf-shaped brooch, set with 3 large *faux* blister pearls and multiple seed pearls, enhanced with marcasites, signed, c1950, 3½in (9cm) wide.
£500–600 *PKT*

A Miriam Haskell three-dimensional yellow filigree metal butterfly stick pin, with flower design fastening, signed, c1955, 3in (7.5cm) long.
£100–125 *PKT*

A Hattie Carnegie brooch, the yellow metal leaves partially painted black, set with variously sized and shaped black and white glass beads, c1955, 2½in (6.5cm) diam.
£80–90 *PKT*

A Norman Hartnell necklace, set with pink and grey oval diamanté and various sized baguette diamanté, signed, c1955, 17in (43cm) long.
£115–135 *PKT*

Two Miriam Haskell two-strand baroque pearl necklaces, 1980s.
£250–300 each *MAU*

A Miriam Haskell blue bead tassel necklace and flower earrings, 1950s, necklace 29in (73.5cm) long.
£500–550 *MAU*

A Hobé silver metal bracelet, outlined with white diamanté, with a central six-strand tapered diamanté drop, signed, c1958, 8in (20.5cm) long.
£125–150 *PKT*

A pair of Schiaparelli citrine, paste and amber smoked glass leaf earrings, 1950s, 1½in (4cm) long.
£225–250 *MAU*

A Hollycraft antique yellow metal brooch, set with variously shaped diamanté and a single faceted diamanté at the centre and 8 pearl overlays, signed, c1953, 2in (5cm) diam.
£110–125 *PKT*

A Schiaparelli green and white cabochon paste and glass 'rock' bracelet and earrings, 1950s, bracelet 7in (18cm) long.
£450–500 *MAU*

A pair of Robert cream and blue bead flower earrings, with baroque pearl and pink paste, 1950s, 1¼in (3cm) diam.
£125–150 *MAU*

A Schiaparelli plastic and brass necklace, and a pair of earrings, 1950s.
£150–180 *GLT*

A Schreiner topaz and citrine paste pin, 1950s, 2¼in (5.5cm) square.
£125–150 *MAU*

A Coppola & Toppo sea-green bead and baroque pearl necklace, 1960s, 15½in (39.5cm) long.
£850–900 *MAU*

A Christian Dior brooch, the yellow metal leaves set with small white round diamanté and marquis blue stones, made in Germany by Henkel & Grosse, signed, c1968, 2in (5cm) diam, with box.
£85–110 *PKT*

A pair of Miriam Haskell baroque pearl drop earrings, with filigree seed pearl and paste surround, 1960s, 2in (5cm) long.
£250–270 *MAU*

l. A Schiaparelli brooch, set with aurora crystals and beads in silver-coloured metal, signed, c1965, 3in (7.5cm) wide.
£150–160 *PKT*

A Vendome 20-strand necklace, with black bead, pearl and faceted aurora strands, the pearls with yellow metal separators, made for Coro, c1960, 14in (35.5cm) long.
£100–125 *PKT*

A Kramer 'trembler' brooch, the body with faceted blue stone surrounded by white diamanté, the head a large faceted white stone with yellow metal whiskers, the tail blue diamanté, the whole set on a yellow metal base, the head mounted on a spring, signed, c1960, 2in (5cm) long.
£125–150 *PKT*

A pair of Babylon red plastic and brass earrings, c1970.
£80–100 *GLT*

A Chanel brown and olive green *faux* pearl bracelet, 1970s.
£150–180 *GLT*

A yellow metal and diamanté brooch, in the form of a Viking longboat, with white enamelled sails and black enamelled hull, signed 'Ciner', c1985, 1½in (4cm) wide.
£90–110 *PKT*

A gilt-metal owl brooch, by Iradj Moini, set with white and coloured rhinestones, Persian, c1980, 2in (5cm) high.
£200–250 *CRIS*

A Sphinx gold metal and black enamel brooch, with central turquoise-coloured stone, simulated pearl and coloured rhinestones, c1980, 3¼in (8.5cm) high.
£35–40 *CRIS*

Hatpins

Five silver hatpins, by Charles Horner and Pearce & Thompson, c1900, largest 11in (28cm) long.
£35–60 each *VB*

An Edwardian metal hatpin, 12in (30.5cm) long.
£15–18 *CHU*

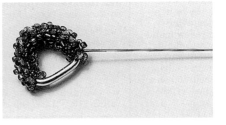

r. A hatpin, with amber-coloured beads, 1950s, 5in (12.5cm) long.
£8–10 *CHU*

Three fabric-wrapped hatpins, 1930s, longest 8in (20.5cm).
£7–10 each *CHU*

A gold-coloured filigree metal hatpin, 1950s, 5in (12.5cm) long.
£8–10 *CHU*

Three sequin-covered hatpins, 1950s, 5in (12.5cm) long.
£8–10 *CHU*

A silver-plated hatpin stand, 1900–15, 7in (18cm) high, and a painted porcelain hatpin stand, 1900–15, 4in (10cm) high.
£25–45 each *VB*

Necklaces & Pendants

A gold-mounted cross pendant, set with bloodstone and cornelian, in an engraved mount, c1840, 2in (5cm) high.
£200–250 *HofB*

A gold-mounted applied cameo pendant, with a locket to the reverse, c1830, 2in (5cm) high.
£170–200 *HofB*

A Victorian heart-shaped gold locket, engraved with scroll foliage, and a 9ct gold belcher chain, c1890.
£200–250 *HofB*

A belcher chain has broad links of equal length, joined alternately horizontally and vertically.

A late Victorian 15ct gold pendant, set with pearls and a peridot, on a 9ct gold chain, c1890, pendant 1in (2.5cm) diam.
£400–450 *HofB*

A Victorian silver engraved locket and chain, c1880, 16in (40.5cm) long.
£200–230 *DAC*

l. An Art Nouveau silver and paste pendant, early 20thC, 2in (5cm) high.
£70–80 *DAC*

r. An Edwardian silver and paste pendant, set with a peridot, 2in (5cm) high.
£60–70 *DAC*

KITCHENWARE

A pewter pepper pot, 19thC,
3¼in (8.5cm) high.
£20–25 *No7*

A Doulton's ceramic water
filter, c1910, 26in (66cm) high.
£130–150 *RAW*

An Irish brass trivet, with
porcelain handle, stamped
'Longfields', late 19thC, c1921,
10in (25.5cm) long.
£80–120 *ET*

A Staines Thermobile hot water
urn, c1940, 14in (35.5cm) high.
£25–30 *UTP*

A set of ceramic kitchen
scales, with metal pan,
1920s, 12in (30.5cm) high.
£60–80 *SMI*

A Ewbank carpet sweeper, 1940s,
14in (35.5cm) wide.
£20–25 *UTP*

A Hygeneware glass and plastic sugar
jar and spoon, glass jug and pourer
jug, 1950s, sugar jar 4in (10cm) high.
£5–8 each *AL*

A Pyrex glass measure,
with plastic lid and handle,
c1960, 10in (25.5cm) high.
£3–4 *AL*

A set of Salter tin scales,
with plastic pan, c1950,
11in (28cm) high.
£15–20 *AL*

A McDougalls Flour ceramic rolling
pin, with wooden handles, 1960s,
16in (40.5cm) long.
£30–35 *SMI*

Butter Churns

An Irish pine butter churn barrel, on stand, c1880, 29in (74cm) high.
£100–120 *ByI*

l. An Irish oak butter churn, c1875, 46in (117cm) high.
£180–200 *ByI*

A stoneware butter churn, late 19thC, 26in (66cm) high.
£150–160 *SMI*

A Welsh wooden butter churn, late 19thC, 42in (107cm) high.
£160–180 *SMI*

Ceramics

Two Avery blue transfer-printed ceramic weights, damaged, c1880, largest 3in (7.5cm) high.
£80–100 *SMI*

A Harriman's stoneware sugar jar, printed in brown, late 19thC, 10in (25.5cm) high.
£50–60 *SMI*

A Kent's ceramic milk saver, late 19thC, 4in (10cm) high.
£60–70 *SMI*

A ceramic new milk pail,
printed in black, late 19thC,
10in (25.5cm) high.
£300–350 *SMI*

A ceramic cream bowl, by Dairy
Supply Co, London, c1900,
14¼in (36cm) wide.
£225–250 *B&R*

An all-white stoneware
banded raisins jar, c1900,
7in (18cm) high.
£20–25 *AL*

A stoneware butter crock,
printed in black, early 20thC,
8in (20.5cm) high.
£80–85 *SMI*

A Grimwade stoneware salt jar,
with advertising on underside of
lid, c1910, 10in (25.5cm) high.
£125–145 *B&R*

A Maling ceramic butter
knives jar, c1910,
8¼in (21cm) high.
£100–120 *B&R*

A Lord Mayor's ceramic patent
pudding basin, printed in black,
early 20thC, 7in (18cm) diam.
£70–80 *SMI*

A Clarke's ceramic 'rigid' icing
bowl, printed in green, 1920s,
6in (15cm) high.
£60–70 *SMI*

A ceramic Weetabix cereal
dish, printed in brown, 1920s,
10in (25.5cm) wide.
£70–80 *SMI*

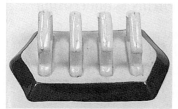

A Cornishware blue and white
ceramic toast rack, c1930,
5in (12.5cm) long.
£120–130 *SMI*

A Cornishware blue and white
ceramic rice jar, black shield
mark, c1937, 5¾in (14.5cm) high.
£30–35 *AL*

A Cornwishware blue and
white ceramic cruet, 1950s,
3in (7.5cm) high.
£20–25 *AL*

A Price Bros blue and white banded mixing bowl, with lip, c1950, 10½in (27cm) diam.
£20–25 *AL*

A blue and white banded mixing bowl, c1950, 10in (25.5cm) diam.
£15–20 *AL*

A yellow mixing bowl, with lip, c1950, 7in (18cm) diam.
£14–16 *AL*

A pottery mixing bowl, 1950–60s, 8½in (21.5cm) diam.
£14–16 *AL*

A brown ceramic pickled onion pot and lid, possibly SylvaC, unmarked, 1950s, 7in (18cm) high.
£3–4 *TRE*

A Poole Pottery cheese dish, with blue base, 1960s, 7in (18cm) long.
£15–20 *AL*

Copper & Metalware

An Irish copper saucepan, with blocked tin interior and wrought iron handle, 19thC, 7¼in (18.5cm) diam.
£50–60 *EON*

A copper milk churn, early 19thC, 18in (46cm) high.
£280–300 *SMI*

A copper jug, with brass mounts, 19thC, 20in (51cm) high.
£300–350 *ANV*

A copper drip tray, for placing under a barrel, 19thC, 6in (15cm) high.
£40–45 *OCH*

A copper kettle, c1890, 14in (35.5cm) long.
£110–130 *AL*

A Kenrick & Sons cast iron coffee grinder, with wooden handle knob, c1890, 8in (20.5cm) high.
£140–160 *SMI*

A Kenrick & Sons cast iron coffee grinder, c1890, 5in (12.5cm) high.
£125–150 *SMI*

A brass and tin one gallon measure, 1930s, 11in (28cm) high.
£65–75 *SMI*

A tin double steamer pan, with ceramic bowls, early 20thC, 5in (12.5cm) high.
£55–60 *SMI*

A Goblin aluminium pudding cover, with wooden knob handle, 1930s, 5in (12.5cm) high.
£5–7 *AL*

An aluminium milk churn and measure, c1940, churn 13in (33cm) high.
Churn   £18–20
Measure   £ 7–9 *AL*

l. Two tin cake moulds, in the shape of '1' and '2', c1950, 8½in (21.5cm) long.
£6–8 each *AL*

r. Two aluminium flour sugar shakers, 1950s, 4½in (11.5cm) high.
£5–8 *AL*

A Guernsey aluminium milk jug, with stamped crest, c1956, 9in (23cm) high.
£10–15 *PPe*

Eggs

A wooden egg stand, painted black, gold and red, late 19thC, 8in (20.5cm) wide.
£85–95 *SPa*

Four graduated Gourmet ceramic egg beaters, with wooden handles, early 20thC, tallest 9in (23cm) high.
£50–60 each *SMI*

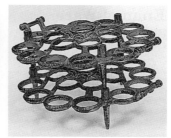

A Salter cast iron double egg rack, early 20thC, 5in (12.5cm) high.
£80–100 *SMI*

A wooden egg delivery box, by Raylite, for B. Duncan, Brook Hall Farm, Wissett, Halesworth, Suffolk, c1920, 7¾in (20cm) wide.
£80–90 *B&R*

A cardboard egg box, c1920, 13in (33cm) wide.
£20–25 *AL*

An aluminium egg poacher, c1950, 7in (18cm) diam.
£4–5 *AL*

A tin of dried eggs, c1940, 4in (10cm) high.
£4–5 *AL*

A stoneware egg crock, printed in black, 1930s, 13in (33cm) high.
£60–70 *SMI*

r. A Tala metal egg slicer, c1950, 6in (15cm) long.
£2–3 *AL*

Enamel Ware

A Granite Ware enamel
Quaker Oats cooker, c1910,
9¾in (25cm) high.
£60–75 *B&R*

An enamel flour bin, with lid,
c1910, 9¾in (25cm) high.
£10–15 *UTP*

An enamel flour bin, printed in
black, c1910, 6¼in (16cm) high.
£25–30 *B&R*

r. A Judge Brand two-pint
double enamel saucepan,
c1940, 8in (20.5cm) high.
£18–22 *UTP*

An enamel teapot, c1950,
6in (15cm) high.
£8–10 *AL*

Homepride

The Homepride men were invented in
1964 and first starred on flour bags and in
TV commercials in 1965. Fred was the
leader of these so-called 'flour-graders'
whose job was to sort out lumps and sift
the grains, hence the famous slogan
'Graded grains make finer flour'. The
smiling bowler-hatted figures were an
instant hit, and in 1969 Homepride
launched the plastic flour grader figure

priced at 3/6d (17½p). Over 500,000 of
these character sifters found their way
into households across the country, and
Homepride went on to create a whole
range of other promotional items from
spice racks to thermometers. These
objects are now increasingly found at
antiques fairs and have even inspired
their own collector's club – The Friends
of Fred.

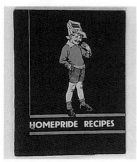

A book of *Homepride
Recipes*, 1930s, 5¼ x 4½in
(13.5 x 11.5cm).
£3–4 *RAD*

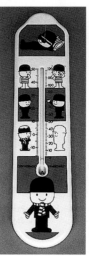

r. A Homepride thermometer,
printed in blue and black,
c1978, 18in (46cm) high.
£30–35 *AL*

A Homepride plastic
biscuit cutter, c1979,
4¾in (12cm) high.
£5–10 *AL*

A Homepride pottery flour
jar, printed in blue and
red to resemble a packet
of flour, with a plastic lid,
c1979, 8in (20.5cm) high.
£30–35 *AL*

Horlicks

James and William Horlick were born in England, where James trained as a chemist, specialising in the production of dried infant food. William emigrated to America, followed by James and together they set up the Horlicks food company, and patented their malted milk in Chicago in 1883.

The advantage of their powdered drink was that it was a complete and sterile food, requiring only the addition of hot water, and doctors instantly recommended it for infants and invalids. The brothers advertised their product widely in the press and with signs on railway stations and omnibuses. Horlicks malted milk was presented to Arctic explorers such as Roald Amundsen and Captain Scott, thus giving the company considerable publicity.

During WWI Horlicks powder and tablets formed part of military rations, and the rise of the soda fountain in America in the 1900s helped transform malted milk into a fun drink. In Britain, however, Horlicks was always associated with health, and in the 1930s, J. Walter Thompson, the advertising company, launched the famous campaign 'Horlicks guards against night starvation', inventing the concept of 'night starvation' and promoting Horlicks as an essential aid to sleep.

Two Horlicks glass and metal mixers, printed in red, 1930s, largest 8in (20.5cm) high.
l. **£8–9** *r.* **£5–6** *AL*

A grey plastic Horlicks mixer, printed in black, 1960s, 8¼in (21cm) high.
£14–16 *AL*

Two Horlicks pottery mugs, 1950–60, 3¾in (9.5cm) high.
£5–8 each *AL*

A yellow and black aluminium Horlicks sign, c1960, 15in (38cm) wide.
£7–8 *AL*

Two ceramic Horlicks mixers, 1960s, 8in (20.5cm) high.
£10–12 each *AL*

Horlicks Home Book, produced for Horlicks by Good Housekeeping, c1964, 9in (23cm) high.
£3–4 *AL*

Moulds

Two Wedgwood jelly moulds, 19thC,
largest 8in (20.5cm) high.
£65–85 each *SMI*

A copper two-piece chocolate
mould, in the form of a nut,
19thC, 2in (5cm) long.
£40–45 *No7*

Two copper and tin jelly moulds,
c1870, 5¼in (13.5cm) high.
£100–120 *MSB*

l. A South German wooden biscuit
mould, 19thC, 20in (51cm) long.
£500–550 *AEF*

A set of 6 copper chocolate
moulds, each engraved with a
'D' under a coronet, 19thC,
2½in (6.5cm) diam.
£250–300 *TMA*

l. Two copper
and tin moulds,
1875–1900, largest
4½in (11.5cm) long.
£135–170 each *MSB*

Six copper pudding moulds,
c1880, 1¾in (4.5cm) high.
£260–280 *MSB*

A copper pudding mould,
1880–1900, 2½in (6.5cm) high.
£70–80 *MSB*

A white ceramic royal
pudding mould, with a black
wire handle, c1880,
5in (12.5cm) high.
£50–70 *SMI*

A white pottery shell-shaped
mould, c1880, 4¾in (12cm) high.
£20–25 *AL*

Two tin moulds, c1890,
largest 11in (28cm) long.
£30–35 each *AL*

A circular tin mould, c1890,
6in (15cm) diam.
£20–25 *AL*

A white pottery jelly mould,
c1900, 4in (10cm) high.
£20–25 *AL*

A Shelley white ceramic mould,
in the form of an armadillo,
c1926, 10¼in (26cm) long.
£125–150 *B&R*

A collection of tin chocolate
Easter egg moulds, c1930s.
£1–6 each *No7*

Three Mickey Mouse
aluminium moulds, c1950,
2in (5cm) high.
£8–9 each *AL*

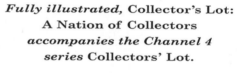

Ovens

A Fletcher Russell
black cast iron four-
burner gas cooker,
no thermostat, c1918,
33in (84cm) high.
£60–80 *VGC*

A Black Prince two-
burner gas cooker, in
unrestored condition
with original black
paint finish, c1915,
37in (94cm) high.
£60–80 *VGC*

A Davis four-burner
gas cooker and stand,
with a white enamel
brick finish, c1920,
51in (129.5cm) high.
£700–800 *SWO*

A New World Eureka
series opaline green
cooker, in original
condition, c1938,
58in (147.5cm) high.
£50–75 *VGC*

Tins

A semi-circular yellow
painted flour bin, late 19thC,
11¾in (30cm) high.
£55–65 *B&R*

A painted flour tin,
1920s, 10in (25.5cm) high.
£45–55 *SMI*

A red and white cake tin,
c1950, 6in (15cm) high.
£8–9 *AL*

A yellow and green coffee tin,
decorated with red and pink
poppies, c1950, 5in (12.5cm) high.
£8–10 *AL*

A biscuit tin, decorated with
Mabel Lucie Attwell scene,
c1950, 5in (12.5cm) diam.
£7–8 *AL*

A Worcester ware cream and
gold aluminium cereal tin, with
red lid, c1960, 6in (15cm) high.
£8–9 *AL*

Utensils

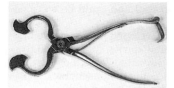

A pair of polished steel sugar nips, c1860, 8½in (21.5cm) long.
£20–35 *WAB*

A cast iron apple peeler, c1880, 10in (25.5cm) high.
£70–80 *SMI*

A cast iron nutmeg grater, c1890, 4in (10cm) long.
£70–80 *SMI*

A Spong No. 630 vegetable slicer, c1940, 12in (30.5cm) high.
£12–15 *UTP*

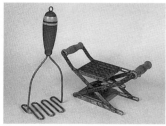

A metal potato masher and chipper, with wooden handles, 1950s, masher 10in (25.5cm) long.
£2–3 each *AL*

A brass crucifix-shaped pastry marker, with wooden handle, late 19thC, 8in (20.5cm) long.
£80–90 *SMI*

Two 'bull' metal tin openers, c1900, 6½in (16.5cm) long.
£8–12 each *WAB*

Three ice cream scoops, 1920s–50s, largest 10½in (26.5cm) long.
£20–30 each *WAB*

A Tala icing syringe and nozzles, 1940, 6in (15cm) high, with original box.
£3–5 *UTP*

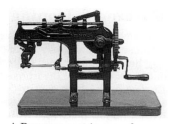

A Bonanza cast iron apple peeler, on a wooden base, by Goodell Co, c1880, 23in (58.5cm) long.
£180–200 *SMI*

An Enterprise cast iron meat press, Philadelphia, USA, c1900, 22¾in (58cm) high.
£80–90 *B&R*

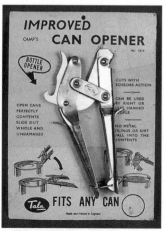

A Tala can opener, with instructions, late 1940s, 8in (20.5cm) high.
£5–6 *UTP*

l. A metal whisk, with a red and yellow wooden handle, c1960, 12in (30.5cm) long.
£5–6 *UTP*

Washing & Ironing

The invention of the iron is credited to the Chinese, who, as early as the 8th century AD, heated saucepan-like items to smooth out their clothes. Flat irons were in use in Europe in the 17th century, and in the 18th century the box iron was developed, with a hollow body into which a heated slug of metal was placed. Ember irons held burning charcoal or embers, while sad irons (a corruption of solid irons), were placed by the fire so that the whole iron could heat up. These irons usually came in pairs, so that one could be warmed while the other was in use.

The Victorians developed irons powered by gas and methylated spirits, and in 1880 the electric iron was invented. This, however, did not become a popular household appliance until the 1920s and 1930s, a period that saw both the introduction of the thermostat, which controlled the electric iron's temperature, and the development of synthetic fabrics, which required pressing with a low and controlled heat.

A Victorian cast iron and brass goffering mangle, on mahogany base, 14in (35.5cm) wide.
£160–180 *AAV*

An Irish cast iron flat iron, late 19thC, 9½in (24cm) long.
£10–15 *EON*

An Irish bog oak clothes plunger, with brass and iron rings, c1850, 49in (124.5cm) long.
£70–80 *EON*

A tin fabric steamer, c1900, 16in (40.5cm) high.
£50–60 *Riv*

A Kenrick Otto gas iron, early 20thC, 7in (18cm) long.
£70–80 *SMI*

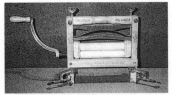

An American salesman's sample wooden mangle, by Lovell Manufacturing Co, in working order, c1900, 7¾in (20cm) high.
£130–145 *B&R*

An Elekira travelling iron and case, with fitting for plug and electric bulb socket, German, 1950s, 7in (18cm) long.
£20–25 *PC*

l. A Davies speckled grey gas iron, early 20thC, 9in (23cm) long.
£60–65 *SMI*

A spirit iron, with wooden handle, early 20thC, 6in (15cm) long.
£60–65 *SMI*

Wood

A Northumbrian riddle board, c1820, 17½in (44.5cm) long.
£250–300   RYA

Riddle boards were used for breaking the husks of oats.

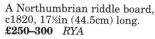

A French baguette tray, 19thC, 43in (109cm) long.
£40–50   DaH

Three sycamore wedding bread boards, late 19thC, 12in (30.5cm) diam.
£80–100 each   SMI

A housemaid's pine box, 1930s, 14in (35.5cm) long.
£70–80   SMI

A wooden bowl, 1850s, 9½in (24cm) diam.
£325–375   A&A

A Provençal walnut bread box, c1870, 30in (76cm) high.
£250–300   LPA

An oak cutlery box, 19thC, 11½in (29cm) long.
£80–100   SWN

A French water ladle or juice spoon, 19thC, 15½in (39.5cm) long.
£35–40   No7

A large bread board, inscribed 'Be Thankful' and carved with wheat and barley, c1900, 15in (38cm) diam.
£125–145   B&R

A wooden rolling pin, with pale blue handles, c1950, 16in (40.5cm) long.
£5–6   AL

FURTHER READING
Christina Bishop, *Miller's Collecting Kitchenware* Miller's Publications, 1995

l. A wooden sugar canister, c1970, 5in (12.5cm) high.
£5–6   AL

LIGHTING

A brass gimballed spring-loaded candle holder, with glass shade, c1840, 13in (33cm) high.
£150–180 *PC*

r. A brass candle lamp, with Burmese glass shade and cranberry font, 19thC, 18in (45.5cm) high.
£170–200 *GAK*

A brass and copper oil lamp, with glass shade, c1890, 29in (73.5cm) high.
£175–200 *TWa*

r. An oil lamp, with alabaster and brass base and moulded green glass font, c1910, 22in (56cm) high.
£75–95 *TWa*

An iron space lamp, 1880s, 20in (51cm) wide.
£60–70 *PC*

A pair of gilt-bronze candlesticks, 19thC, converted for electricity, 22in (56cm) high.
£350–400 *Doc*

A German oil lamp, the white ceramic base decorated with brown flowers, c1890, 8½in (21.5cm) high.
£25–35 *TWa*

A French oil lamp, with green glass font and opaque glass shade, on marble column, c1880, 30in (76cm) high.
£250–300 *TWa*

An oil lamp, with pink painted metal base, 1920s, 10¼in (26cm) high.
£8–10 *TAC*

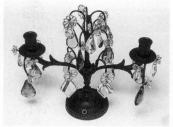

A pair of girandoles, with amethyst and smoked glass drops and black metal candle holders, 1930s, 8in (20.5cm) high.
£450–550 *JPr*

The word 'girandole' derives from the Italian girandola, *a kind of revolving firework. It was used in England from the 18thC to describe candelabra and sconces.*

An Art Deco chrome-plated chandelier, the circular drum body supporting 3 arms with drop fittings on a vase-shaped drop, 1920s, 19¼in (49.5cm) high.
£80–100 *P(B)*

A black iron-framed chandelier, with two-dimensional lyre-shaped pendant amethyst, smoke and crystal cut-glass drops, 1920–30, 21in (53.5cm) high.
£450–550 *JPr*

A multi-coloured glass ceiling bowl, 1930s, 12in (30.5cm) diam.
£30–40 *TWa*

A Continental porcelain lamp base, with figure dressed in blue and white, 1930s, 6in (15cm) high.
£20–30 *MEG*

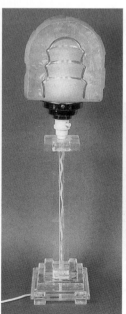

A black and chrome table lamp, c1930, 23in (58.5cm) high.
£85–95 *CAB*

r. A clear Perspex table lamp, 1940s, 24in (61cm) high.
£85–95 *CAB*

A French gilt-brass chandelier, with crystal glass drops, 1930s, 20in (51cm) high.
£350–400 *JPr*

A green plastic bedside lamp, with white glass shade, c1945, 13in (33cm) high.
£35–45 *CAB*

An Ever Ready wooden battery hand lamp, with sliding door at back, mid-20thC, 5in (12.5cm) high.
£30–35 *DOM*

A hanging ceiling light, with yellow glass shade and metal fittings, 1950s, 24in (61cm) high.
£30–40 *TWa*

l. A brass oil lamp, with orange glass shade, 1950s–60s, 29in (73.5cm) high.
£100–120 *TWa*

r. A hanging light, with 5 graduated height chrome balls, 1960s, 35in (89cm) high.
£50–70 *TWa*

Fascination with space imagery in the 1960s profoundly influenced lighting design. Seminal sixties designers such as the Italian Castiglioni brothers and the Danish architect Verner Panton paved the way in modern lighting, and their radical designs were soon copied and reinterpreted in high street shops. Manufacturers used plastic and chrome to create lights that were futuristic in style and that reflected the swinging fashions of the pop generation. Growing interest in post-war design has stimulated demand for lighting from the 1950s–70s and while big-name pieces command the highest prices, stylish non-designer lighting is also becoming increasingly collectable.

A ceiling light, the 5 glass shades with pierced chrome fittings and orange linings, 1960s, 26in (66cm) high.
£70–80 *TWa*

A chrome table lamp, in the form of a mushroom, with both uplight and downlight, 1960s, 16½in (42cm) high.
£120–140 *P(B)*

A Coalport Paddington bear lamp, c1974, 9¾in (25cm) high.
£120–150 *WWY*

A Wedgwood Peter Rabbit light switch cover, 1970s, 4¾in (12cm) high.
£20–25 *WWY*

LUGGAGE & TRAVEL GOODS

A campaign cutlery set, c1890, 5in (12.5cm) long.
£135–155 *DQ*

A copper tea-for-two picnic set, in leather case, c1920, 8in (20.5cm) high.
£120–140 *DQ*

A brown pigskin Gladstone bag, c1930, 15in (38cm) long.
£60–70 *BYG*

A rattan suitcase, c1940, 16in (40.5cm) wide.
£25–35 *DQ*

A wicker picnic basket, fitted with tinplate spirit kettle and burner, spirit canister, glass flask, tea caddy, biscuit box and 4 spiral moulded white and gilt china cups and saucers, with pigskin and leather straps, c1900, 21in (51cm) wide.
£250–300 *AP*

A French wooden hat box, c1920, 18in (45.5cm) diam.
£50–60 *DQ*

A tan leather suitcase, with cloth interior, monogrammed with the initials 'R.M.C.', c1930, 26in (66cm) wide.
£90–100 *BYG*

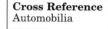

Cross Reference
Automobilia

r. A Brexton light blue picnic hamper, the crockery decorated with forget-me-nots, complete with original label and keys, c1960s, case 23in (58.5cm) wide.
£100–125 *AL*

An English stitched crocodile skin suitcase, c1900, 25in (64cm) wide.
£450–500 *CAT*

A German six-person silver-plated cocktail set, the leather case lined in burgundy velvet with leather strap, opening to reveal drinks flask, ice bucket, cocktail shaker with 6 metal tots, broken zip, c1920, 14½in (37cm) wide.
£350–400 *S*

A pair of Louis Vuitton suitcases, with leather trimming, and a Louis Vuitton holdall, early 20thC, suitcases 31in (78.5cm) wide.
£700–800 *LAY*

MEDALS
Commemorative

Medals have been struck to commemorate every conceivable theme, from great historical events to sporting occasions. Values depend on subject, age, rarity and condition. The appeal of the image is a major factor; the name of the designer can also be important, particularly if the medal is by a well-known artist.

A silver medal, commemorating the death of Charles I, by T. Rawlins, with a draped bust of Charles with long hair and a salamander amid flames on the reverse, 1649, 42mm diam.
£320–350 *BAL*

The salamander on the reverse is used as an emblem of fortitude and patience under sufferings.

A silver medal, commemorating the victories of Anne over Louis XIV, by P. H. Müller, the reverse with a tower besieged, the edge inscribed 'Dominus Tradidit Eum In Manus Foeminae Iudith XVIc', 1706, 43mm diam.
£200–225 *BAL*

The imagery of this medal is designed to satirize Louis XIV for calling himself Magnus while at the same time being defeated by a woman, so making Anne 'greater'.

A silver medal, commemorating the Act of Union Between England and Scotland, 1707, by J. Croker, with a crowned bust and a statue of Anne as Pallas on the reverse, 69mm diam.
£220–250 *BAL*

A bronze medal, commemorating Hans Sloane, founder of the British Museum 1745, signed by J. A. Dassier, a festoon of flowers on reverse, 55mm diam.
£60–70 *EIM*

A gold, red, white and blue enamel badge, commemorating George III's recovery from illness, 1789, 36mm diam, with integral loop for suspension.
£550–650 *BAL*

On March 10th 1789, Parliament presented congratulatory addresses to the King and the nation celebrated his return to health with enthusiasm. On March 14th the King returned to Windsor, with large crowds cheering his progress.

A George Washington, Comitia Americana medal, commemorating the Taking of Boston, 1776, struck in bronze from the original dies by Pierre DuVivier, 68mm diam, in late 19thC leather fitted case embossed with inscription.
£1,700–2,000 *S(NY)*

r. A Dublin York Club silver ticket, by I. Parkes, with bust of the Duke of York and bar loop for suspension inscribed 'Honi Soit Qui Mal y Pense', 1825, 36mm diam.
£145–165 *BAL*

A white metal medal, commemorating the Reform Bill, 1832, by T. Halliday, with conjoined busts of Grey, Russell and Brougham and inscribed 'The Confidence of the People', 38mm diam.
£25–30 *BAL*

A white metal medal, commemorating the Orphan Working School, Hampstead, 1847, with view of the school and inscribed on reverse, 48mm diam.
£40–50 *BAL*

Ally Sloper's silver medal for valour, the reverse inscribed 'To William J. Osborn for his Courageous Conduct at the Fire at Coast Guard Station, Castle Townshend, Co Cork, 7 July 1888', fitted with small ring for suspension, 36mm diam.
£280–320 *DNW*

Ally Sloper was a favourite Victorian cartoon character and this medal was awarded by The Sloperies magazine to a reader who had saved some children from a fire.

The Gallantry Fund Award silver medal, the reverse inscribed 'James Rowley, Decr. 15. 1894', 38mm diam, in fitted case of issue.
£400–450 *DNW*

This medal was awarded by Today magazine in 1894 to a reader who had saved 4 people from drowning.

A bronze medal, commemorating the Penny Post Jubilee, 1840–90, signed by L. C. Lauer, with facing bust of Rowland Hill, founder of the Penny Post, 65mm diam.
£120–150 *EIM*

The Pluck silver medal for heroism, the reverse scroll inscribed 'Sgt Beisly', marked 'Birmingham 1897', with ring suspension and ribbon bar inscribed 'Special Service', 32mm diam.
£350–380 *DNW*

Pluck magazine was established in 1895 to counteract the influence of the 'Penny Dreadful' and celebrate the adventures of British heroes. Like other journals of the period, it awarded its own medals for brave and exceptional deeds.

A silver medal, commemorating the Dublin Brewers and Distillers Exhibition, 1894, by Vaughton, with a large statue, 51mm diam.
£230–260 *DNW*

l. A silver medal, commemorating the National Pig Breeders' Association, founded 1886, by Restall, c1900, 51mm diam.
£55–65 *BAL*

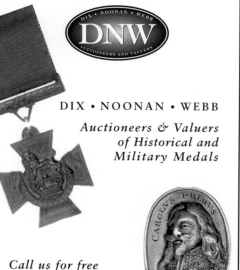

A gold presentation medal, commemorating the opening of the New York Stock Exchange, 1903, by Tiffany & Company, 126mm, in the original maroon leather case of issue, the inner satin cover stamped 'Tiffany & Co, New York, Paris, London', together with the original 7 page illuminated certificate of presentation,
£15,000–17,000 *S(NY)*

The price of this gold medal reflects its rarity, the fact that only 6 were struck, its quality (gold and by Tiffany) and above all its historical and symbolic importance. The New York Stock Exchange is at the heart of the international market, and its building, opened in 1903, is a city landmark and among the most famous financial edifices in the world.

A silver-gilt medal, a prize from Cowes Royal Southern Yacht Club, Isle of Wight, with a view of the club house with flag flying, 1937, 44mm diam.
£55–65 *BAL*

The Golden Penny Award for Bravery, silver, the reverse inscribed 'Owen Holman 1903', 36mm diam.
£550–600 *DNW*

The Golden Penny was a London Newspaper established in 1895. It awarded this medal to policeman Owen Holman for rescuing the victims of a fire.

r. An iron medal, 'Death from the Air', by Arnold Zadikow, with a skeletal figure of Death holding 3 zeppelins with ropes, 1915, 72mm diam.
£240–280 *DNW*

An Art Deco silver medal, by P. M. Dammann, depicting a female head, and a female figure and Paris on the reverse, 1907, 64mm diam.
£200–220 *DNW*

The 1907 date on the medal is that of the founding of the Compagnie Pour La Diffusion d'Electricité. The medal is thought to have been struck to mark an anniversary, either the 20th in 1927 or the 25th in 1932.

A bronze Olympic Games medal, London, 1948, by B. MacKennal and J. Pinches, depicting a quadriga being driven, the reverse with Big Ben and the Houses of Parliament, 51mm diam.
£120–140 *DNW*

A white metal medal, commemorating the opening of the Queen Alexandra Bridge, 1909, by Elkington & Co, 64mm diam.
£40–45 *BAL*

The Women's Social and Political Union Medal for Valour, silver, inscribed 'Hunger Strike', the reverse inscribed 'Isabel Kelley', the suspension bar inscribed with the date 'July 30th 1909', the top suspension brooch bar inscribed 'For Valour', with original ribbon, 22mm diam.
£2,700–3,000 *DNW*

This medal was awarded to suffragette Isabel Kelley for maintaining a five-day hunger strike in Holloway prison. A fearless woman, Kelley later went on to protest at a Budget meeting in Dundee by abseiling from the roof of the Bank of Scotland.

A football medal, 1950s, 50mm diam.
£2–3 *TRE*

Military

The value of military decorations lies not just in the medal itself, but in the bars attached to the ribbon, signifying that a man served at a certain battle or during a specific period of time. 'I am often asked how much bars affect the price of medals,' says Jim Bullock of Romsey Medal Centre. 'Take the example of the Indian Mutiny Medal 1857–58. Without a bar, it is worth £80–100; with a Delhi bar, (showing that the man served at the Battle of Delhi), it goes up to £160, and with a Defence of Lucknow bar the value rises to £650. Another case in point is the Queen's South Africa Medal 1899–1902. On its own it is worth around £40 but with a bar for the Defence of Mafeking, the same medal can fetch £600. There are many different examples one could cite, and bars are a very complex subject, but safe to say, they can make a huge difference to the value of a medal.'

r. A South Africa medal, 1834–53, and Victorian Long Service and Good Conduct Medal, awarded to Private J. Crawforth, 73rd Foot, Black Watch. **£275–350** *RMC*

A Royal Tyrone Regiment struck silver medal, inscribed 'For Soldierly Merit', fitted with steel clip and ring, c1797, 38mm diam. **£320–360** *DNW*

The Marquess of Abercorn established this badge of merit on June 3, 1797. It was to be given to 100 soldiers, selected from men of at least 3 years service.

The Waterloo Medal, with Peninsula bar clasp, impressed 'Jos. Ingea. 15th King's Reg. Hussars', 1815. **£380–450** *Bea(E)*

Four medals: Crimea, with one bar Sebastopol, China 1857 with 2 bars, T Forts 1860, Pekin 1860, Army Long Service and Good Conduct later type, and Turkish Crimea British issue, awarded to W. Daulby, 1st Dragoon Guards. **£300–350** *WAL*

The New Zealand Medal, 1865–66, awarded to Adam Crawford, 4th Battalion Military TRn.
£200–230 *Bea(E)*

A North West Canada medal, 1885, awarded to Private George Rogers, 10th RC.
£130–160 *WAL*

The Ashantee War Medal, 1873–74, awarded to R. Turner, Ship's Corpe, HMS Simoon 73–74.
£140–160 *Bea(E)*

An Indian General Service medal, 1895–1902, with bar 'Relief of Chitral', awarded to Private E. Deerie, King's Own Scottish Borderers.
£60–70 *RMC*

A George V Distinguished Conduct medal, British War medal, Victory medal, Army Long Service and George V Good Conduct Medal, awarded to Lancashire Fusiliers.
£400–450 *RMC*

A General Service medal, 1918–62, 2 bars Palestine 1945–48 and Malaya George VI, awarded to Sergeant R. A. Taylor, REME.
£35–45 *RMC*

An Army Long Service and Good Conduct Medal, Elizabeth II, 2nd issue, with suspension bar Somaliland Scouts.
£550–600 *DNW*

An 1939–45 Star, Atlantic Star, Burma Star, 1939–45 War medal, Naval Long Service and Good Conduct medal, awarded to E.R.A. H. H. Tink, HMS *Drake*, Royal Navy.
£70–80 *RMC*

According to records at the Public Record Office, 10 medals with the suspension bar worded 'Somaliland Scouts' were ordered from the Royal Mint in 1954. British Somaliland ceased to exist shortly afterwards and this, therefore, is probably the rarest variety of this series.

l. A 1935 Jubilee medal, unnamed as issued.
£14–16 *RMC*

METALWARE

A French bronzed spelter
figure after Moreau,
of a fisherman, on a
turned base, 19thC,
28in (71cm) high.
£275–325 *CAG*

A cast iron Amos 'n'
Andy group, 1930s,
4½in (11.5cm) high.
£150–170 *AWT*

*Amos 'n' Andy was a hugely
successful US radio comedy act
in the 1930s, featuring 2 black
characters, Amos and Andy,
portrayed by white actors.*

A tin 'Farmers' fire mark, mid-
19thC, 10in (25.5cm) high.
£120–150 *ET*

*Metal fire marks were affixed to the
front of buildings to prove that they
were insured.*

A Viennese School cold-painted
bronze kingfisher, c1900,
4½in (11.5cm) long.
£150–175 *WeH*

A chrome fox paperweight,
c1920, 8¾in (22cm) long.
£115–135 *RTh*

l. An enamel powder compact, in
the form of an envelope bearing a
postmark 'London, April 18th, 1939',
3¾in (9.5cm) square.
£60–70 *HYD*

A lead thrush, with base to
fit on a garden post, c1860,
10in (25.5cm) high.
£200–225 *INC*

A spelter fox, with a partridge
in its mouth and 2 front paws
on a log, with marble base,
c1900, 5in (12.5cm) high.
£115–135 *WeH*

A French silver-coloured
metal compact, c1930,
2in (5cm) square.
£10–12 *PC*

A French compact, in blue, cream and grey enamel and chrome geometric pattern, by Houbigant, 1930s, 3¼in (8.5cm) wide.
£10–12 *PC*

A base metal bottle pourer, in the form of a knight's head, 1930s, 3½in (9cm) high.
£7–9 *GIN*

An Elizabeth Arden mask compact, c1940, 3in (7.5cm) wide.
£100–120 *LBr*

Brass

An adjustable brass tapestry holder, to act as a firescreen when clamped on a mantle, c1870, 14in (35.5cm) long.
£75–85 *LIB*

A Henry Fearncombe & Sons brass jug, c1880, 9in (23cm) high.
£550–650 *NCA*

The initials 'C.D.' on base may indicate that the designer was Christopher Dresser.

A brass desk bell, in the form of a Dutch woman, 1900–10, 2½in (6.5cm) high.
£20–25 *CHe*

A brass slip jug, 19thC, 6in (15cm) high.
£32–36 *No7*

Cross Reference
Art Deco
Art Nouveau

A brass spring-loaded candlestick, c1890, 14½in (36.5cm) high.
£125–145 *WAB*

l. A brass box, the cover engraved with an owl with glass eyes, 1930s, 2¼in (5.5cm) diam.
£45–50 *CHe*

A brass string box with scissors, c1900, 3¾in (9.5cm) high.
£80–90 *CHe*

A brass photograph frames, early 20thC, 5in (12.5cm) high.
£60–70 *MSB*

Bronze

An English bronze mortar, with the coat-of-arms of Charles II, late 17thC, 4¼in (11cm) high.
£250–350 *KEY*

Two bronze and iron mannequin boots, 19thC, 5¼in (13.5cm) high.
£50–60 each *ASM*

A French Second Empire bronze coppered dish, sculpted by Lielierre and edited by Susse Frères, c1870, 5in (12.5cm) diam.
£180–220 *BKK*

l. A French Art Nouveau bronze frame, the sides formed as nymphs, with waterlilies, butterflies and a moon, late 19thC, 9¾ x 11in (25 x 28cm).
£250–300 *HOK*

r. A bronze bowl, engraved and relief-moulded with Art Nouveau style decoration, c1900, 15in (38cm) high.
£1,200–1,400 *DQ*

Copper

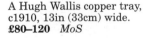

l. An Art Nouveau wall mirror, the copper frame decorated with a sun motif, flowering plants and a peacock with turquoise enamelled plumage, with metal label for Goodyears, Regent St, London, c1900, 22 x 31¾in (56 x 81cm).
£650–750 *Bea(E)*

A Hugh Wallis copper tray, c1910, 13in (33cm) wide.
£80–120 *MoS*

l. A copper wire muffin fork, 19thC, 8½in (21.5cm) long.
£30–35 *No7*

Pewter

A Hugh Wallis pewter tray, c1900, 17¼in (44cm) wide.
£30–40 *WAC*

A Liberty & Co Tudric pewter wine taster, c1900, 5in (12.5cm) diam.
£50–60 *WAC*

An oval planter, on 4 pad feet, stamped 'Tudric', 1920s, 13in (33cm) long.
£220–250 *P(B)*

Silver

A cylindrical nutmeg grater, with side opening, by Mary Anne & Charles Reily, London 1826, 3in (7.5cm) long.
£500–550 *TC*

A silver tea caddy, by William Comyns, the vase-shaped body chased and embossed with floral and foliate decoration, vacant cartouche to front, the concave hinged lid with engraved edge and plain top, complete with key, London 1889, 4½in (11.5cm) high.
£550–600 *GAK*

An Arts and Crafts silver bowl, the hammered body with 3 open leaf petal-embossed handles, by Florence and Louise Rimmington, London 1903, 4¼in (11cm) diam.
£180–200 *WW*

A George III silver cream jug, with prickwork engraving, 4in (10cm) high.
£150–180 *PSA*

A silver pin tray, London 1895, 4½in (11.5cm) wide.
£70–80 *PSA*

A pair of Britannia standard Georgian style sauceboats, with crinkle rims, scroll handles, bulbous bodies and hoof supports, London 1901, 4¾in (12cm) long.
£130–150 *DDM*

A candle snuffer, with silver handle, c1880, 10½in (26.5cm) long.
£35–45 *TAC*

A silver egg-shaped vinaigrette, marked London 1881, 1½in (4cm) high.
£55–65 *VB*

A half-fluted rose bowl, with a moulded rim over a band of embossed ribbon festoons, on black plinth with presentation plaque, London 1897, 9in (23cm) diam.
£350–400 *AH*

l. Three silver nail buffers, marked Birmingham 1899, 1904 and 1910, largest 3½in (9cm) long.
£30–40 each *VB*

Two silver sovereign cases, with slide top openings, by Levi & Saloman, Birmingham 1902, 1in (2.5cm) diam.
£265–300 *THOM*

A silver sauce bottle coaster, London 1907, 1½in (4cm) high.
£20–25 *HEI*

An octagonal silver sugar caster, maker J. R., Glasgow 1904, 8½in (21.5cm) high.
£175–200 *PC*

r. A silver and steel buttonhook, depicting Mr Punch, by Crisford & Norris, Birmingham 1904, 4in (10cm) long.
£125–155 *BEX*

A silver epergne, by W. Hutton & Sons, London 1908, 12in (30.5cm) high.
£1,000–1,250 *THOM*

A silver sweetmeat dish, c1910, 10⅛in (26cm) wide.
£220–250 *WeH*

A crocodile-skin flask, with silver base and top, initialled 'E.W.E.', c1910, 6in (15cm) high.
£225–245 *RTh*

A French silver watch/key ring, in the form of a rifle, c1910, 2in (5cm) long.
£275–325 *BEX*

A silver top rouge pot, Birmingham 1915, 1½in (4cm) high.
£25–35 *PSA*

r. A silver novelty ship's ventilator, by S. Jacob, London 1911, 4⅜in (11cm) high.
£250–275 *TC*

Three silver napkin clips, c1910, 1–1½in (2.5–4cm) long.
£85–95 each *BEX*

Napkin clips were used by gentlemen to pin their napkins to their shirts.

A silver commemorative spade, inscribed 'A Memento of Cutting Sod of No. 3 Pit from Welsh Colliery', by J. R., Glasgow 1919, 8in (20.5cm) high.
£300–345 *BEX*

A cut-glass flask, with silver base and top, hallmarked, c1920, 5¼in (13.5cm) long.
£160–180 *RTh*

A Liberty & Co silver covered bowl, with twin handles, foliate decoration and openwork finial, Birmingham 1930, 6¼in (16cm) wide.
£450–500 *TC*

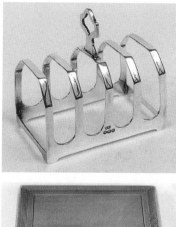

r. A silver toast rack, by E. V., Sheffield 1937, 5in (12.5cm) long.
£65–70 *WAC*

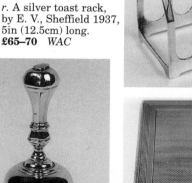

A silver table bell, with ivory handle, by J. H. S., London 1935, 4½in (11.5cm) high.
£500–550 *TC*

An Asprey's sterling silver compact, with gold inlay, ruby thumb catch, and inner lid, Birmingham 1964, 2¾in (7cm) square.
£85–95 *PC*

r. A silver orange peeler, by Tom Marshall, 1998, 1¾in (4.5cm) long.
£70–80 *STG*

A silver fox corkscrew, with red garnet eyes, hallmarked, 1920, 3½in (9cm) wide.
£125–145 *RTh*

A silver napkin ring, Birmingham 1926, 1½in (4cm) high.
£80–100 *MRW*

A silver napkin ring, egg cup and spoon, by Harry Atkin, Sheffield 1937–39, egg cup 2½in (6.5cm) high.
£200–225 *BEX*

Cruets & Salts

A pair of silver salts, by Robert
Hennell, London 1859,
1½in (4cm) high.
£200–250   *CoHA*

A Victorian seven-bottle cruet
set, on ornate scroll feet,
3 bottles with silver covers,
maker's mark J. E., London
1861, 10¼in (26cm) high.
£600–700   *DDM*

A pepper pot, in the form
of a fighting cock, by John
Aldwinkle and Thomas Slater,
London 1888, 3½in (9cm) high.
£300–350   *TC*

A novelty silver pepper, in
the form of a Toby jug with
scrolled handle, Birmingham
1911, 3in (7.5cm) high.
£300–350   *GAK*

A pair of pierced silver salts,
with original green glass liners,
Chester 1909, 2in (5cm) high.
£200–230   *CoHA*

A novelty chick pepper pot, by
William Hornsby, London 1902,
1½in (4cm) high.
£200–230   *TC*

Cups & Mugs

A silver-mounted coconut cup,
by Matthew Brutton and John
Fothergill, Birmingham 1776,
7½in (19cm) high.
£900–1,000   *AMH*

A silver beaker, with
contemporary crest, by John
Hampston and John Prince,
York 1788, 3in (7.5cm) high.
£850–950   *DD*

FURTHER READING
Silver & Sheffield Plate Marks,
Miller's Publications, 1993
*Silver & Plate Antiques
Checklist,* Miller's
Publications, 1994.

A silver mug, with leaf capped
scroll handle and engraved
floral decoration, by Robert
Hennell, London 1872,
4¾in (12cm) high.
£230–260   *Bea(E)*

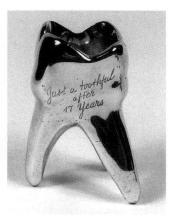

A tumbler cup, engraved with crests and initials, by McHattie & Fenwick, Edinburgh 1802, 3in (7.5cm) high.
£450–500 *HofB*

A thimble tot cup, inscribed 'Just a Thimble Full', by Hilliard & Thomason, Birmingham 1876, 2¼in (5.5cm) high, in original case.
£250–285 *TC*

A silver tooth tot cup, inscribed 'Just a Toothful after 17 years', by William Frederick Wright, London 1906, 3¼in (8.5cm) high.
£475–535 *TC*

Cutlery & Flatware

A silver caddy spoon, by Abraham Taylor, London 1797, 2½in (6.5cm) long.
£335–365 *BEX*

A silver caddy spoon, London 1795, 2¼in (5.5cm) long.
£225–245 *BEX*

r. Two pairs of steel knives and forks, stained ivory and silver collars, with mark of the London Cutlery Co, c1730, longest 7in (18cm).
£100–120 *ET*

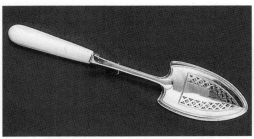

A George III chop server, with pierced and sprung spade-shaped blades and plain ivory grip, by William Eley I, London 1796, 12in (30.5cm) long.
£350–400 *HofB*

A pair of silver tablespoons, by Peter Bateman, London 1799, 9in (23cm) long.
£165–185 *CoHA*

A pair of silver sugar tongs, by Peter & Ann Bateman, London 1801, 5½in (14cm) long.
£40–50 *DIC*

A silver caddy spoon, by Gervaise Wheeler, Birmingham 1834, 3¼in (8.5cm) long.
£250–275 *BEX*

An oak canteen of matched silver fiddle pattern cutlery and flatware, London 1836–74, knives Sheffield 1966.
£1,000–1,200 *WL*

A Russian presentation spoon, the reverse of the bowl engraved with an inscription and scroll foliage, Moscow 1867, 7in (18cm) long.
£200–235 *HofB*

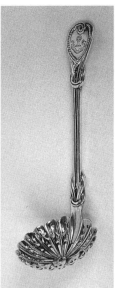

A silver sifter spoon, by Lias, London 1854, 5½in (14cm) long.
£200–220 *AMH*

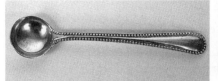

A silver salt spoon, London 1876, 3¼in (8cm) long.
£20–22 *AMH*

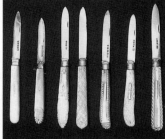

Seven silver-bladed folding fruit knives, with mother-of-pearl handles, 1870–1900.
£50–70 *MB*

A silver caddy spoon, by John, Henry & Charles Lias, London 1874, 4in (10cm) long.
£30–35 *BEX*

A silver cake knife, by L. E. & S., Sheffield 1898, 10½in (26.5cm) long.
£200–225 *BEX*

A pair of silver-handled nut crackers, Birmingham 1899, 4½in (11.5cm) long.
£170–200 *CoHA*

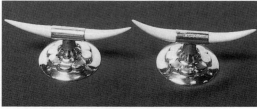

A pair of Edwardian silver and ivory knife rests, by T. Wooley, Birmingham 1903, 3½in (9cm) long.
£225–265 *BEX*

A silver sifter spoon, Sheffield 1900, 4¾in (12cm) long.
£120–140 *AMH*

A pair of Edwardian silver grape scissors, by Elkington, Birmingham 1903, 7in (18cm) long.
£375–425 *BEX*

A silver jam spoon, Sheffield
1903, 5½in (14cm) long.
£20–22 *AMH*

A pair of silver teaspoons,
the terminals decorated with
crossed tennis rackets and
inscribed 'S.G.L.T.C.', c1910,
7in (18cm) long.
£80–100 *WaR*

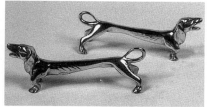

l. A pair of dachshund knife
rests, by William Hutton &
Sons Ltd, Sheffield 1908,
3¼in (8cm) long.
£350–400 *TC*

Two silver souvenir
spoons, St Louis 1904
and Alaska 1909,
5in (12.5cm) long.
£60–70 each *YAN*

Figures & Sculpture

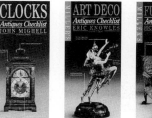

l. A Continental silver
group of a barrel
organ player, 1930s,
4in (10cm) wide.
£65–80 *TAR*

A silver figure of a
slave, on a marble
base, by John S.
Hunt, c1860,
13¼in (33.5cm) high.
£2,250–2,500 *SFL*

A silver deer, by
E. Barnard & Sons,
with Victorian duty
stamp pre-1891,
3½in (9cm) high.
£145–165 *WeH*

A Continental silver cock pheasant, c1924,
9in (23cm) long.
£800–900 *DIC*

Menu Holders

Four Scottish silver menu
holders, by Hamilton &
Inches, Edinburgh 1896,
2¾in (7cm) long.
£550–600 *BEX*

A silver menu holder,
Birmingham 1893,
3½in (9cm) wide.
£70–80 *PSA*

A set of 4 artist's palette menu
holders, by Martin Hall & Co,
Birmingham 1904,
1½in (4cm) high.
£475–525 *TC*

l. A pair of silver lobster claw
menu holders, by Sampson
Mordan & Co, Chester 1907,
1¾in (4.5cm) high.
£300–350 *BEX*

r. A pair of Edwardian
silver duck menu holders,
by Crisford & Norris,
Birmingham 1909,
1½in (4cm) wide.
£325–365 *BEX*

Photograph Frames

A Victorian silver photograph
frame, slight damage,
6½in (16.5cm) high.
£65–75 *Q2*

A silver photograph frame,
by W. Comyns, London 1905,
7¼in (18.5cm) high.
£450–500 *THOM*

A silver photograph frame,
Birmingham 1904,
6in (15cm) high.
£325–375 *THOM*

l. A silver photograph frame,
by R. Pringle, Birmingham
1908, 5in (12.5cm) high.
£200–235 *THOM*

r. A silver photograph frame,
by Richard Cooper, Birmingham
1911, 5½in (14cm) high.
£200–220 *THOM*

Silver Plate

A silvered bronzed model of Hippocampus, c1862, 9½in (24cm) high.
£240–280 *SUC*

Hippocampus was the steed of Neptune, Roman god of the sea. The mythical sea creature has the head and forelegs of a horse and the hindquarters and tail of a fish.

A silver-plated spoon warmer, in the shape of an egg with a chick perched on the shell, c1890, 5in (12.5cm) wide.
£230–260 *SSW*

A Mappin & Webb silver-plated revolving tureen, with ivory handle, c1930s, 12½in (32cm) wide.
£200–220 *TAC*

A Victorian silver-plated flask, with snuff box, 5½in (14cm) long.
£120–150 *ET*

l. A barrister's silver-plated hammer, c1900, 7¼in (18.5cm) long.
£60–70 *WAB*

The pointed end was used to break the seal on documents, and the hammer end to reseal them.

A silver-plated commemorative teaspoon, with enamelled terminal inscribed 'Canada' and embossed city scene on bowl, 4½in (11.5cm) long.
£9–10 *TRE*

A silver-plated biscuit barrel, by Elkington & Co, decorated with figures in high relief, the hinged cover embossed with an ale-drinking figure sitting on a barrel, the spreading base with a band of flowers and leaves, 1874, 8¼in (21cm) high.
£330–360 *P(EA)*

A silver-plated pepper mill, in the form of a caster, c1920, 4¼in (10cm) high.
£60–70 *CoHA*

r. A Stratton silver-plated 'Princess' compact, with metal gravure 'Old Master' design on lid and automatic opening inner lid, c1960, 3in (7.5cm) diam, with original figured grosgrain pouch.
£30–40 *PC*

MILITARIA, ARMS & ARMOUR

l. A Georgian tipstaff, the top in the form of brass openwork crown, polished turned wood grip, 8½in (21.5cm) high.
£330–380 *WAL*

r. A French Dragoons leather saddle, and a pair of French leather saddle holsters, late 19thC.
£700–800 *Bon*

A mounted infantry officer's horse's bit, 19thC, 5in (12.5cm) wide.
£70–80 *ET*

A James Burrows stonebow, with slender steel bow, retaining its original strings, slight damage, early 19thC, 32¾in (83.5cm) long.
£400–450 *Bon*

A brass-mounted cow horn powder horn, for the Baker Rifle of the Percy Tenantry, end cap engraved with ducal coronet above crescent, c1800, 14in (35.5cm) long.
£250–280 *WAL*

A framed fragment of an L32 zeppelin, c1916, 11in (28cm) high.
£100–110 *NC*
Signed by the lieutenant who shot it down over Billericay, Essex.

A cream jug, from a Luftwaffe officers' mess, 1940s, 2in (5cm) high.
£30–35 *COB*

A WWII Japanese military split image range finder, 3½in (9cm) long.
£125–150 *ET*

l. A photographic postcard of military money, 1940s.
£5–8 *WP*

A painted wooden side drum of the London Irish Rifles, with green and black painted rims, black cords and tensioners, title scroll, regimental badge and 21 battle honours, signed M. O'Donnell, c1960, 20in (51cm) high.
£200–220 *WAL*

Armour & Uniforms

A breastplate, rope-turned at the neck, pierced on the right side for a lance-rest, slight pitting, probably German, late 16thC, 11¾in (30cm) high.
£450–500   *Bon*

A cabasset, formed in one piece with vestigial pear-shaped finial and brass rosettes around base, slight damage, c1600.
£160–200   *WAL*

A lobster-tailed pot helmet, the ribbed skull with ring-shaped finial, pointed fixed peak with turned edge, probably German, mid-17thC, 7⅜in (20cm) high.
£650–750   *Bon*

r. A French Second Empire cuirassier's breastplate and backplate, each of bright steel, the interiors with dated etched inscriptions, complete with original brass shoulder chains and retaining plates, leathers replaced, 1863, 19in (48.5cm) high.
£450–500   *Bon*

A French czapka of the 8th Chevau Legers Lanciers Polonais, with leather headband and peak, green cloth sides and tip with white braid trim, later long white feather plume and chinchain, c1812.
£3,700–4,000   *WAL*

A captain's uniform, comprising full dress blue tunic, patrol jacket, mess jacket, pill box hat and several other items, all contained in tin trunk with nameplate 'Lieut Bartlett, 8th Lancashire Artillery Volunteers', c1865.
£900–1,000   *WAL*

r. A Victorian military style horse-hair sporran, c1880, 18in (45.5cm) long.
£120–150   *BWA*

A Prussian Landwehr other rank's picklehaube, black leather with pierced and embossed Prussian eagle helmet-plate, central brass spike, original cockades and chinstrap, complete with original field service cover, c1914, 9in (23cm) high.
£330–380 *Bon*

A WWI tank driver's mask, the leather-covered front with chainmail mouth protection, chamois-lined with ties.
£200–220 *Bon*

l. A Victorian officer's silver-plated helmet, of the 1st (Royal) Dragoons, in tin case with nameplate 'M. R. Burrell Esq, Royal Dragoons'.
£1,600–1,800 *WAL*

Sir Merrik Raymond Burrell, CBE, 7th Baronet, served in S. Africa, Inspector of Remounts, 1915, CBE 1919.

A WWI Austrian 1916 pattern Berndorfer steel helmet, with protecting front plate attached and triple leather pad liner.
£200–220 *Bon*

A post warden's uniform, comprising jacket with badge 'CD Birmingham', skirt and hat, c1942, jacket 28in (71cm) long.
£80–100 *PC*

Two WWII German steel helmets.
£200–240 each *FAM*

A Russian tank crew helmet, with built-in headphones and throat mike, 1950s.
£25–30 *FAM*

Badges & Helmet Plates

An officer's silver-plated helmet plate, of the 1st Cheshire Rifle Volunteers, with maker's tablet for Hobson & Sons on back, 1902–08.
£240–280 *WAL*

A Victorian West Kent bronze helmet plate, 4in (10cm) high.
£80–100 *PC*

l. A bronze cap badge, of the Charterhouse Officers' Training Corps, 1914–18.
£18–20 *PC*

A bronze badge, of the Queen's Own Worcestershire Hussars, 1908–56.
£18–20 *PC*

A silver and green enamel commemorative lapel badge, entitled 'Easter Rising 1916', the reverse with lapel stud fitting.
£160–180 *DNW*

Edged Weapons

l. Captain Bligh's court sword, the steel hilt with urn pommel, with single knuckle bow, single rear quillon, pierced grip, circular pierced guard and original leather washer, late 18thC, blade 32in (98cm) long.
£8,500–9,500 *LAY*

William Bligh (1754–1817) became famous as being Captain of HMS Bounty at the time of the celebrated mutiny in 1789. Partly thanks to films, huge interest still surrounds this event and the much debated character of Bligh, which explains the value of this sword.

A 1788 pattern heavy cavalry trooper's sword, with spear point, steel basket guard, ovoid pommel, and brass wire-bound fishskin-covered grip, iron scabbard, slight pitting and scabbard lug missing, 35in (89cm) long.
£750–850 *WAL*

A basket-hilted back-sword, with single-edged blade, the hilt of flattened bars framing shaped panels pierced with designs of circles and triangles, domed pommel and spirally grooved shagreen-covered wooden grip, late 18thC, 31¾in (81cm) long.
£1,200–1,400 *Bon*

A German carved dagger, the hilt representing a suit of armour, 19thC, 10in (25.5cm) long.
£850–950 *AEF*

Firearms

A pair of rifled flintlock box-lock pocket pistols, by John Collis, Oxford, with signed actions engraved with a trophy of arms on each side, late 18thC, 6in (15.5cm) long.
£500–550 *Bon*

r. A pair of officer's percussion pistols, by E. M. Reilly, London, with accessories, maker's label on inside of case, c1840, 6in (15cm) long.
£900–1,000 *WA*

MONEY BOXES

A Nottingham slipware brown-glazed money box, inscribed 'Dorothy Blacow', c1866, 11in (28cm) high.
£380–420 *SER*

A Nottingham slipware money box, impressed 'Thomas Harold Preston, c1884, 11in (28cm) high.
£370–400 *SER*

l. An American cast iron mechanical money box, in the form of a jockey riding a mule, with original paintwork, patented April 22nd, 1879, 10in (25.5cm) long.
£450–500 *FW&C*

An iron and brass money bank, c1890, 7½in (19cm) high.
£180–200 *INC*

A tin money box, in the form of a toadstool, with red and white spotted top, with key, 1930s, 3in (7.5cm) high.
£24–28 *GrD*

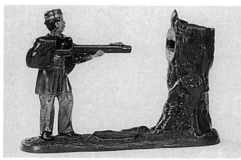

A cast iron Creedmore money bank, by J. & E. Stevens & Co, modelled as a rifled marksman in red jacket with blue cape and trousers, slight damage, patent date 1/6/1877, 10in (25.5cm) long.
£200–220 *S(S)*

A cast iron money bank, with a frog on a penny farthing bicycle, repainted in red, yellow and green, c1880, 10½in (26.5cm) wide.
£10–15 *MAC*

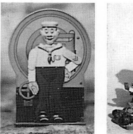

A SylvaC brown-glazed
money box, in the form of
a bulldog, No. 5096, 1930s,
5½in (14cm) high.
£45–55 *TAC*

A composition Hovis money
box, 1960s, 5in (12.5cm) long.
£5–7 *CMF*

A brown-glazed pottery
football money box, 1960–70,
5in (12.5cm) high.
£5–6 *TRE*

r. A plastic Winnie-the-
Pooh money box, 1970s,
3in (7.5cm) high.
£5–7 *CMF*

A Winston Churchill money
box, 'Save for Victory', 1940s,
5in (12.5cm) high.
£20–25 *JUN*

A blue plastic owl savings
bank, by Cowan de Crest Ltd,
c1965, 7¼in (18.5cm) high.
£16–18 *CMF*

A ceramic Noddy money box,
1970s, 4in (10cm) high.
£14–16 *CMF*

A blue plastic piggy bank,
1950s, 6½in (16.5cm) high.
£4–6 *CMF*

A Butlin Beavers' papier
mâché money box, 1960s,
6in (15cm) high.
£20–24 *Rac*

A plastic National Westminster
Bank globe money box, 1980s,
4½in (11.5cm) high.
£8–9 *CMF*

NEWSPAPERS & MAGAZINES

Newspapers began in the late 16th/early 17th century when continental printers, principally in Germany, produced 'relations' – single sheets of paper reporting a specific event. Over a week or more, several sheets might be gathered into a newsbook. One of the earliest examples was the weekly relation published by Johann Carolus of Strasbourg from January 1609, which included in September of that year an account of Galileo's telescope.

The first newsbook or *coranto* (from the Latin 'to run') published in England was issued in London in 1621 by Thomas Archer, who was quickly imprisoned for embellishing his stories. Censorship was draconian, and early newspapers such as *The Weekly News* (est. 1622) restricted themselves to reporting foreign affairs for fear of attracting unwelcome attention from politicians and the courts. The Civil War, 1642–46, however, stimulated huge demand for home news, and both Parliamentarians and Royalists produced their own news-books, engaging in a war of propaganda as well as military battles. Newspapers were strictly controlled both under Oliver Cromwell and Charles II, but at the end of the 17th century regulations were relaxed and there was a rise in demand for newspapers, stimulated by the development of London coffee houses. The two outstanding coffee-house journals were *The Tatler* (est. 1709) and *The Spectator* (est. 1711).

The 18th century was a golden age for newspapers, witnessing the launch of local and Sunday newspapers and the founding of *The Times* in 1785, which became the leading journal of the day. In the 19th century, with developing literacy and prosperity, the press expanded enormously with publications for every taste ranging from the radical *Poor Man's Guardian* (1831) dedicated to protecting public liberty and the freedom of the press, to comic papers such as *Ally Sloper's Half Holiday*, aimed at a largely working-class readership. The Victorian period saw the introduction of the pictorial newspaper, most famously *The London Illustrated News* (1842), and the launch of many great dailies including *The Daily Mail* (1896), which sold for ½d and within 10 years had achieved a readership of one million.

The most important factors for collectors tend to be content (the news events reported), newspaper title and condition. Early newspapers (before the mid-19th century) are often very rare, because only a small number were printed originally, from which only a few survive today. Condition of antique pieces, however, can often be better than more recent examples, because the paper quality was higher. Pulp paper was introduced in the 1900s, making 20th-century newspapers difficult to conserve, and prone to disintegration. Look out for early pieces, first editions and newspapers recounting events of major interest.

Newspapers

The Perfect Diurnall, 21st–28th August, 1654, 8 x 6in (20.5 x 15cm).
£80–90 *HaR*

Published by Parliament in 1642 at the outbreak of the Civil War.

The Newes, 26th May, 1664, 8 x 6½in (20.5 x 16.5cm).
£70–80 *ANN*

The Impartial Protestant Mercury, 10th–14th March, 1684, 11 x 7in (28 x 18cm).
£60–80 *HaR*

Cross Reference
Comics

The London Gazette, 6th–9th July, 1685, 11¼ x 7in (28.5 x 18cm).
£250–300 *ANN*

Includes a report of the Battle of Sedgmoor, a rare and sought-after copy.

The London Gazette,
9th–12th June, 1673,
11¼ x 7in (28.5 x 18cm).
£35–40 *HaR*

*In 1665 the Court moved
to Oxford to avoid the
plague. Even newspapers
from London were feared
to be infected, so Charles
II authorised Lord
Arlington to publish* The
Oxford Gazette. *When
the Court returned to the
capital the newspaper
followed, changing its
name to* The London
Gazette *and becoming
the leading official
journal of Charles's reign.*

Jackson's Oxford Journal,
31st March, 1792,
18½ x 12½in (47 x 32cm).
£12–15 *ANN*

New Observator, 10th
January, 1691, 8 x 12¾in
(20.5 x 32.5cm).
£40–50 *ANN*

The London Courant,
24th September, 1746,
17¼ x 11¾in (44 x 30cm).
£35–40 *HaR*

*The Westminster
Journal and Old British
Spy,* 2nd–9th October,
1802, 18¾ x 13½in
(47.5 x 34.5cm).
£20–25 *HaR*

l. The London Chronicle, reporting the
Battle of Vittoria, a Wellington victory,
3rd–5th July, 1813, 11¾ x 9in (30 x 23cm).
£100–120 *ANN*

The Norwich Gazette,
24th February, 1728,
10½ x 8½in
(26.5 x 21.5cm).
£80–90 *HaR*

*The Middlesex Journal
or Chronicle of Liberty,*
17th–19th January,
1771, 18 x 11¾in
(45.5 x 30cm).
£15–20 *HaR*

Bell's Weekly Messenger,
including Nelson's
funeral edition,
12th January, 1806,
14½ x 10in (37 x 25.5cm).
£180–200 *ANN*

The Post Boy, 8th–10th
August, 1723, 14 x 8in
(35.5 x 20.5cm).
£35–40 *HaR*

*The Morning Post and
Daily Advertiser,*
12th March, 1783,
18 x 12½in (45.5 x 32cm).
£10–12 *ANN*

The Times, reporting
the Drury Lane
Theatre fire disaster,
25th February, 1809,
12½ x 19½in
(32 x 49.5cm).
£30–35 *HaR*

The Sun, 4th March
1815, 20 x 13½in
(51 x 34.5cm).
£10–15 *ANN*

The Black Dwarf,
10th September, 1817,
11 x 8¾in (28 x 22cm).
£12–15 *HaR*

The Black Dwarf
*was an important
radical paper.*

Bell's Weekly Messenger,
issue No. 5, 16th
September, 1827,
16 x 11½in (40.5 x 29cm).
£10–15 *HaR*

*The Illustrated London
News*, issue No. 1,
14th May, 1842,
16 x 11in (40.5 x 28cm).
£3–5 *HaR*

The Guardian,
16th April, 1856,
15¾ x 11in (40 x 28cm).
£5–10 *ANN*

Cross Reference
Shipping

*The Exchange and
Mart*, priced one penny,
13th May, 1868, 16½ x
10¾in (42 x 27.5cm).
£8–10 *ANN*

Daily Mail, No. 1,
4th May, 1896,
23¾ x 17¼in (59 x 44cm).
£40–50 *HaR*

Daily Mail, Queen
Victoria's Diamond
Jubilee edition,
with 2 photographs,
23rd June, 1897,
24 x 17½in (61 x 44.5cm).
£65–80 *HaR*

Cross Reference
Comics

*Ally Sloper's Half
Holiday*, a comedy
magazine, 21st August,
1897, 15½ x 11in
(39.5 x 28cm).
£5–6 *ANN*

The Daily Mirror,
recording the sinking
of *Titanic*, inside story
proclaims 'All Lives
Safe', Tuesday 16th
April, 1912.
£90–100 *MED*

A newspaper vendor's
stand poster, entitled
'*The Daily Mirror*,
Saturday April 20,
1912, Hymn Played
While The Titanic
Sank', showing part of
sheet music, 30 x 20in
(76 x 51cm).
£500–550 *ONS*

The British Worker,
13th May, 1926,
12½ x 10in (32 x 25.5cm).
£45–50 *HaR*

Daily Mirror, Festival
of Britain edition,
priced one penny,
3rd May, 1951,
14 x 11½in (35.5 x 29cm).
£4–5 *GIN*

Ocean Times, a ship's
daily newspaper from
RMS *Franconia*,
31st March, 1953.
£3–5 *BAf*

News Chronicle,
Coronation issue,
3rd June, 1953,
24 x 16½in (61 x 42cm).
£1–3 *HaR*

Daily Herald,
Coronation issue, 3rd
June, 1953, 21 x 16½in
(53.5 x 42cm).
£1–3 *HaR*

*The Times, Survey of
British Aviation*,
1953, 24 x 17½in
(61 x 44.5cm).
£3–5 *HaR*

*The Times, The First
Ascent of Mount
Everest*, July 1953,
18 x 12½in (45.5 x 32cm).
£4–5 *HaR*

Sunday Citizen,
23rd September, 1962,
16 x 12in (40.5 x 30.5cm).
£4–5 *HaR*

The Times, moon
landing edition, 3rd
June, 1969, 24 x
17½in (61 x 44.5cm).
£4–5 *HaR*

Magazines

The War Budget, 1st
June, 1916, 14 x 6in
(35.5 x 15cm).
£2–3 *MRW*

l. Two *John Bull* magazines,
10 x 10in (25.5 x 25.5cm) 1950s.
£1–2 each *Rac*

r. Picture Post, 4th April
1942, 13 x 10½in
(33 x 26.5cm).
£2–3 *RAD*

l. Vogue Beauty Book,
1953, 11 x 9in
(28 x 23cm).
£6–8 *RAD*

Vogue, July 1958,
13 x 9¾in (33 x 25cm).
£6–8 *RAD*

A blue jasper scent bottle, each side decorated with a figure within swag, ribbon and floral borders, probably Wedgwood, 19thC, 4in (10cm) high.
£240–260 *AAV*

A French turquoise opaline glass scent bottle, with gold top and panel decorated in coloured enamels, c1830.
£1,800–2,000 *BHa*

Six Victorian scent bottles, with glass, silver and brass stoppers, largest 1½in (3.5cm) high.
£20–80 each *VB*

A blue glass overlay double scent bottle, with continental silver tops, possibly Bohemian, c1870, 5in (12.5cm) long.
£300–325 *THOM*

A French opaline glass scent bottle, c1880, 1½in (3.5cm) high.
£180–200 *LBr*

A French blue cut-glass scent bottle, c1900, 5½in (14cm) high.
£140–160 *LBr*

l. A ceramic Bonzo scent atomiser, with a white metal chain around neck, c1930, 5in (12.5cm) high.
£125–150 *LBr*

A Lalique glass scent bottle, with a fan top, c1920, 5½in (14cm) high.
£1,000–1,200 *LBr*

A Ricksecker Bohemian glass cologne bottle with tassel, American, c1910, 9in (23cm) high.
£120–160 *LBr*

l. A Wiesner of Miami scent bottle and lipstick, c1950, 4½in (11.5cm) high.
£80–100 *LBr*

A boxwood and brass folding rule and sundial, with compass and folding gnomon, by J. Parkes & Son, Registered June 28, 1853, 6in (15cm) long.
£250–300 *TOM*

An aneroid barometer, with cast iron base and ceramic dial, c1880, 6in (15cm) diam.
£100–120 *RTw*

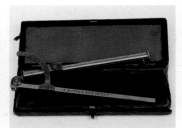

A brass inclinometer, by J. Davis & Son, Derby, with fitted case, c1890, 7in (17.5cm) long.
£80–120 *TOM*

An American electric fan, with brass blades and cast iron base, c1906, 13in (33cm) diam.
£220–250 *EKK*

A live-steam model overdrive engine, c1910, 12in (30.5cm) long.
£500–575 *DQ*

A copper and brass electric fire, 1920s, 21in (53.5cm) high.
£50–70 *JUN*

The British Calculator model B, 1920s, 5in (12.5cm) diam, in original fitted box.
£30–40 *TOM*

A gas meter, by T. C. Glover Co, c1930, 15in (38cm) high.
£50–60 *JUN*

l. A coin-operated gas meter by A. G. Sutherland Ltd, c1930, 15in (38cm) high.
£70–80 *JUN*

A bombardment spotting disc MK2 and line spotting conversion disc, in wooden box, 1940s, 14in (35.5cm) wide.
£220–250 *ET*

A turned beech and walnut bodkin case, with needles, 19thC, 6½in (16.5cm) long.
£55–65 *BIL*

Two beaded and overlay glass needle tubes, c1850–70, 3½in (9cm) long.
£25–50 each *VB*

A novelty chair pin cushion and thread holder, 1930s, 5in (12.5cm) high.
£40–45 *DHA*

A Stuart tartan needle case, c1870, 2in (5cm) high.
£70–80 *VB*

A Tunbridge Ware acorn tape measure and a thimble case, c1870, largest 1½in (3.5cm) long.
£125–150 each *AMH*

r. Two Mauchline Ware thimble holders, c1870–80, 2in (5cm) high.
£35–55 each *VB*

A brass egg-shaped thimble holder, and silver thimble, c1898, 2in (5cm) long.
£90–100 *DHA*

l. A silver pincushion, modelled as a lady's high-heeled shoe, decorated with a bow and scrolling foliage, Birmingham 1896, 3in (7.5cm) long.
£140–175 *GH*

A silver pincushion, in the form of an elephant, by A. & L. L., Birmingham 1909, 2¾in (7cm) long.
£170–200 *GH*

A Glista Mendarn card of thread for mending stockings, 1930s, 4in (10cm) square.
£8–10 *DHA*

A velvet pincushion, in the form of an apple, 1930s, 5in (12.5cm) wide.
£40–45 *DHA*

A carved bone model of a two-masted schooner, 19thC, 19in (48cm) long, in a glass case.
£600–700 *TMA*

A 1912 calendar on card, advertising the White Star Line Fleet, with illustration of a liner by Montague B. Black, 11¾ x 19¾in (30 x 50cm).
£2,400–2,800 *ONS*

A tissue print, issued to commemorate the sinking of RMS *Titanic*, c1913, 15 x 14in (38 x 35.5cm).
£200–250 *DQ*

An RMS *Arundel Castle* silver-plated ink pot, with glass well, 1920–50, 2in (5cm) high.
£35–45 *BAf*

An original advertisement for the Cunard Line, c1930, 15in (38cm) high.
£100–125 *COB*

A limited edition book, No. 395/1000, entitled *Royal Yachts*, with full colour and over 30 half tone illustrations, by Paymaster Commander C. M. Gavin, 1932.
£40–50 *MED*

A box of P & O matches, c1937.
£6–8 *BAf*

A diorama of a sailing ship, c1950, 18in (45.5cm) wide.
£180–200 *NC*

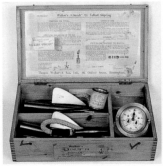

A Walker's 'Cherub' III ship's log, c1970, 19in (48cm) wide.
£250–300 *NC*

An illuminated azimuth circle, used for taking compass bearings, 1940s, box 12in (30.5cm) wide.
£70–80 *ET*

A red tanned cotton sail, 1970s, 180in x 120in (457 x 304cm).
£50–60 *NC*

An alloy shipbuilder's plate, Drypool Group, c1975, 18in (45.5cm) wide.
£85–95 *BAf*

A box of 12 stainless steel and plastic cocktail forks, c1960, box 5½in (14cm) wide.
£4–5 *AL*

A Poole Pottery spill vase, with abstract design, marked 'Poole, England', 1960s, 6in (15cm) high.
£40–50 *P(B)*

r. A Miss Nowell brown, orange and gold striped dress, 1960s, 50in (127cm) long.
£18–22 *BOH*

A Texas Ware melamine plate, commemorating the Apollo spaceships and the moon landing, 1970s, 10in (25.5cm) diam.
£16–18 *PB*

A Pressflags Production *Thunderbirds* shop display card for pencil sharpeners, c1966, 9in (23cm) wide.
£150–175 *TOY*

A red plastic portable 'Valentine' typewriter and case, designed by Ettore Sottsass for Olivetti, c1969, 15in (38cm) wide.
£75–100 *PLB*

A JVC orange plastic portable television, with hanging chain, on a square platform with integral clock alarm, c1970, 14in (35.5cm) high.
£250–300 *CSK*

A squeaky rubber Womble, by Combex Models, c1974, 6in (15cm) high.
£15–20 *CWo*

A Six Million Dollar Man, by Denys Fisher, 14in (35.5cm) high.
£100–120 *TOY*

r. A *New Avengers* photograph, signed by Patrick Macnee, Joanna Lumley and Gareth Hunt, 1970s, 8 x 10in (20.5 x 25.5cm).
£30–40 *VS*

A painted tobacco tin,
c1815, 5in (12.5cm) wide.
£150–175 *MB*

A French ebony and composite
snuff box, with hand-coloured
print on paper under glass,
c1840, 2¼in (5.5cm) diam.
£90–100 *BIL*

An applewood and pearwood
cedar-lined cigar box, inlaid
with ebony and mother-of-pearl,
c1860, 12in (30.5cm) wide.
£450–500 *MB*

A Staffordshire pottery
tobacco jar, c1880,
12½in (32cm) high.
£200–220 *SER*

A silver and enamel vesta
case, decorated with a
match and inscribed 'A
match for any man', maker
D & F, Birmingham, c1887,
1½in (3.5cm) high.
£320–350 *GH*

A Royal Doulton
'Princes Mixture
Snuff' jar, c1890,
7¼in (18.5cm) high.
£160–200 *INC*

A Continental white
metal and enamel
vesta case, with red
and blue engine-turned
diagonal pattern, 1930s,
1¾in (4.5cm) high.
£80–100 *GH*

A pair of Goebel stylised donkey
bookends, with ashtrays, c1933,
5in (12.5cm) high.
£180–220 *BKK*

Two Dunlop ashtrays, by
Roanoid Ltd, with 3 arms
closing to keep ash inside,
with black Bakelite bases,
c1934, 4in (10cm) high.
£20–25 each *BKK*

A selection of cigarette packets,
De Reszke Minors, Churchman's
Tenner Green Label and
Gallaher's Park Drive, 1930–50,
2¼in x 1½in (5.5cm x 4cm).
£2–3 each *MRW*

l. A cigarette lighter, in the form of
a table lamp, with enamelled metal
shade, c1950, 3½in (9cm) high.
£25–30 *WAB*

r. A metal cigarette lighter,
decorated with enamel, c1950,
2¼in (5.5cm) high.
£25–30 *WAB*

A Stevengraph entitled 'The First Touch', No. 173, c1881, 5 x 8in (12.5 x 20.5cm) wide.
£380–420 *VINE*

Six plastic beakers, contained in a leather carrying case, c1890, 5½in (14cm) high.
£120–140 *WAB*

A Turkey Red Cigarettes baseball card, c1911, 8 x 5¾in (20.5 x 14.5cm).
£280–310 *HALL*

A French weave creel for trout, c1930, 10in (25.5cm) long.
£70–85 *WAB*

A mounted African Cokes hartebeest, from the Gerard collection, 19thC, 32in (81cm) high.
£500–550 *BS*

A Yorkshire County Schools velvet sports cap, 1926–27.
£75–85 *WAB*

r. A red and white hockey club cap, from Military Outfitters in Camberley, 1931–32.
£25–35 *WAB*

An enamelled Dunlop caddy brooch, c1930, 1¼in (3cm) high.
£30–35 *DAC*

A Parvo garden tennis set, with original contents, c1890, 35in (89cm) long.
£200–250 *STK*

A pair of lady's metal ice skates, with detachable leather boots, c1910.
£40–50 *JUN*

A pottery golfing figure, signed by T. S. Chudin, c1930, 16in (40.5cm) high.
£150–200 *WaR*

A leather football, 1940s,
10in (25.5cm) diam.
£24–28 *DQ*

A Penfold Patented golf balls
box, 1950s, 6¾in (17cm) wide.
£15–20 *WaR*

A cardboard die-cut stand-up sign,
of Ted Williams advertising Moxie,
with red background, 1950s,
framed, 10 x 15in (25.5 x 38cm).
£1,000–1,250 *HALL*

A Chicago Blackhawks player's
jacket, wool with leather
sleeves, c1971.
£325–375 *HALL*

l. A green plastic table tennis
bat, advertising BP, c1960,
10in (25.5cm) high.
£10–15 *JUN*

A photo-montage, signed by Sam
Snead, Gene Sarazen and Byron
Nelson, 1980s, 11 x 14in (28 x 35cm).
£85–95 *HALL*

A hand-painted terracotta
model of Hakata Mimas Dilly,
a Japanese master tattoo
artist, tattooing a geisha girl,
1950s, 8in (20.5cm) high.
£180–200 *Ram*

A watercolour painting, by London tattoo
artist Albert Gordon, for a window display,
signed, c1922, 27 x 61in (68.5 x 155cm).
£350–400 *Ram*

*This painting was copied by a German
tattooist for use as posters in the 1940s.
These posters would be worth £80–100 each.*

A travelling tattoo kit,
in a leather case, 1950s,
12in (30.5cm) wide.
£150–170 *Ram*

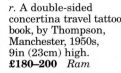

r. A double-sided
concertina travel tattoo
book, by Thompson,
Manchester, 1950s,
9in (23cm) high.
£180–200 *Ram*

l. Three tattoo-related
postcards, 1950s,
5 x 3in (12.5 x 7.5cm).
£1–5 each *Ram*

ORIENTAL

l. A Chinese export lacquer tea caddy, in the shape of a melon, c1800, 9½in (24cm) diam.
£340–380 *SSW*

Two carved ivory clam's dreams, the interiors depicting figures in landscape scenes, 19thC, 5in (12.5cm) diam.
£90–100 each *JaG*

A Gandharan stucco Buddha head, 4th–5th century AD, 5in (12.5cm) high.
£425–475 *SAM*

An ivory netsuke, depicting Urashima Taro, late 19thC, 2in (5cm) high.
£240–280 *JaG*

A Chinese framed appliqué, depicting figures by a pagoda with branches of blossom, late 19thC, 8in (20.5cm) diam.
£145–185 *PBr*

A carved wood netsuke, Edo period, c1800, 1½in (4cm) high.
£250–300 *JaG*

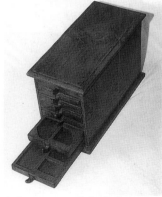

A pair of Chinese rank badges, depicting a mandarin duck for 7th Civil Rank, late 19thC, 12in (30.5cm) square.
£325–375 *PBr*

r. An Indian madu, consisting of 2 opposing buck horns fixed behind a pierced dahl, decorated with birds among foliage, early 19thC, 24in (61cm) wide.
£300–350 *GV*

A Javanese teak herbal remedy chest, c1890, 11in (28cm) high.
£350–400 *SAM*

A bronze Shiva, mounted on a radiator cap as a car mascot, 1930s, 6in (15cm) high.
£85–95 *DHA*

Ceramics

In the 17th and 18th centuries, Europeans were fascinated by the ceramics of China and Japan and vast amounts of porcelain were exported to the West. Not all trading ships reached their destinations successfully, and this section includes ceramics rescued from three shipwrecks. The Vung Tau cargo, dating from circa 1690, was discovered in 1989, when a fisherman, some 100 nautical miles from Vung Tau, snagged his nets on a sunken vessel that was carrying Chinese export porcelain. The Diana cargo was salvaged from the wreck of the *Diana*, an English ship that foundered in 1817 in the straits of Malacca, en route from China to Madras in India, and was packed to the gunnels with 'China articles'. Most famous of all, however, is the Nanking cargo, the vast haul of Chinese porcelain retrieved by Mike Hatcher in 1985 from a Dutch East Indiaman, the *Geldermalsen*, wrecked in 1752 in the South China Seas. When it was sold at Christie's in Amsterdam in 1986, the cargo attracted huge publicity and made over £10 million, establishing Hatcher as perhaps the most celebrated and controversial treasure hunter of his day.

An Annamese blue and white baluster vase, Ming Dynasty, 1368–1644, 10in (25.5cm) high.
£400–450 *ORI*

A painted pottery horse, Tang Dynasty, AD 618–907, 13in (33cm) high.
£1,650–1,850 *ORI*

A Chinese blue and white charger, Kangxi period, 1662–1722, 13½in (34.5cm) diam.
£1,450–1,650 *ORI*

Three Chinese blue and white custard cups, with covers, painted on the exterior with butterflies among flowers beneath a latticed border at the rim, with applied woven bracket handle, the covers similarly painted and surmounted by a finial in the form of a flower, 18thC, 3in (7.5cm) high.
£330–360 *P*

A Chinese blue and white octagonal teabowl and saucer, from the Vung Tau cargo, c1690, saucer 5¼in (13.5cm) diam.
£400–450 *RBA*

FURTHER READING
Miller's Chinese & Japanese Antiques Buyer's Guide,
Miller's Publications, 1999

A Chinese Imari spoon tray, Qianlong period, mid–18thC, 5in (12.5cm) wide.
£140–160 *GeW*

A Chinese teapot, painted *en grisaille* with figures in black on a white ground, 18thC, 5in (12.5cm) high.
£400–450 *MBo*

A Chinese blue and white saucer, from the Nanking cargo, painted in underglaze blue with a pagoda riverscape, c1750, 4¾in (12cm) diam.
£110–125 *RBA*

A Chinese blue and white vase, decorated with flowerheads, Ming Dynasty marks, 19thC, 9½in (24cm) high.
£230–260 *HOK*

A pair of Japanese earthenware vases, decorated in gilt and rusts, with continuous scenes of elegant ladies on terraces, 19thC, 14½in (37cm) high.
£1,600–1,800 *HOK*

An encrusted brown glazed stoneware storage jar, from the *Diana* cargo, c1816, 15½in (39cm) high.
£750–900 *RBA*

A Japanese Kyoto pottery hand warmer, decorated with white storks, 19thC, 4in (10cm) high.
£700–800 *BOW*

A Chinese *famille rose* oblong octagonal jardinière, the everted rim with trellised patterns in coral red, painted on each side with a figural or floral scene, minor rubbing, with apocryphal Yongzheng mark in coral red, late Qing Dynasty, 11in (28cm) wide.
£260–300 *P*

r. A Japanese brushwasher, painted with a crane standing by a lake into which the sun sets, signed and sealed by Rung gou, 1930s, 3¾in (9.5cm) diam.
£350–400 *Wai*

A Chinese blue and white provincial bowl, from the *Diana* cargo, painted with Petal pattern, c1817, 6½in (16.5cm) high.
£140–180 *RBA*

A Chinese crackleware bowl and cover, the grey body decorated with blue Chinese characters, 19thC, 10in (25.5cm) diam.
£230–260 *AP*

A pair of Japanese porcelain cups and saucers, by Koransha, c1860, 2½in (6.5cm) high.
£150–175 *MCN*

Noritake

The Noritake China Company was founded by the Morimura brothers in Nagoya, Japan, in 1904. The firm specialized in affordably priced, hand-painted porcelain dinnerware. Noritake was exported across the world, particularly to the USA. The major American retailer was the Larkin Company of Buffalo, New York, who, trading via catalogues, helped to make Noritake some of the most popular household china in America.

During the 1920s and 1930s, Noritake established a design team in New York, and as well as producing conventional wares,

employed designers such as the architect Frank Lloyd Wright to create more modernist patterns. Many different backstamps were used. In 1891 the American Congress had passed an act requiring that foreign articles be stamped in English with their country of origin. The Japanese chose to use the word 'Nippon', their own word for Japan. Noritake was marked 'Hand painted Nippon' until 1921, when Congress decided that 'Nippon' was a Japanese word and should be replaced by the more familiar 'Japan'. Noritake ceramics produced after this date are inscribed 'Hand painted, Made in Japan'.

A Noritake coffee can and saucer, decorated in gilt on a cream ground, with black rims, c1920, saucer 4½in (11.5cm) diam.
£25–35 *DgC*

A Noritake tea-for-one pot, decorated with gold and cream on a white ground, c1925, 7in (18cm) wide.
£40–50 *DgC*

A Noritake trio, decorated with Tree in the Meadow pattern, marked 'Made in Japan', 1920s, cup 2½in (6.5cm) high.
£35–40 *EAS*

A Noritake part dressing set, comprising a candlestick, ring tree, pot and cover, decorated with lustre blue and gold on a white ground, 1920s, candlestick 5½in (14cm) high.
£45–55 *DgC*

A Noritake ten-piece coffee set, decorated with flowers on a yellow ground, with green and gold rim, 1930s, jug 2½in (6.5cm) high.
£120–150 *DgC*

A Noritake hair tidy, the upper section decorated with gold and red pattern, on cabriole legs, 1920–30s, 4in (10cm) square.
£45–55 *EAS*

A Noritake punchbowl, with gilt ram's head handles, decorated in shades of blue and pink, with floral painted panels, c1925, 9in (23cm) diam.
£170–200 *DgC*

A Noritake plate, decorated with figures in a river landscape, marked 'Made in Japan', 1930s, 6¼in (16cm) diam.
£17–20 *EAS*

A Noritake cup and saucer, decorated with red and gold floral pattern, marked 'Made in Japan', c1930, 2½in (6.5cm) high.
£18–22 *EAS*

PAPER MONEY

An Isle of Man Castle Rushen one guinea note,
unissued, c1790.
£140–160 *WP*

A Stourbridge & Kidderminster Banking
Company £20 note, unissued, 1830s.
£65–80 *WP*

A Bank of England £5 note, in favour of
Matthew Marshall, split and rejoined,
pinholes and red 'M' across date line,
dated '2nd February 1842'.
£3,000–3,300 *P*

This £5 note is an early and rare example.

A Swaledale & Wensleydale Bank £20 note,
unissued, 1860s.
£15–20 *WP*

A Craven Bank £10 note, unissued, 1860s.
£30–40 *WP*

An Irish Republic $5 Fenian Bond, signed
'O'Sullivan' and 'O'Mahony', vignette of Wolfe
Tone, creased, slight tears, dated '1866'.
£170–200 *WA*

A specimen 1/- postal order, c1880.
£20–25 *WP*

A United Kingdom of Great Britain and
Ireland 10/- Treasury note, John Bradbury
signature, c1918.
£180–200 *WP*

A United States of America $1 silver certificate, the
reverse inscribed in pen 'Handed to my friend, M. Etris.
This note was in my pocket when I was picked up out
of the sea by the SS *Carpathia*, from the wreck of the
SS *Titanic*, April 15th, 1912', signed 'A. H. Weikman,
Palmyra, N J', creased and discoloured, c1899.
£4,200–4,600 *S(NY)*

This worn dollar bill was in the back pocket of
Mr A. H. Weikman, the saloon barber of the Titanic
when it sank on April 15th 1912. Both barber and
bill survived the shipwreck, and Weikman later
autographed the note and gave it to a friend.

A United Kingdom of Great Britain and
Ireland 5/- note, unissued, c1919.
£850–1,000 *WP*

An Isle of Man £1 note, c1921.
£180–200 *WP*

A Barclay's Bank $20 note,
Trinidad, unissued and
perforated, cancelled, c1926.
£500–550 *P*

A North of Scotland Bank
£5 note, c1928.
£130–150 *WP*

A Bank of England £1 error
note, with white streak, c1971.
£25–30 *WP*

A Bank of Zambia £1 note,
by Harrison & Sons, with
fisherman at left and Queen
Elizabeth at right, lion's
head sketched in on surface
of watermark, 3 punch
holes, c1963.
£1,500–1,800 *P*

A Bank of England £5 note,
dated '17th October 1941'.
£70–80 *NAR*

r. A Bank of England specimen
£20 note, with extra paper and
missing serial numbers, c1991.
£100–120 *WP*

PENKNIVES

A silver penknife, decorated with flowers and leaves, c1880, 3in (7.5cm) long.
£70–80 *MB*

A fleime, with horn handle, c1860, 3in (7.5cm) long.
£60–65 *MB*

For veterinary use.

A multi-bladed penknife, with tortoiseshell handle, c1880, 3in (7.5cm) long.
£70–80 *MB*

A multi-bladed penknife, with ivory handle, c1880, 3in (7.5cm) long.
£20–25 *MB*

A multi-bladed penknife, with tortoiseshell handle, some damage, c1860, 3in (7.5cm) long.
£25–30 *MB*

A penknife, in the form of a shield, with button hook, c1880, 1in (2.5cm) square.
£50–60 *MB*

A French penknife, with horn handle, in the form of a shoe, c1880, 3in (7.5cm) long.
£60–65 *MB*

l. A Scandinavian folding knife, with boxwood handle, c1880, 5½in (14cm) long.
£70–80 *MB*

A silver combination fruit knife and button hook, with mother-of-pearl handle, c1890, 2¼in (5.5cm) long.
£60–65 *MB*

A silver folding blade and combination fruit knife and fork, with mother-of-pearl handle, c1880, 3in (7.5cm) long.
£80–90 *MB*

A base metal penknife, in the form of an aeroplane, 1950s, 4in (10cm) long.
£55–65 *BCA*

Two brass cat and rabbit penknives, 1910–20, rabbit 2½in (6.5cm) long.
£18–25 *WAB*

PHOTOGRAPHS

A black and white photograph on glass, in a leather case, c1860, 4¾in (12cm) high.
£60–70 *CHe*

A selection of tintypes, in fancy mounts, c1900, 4 x 2½in (10 x 6.5cm).
£3–8 *HEG*

Tintypes or ferrotypes were invented by an American, Hamilton Smith, c1856. The film was supported on a thin sheet of black or dark brown enamelled iron. Comparatively simple to produce and more affordable than other photographic processes, tintypes were popular with seaside and local photographers.

A photograph of a young American lady, impressed on back for 3D effect, St Louis, c1906, 10 x 8in (25.5 x 20.5cm) in a wooden frame.
£35–40 *DOM*

A hand-coloured ambrotype of a little girl holding flowers, in a leather case, c1880, 2½ x 2in (6.5 x 5cm)
£20–25 *HEG*

A Victorian figured walnut stereograph viewer, with decorative fretwork panels and bracket support to rising platform, with adjustable lens, inscribed 'London Stereoscope Co', 16in (40.5cm) wide.
£220–250 *WBH*

A French stereoscope, with a collection of glass slides, c1910, 5in (13cm) wide.
£20–30 *ET*

l. A hand-tinted daguerreotype, in a leather case, American, 1850s, 4 x 3½in (10 x 9cm).
£35–45 *HEG*

An ambrotype of a young boy with book, in a leather case, c1880, 2½ x 3in (6.5 x 7.5cm).
£25–35 *HEG*

An album of 10 photographs of the American Civil War, by Matthew Brady, containing signed photographs of General Grant, General Meade, General Butler and staff, c1865.
£6,500–7,000 *WA*

This album was assembled by Lt General Sir Charles Hastings Doyle, Governor General of Nova Scotia, who was on a confidential visit to General Grant's headquarters during the American Civil War. There is some speculation that this visit by a leading military officer was part of a covert British military advice mission to the Union side. This album contains original photographs all annotated by Doyle, who joined the 87th Royal Irish Regiment in 1819 and was Colonel-in-Chief 1870–81.

PIN-UPS

Pictures of scantily clad women have always appealed to a proportion of the male population. The earliest objects shown here are smoking accessories from the 19th century, when nude images were given a spurious respectability by being portrayed as classical or Oriental maidens. Naughty postcards were popular in the 1900s, but the golden age of the pin-up was the 1940s and 1950s. The term is said to derive from WWII, when servicemen pinned up pictures of film stars in their quarters, and the period saw an explosion of pin-up material,

with busty blondes in various stages of undress decorating everything from calendars to cocktail glasses, to ashtrays (pin-up imagery is often found on objects associated with smoking and drinking). Pin-up material from this period is very collectable and popular with women as well as men.

Changing fashions and sexual liberation in the 1960s heralded the end of pin-up art. In more recent times, drawings of glamour girls have been replaced by 'page three' girls and a more explicit photographic sexuality.

A white metal and enamel vesta, painted with a nude young woman wading through a pool, c1900, 2in (5cm) high.
£520–550 *GH*

A silver and enamel cigarette case, decorated with a picture of Leda and the Swan, c1900, 3½ x 2⅛in (9 x 5.5cm).
£1,800–2,000 *SFL*

A silver and enamel cigarette case, with oval painted picture, c1900, 3½ x 3in (9cm x 7.5cm).
£800–1,000 *SFL*

A set of 7 postcards, by Alb Jarach, entitled 'Rue de la Paix', Nos. 156–162, signed, c1914.
£45–55 *SpP*

A red tin ashtray, advertising M. & J. Bonded Cigarettes, Philadelphia, USA, 1950s, 3½in (9cm) wide.
£16–18 *SpM*

l. A set of 7 postcards, by Suzanne Meunier, entitled 'Les Seins de Marbre', signed, c1914.
£40–50 *SpP*

A pack of Fortune Brand playing cards, entitled 'Girls of Nations', made in Hong Kong, 1950s, 3½ x 2½in (9 x 6.5cm).
£25–30 *SpM*

These nudes are photographic. Playing cards with painted pin-ups are rarer and more sought-after, and can be worth twice as much as examples decorated with photographs of real women.

A watercolour drawing, by Dickens, showing a naked model partially covered by a pink and white striped beach towel, artwork for a calendar, slight damage, 1950s, 17 x 23in (43 x 58.5cm).
£300–350 *VS*

A pin-up glass tumbler, with a scantily dressed lady on the front, undressed on the reverse, 1950s, 4½in (11.5cm) high.
£12–15 *SpM*

A pin-up book of matches, advertising Schiller Gifts, Palisade, New Jersey, 1950s, 1½in (4cm) wide.
£3–5 *SpM*

A pair of Pin Up Girl seamfree mesh stockings, 1950s, packet 9½in (24cm) high.
£4–6 *HUX*

A *Man Senior* magazine, August 1955, 12 x 9in (30.5 x 23cm).
£6–8 *RAD*

Two fans' booklets, with 66 photographs of Gina Lollobrigida, 2 styles, late 1950s, 6 x 4in (15 x 10cm).
£30–40 *VS*

A signed photograph of Marilyn Monroe, promoting the film *Bus Stop*, c1956, 10 x 8in (25.5 x 20.5cm).
£9,000–10,000 *FRa*

r. A colour photograph of Traci Lords, signed, 1990s, 10 x 8in (25.5 x 20.5cm) high.
£100–125 *FRa*

A colour photograph of Kim Basinger, full-length naked, signed, c1996, 10in (25.5cm) high.
£50–60 *VS*

POSTCARDS

A postcard, commemorating Queen Victoria's Diamond Jubilee, 1897.
£90–110 *VS*

A postcard by Lessieux, entitled 'Orientale', showing a belly dancer and a seated musician, signed, dated '1900'.
£10–15 *SpP*

Two Charlie Chaplin Red Letter Photocards, 1900s.
£2–3 each *MRW*

A postcard, by J. Damberger, entitled 'Erste Liebe', published by Hirth, Munich, c1900.
£30–40 *SpP*

A glamour postcard, by Philip Boileau, entitled 'From Him', No. 2066, published by Reinthal & Newman, New York, c1900.
£5–6 *JMC*

l. A set of 5 Art Nouveau postcards, by Raphael Kirchner, from series 4140, 'Marionettes', published by Pascalis Moss & Co, each depicting a scantily clad lady on a perforated gold background, operating a pair of puppets, all inscribed and post-marked 'October 1902'.
£80–100 *DN*

A postcard, by Philip Boileau, entitled 'The Little Neighbors', No 828, published by Reinthal & Newman, New York, c1910.
£5–6 *JMC*

A Suffragette postcard, depicting Mrs Pethick Lawrence, Treasurer of the National Women's Social and Political Union, c1910.
£35–45 *VS*

A set of 7 postcards, by Suzanne Meunier, 'Le Vin de Champagne', 'Whisky', 'Pomard', 'Lacryma-Christi', 'Rhin Français', 'Vouvray', 'Sauternes', Nos. 200–206, c1914.
£45–55 *SpP*

A glamour postcard, entitled 'La Parisienne de 1911', series No. 31.
£5–6 *JMC*

A WWI woven postcard, entitled 'Le Filleul', a study of 4 people at table.
£15–20 *SpP*

A greetings postcard, 'A Birthday Wish and Greeting' with rhyme and violets, c1916.
£2–3 *THA*

Two brightly-coloured embroidered silk postcards, c1915.
£4–5 each *MAC*

Two brightly-coloured embroidered silk postcards, WWI, 3½ x 5½in (9 x 14cm).
£4–5 each *MAC*

A woven silk postcard, embroidered 'Bonnie Scotland' in red and yellow, a bagpiper and 'For Auld Lang Syne', published by W. M. Grant & Co, Coventry, c1905.
£22–26 *SpP*

l. A set of 12 Allies postcards, by Dupuis, signed, WWI.
£25–35 *SpP*

r. An Art Deco postcard by Mela Keohler, with a girl dressed in green, holding a posy of flowers at neck, Ser. 1936, No. 1.
£15–20 *SpP*

Two nursery rhyme postcards, 1920s.
£6–8 each *MRW*

A 'magic' hold-to-light postcard, early 1920s.
£10–12 *MRW*

l. Two postcards, by Louis Wain, entitled 'The Pierrots' and 'Marketing', 1920s.
£20–30 each *MRW*

A *Grimm's Fairy Tales* postcard book, with pictures by Mabel Lucie Attwell, published by Raphael Tuck, 1920, 7 x 6in (18 x 15cm).
£30–40 WWY

l. An aviation postcard, entitled 'Le premier avion au Dahomey', May 1926'.
£25–30 VS

A postcard, depicting a £1 note, c1920.
£4–5 WP

Two comic postcards, depicting seaside views, 1930s.
£4–6 each MRW

A postcard, depicting the swimming bath from Cunard Line, RMS *Berengaria*, 1930s.
£3–5 COB

A birthday postcard, entitled 'Tuesday is your Birthday', with poem, 1930s.
£3–5 COB

l. A watercolour on board, artwork showing a policeman at a motor crash, with caption to reverse, 1930s.
£180–220 VS

A Mabel Lucie Attwell postcard, 1930s.
£3–6 CMF

A woven postcard, with a view of Prague, stamp on front, 1930s.
£12–15 SpP

RADIOS, TVs & SOUND EQUIPMENT
Radios

A crystal set, made by
A. E. Woodward, Cheltenham,
1920s, 10in (25.5cm) wide.
£50–60 *OTA*

l. A Philips Superinductance model
830A radio, brown Arbolite case
with Bakelite trim, c1932,
16in (40.5cm) wide.
£300–350 *OTA*

A Sentinel Cadillac grille Bakelite
radio, 1930s, 11in (28cm) wide.
£1,800–2,200 *YAN*

An Ekco A23 three-band
brown Bakelite radio, with
pre-set tuning, c1946,
22in (56cm) wide.
£100–175 *OTA*

A Strad brown Bakelite valve
wireless set, No.511, by RM
Electric Ltd, Gateshead,
1947–48, 15in (38cm) wide.
£45–50 *DOM*

A Derwent three-band brown
Bakelite radio, c1947,
14in (35.5cm) wide.
£70–80 *OTA*

A Roberts valve portable radio, c1952, 10in (25.5cm) wide.
£40–50 *OTA*

An Ever Ready Sky Casket valve radio, c1957, 9in (23cm) wide.
£75–85 *GIN*

An Ultra Coronation Twin mains or battery portable black Bakelite radio, 1953, 11½in (29cm) wide.
£60–80 *OTA*

A Roberts R300 transistor radio, c1959, 9in (23cm) wide.
£10–20 *OTA*

A Murphy B818 chrome and grey PVC battery radio, restored, late 1950s, 9in (23cm) wide.
£55–65 *TIH*

A Bush white radio, with brass fittings, 1950s, 13in (33cm) wide.
£35–45 *PPH*

An Ekco portable transistor radio, the wooden case covered with red vinyl-plastic and metal control knobs, requires repair, c1960, 10in (25.5cm) wide.
£20–25 *DOM*

A Dynatron Nomad portable transistor radio, with red leather-covered casing and plastic control panels, battery only, c1961, 12in (30.5cm) wide.
£35–40 *DOM*

A Roberts Rambler radio, 1960s–70s, 8½in (21.5cm) wide.
£30–35 *GIN*

Pocket Transistor Radios

The pocket transistor radio is one of the icons of post-war youth culture. The transistor was invented by Bell Laboratories USA in 1948, paving the way for the creation in 1955 of the world's first transistor radio, the TR1, marketed by Regency Electronics of Indianapolis, which measured 3 x 5 x 1¼in (7.5 x 12.5 x 3cm) and weighed only 12oz (340g).

Japanese competition soon followed, and in 1957 Sony introduced the first pocket-sized transistor radio, the Sony TR63. Intent on capturing the US market, Japanese designers borrowed their stylistic vocabulary from America, drawing on sci-fi graphic art, contemporary architecture and even automobile design. Trade names such as Global, Zephyr and Aero reflected period fascination with space travel, and on a

more serious note CD (Civil Defence) marks – small triangles on the tuning dial indicated emergency frequencies of 640am and 1240am – for use in the event of nuclear attack. These are found only on pieces manufactured before 1963 and are a good way of dating early transistor radios.

After 1964 the market was flooded with cheap imports, particularly from Hong Kong, and design quality deteriorated. Collectors tend to focus on early models, and high-quality Japanese transistors, often command the highest prices.

Condition is of huge importance; original boxes and instruction leaflets will add to a radio's value, as will an unusual coloured case and typical period motifs such as a boomerang or orbiting satellite symbols.

A Sony model TR63 green shirt-pocket transistor radio, Japanese, c1957, 4¼in (11cm) high.
£225–275 *OVE*

A Toshiba 'Lace' model TR193 red shirt-pocket transistor radio, with real lace under the clear plastic speaker grille, Japanese, c1959, 4¼in (10½cm) high.
£150–175 *OVE*

An Emerson Explorer model 888 black coat-pocket transistor radio, American, c1960, 6½in (17cm) high.
£65–85 *OVE*

A Global model GR711 red shirt-pocket transistor radio, Japanese, c1961, 4in (9½cm) high.
£75–100 *OVE*

A Dansette model RT66 red
shirt-pocket transistor radio,
c1961, 4¼in (11cm) wide.
£25–35 *OVE*

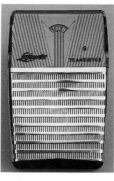

l. A Lafayette
model FS-91 black
shirt-pocket
transistor radio,
Japanese, c1961,
4½in (11.5cm) high.
£75–100 *OVE*

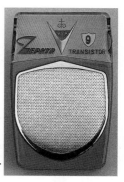

r. A Zephyr model
ZR930 beige shirt-
pocket transistor,
Japanese, c1962,
4½in (11.5cm) high.
£75–100 *OVE*

Gramophones

l. An American miniature
folding Mignophone
gramophone, by Walker
Products, with leather
horn and case, c1925,
9in (23cm) high.
£180–200 *ET*

r. A Walker Bros
wooden gramophone
speaker, British, c1926,
21in (53.5cm) high.
£180–200 *OTA*

A Trek 505 portable
gramophone, c1947,
12in (30.5cm) wide.
£100–110 *DAC*

A gramophone, 1930s,
20in (51cm) wide,
on an Edwardian
pot cupboard.
£300–350 *MiA*

r. An Antoria portable
gramophone, in
blue case, c1954,
11in (28cm) wide.
£120–130 *DAC*

Microphones

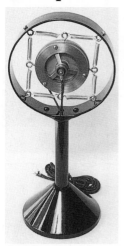

A carbon-spring
microphone, 1920s,
14in (35.5cm) high.
£270–320 *EKK*

A Western Electric 1-B
double-button carbon-
spring microphone
element, 1920s,
9in (23cm) high.
£700–800 *EKK*

r. A Turner U9S dynamic
microphone, 1940s,
10in (25.5cm) high.
£130–150 *EKK*

An RCA 77-B1 ribbon
microphone, 1930s,
13in (33cm) high.
£900–1,100 *EKK*

r. A Reslo ribbon
microphone, 1960s,
5in (12.5cm) high.
£50–60 *JON*

A Great Western Railway
tannoy microphone,
1930s, 9in (23cm) high.
£50–60 *DAC*

Televisions

l. A KB Stargazer brown
Bakelite television set, c1951,
36in (91.5cm) high.
£350–400 *OTA*

*When produced this was the
largest Bakelite radio or
television cabinet made.*

A Bush brown Bakelite television,
1950s, 14in (35.5cm) high.
£200–250 *JUN*

A Philco Predicta black and
white television, c1958,
28in (71cm) high.
£900–1,100 *EKK*

*The Predicta television had a
swivel screen, a 25ft (762cm)
cable and could be detached
from its base. The controls,
remained on the console and
this design was superseded
by the more practical
portable TV.*

RAILWAYANA

A pottery water jug, transfer-printed in shades of brown with 'Entrance to the Liverpool–Manchester Railway', 1830s, 7in (18cm) high.
£550–600 *SRA*

A black and white mug, decorated with an early 2-2-2 locomotive 'Express' tender and 2 coaches in red and yellow, 1840s, 3½in (9cm) high.
£120–140 *SRA*

A pair of Edwardian Great Central Railway glass spirit flasks, with their original glass and cork stoppers, both inscribed, 6in (15cm) high.
£140–160 *SRA*

A Victorian Improved McInnes-Dobbie Pattern Steam Engine Indicator, by Hannan & Buchanan, Glasgow, in a polished wood carrying case, 6½in (16.5cm) high.
£450–500 *SRA*

An SE & CR. Carriage Department brass 'T' fire hydrant, c1890, 15in (38cm) long.
£25–30 *HAX*

A railway whistle and key for private compartments, c1880, 3¼in (8.5cm) long.
£60–70 *WAB*

An LMS brass arm badge, engraved 'LMS Out Porter 1', 1930s, 4¼in (11cm) wide.
£120–140 *SRA*

A BRE premier alloy gas lamp, by Cresteella Engineering Co, Leeds, with wooden handle and brass fittings, 1940s, 10in (25.5cm) high.
£45–50 *DOM*

A Birmingham Stage Carriage Driver's badge, c1925, 2in (5cm) diam.
£40–45 *INC*

Books & Ephemera

A black and white postcard, with of Shawford Station, c1915.
£18–20 *SpP*

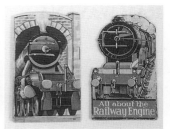

All about the Railway Engine, c1926, 6½ x 4in (16.5 x 10cm) and an untitled book.
£16–18 *SRA*

A Wallis's New Railway Game, printed by Passmore, 1870s, 7 x 5in (18 x 12.5cm).
£160–180 *SRA*

A Chad Valley board game, entitled 'The Down Mail', 1930s, 8½ x 5½in (21.5 x 14cm).
£60–70 *J&J*

The Book of Railways, written by Arthur Groom and published by Birn Bros Ltd, London, 1950s, 11 x 8in (28 x 20.5cm).
£12–15 *J&J*

A 'Coronation Scot' railway game, 1950s, 6 x 11in (15 x 28cm).
£15–20 *J&J*

Enamel & Metal Signs

An L&SWR red sign, with raised white lettering, slightly corroded, c1880, 26in (66cm) wide.
£70–80 *SOL*

An SE&CR dark green sign, with white raised lettering, 1901–22, 26in (66cm) wide.
£90–120 *SOL*

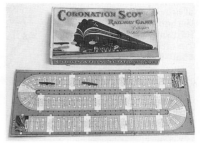

A Southern Railway green cast iron sign, with white lettering, 1930s, 25in (63.5cm) wide.
£80–90 *RAR*

A London Underground enamel sign, 1950s, 36in (91.5cm) wide.
£30–35 *RAR*

A British Rail maroon enamel sign, 1950s–60s, 30in (76cm) wide.
£50–60 *RAR*

A British Rail (Midland) white enamel car platform sign, with brown lettering, c1960, 18in (46cm) high.
£15–20 *SOL*

Nameplates

Nameplates are the most sough after and expensive items of railwayana. Even during the 1950s and 1960s, when many old locomotives were broken up, railway enthusiasts were already preserving the nameplates. By the 1970s, these items were fetching hundreds of pounds, and today prices are more likely to be in the thousands. 'In the last five years interest has gone through the roof,' says auctioneer Patrick Bogue, 'and there is a large, very

dedicated collecting base in England. What collectors tend to want is a plate from a good class of locomotive running on a particularly nostalgic route, for example the Great Western is a popular favourite.' Plates from the most famous trains tend to be in museums such as the National Railway Museum in York, but there is still enough quality material on the market to attract keen response and ever-rising prices.

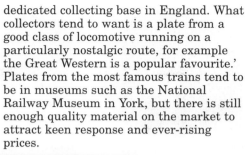

l. A GWR curved brass and steel nameplate, 'Saint Dunstan', 1907, 68in (172.5cm) wide.
£8,500–10,000 *SRA*

A GWR nameplate, 'Kenilworth', 1899, 34in (86.5cm) wide.
£15,000–17,000 *SRA*

r. A GWR nameplate, 'Moreton Hall', 1931, 54in (137.5cm) wide.
£5,000–5,500 *SRA*

An LMS nameplate, 'Kempenfelt', 1934, 31½in (80cm) wide.
£8,500–10,000 *SRA*

A BR nameplate, 'Clive of India', 1953, 47in (119.5cm) wide.
£13,500–15,000 *SRA*

A BR nameplate, 'Royal Oak Warship Class', 1960, 39½in (100.5cm) wide.
£5,000–5,500 *SRA*

Plates & Plaques

A WWI Prussian Railway cast iron locomotive motif, displaying the eagle and 'KPEV', 9½in (24cm) diam.
£750–850 *SRA*

A South African Railways brass cabside plate, from Beyer Garratt locomotive, c1925, 16in (40.5cm) wide.
£650–700 *RAR*

r. A BR electric locomotive alloy logo, showing the Crewe Eagle in outline, signifying Crewe Electric Depot, c1985.
£120–150 *SOL*

A diesel depot plaque, showing a Flying Cockney Sparrow wearing a loco driver's black greasetop hat, c1987/8, 12¾in (32.5cm) square.
£200–250 *SOL*

This type of plaque was introduced by British Rail in October 1987 to promote rail freight business and were fitted on the side of diesel locos to show which depot they were based at, using a different symbol for each depot. They are now gradually being removed. There were 3 sizes, 17½in (44.5cm) square, 12¾in (32cm) square and 11in (28cm) square and plaques were fitted as diamonds.

Tickets & Tokens

Early railway tickets are extremely rare, and when a collection comes up for auction lots are hotly contested and can make exceptionally high sums. At a recent auction an 1853 First Class Leominster to Berrington ticket issued by the Shropshire and Hereford Railway made a world record price of £640, and the same passionate

train spotter paid £600 for another Victorian ticket at the sale.

Collectors tend to prefer travel tickets, as opposed to platform or any other type of rail ticket. Some general railwayana enthusiasts concentrate on tickets alone, while others will collect tickets pertaining to the network or trains that interest them.

A S&HR Leominster to Berrington First Class ticket, c1853.
£650–750 *ONS*

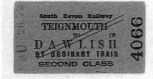

A SDR Teignmouth to Dawlish by ordinary train, Second Class ticket, c1872.
£600–700 *ONS*

A railway ticket punch, c1900, 2½in (6.5cm) high.
£10–15 *WAB*

A Kington & Eardisley Railway Free Pass, Thursday September 9th 1875, signed by Edmund H. Cheek, secretary.
£80–100 *ONS*

A L & NW payment token, c1930, 1¼in (3cm) diam.
£9–12 *DAC*

Did you know?

The pasteboard railway ticket was invented in 1837 by Thomas Edmondson, a clerk on the Newcastle and Carlisle railway.

Totem Signs

A BR(W) cream on chocolate enamel station totem, 'Stourbridge Junction', 1950–55, 36in (91.5cm) wide.
£160–180 *SOL*

A BR(E) dark blue totem, 'Wood Green', 1950s, 36in (91.5cm) wide.
£350–400 *SRA*

A BR(W) chocolate and cream totem, 'Gobowen', 1950s, 36in (91.5cm) wide.
£240–270 *SRA*

A BR(S) dark green totem, 'Hastings', 1950s, 36in (91.5cm) wide.
£270–320 *SRA*

A BR(W) chocolate and cream totem, 'Westbourne Park', 1950s, 36in (91.5cm) wide.
£270–300 *SRA*

A BR(E) dark blue totem, 'Althorpe', 1950s–60s, 36in (91.5cm) wide.
£475–525 *RAR*

Works Plates

l. A brass works plate, 'Hunslet Engine Co, Leeds, No. 498 1890', on a polished wood mount, 15in (38cm) wide.
£1,600–1,800 *SRA*

r. A red works plate, 'Hudswell, Clarke & Co, Ltd, Leeds, No.1774 – 1944' in raised black letters, 11½in (29cm) wide.
£150–180 *SOL*

A triangular cut-brass works plate, 'Nasmyth Wilson & Co Limited No. 1414 – 1923, Patricroft Manchester', 13¾in (35cm) wide.
£650–700 *SRA*

ROCK & POP

The rock and pop collectables market is very fluid, rising and falling with the popularity of the stars. All Saints and Boyzone items might be in demand at the moment, but today's teen rave can very easily become tomorrow's forgotten memory. 'I'm having great difficulty selling some Bay City Rollers' lampshades, even at £3 each,' says Paul Wane at Tracks, dealers in rock memorabilia. Consistent best sellers tend to be those who have made a major artistic contribution to music and whose work lives on. Although it might sound a bit macabre, if a star or member of the band has died, memorabilia is even more valuable. Top of the collectable pops include The Beatles, Elvis Presley, Jimmy Hendrix and The Rolling Stones.

The most desirable objects tend to be personal items belonging to the stars –

clothes, instruments etc – preferably accompanied by a photograph of the personality wearing or using them, thus proving that they are genuine. Signatures are always sought after, particularly if they are on an album, programme or something more personal than just an autograph book (this section includes a pair of signed All Saints thong knickers!). Mass-marketed memorabilia created for the fans (T-shirts, toys etc) generally comes at the bottom of the collectable pile. Although Beatles material is very sought after, with more recent bands, such as the Spice Girls (to whom we devote a page at the end of this section), objects have been created in such vast quantities that it will be a very long time before most mass-produced items become rare or collectable.

A pair of Melanie of All Saints white knickers, by La Senza Lingerie, signed 'Lots Of Love Mel xx' in black pen on the waist band, with a copy of a letter of authenticity from 'Eargasm Music Management', 1990s.
£250–300 *Bon*

A pair of black stretch leather stage boots, worn by Debbie Harry of Blondie, 1970s–80s.
£450–500 *Bon(C)*

The parachute fatigues, worn by Ronan Keating of Boyzone on the 1997 Boyzone Tour.
£130–150 *Bon*

© *Philip Ollerenshaw / Idols Licensing & Publicity Ltd.*

r. An M. Hohner mouth organ, used by Bob Dylan at the Pelle Rossa Festival, Italy, July 1998, signed 'Bob Dylan'.
£450–500 *Bon*

The lyrics for Jimi Hendrix's 'Coming Down Hard On Me, Baby', in blue felt pen on 2 sheets of legal paper, mounted and framed with a colour picture of Jimi, c1970, each 8 x 12¼in (20 x 31cm), framed and glazed.
£11,000–12,000 *S*

This track was being worked on by Jimi around June / July 1970 and a version was recorded at the Electric Lady Studios. It appeared on the 'Loose Ends' and 'Crash Landing' albums.

r. A CD award, presented to EMI International to recognize Gold sales in Japan of 100,000 units for 'Eternal – Always and Forever', mounted, framed and glazed, 1990s, 16in (40.5cm) square.
£220–250 *Bon*

A gold disc and cassette for the INXS album 'Listen Like Thieves', presented to Pat Evans of WXRK to commemorate sales of more than half a million copies of the 1985 album and cassette, framed and glazed.
£350–400 DN

INXS was the band headed by the late Michael Hutchence.

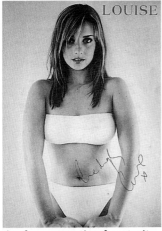

A colour promotional portrait poster depicting Louise, signed 'Love Always Louise x' in black marker pen, framed and glazed, 37 x 26in (94 x 66cm).
£100–120 Bon

r. Elvis Presley's black leather motorcycle jacket, with red lining, 1960s.
£6,500–7,000 S

According to Elvis's cousin Patsy Presley, from whom the item was obtained, he used to wear this for riding his Harley-Davidson and she believes it may have been worn in one of his movies.

A Premier International leather football, signed in black by the various 1998 band members of Iron Maiden and former England Internationals Neil Webb, Tony Woodcock and Terry Butcher.
£60–80 Bon

A Posh Boy black and white striped T-shirt, worn by Chris Lowe on the cover of the album Suburbia, signed by Lowe, 1980s.
£220–250 Bon

A pair of black circular rimmed glasses, worn by Elton John during a 1990 concert, cased and with a letter of authenticity, 1990s.
£275–325 RBB

A double platinum award, for the CD 'Older' by George Michael, 1996.
£1,400–1,600 S

This award was presented to George Michael for sales in the UK of more than 600,000 copies of 'Older', BPI certified, together with a copy letter from Andy Stephens Management regarding the donation of this disc to a charity.

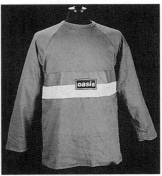

A T-shirt signed by Oasis, in blue cotton with logo and red and white stripes, signed in black marker by all members of the band, 1990s.
£450–500 S

Donated by the band to raise money on behalf of St Mary's Catholic Church, Camarthen.

A poster for Pink Floyd and the Jeff Beck group, at the Shrine Auditorium, July 1968, designed by Pinnacle artists John Van Hammersfeldt and Bob Fried, 18in (46cm) square.
£500–550 *S*

An autographed programme for the Rolling Stones' UK tour, September/October 1965, the colour front cover signed by members of the band in black ballpoint.
£900–1,100 *S*

Tina Turner's Versace dress, in black mesh with diamanté studs, with designer's motif, labelled 'Atelier Versace', together with a pair of black satin stilettoe shoes, each with black beaded No. 1 on the toe, by Gianni Versace, 1980s.
£5,000–5,500 *S*

A pair of yellow and black lace-up Vans Motorcycle boots, with personalised yellow embroidered 'Maxim' logo, worn by Maxim from The Prodigy on the US tour, 1998 Spanish tour and the 4th June Tel Aviv concert, together with letter of authenticity, 1990s, size 11.
£120–150 *Bon*

A ticket for the Sex Pistols' first UK gig at Ivanhoes, 1970s, 3½ x 4½in (9 x 11.5cm).
£1,500–1,750 *FRa*

A Gianni Versace white silk shirt from Robbie Williams's personal wardrobe, signed in black pen on the front, with a letter of authenticity from 'Ie Music Ltd', 1990s.
£200–250 *Bon*

A Queen tour programme, signed, 1980s, 11¼in (28.5cm) square.
£400–450 *PC*

Johnny Rotten's red, blue and black mohair sweater, worn by him for numerous public appearances and band performances, 1970s.
£2,000–2,500 *FRa*

A Gold Record Award presented by PolyCosmic Records to Wet Wet Wet, whose album 'End of Part One' achieved sales of more than 20,000 units, mounted CD and commemorative plaque, framed and glazed, 1997, 16 x 12in (40.5 x 30.5cm).
£220–260 *Bon*

The Beatles

A black and white photograph of the Beatles, together with a card signed by the group in blue ballpoint, 1963, photograph 8 x 10in (20.5 x 25.5cm).
£2,000–2,200 *S*

r. 'The Beatles Illustrated Lyrics Puzzle', 1960s, 21in (53.5cm) wide, including poster.
£40–50 *BTC*

A Beatles 1964 tour programme, 10½ x 8in (26.5 x 20.5cm).
£40–50 *BTC*

John Lennon's green corduroy jacket, round necked with stud fastening to front and cuffs, elasticated panels to sides, together with a black and white photograph of John wearing the jacket, c1966.
£9,500–10,000 *S*

This was worn by John during the Beatles' last tour. Photographs exist of him wearing it backstage at Candlestick Park. With the item is an affidavit from Dot Jarlett, the Lennons' former Kenwood housekeeper.

The Beatles Flip Your Wig Game, by Milton Bradley Co, 1960s, box 19in (48.5cm) wide.
£80–100 *BTC*

A set of American Beatles cake decoration figures, 1960s, 3¼in (8.3cm) high.
£80–100 *SAF*

l. A postcard from John Lennon to a fan, written in black ink on an Artist's Space exhibition card, signed and stamped '9 Feb 1979'.
£3,750–4,250 *S*

Instruments & Musical Equipment

l. A Hofner Committee guitar, Serial No. 2437, with maple faced back and sides, maple neck and frog head, bound rosewood fingerboard with pearl inlays to head, and individual machines with pearloid butterfly buttons and ebony adjustable bridge, c1957.
£700–800 *Bon(C)*

This model was so called because it was designed by a committee of 6 of Britain's top guitarists – Ike Isaacs, Roy Plummer, Bert Weedon, Freddie Phillips, Jack Llewellyn and Frank Deniz.

A Gibson SG special guitar, Serial No. 917512, belonging to Pete Townshend, in cherry finish, with hard Gibson case, c1969, together with a letter of provenance, laser copies of 3 photographs of Townshend playing a similar guitar and a copy of an interview in *Guitarist* magazine, June 1990.
£6,000–7,000 *S*

A Besson & Co cornet, No. 126699, played by Derek Watkins on several Beatles' recordings, including 'Strawberry Fields Forever', in leather carrying case with 2 mouthpieces and letter from the musician confirming its use, 1967–68.
£4,200–4,600 *S*

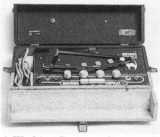

A Watkins Copicat echo unit, made of wood with metal inners, loop tape and mains power, c1967, 15in (38cm) wide.
£100–120 *DOM*

This unit was used by performers for effects for electric guitar and microphone. The 3 presets provided 3 different effects of echo and reverb, giving some very distinct spacey sounds from the valves inside. The tape running in a loop would sometimes break unexpectedly during performances and would have to be replaced when worn. Self-contained in a vinyl and cloth-covered wooden case with carrying handle, this unit was an essential piece of equipment to performers and budding guitarists of the period.

A Fender Bandmaster reverb amplifier, Traynor topbox and 150W Fender cabinet, with original owner's manual, 1970s.
£160–200 *Bon(C)*

A Dick Knight special guitar, with spruce arched top and a pearl engraved flower to back of head and larger one to head face with pearl logo, all hardware gold-plated, in hard case, c1973.
£1,400–1,800 *Bon(C)*

r. A Fender Squire Stratocaster Serial No. MN8273817, autographed by Bob Dylan, with black finish, signed on the scratchplate in black pen, 1990s.
£900–1,000 *S*

l. A Gibson Epiphone guitar, Serial No. 9400638, autographed by Noel Gallagher, the light sunburst body signed in black marker and inscribed 'Play it louder Best Wishes', 1990s.
£1,600–2,000 *S*

Records

An autographed red label copy of 'Love Me Do', by the Beatles, the A side signed in blue ballpoint by George, the other side by John and Paul, with dedications 'To Marg', 1960s.
£1,300–1,500 *S*

Earl Grant, 'Swingin' Gently with Earl Grant' EP, c1960.
£6–7 *ED*

An original soundtrack album 'Mondo Cane', by United Artist Records, c1962.
£25–30 *TOT*

Kate Bush, 'The Kick Inside' LP, signed, c1978.
£20–25 *SAF*

Electric Prunes, 'I Had Too Much to Dream (Last Night)' LP, c1967.
£20–30 *TOT*

Dickie Henderson & Cheryl Kennedy singing songs from Walt Disney's 'Mary Poppins' LP, c1970.
£8–10 *PC*

l. Buddy Holly 'Showcase' LP by Coral, c1964.
£15–20 *TOT*

Oasis, '(What's The Story) Morning Glory?' LP, boldly signed by all band members, 1990s.
£500–550 *Bon(C)*

Oasis, 'Definitely Maybe' LP, signed by all 5 current members, Noel Gallagher, Liam Gallagher, Paul Arthurs, Paul McGuigan and Alan White, 1990s.
£450–500 *Bon(C)*

Rolling Stones, 'Big Hits (High Tide and Green Grass)' LP, c1966.
£16–20 *ED*

An autographed copy of the 'Radio Promotional Album', the back cover signed by the Rolling Stones in various inks, c1969.
£2,000–2,500 *S*

The pressing of this promotional compilation was restricted to about 400 copies, with half going each to the US and the UK.

l. Cat Stevens, 'The World of Cat Stevens' LP, c1970.
£8–10 *PC*

r. The Sex Pistols 'God Save the Queen' single, c1977.
£8–10 *SAF*

Sex Pistols 'God Save the Queen' single, signed on the Queen's image by Sid Vicious, Johnny Rotten, Steve Jones and Paul Cook, c1977.
£350–400 *Bon(C)*

l. Larry Williams, 'Bony Moronie' single, London label, 1958.
£15–20 *TOT*

Tudor Lodge, black and white record cover with record, Vertigo Label, c1971.
£125–150 *CTO*

Spice Girls

When Geri Halliwell turned out her Ginger Spice wardrobe for charity at Sotheby's recently, it was one of the sensations of the auction season. 'The atmosphere was electric, it was the most extraordinary experience of my career,' says auctioneer Kerry Taylor. 'The best bit was when Geri herself turned up as a surprise to auction the last lot; there was such a cheer I thought the roof would lift off.' The room was packed with TV crews, fans and bidders, watching models strutting around in Geri's eye-poppingly short outfits. The top lot was the Union Jack dress worn at the 1997 Brit Awards and bought for £41,320 by Peter Morton for the Hard Rock Hotel in Las Vegas. A symbol of Cool Britannia, this was the Spice Girls' most famous outfit. It was also a great purchase in terms of publicity, as the frock and the name of the hotel were splashed across the world's press and TV – saturation advertising that would otherwise have cost a fortune.

Some were clearly bidding for promotional purposes, others were genuine fans. Everything at the sale sold and, for the moment at least, Spice Girls' material is hot. But is it a good investment for the future, and could the Spice Girls' merchandise, filling children's cupboards across the country, ever become collectable? 'I think it's very unlikely,' says Taylor. 'The cheaper objects have been manufactured in their millions, and what collectors want is rarity and one-off items. With the personal memorabilia, values will obviously depend on how long people go on listening to the music and what the girls do in future. But Geri has become an icon, and I think people will remain interested in her. My personal tip for the future is her shoes. Just like Geri, they're colourful, humorous, outrageous and utterly distinctive. One look at those platforms and buffalo wedges and you automatically think "Girl Power".'

Four pairs of buffalo wedges, worn by Ginger Spice, Geri Halliwell, in pink and plum, black, blue and beige and red and blue, 1990s, soles 6in (15cm) high.
£450–500 each pair *S*

The black PVC outfit and red thigh-length boots worn by Ginger Spice, Geri Halliwell, in the video 'Say You'll Be There', with signed photograph, c1996.
£2,400–2,800 *S*

The black rubber fetish outfit, worn by Ginger Spice, Geri Halliwell, in the video 'Spice Up Your Life', c1997.
£1,900–2,200 *S*

The 'painted face' dress worn by Ginger Spice, Geri Halliwell, during the Spice Girls' first trip to Japan, with airbrushed painting in blue, black and white, oval cut-out between shoulders, labelled 'Prizzi', 1990s.
£700–800 *S*

l. A colour photo of the Spice Girls, signed in black marker pen by all 5 band members, 1990s, 8 x 10in (20.5 x 25.5cm).
£250–275 *FRa*

A silver ball tongue stud, from the mouth of Scary Spice, 1990s, 1in (2.5cm) long, with letter of authenticity on 'The Spice Girls Ltd' headed paper.
£275–325 *Bon*

SCENT BOTTLES

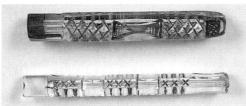

Two white and amber coloured cut-glass attar bottles, mid-19thC, 5in (12.5cm) long.
£35–40 each *DAC*

A silver-topped scent bottle, Birmingham 1882, 2in (5cm) high.
£25–35 *DAC*

A cut-glass scent bottle, with silver ring, Birmingham 1907, 5½in (14cm) high.
£40–50 *DAC*

A Wade ceramic mustard-coloured scent bottle, with crown-shaped stopper, c1910, 3in (7.5cm) high.
£90–100 *LBr*

A Russian dark blue enamelled scent bottle, decorated in light blue and red, c1910, 2¼in (5.5cm) high.
£135–140 *LBr*

A glass and gilt scent bottle, with chain, c1910, ¾in (2cm) high.
£65–75 *LBr*

A cologne bottle, modelled as a hand holding a bottle, c1920, 10in (25.5cm) high.
£25–30 *DAC*

A large silver-mounted scent flask, the cut-glass body with basket-weave design and plain silver mounts, by Joseph Gloster & Sons, Birmingham 1919, 10in (25.5cm) long.
£400–450 *HofB*

A Lalique Perles scent bottle, 1930s, 6¾in (17cm) high.
£400–450 *LBr*

A bottle of Lenthéric perfume, Maharajah de Kapurthaj, boxed, c1920, 4in (10cm) long.
£90–100 *LBr*

r. A bottle of Evening in Paris perfume, by Bourjois, in a horse-shoe container, 1930s, 4in (10cm) long.
£140–160 *LBr*

A shell-shaped plastic container, with a glass bottle of Evening in Paris perfume, by Bourjois, c1930, 4in (10cm) long.
£120–160 *LBr*

A gilded plaster display bottle, Guerlain shape, 1930s, 14in (35.5cm) high.
£200–250 *LBr*

A Ronson perfume atomiser, with blue and yellow pattern, marked 'Ronson Perfu-Mist', made in USA, 1930s, 1¾in (4.5cm) high.
£75–85 *PC*

A cut-glass scent bottle, with silver and blue enamel top, London 1927, 8in (20.5cm) high.
£145–155 *DAC*

FURTHER READING

Miller's Perfume Bottles: A Collector's Guide
Miller's Publications, 1998

A glass scent bottle, with pink atomiser and tassel, 1930s, 3½in (9cm) high.
£25–35 *DAC*

A Coty scent bottle, with gilded decoration and blue atomiser, c1940, 2½in (6.5cm) high.
£70–80 *LBr*

A Vasart green glass scent bottle, with cut-cane pink millefiori decoration, 1950s, 4½in (11.5cm) high.
£145–165 *SWB*

r. A Fiorinelli limited edition scent bottle, by Saint Louis, France, c1995, 8½in (21.5cm) high, with box and certificate.
£1,500–1,800 *STG*

A Lalique eau de cologne bottle, Je Reviens for Worth, c1955, 3in (7.5cm) high.
£80–90 *Rac*

Two Glasform glass scent bottles, coral and green, 1995, largest 4¼in (11cm) diam.
£100–120 *GLA*

SCIENCE & TECHNOLOGY
Scientific Instruments

A folding botanical microscope, with ivory eyepiece, in mahogany case, c1790, 5in (12.5cm) long.
£250–300 *TOM*

l. A brass sunshine recorder, with fixed latitude, on a slate bed, c1890, 7in (18cm) square.
£550–650 *RTw*

A Victorian stationary steam engine, 25in (63.5cm) high.
£1,000–1,200 *SPU*

A brass mining surveying dial, by W. & S. Jones, London, with calibrated rim and brass cover, c1870, 8in (20.5cm) diam.
£180–200 *MR*

A Crooks 'Maltese Cross' cathode ray demonstration tube, by Becker & Co, London, c1920, 9in (23cm) high.
£70–80 *ET*

A medical head mirror, by Meyer Meltzer, c1890, 7in (18cm) long.
£80–100 *ET*

A Russian Meteorolocial Office barograph, in Bakelite case, c1955, 9in (23cm) wide.
£400–450 *RTw*

A silver pocket medical kit, by Corke Brothers & Co, London, c1910, 4in (10cm) long.
£1,650–1,850 *BEX*

l. A Philips 2000w light bulb, 1950s, 18in (45.5cm) high.
£25–30 *ET*

Calculating Machines

The earliest calculating device was the abacus, which has been in constant use from ancient times to the present day. In the 17th century scientists invented various adding machines, the most famous of which was a metal calculator, manipulated by a stylus and developed in 1642 by the 21-year-old Frenchman, Blaise Pascal, the son of a tax inspector, whose job necessarily involved complex calculations.

By the Victorian period, compact machines were being created for office use, and in the 20th century there was a huge variety of mechanical calculating machines, ranging from pocket-watch calculators, to large lever-operated machines, to hand-held models operated with a stylus. These mechanical calculators were supplanted by the electronic calculator. The first desk-top versions appeared in the 1960s, followed by the creation of the pocket electronic calculator in 1970. Produced by the manufacturers Sharp and Canon, these pioneering pocket models retailed for around £250–300 each, an astonishing thought today, when a calculator can be bought for under £5. Vintage mechanical and electronic calculators are sought after by enthusiasts, particularly in the USA.

A Brunsviga System Trinks calculating machine, 1930s, 12in (30.5cm) wide.
£50–60 *ET*

A Fowler's Universal Calculator, with Bakelite back case, and original instructions, c1920, 4in (10cm) diam.
£80–100 *TOM*

A beech abacus, with coloured beads, early 20thC, 32½in (82.5cm) high.
£60–70 *FOX*

A Fowler's Textile Calculator Type E1, in original metal case, 1920s, 3in (7.5cm) diam.
£50–60 *TOM*

A Bri-Cal oxidized and lacquered brass adding machine, 1930s, 8in (20.5cm) diam, in original box.
£40–50 *TOM*

Electrical Household Appliances

The first commercial electric fan, a two-bladed desk model, was created in 1882 by Dr Scuyler Skaats Wheeler, chief engineer of the Crocker & Curtis Electric Motor Co, New York. The next major development was the gear-driven oscillating electric fan produced in the USA in 1908 by the Eck Dynamo & Electric Co, and soon imitated by other companies.

Production in Britain started around 1888, when B. Verity & Co began manufacturing electric fans for various electrical firms including GEC. Largely by virtue of the climate, however, electric fans were more popular in the USA than the in UK, and the former remains the major centre for collectors today. Early models are rare and can command surprisingly high prices.

l. A Biehl six-blade oscillating fan, with brass-plated guard and blades, 1916–21, blades 9in (23cm) long.
£75–85 *MRo*

A Trojan brass and cast iron fan, type 5310, by Emerson Electric Manufacturing Co, St Louis, c1905, 16in (40.5cm) high.
£500–550 *EKK*

A Westinghouse six-blade stationary fan, with brass blades and guard, lightweight steel base and open ring guard, 1918–20, blades 12in (30.5cm) long.
£80–100 *MRo*

An electric fan, by Verity's Fans Holdings Ltd, England, 1930s, 12in (30.5cm) diam.
£100–125 *HHa*

A Dazzling cast iron portable electric fire, with dual switch, c1920, 22in (56cm) high.
£140–160 *JUN*

A Super Electric Water Heater, 1930s, 7in (18cm) long.
£18–22 *EKK*

r. A Hamilton Beach No. 18 one-speed milk shake mixer, 1940s, 18in (45.5cm) high.
£110–130 *EKK*

A Hoover Junior vacuum cleaner, 1950s, 47in (119.5cm) high.
£10–20 *JUN*

Rulers

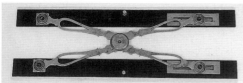

An ebony and brass parallel rule, with ivory edges, 18thC, 12in (30.5cm) long.
£150–200 *TOM*

A boxwood and nickel-silver two-fold rule, with ivory slide, by Stanley, London, with engineer's scales by Routledge, Bolton, c1860, 24in (61cm) long.
£40–50 *TOM*

An ivory and brass sliding caliper, with advertising and scales for the weight of steel, c1880, 4in (10cm) long, in original case.
£70–80 *TOM*

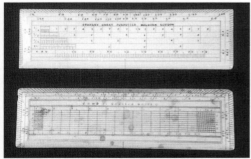

Two English ivory protractors, c1900, 12in (30.5cm) long.
£25–35 *WO*

A boxwood and brass textile calculating slide rule, compiled by James Holmes of Burnley, made by E. Preston and Sons, Birmingham, c1890, 12in (30.5cm) long.
£100–120 *TOM*

A farmer's boxwood, ivory and brass slide rule farm animal carcase calculator, by J. Tree, London, 19thC, 6½in (16.5cm) long.
£170–220 *ET*

l. A boxwood six-fold barrel dip rule, by J. Long, London, 19thC, 9in (23cm) long folded.
£65–75 *WO*

A brass folding rule, with ornate hinge, by John Rabone & Sons, Birmingham, c1870, 24in (61cm) long.
£50–60 *TOM*

Optical Equipment

A pair of tinted glass spectacles, in a papier mâché case, early 19thC, 6in (15cm) long.
£45–50 *CHU*

Five monocles and eye-glasses, 1840–1900, 1–2in (2.5–5cm) diam.
£12–25 each *VB*

A pair of folding opera glasses, stamped 'Aitchison's Patent 24883', c1870, 5in (12.5cm) wide.
£120–150 *TOM*

A pair of brass extending opera glasses, with green enamel decoration, made in Paris, c1890, 4in (10cm) wide.
£140–160 *CHe*

l. A set of optician's test lenses for bifocals, early 20thC, box 5in (12.5cm) wide.
£50–60 *ET*

An Edwardian silver spring clip lorgnette, 3½in (9cm) long.
£220–250 *WIM*

l. A pair of mother-of-pearl and brass opera glasses, 1970s, 3¾in (9.5cm) wide.
£100–125 *DKH*

Telescopes & Binoculars

A brass telescope, with stand and case, c1880, 60in (152.5cm) high.
£2,000–2,500 *SPU*

A French brass marine single draw telescope, with fine ropework, by Legris, Optician, c1860, 42in (106.5cm) long.
£80–120 *TOM*

A pair of 'cow udder' binoculars, by Carl Zeiss, late 19thC, 7in (18cm) wide.
£800–1,000 *ET*

A Royal Naval signalman's nickel and leather single draw telescope, by Ross, 1920s, 25in (63.5cm) long.
£145–175 *NC*

A Brocklebank Line brass and leather ships' telescope, by Heath, c1950, 30in (76cm) long.
£250–300 *NC*

SCRIPOPHILY

An American Express share
certificate, signed by
Butterfield as President,
Fargo as Secretary and
Holland as Treasurer,
slight damage, c1859.
£700–800 *P*

A State of Arkansas Levee bond,
issued to the Memphis and
St Louis Railroad Co, 1870,
8%, $1,000 bond, with vignettes
of steamboats, allegorical
figures and state seal, repaired.
£75–95 *P*

An Oregon Pacific Railroad
Company $1000 gold bond,
1880, depicting loco
and dock scenes with
20 coupons attached.
£175–195 *SCR*

An Edison Phonograph Toy
Manufacturing share certificate,
with vignette of Santa Claus on
sledge drawn by reindeer, 1890.
£750–850 *P*

l. A share certificate for The
Channel Tubular Railway
Preliminary Co, 1892, 'Parts de
Fondateurs', with vignettes of
warships, a train in a tubular
tunnel and English and French
flags, text in French and English.
£180–200 *P*

r. A 100 francs
share certificate
for Mines D'Or
de la France, red
and yellow with
a full sheet of
coupons, 1895.
£35–45 *GKR*

A Chicago & Alton
Railroad Co $1,000
cancelled bond, with
loco vignette, green
and black, dated '1899'.
£15–20 *SCR*

A 1,000 Crowns bond,
4% loan of 1908, with
vignette of a maiden
overlooking the City
of Vienna, 1908.
£23–27 *GKR*

A City of Montreal certificate, for 3% debenture stock of 1890, engraved with vignettes of sea front and beaver, black and white, c1903.
£15–20 *SCR*

A Canadian Mortgage Association share certificate, with vignettes of farming and city scenes, brown, blue and beige, dated '1910'.
£35–45 *SCR*

A £20 bond, 5% Anglo-French loan of 1908, for redemption of Peking–Hankow Railway loan, with vignette of West Gate of Peking, green and cream, c1908.
£75–85 *GKR*

A Banana du Rio-Grande Nicaragua share certificate, depicting the ship *Banana X*, loco & banana plantations in yellow, issued in Paris, c1918.
£55–65 *SCR*

l. A Compania Huanchaca de Bolivia bearer share, with coupons in copper mining company, issued in Valparaso, with vignette of factory entrance, text in English, French and Spanish, 1928.
£15–20 *SCR*

A Big Pete Canadian Mines Ltd bearer share certificate, with crest, decorative border and full coupons attached, text in English and French, issued in New Liskeard, near Cobalt, Canada, 1910.
£18–20 *SCR*

A bond for the Kingdom of Roumania, depicting the castle of Vlad the Impaler, blue and black, issued in 1929.
£30–35 *SCR*

l. A Fox Theatres Corporation stock certificate, with vignette of reclining figure of Britannia, in brown/black, dated '1929'.
£15–20 *SCR*

SEWING

Four mother-of-pearl sewing items, 1840–80, 1½–2in long:
Needle book   £40–50
Cotton spool   £15–25
Folding scissors £10–20
Stiletto   £15–25 *VB*

r. A black hand sewing machine, decorated in gold, 19thC, 12in (30.5cm) long.
£55–65 *TRU*

A Mauchline ware bell-shaped tape measure, depicting the pier at Walton-on-the-Naze, late 19thC, 2in (5cm) high.
£90–100 *DHA*

A Victorian glass thimble holder, in the shape of a shoe, 2½in (6.5cm) long.
£40–45 *VB*

A Prince Charles tartan needle tube, c1880, 3¾in (9.5cm) long.
£60–70 *VB*

A hand-painted silk and ribbon pincushion, decorated with forget-me-nots, c1860, 6in (15cm) square.
£50–60 *JPr*

A silver needle book, Birmingham 1909, 1¾in (4.5cm) high.
£30–35 *VB*

A Tunbridge ware needle case, c1860–70, 2½in (6.5cm) high.
£220–270 *AMH*

r. Two French Lyonnais wooden cord winders, used for making silk cords and tassels, with steel hooks, c1880, 17in (43cm) long.
£250–300 *MLL*

SHIPPING

An ebony octant, with ivory scales, by Crichton, London, with 7 filters, in a mahogany case, c1850, 13in (33cm) wide.
£450–500 *TOM*

A brass plaque from the German warship SMS *König Albert*, c1909, 5 x 6in (12.5 x 15cm).
£80–100 *COB*

A Philips Universal map measurer, 1920s, 1¾in (4.5cm) long.
£15–20 *VB*

A scrimshaw horn, engraved with 3 architectural coastal scenes, one possibly St Petersburg, a whale and a leaf border, 19thC, 5½in (14cm) long.
£400–450 *DN*

A Radiguet gun boat in live steam, with original rigging and paintwork on hull and scribed wooden deck, c1900, 25in (63.5cm) long.
£6,300–7,000 *BKS*

r. A ship's galley pine fitment, c1900, 20in (51cm) high.
£250–300 *MLL*

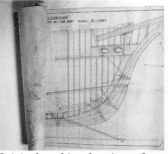

Original working drawings of HMS *Cormorant*, scale ¾in–12in, c1909, 31 x 52in (78.5 x 132cm).
£150–200 *NC*

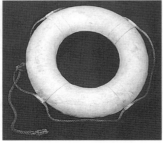

r. A white stitched canvas life preserver, 1920s, 22in (56cm) diam.
£35–45 *ASM*

An original blue back chart of the Azores, by Wilson, 1861, 30 x 40in (76 x 106.5cm).
£80–100 *NC*

A ship's galvanized anchor lamp, with brass fittings, c1920s, 24in (61cm) high.
£50–75 *JUN*

l. A pair of brass rowlocks, 1930s, 10in (25.5cm) long.
£25–30 GWA

A Royal Navy Aldis light, in box, c1944, 13in (33cm) wide.
£25–30 NC

A chrome-plated brass and wood steering wheel, 20thC, 15¼in (38.5cm) diam.
£90–100 ASM

A WWII German Naval issue station pointer, by E. D. Sprenger, Berlin, of japanned brass construction, in original fitted case, c1944, 26in (66cm) long.
£400–450 MJa

r. A brass bell from the BR ferry MV *Cambria*, engraved 'Cambria 1949' on the side, 12in (30.5cm) high.
£180–220 SOL

r. A ship-builder's brass plate, inscribed 'John Harker Ltd', c1950, 9 x 14in (23 x 35.5cm).
£100–150 NC

l. A ship's bridge brass window frame, 1950s, 27in (68.5cm) wide.
£300–330 NC

A ship's chrome voice pipe, 1950s, 6in (15cm) long.
£35–40 NC

Ephemera

A bridge score pad,
with yellow cover
marked 'Elder Dempster
Lines', 1920–30,
8in (20.5cm) high.
£10–12 *BAf*

A pack of playing
cards, depicting
British Tankers, 1950s.
£10–12 *BAf*

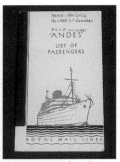

A passenger list from
the *Andes*, Royal Mail
Lines, c1963, 7 x 4in
(18 x 10cm).
£3–5 *BAf*

A TSS *Duke of
Lancaster* menu,
27th May 1960,
6 x 4in (15 x 10cm).
£3–6 *COB*

A SR.N5 hovercraft brochure,
1960s, 6 x 10in (15 x 25.5cm).
£15–20 *COB*

Metalware

r. A Victorian White
Star Line silver-
plated toast rack,
4in (10cm) wide.
£24–28 *CaC*

l. A Union Castle
passenger ship's
silver-plated
sugar bowl, c1930,
4in (10cm) high.
£60–70 *NC*

A P&O passenger ship's set of 12 dessert knives
and forks, and a set of 6 spoons, 1980s.
£30–50 each set *NC*

Titanic Memorabilia

One of the most celebrated maritime disasters of all time was the sinking of the *Titanic*. The largest and most luxurious passenger liner of its day, the British ship was considered unsinkable because its double-bottomed hull was divided into 16 watertight compartments, up to four of which could be flooded without endangering the vessel's safety. On its maiden voyage to the USA however, shortly before midnight on the April 14, 1912, the *Titanic* struck an iceberg that ripped a 300-foot gash in its side, rupturing five compartments. By 2.20am the next morning, the *Titanic* had sunk. Of the 2,224 persons on board, 1,513 lost their lives, and only the arrival of the Cunard liner *Carpathia*, 1 hour 20 minutes after the vessel had gone down, prevented further deaths in the icy waters off Newfoundland.

From the moment the disaster was known, many preserved their *Titanic* mementos, and during the 20th century fascination with the story has been kept alive by such motion pictures as *Titanic* (1953), *A Night to Remember* (1958), and, in 1998, the most recent *Titanic* blockbuster movie.

'Interest has grown hugely in *Titanic* material,' says Peter Bogue from Onslow's Auction House in London, which began holding annual *Titanic* sales in 1987. 'Over the past year there have been some staggering prices, certainly helped by the new *Titanic* film.' The most expensive items tend to be objects rescued from the vessel: a collection of water-damaged personal effects belonging to a steward who perished on the *Titanic*, sold for £15,000 at Onslow's most recent sale. Postcards sent from the ship fetch high prices, and there is also strong interest in contemporary newspaper reports and commemorative ephemera recording the disaster.

A group of personal effects belonging to Edmond J. Stone, First Class Bedroom Steward, RMS *Titanic*, comprising a water damaged pocket watch stopped at 2.16am (the ship's lights went out at 2.15am and she disappeared under the water at 2.20am) and chain with propelling pencil attached, slightly rusted penknives, White Star Company keys, a tailor's bill, the larger fragmented part of a memorandum to Stone from the P&O Steam Navigation Company dated 2nd Feb 1912, a white canvas bag and papers addressed to Mrs E. Stone.
£15,000–17,000   *ONS*

A Continuous Certificate of Discharge for Fireman William Nutbeam, a survivor of RMS *Titanic*, entry No 6 for *Titanic* 10th April 1912, with photographic study of William Nutbeam and associated National Health Cards.
£1,800–2,000   *ONS*

A White Star Line TSS *Titanic* colour art postcard, from Thomas Mudd to his mother, 1912.
£3,000–3,500   *ONS*

Tom Mudd, a young man of 19, was emigrating to the USA to start a career. He was sailing as a second-class passenger and perished in the disaster.

r. A copy of a magazine *The Deathless Story of the 'Titanic'*, by Phillip Gibbs, including passenger list, poor condition, c1912.
£30–35   *MED*

Peter Boyd-Smith, *Titanic*, first edition, signed by a survivor, c1992, 10 x 8in (25.5 x 20.5cm).
£30–40   *COB*

SIXTIES & SEVENTIES

A Hornsea coffee pot, decorated with orange and green fruit and with orange cover, 1960s, 9in (23cm) high.
£15–18 *UTP*

A Royal Tudor Ware dinner plate, side plate and bowl, decorated with orange and black flowers, 1960s, dinner plate 10in (25.5cm) diam.
£6–8 each *UTP*

Sheet music for 'Long Live Love', by Sandie Shaw, c1965, 11 x 8½in (28 x 21.5cm).
£2–3 *RAD*

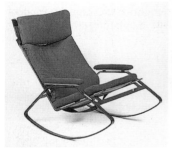

A Reigate rocking chair, by William Plunkett Ltd, the grey nylon-finished steel frame with red fabric cushioned back, arms and seat, 1960s.
£180–220 *Bri*

A PVC tub-shaped armchair, on a swivel chrome base, 1960s, 27in (68.5cm) high.
£50–60 *P(B)*

A chrome 'space' lamp, with smoked glass bowl and chrome stand, 1960–70, 68in (172.5cm) high.
£130–150 *RAT*

A black plastic beaded handbag, 1960s, 6in (15cm) wide.
£10–12 *Har*

A Tiffany silver bracelet, 1960s.
£230–250 *GLT*

A pair of Gold Fan nylons, 1960s.
£4–6 *RAD*

l. A Sindy doll, in original orange dress, 1960s, 12in (30.5cm) high.
£40–50 *CMF*

A pair of Courtelle jersey hot pants, by Donbros, 1960s.
£5–7 *BOH*

An Ossie Clark crêpe top, decorated with black and red flowers, designed for Radley, 1970s.
£20–25 *BOH*

A silk-lined black and pink sequinned top, made in Hong Kong, 1970s.
£24–28 *BOH*

A Ben Sherman red checked shirt, 1970.
£6–7 *BOH*

A Richard Lewis 1930s-style silk chiffon wedding dress, decorated with sequins and pearls, with a short train, 1970s.
£110–130 *JVa*

r. A Poole Pottery orange fruit bowl, 1970s, 8in (20.5cm) diam.
£50–60 *PrB*

A *Clockwork Orange* programme, with press release notes, c1971, 11 x 8½in (28 x 21.5cm).
£25–30 *SAF*

l. A Biba shop display for eyeshadows, complete and unused, 1970s, 15in (38cm) wide.
£100–125 *PLB*

A Big Ben alarm clock, with blue dial and repeater, by Westclox, 1970s, 7½in (19cm) high.
£20–25 *PLB*

A Referendum on the European Community leaflet, 1975, 8 x 6in (20.5 x 15cm).
£3–4 *SVB*

SMOKING

A Welsh oak pipe rack, with shaped back and frieze, c1760, 15in (38cm) wide.
£350–400 *CoA*

Four brass novelty pipe tampers, 1880–1920, 1½–2in (4 x 5cm) high.
£20–40 each *VB*

A brass milk churn match holder/striker, c1920, 3¾in (9.5cm) high.
£35–40 *CHe*

An anti-dust pipe hanger, in original packaging, 1940–50, 6in (15cm) long.
£15–20 *DAC*

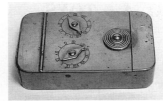

A brass two-clock combination lock tobacco tin, c1800, 2¾in (7cm) wide.
£250–300 *PC*

A silver cigarette case, originally for cartridges, Birmingham 1904, 2¾in (7cm) long.
£130–150 *GIO*

Six ivory cigarette holders, on original sales card, unused, 1930s, card 5 x 7in (12.5 x 18cm).
£25–30 *DAC*

A Zippo chrome cigarette lighter with leather case, 1930s, 6¾in (17cm) high.
£200–220 *CHe*

r. A chrome lighter, in the form of an aeroplane, 1950s, 4in (10cm) wide.
£120–140 *JUN*

An iron tobacco plug cutter, with wood and brass handle, on a wooden base, c1890, 13in (33cm) long.
£50–60 *WAB*

A silver caricature vesta of a WWI soldier, with pronounced nose and wearing a cap, maker AWH, London 1917, 3in (7.5cm) high.
£1,400–1,600 *GH*

Named after the Roman goddess of the hearth, vesta match boxes were made in a huge variety of novelty designs. Prices depend on age, rarity, material and shape, with interesting designs, such as the above example, commanding high sums.

A Cartier silver and gold cigarette case c1930, 4½in (11.5cm) square, and lighter.
£1,650–1,850 *BEX*

SPACE MEMORABILIA & TOYS

Space travel has been one of the most significant achievements of the last half of the 20th century. The space race really took off in October 1957, when the USSR launched the first satellite, Sputnik I, which circled the globe in 96 minutes. One month later, Laika became the first dog in space on Sputnik II.

Initially America lagged behind the USSR. The Soviets were responsible for the first successful manned space flight, piloted by Yuri Gagarin in April 1961; they put the first woman (Valentina Tereshkova) into orbit in 1963; and in 1965 astronaut Alexei Leonov made the first space walk. But the most famous space achievement of the 1960s, and indeed of the 20th century, was an American triumph when, on July 20, 1969, Neil Armstrong became the first man in history to set foot on the moon – 'That's one small step for a man, one giant leap for mankind'.

Space memorabilia, such as the autographs shown here, are highly collectable. Fascination with space also launched a whole generation of sci-fi toys, comics, films and TV shows, celebrating fantasy galactic adventurers and exploration.

A signed colour photograph of cosmonauts Valentina Tereshkova and Valery Bykobsky (husband and wife), wearing uniforms, 1960s, 12 x 9½in (30.5 x 24cm).
£180–200 *VS*

A signed commemorative cover and postcard, both depicting Alexei Leonov's walk in space, c1966.
£50–60 *VS*

A signed colour photograph of Apollo II astronauts Neil Armstrong, Buzz Aldrin and Michael Collins, seated together in space suits with image of moon in the background, 8 x 10in (20.5 x 25.5cm).
£900–1,000 *VS*

A green card signed by Jim Irwin, with Apollo XV beneath and a small doodle of the moon, 1990s, 3 x 5in (7.5 x 12.5in).
£45–55 *VS*

Two colour photographs of astronauts, Fred Haise and James McDivitt, 8 x 10in (20.5 x 25.5cm), together with a signed and inscribed colour booklet by Jim Irwin entitled 'Footprints on the Moon', 1980–90s.
£50–60 *VS*

An Astronaut card game, by Pepus, 1960s, 5in (12.5cm) high.
£15–20 *J&J*

Cross Reference
Comics
Toys

l. A Micronauts Time Traveller action figure, on card, c1976, card 8 x 7in (20.5 x 18cm).
£12–15 *OW*

A Mattel's space station, 1960s, 16 x 14in (40.5 x 35.5cm).
£110–125 *OW*

SPORT

A wooden decoy duck, c1895,
10½in (26.5cm) long.
£135–155 *RTh*

A set of *lignum vitae* bowls, in an oak
rack, c1910, 38in (96.5cm) wide.
£200–225 *GBr*

A child's boxing outfit, comprising black
shorts, white socks, black gloves and
shoes, c1920.
£60–70 *WAB*

A navy blue velvet Kent rugby
cap, with gold binding and
tassel, worn by G. Hubbard,
1925–26.
£75–100 *WaR*

l. A Victorian mahogany billiard/
snooker cue stand, the rotating
frame crested with ball finials,
fitted with clips on a circular
base with compressed bun feet,
together with various cues, spider
and rests, 19in (48.5cm) diam.
£750–850 *GAK*

A brown and black leather
American football
helmet, 1930s.
£280–310 *SMAM*

A pair of black leather
riding boots and trees,
by Maxwell, Dover
Street, London, 1930s,
15in (38cm) high.
£70–80 *WAB*

Baseball

A Playball Gum card,
depicting Joe Di
Maggio, c1941.
£575–625 *HALL*

A Welsh baseball bat, stamped 'WBU' (Welsh
Baseball Union), c1920, 30in (76cm) long.
£50–65 *WAB*

l. An autographed
baseball, from the
Navy Flight Training
School baseball
team, includes
Ted Williams'
signature, c1943.
£325–375 *HALL*

Ted Blood, *The
Splendid Splinter*,
first edition, with
dust jacket, c1960.
£200–250 *HALL*

Cricket

A pair of Victorian boy's cricket pads, 22½in (57cm) high.
£75–95 *WAB*

l. A Victorian one-piece cricket bat, 32in (81.5cm) long.
£55–65 *DQ*

A Victorian silver and enamel cricketing vesta, decorated with a batsman at the wicket, maker J. G., Birmingham 1892, 1½ x 1¼in (3.5 x 3cm).
£450–500 *GH*

l. A Chad Valley mechanical table cricket game, 'The Test Match', 1920s, 13 x 16in (33 x 40.5cm).
£100–120 *J&J*

A silver cricket bat brooch, with agate handle, Birmingham 1900, 1⅜in (3.5cm) high.
£200–225 *BEX*

A Slazenger cricket bat, inscribed with the signature and printed name of Garfield Sobers, and 'World Test Record 365 Not Out', 1960s, 34in (86.5cm) long.
£20–30 *WAB*

Sir Garfield Sobers' record was beaten by Brian Lara in 1994.

A brass cricket ball gauge, 1930s, 3⅜in (9cm) diam.
£35–40 *WAB*

> **Cross Reference**
> Games

A box of 6 Deck Cricket Balls, by John Jaques & Son Ltd, 1930s–1950s, box 5½ x 8½in (14 x 21.5cm).
£10–20 each *WAB*

Fishing

A black japanned salmon fly reservoir, fitted with 5 lift-out trays with 345 nickel-silver spring clips and containing approximately 190 fully dressed and hairwing salmon flies including doubles, c1930, 10½in (26.5cm) wide.
£1,000–1,200 AGA

A Victorian brass salmon gaff, with rosewood handle, 17in (43cm) long.
£120–140 WAB

A galvanised iron fishing bait box, c1880, 10in (25.5cm) wide.
£25–30 MLL

Two metal spikes, with wooden handles, used for making heavy fishing nets, c1880, 8in (20.5cm) long.
£35–40 WAB

l. A Victorian lead weed grapnel, 4in (10cm) high, in original leather pouch.
£25–30 WAB

A Hardy gut cutter and tweezers, engraved with registration number, c1890, 3in (7.5cm) long.
£30–35 OTB

A split-willow salmon creel, Maine, USA, 1910–20, 10in (25.5cm) high.
£200–220 JVM

A fly tying vice, c1900, 7in (18cm) long.
£45–50 WAB

l. P. D. Malloch, *Life History and Habits of The Salmon Sea-Trout and other Freshwater Fish*, second edition, 1912.
£25–30 MUL

A Heddon's Dowagiac Game Fish Minnow lure, 1913–20, 4¼in (11cm) long, boxed.
£330–360 *JVM*

Many different lure patents were issued between 1900 and 1930. Values depend on rarity, and items in original containers and in mint condition command the top prices. Lures are very sought-after particularly in the USA where there is even a National Fishing Lure Collectors' Club, with a large and active membership.

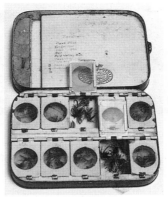

An Ogden Smith black japanned dry fly box, with a large quantity of flies, c1920, 3½ x 5in (9 x 12.5cm).
£125–145 *RTh*

A Hardy fly wallet, with a selection of salmon flies, c1930, 6½in (16.5cm) long.
£350–400 *RTh*

FURTHER READING
Malcolm Greenhalgh, *Fly-Fishing*, Mitchell Beazley, 1998

l. A Hardy 'album' Bakelite fly cast case and damper, with salmon flies in relief on the lid, c1930, 4in (10cm) diam.
£50–60 *OTB*

A Hardy fish-tailer, c1920.
£70–80 *AL*

A dry fly drier and dresser, in the form of a pocket watch, c1920, 1¾in (4.5cm) diam.
£60–70 *OTB*

An angler's knife, with 6 attachments, the side-plates marked with hook sizes, c1930, 4in (10cm) long.
£225–245 *RTh*

l. A wicker fishing creel, c1930, 7in (18cm) high.
£40–45 *DQ*

A Hardy nickel-silver 'Drop Knife No 1', with dropping blade and screwdriver/file, 1930–34, handle 3¼in (8.5cm) long.
£650–800 *OTB*

A Hardy aluminium salmon gaff, 1930s, 23½in (59.5cm) long.
£50–60 *WAB*

l. A glass dry fly oiler, with wooden stopper, brush and leather button tab, 1930s, 3in (7.5cm) high.
£20–25 *OTB*

r. A leather-bound split-willow trout creel, Maine, USA, 1930–40, 10in (25.5cm) wide.
£110–140 *JVM*

Reels

A 3¾in brass crank-wind reel, by Phin of Edinburgh, with wooden handle on serpentine crank arm, c1860.
£150–200 *OTB*

A 3½in brass salmon reel, with folding handle and raised rear check housing, c1870.
£400–500 *OTB*

A 4¾in brass crank-wind salmon reel, with ebonite handle on straight crank arm turning in flanged anti-foul rim, c1870.
£150–175 *OTB*

l. A 3½in brass crank-wind salmon reel, with unusually shaped crank arm, c1880.
£200–250 *OTB*

r. A Slater of Newark 'S.E.J.' fly fisher's 3¼in winch, with ebonite backplate and front rim, brass faceplate with nickel-silver rims, c1895.
£250–300 *OTB*

A Farlow 4in Patent Lever brass salmon fly reel, c1920.
£80–100 *OTB*

A Hardy Bros 3¼in Super Silex Multiplier, with black leaded finish, c1935.
£280–350 *OTB*

A Hardy Zane Grey 8½in multiplier big game reel, with circular Royal Appointment medallions and faceplate with a further circular medallion reading 'The Hardy Zane Grey Reel, 8½in', in original fitted block leather case, 1928–49.
£7,000–7,500 *AGA*

The largest of the range of Zane Grey reels, the 8½in is very rarely seen and the Hardy Production book shows only twenty-one examples having been made between 1928 and 1949.

A Starback 3½in wood and brass fishing reel, c1940.
£55–65 *DQ*

A Hardy The Hardex-Hydra Reel No 2, Mk 2, unused, in maker's original leatherette box, with instructions, 1930s.
£130–150 *MUL*

r. A Julius Vom Hofe nickel-silver multiplier reel, with ebonite handle, c1935.
£500–550 *AGA*

Four Nottingham wood and brass reels, 1930s, largest 6in diam.
£25–65 each *WAB*

r. An Allcock Sea Knight 4½in alloy centre pin sea reel, in original red box, c1968.
£50–60 *OTB*

Football

A Bristol blue and white twelve-sided pottery plate, printed for Football Association English League 1st Division with positions and club crests, 1906–7, 12in (30.5cm) diam.
£500–550 *MUL*

Two pairs of brown leather football boots, with white laces, 1930s–50s.
£65–95 each *WAB*

A 1968 European Cup programme, signed by Matt Busby, Dennis Law etc, with signed 1966 photograph of German International Uwe Seeler, programme 7½ x 7¼in (19 x 18.5cm).
£35–45 *SAF*

A wooden football rattle, with original red and white paint, c1910, 10in (25.5cm) long.
£40–45 *DQ*

A 'U-Select-It' football wall machine, with keys, 1930s, 31¾in (80.5cm) high.
£475–525 *SAF*

> **Cross Reference**
> Amusement &
> Vending Machines

Three silver Heathfield Football Club League medals, 1920–22, 1in (2.5cm) diam.
£4–6 each *HEI*

A green glass ashtray, inscribed in yellow 'The National Sporting Club Honours World Cup Winners', above a colour photograph of the team and inset portrait of manager, Sir Alf Ramsey, 1967, 8½in (21.5cm) wide.
£15–20 *WaR*

A set of 18 European trade cards, depicting Manchester United Footballers, c1997.
£4–5 *LCC*

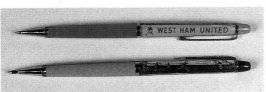

Two Biro pens, in West Ham United and Chelsea colours, with team players in liquid, 1950s–60s, 4½in (11.5cm) long.
£10–12 each *WaR*

Fifty-two football programmes, 1970s and 1980s.
£8–10 *MED*

Golf

A long-nosed golden beechwood scare neck driver, stamped 'D. Anderson', c1880, 38in (96.5cm) long.
£420–460 *MUL*

A Gibson's Burslem pottery bowl, with an orange rim, decorated with golf scene transfers of 'brownies', c1910, 4in (10cm) high.
£90–110 *WaR*

These transfers of figures in brown tones were known as 'brownies'.

l. A North British Golf Ball box, 1920s, 7¼in (18.5cm) wide.
£25–35 *WaR*

A silver-plated golf player trophy, on a wooden plinth, c1935, 6in (15cm) high.
£100–120 *WaR*

An enamel golf brooch, the clubs painted red, green, white and yellow, 1930s, 2in (5cm) long.
£35–40 *DAC*

A golf ball cigarette lighter, on a stand of miniature clubs, c1940, 5½in (14cm) high.
£35–40 *DAC*

A cold-painted bronze lady golfer, with a cigarette lighter in the form of a golf ball, on an onyx ashtray, 1920s, 7½in (19cm) high.
£150–175 *WaR*

r. A cast iron golf ball cleaner, 8½in (20.5cm) diam.
£125–145 *WAB*

Table Tennis

A pair of carved wooden table tennis bats, 1880s, 12¾in (32.5cm) long.
£100–125 *WaR*

A pair of vellum table tennis bats, with tooled-leather frames, by Hamleys, London, c1910, 13¾in (35cm) long.
£30–40 *WAB*

A cork-handled table tennis bat, 1920s, 12in (30.5cm) long.
£5–10 *WaR*

Tennis

l. A convex wedge lady's tennis racket, with flat top, c1900, 26in (66cm) long.
£100–110 *WaR*

A French one-piece garden tennis racket, c1880, 15in (38cm) long.
£40–45 *WaR*

A ceramic tennis racket, with St Leonard's crest, 1920s, 3½in (9cm) long.
£30–35 *WaR*

A lawn tennis tape measure, c1910, 4¼in (11cm) diam.
£45–50 *WAB*

A Spalding open throat tennis racket, 1920–30, 27in (68.5cm) long.
£55–65 *WaR*

A display tennis racket, 1950s–60s, 60in (152.5cm) long.
£175–225 *WAB*

Cross Reference
Goss & Crested China

l. A German porcelain match holder, in the form of a girl holding a tennis racket, with Blackpool crest, 1920–30s, 3in (7.5cm) high.
£20–25 *JMC*

A box of Slazenger Lawn Tennis balls, used condition, 1940s, 8in (20.5cm) wide.
£25–30 *WaR*

STEVENGRAPHS

A Stevengraph is the trade name given to the woven silk picture invented by Thomas Stevens (1828–88) of Coventry. The Midlands city had long been famous for the manufacture of silk ribbons, and Stevens adapted the Jacquard loom to produce decorative bookmarks, postcards and, most famously, pictures. The first examples were woven before an admiring audience at the 1879 York Exhibition. They were an instant success, and soon new titles were being issued every few weeks. Favourite subjects included sporting scenes, historical tableaux, celebrity portraits, transport pictures and American themes, reflecting the popularity of Stevengraphs in the USA.

By the 1900s the market was in decline, and comparatively few Stevengraphs were produced in the Edwardian period. Prices are affected by subject, rarity and condition. Stevengraphs are prone to fading, and some have been rendered almost worthless by the removal of the coloured silk from the card base. Some collectors will insist on a titled mount and Stevens's advertising label on the reverse, although, particularly in the final years of production, these labels were not always applied to pictures.

A Stevengraph, No. 148a, entitled 'Dick Turpin's ride to York...', York Exhibition version with 8 line poem, silk foxed, c1879, 5 x 8in (12.5 x 20.5cm).
£280–300 *VINE*

A Stevengraph, No. 157, entitled 'The Start', c1879, 5 x 8in (12.5 x 20.5cm).
£180–200 *VINE*

A Stevengraph, No. 194a, entitled 'The Present Time', c1880, 5 x 8in (12.5 x 20.5cm).
£350–400 *VINE*

This subject is very common, but this particular example is in superb condition. In average condition the same title might be worth only £80–100.

A Stevengraph love token bookmark, 'Forget Me Not', c1880, 9in (23cm) long.
£80–90 *YAN*

A Stevengraph commemorative bookmark for 150th anniversary of George Washington's birthday, 1882, 8in (20.5cm) long.
£90–110 *YAN*

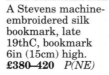

A Stevens machine-embroidered silk bookmark, late 19thC, bookmark 6in (15cm) high.
£380–420 *P(NE)*

A Stevengraph, No. 150 entitled 'The Lady Godiva Procession', No. 150, some fading, c1884, 5 x 8in (12.5 x 20.5cm).
£80–90 *VINE*

A Stevengraph, No. 191, entitled 'The Mersey Tunnel Railway', c1887, 5 x 8in (12.5 x 20.5cm).
£500–550 *VINE*

A double Stevengraph, No. 199, entitled 'Stephenson's Triumph', from the York Exhibition, c1879, 7 x 8in (18 x 20.5cm).
£550–600 *VINE*

A Stevengraph, No. 141, entitled 'The Forth Bridge', depicting the bridge under construction, label gives completion date, c1890, 6½ x 9½in (16.5 x 24cm).
£500–550 *VINE*

A Stevengraph, No. 2, entitled 'Her Majesty Queen Victoria', c1897, 7x 5in (18 x 12.5cm).
£110–130 *VINE*

l. A Stevengraph, No. 180, entitled 'Grace Darling', the girl with blue and red clothing, on a green mount, c1906, 5 x 8in (12.5 x 20.5cm).
£330–360 *VINE*

A Stevengraph, No. 176, entitled 'The Last Lap', c1880, 5 x 7in (12.5 x 18cm).
£400–440 *VINE*

A Stevengraph, No. 152, entitled 'The Death of Nelson, c1893, 7 x 10in (18 x 25.5cm).
£160–180 *VINE*

r. A Stevengraph, No. 134, entitled 'Crystal Palace', c1893, 5 x 8in (12.5 x 20.5cm).
£280–320 *VINE*

Stevengraphs
All Stevengraphs are numbered according to the sequence used by Austin Sprake in *The Price Guide to Stevengraphs,* Antique Collectors' Club, 1972.

A Stevengraph, No. 179, entitled 'Called to the Rescue', with label on reverse showing a list of Stevengraphs, c1897, 5 x 8in (12.5 x 20.5cm).
£260–280 *VINE*

A Stevengraph portrait, No. 76, R. Howell, Champion of the World, with images of bicycles, re-mounted, 1880s, 4¼ x 2½in (11 x 6.5cm).
£200–220 *P(NE)*

TATTOOING MEMORABILIA

The ultimate in youthful fashion today, tattooing has a long history. Egyptian mummies have been found with tattooed decoration, many ancient peoples decorated their skins with tribal patterns, and the Romans tattooed marks on slaves and criminals. With the advent of Christianity, tattooing disappeared from the West although it flourished in other cultures – amongst the Maoris and Native American Indians; in Japan and Polynesia.

The word tattoo is Tahitian (from 'tatau' – mark) and was introduced into the English language when Captain Cook visited Tahiti in 1769 and witnessed this native craft. In the 18th and 19th centuries, tattooed Indians, Polynesians and later Europeans became popular fairground attractions. Tattooing parlours opened up in towns and ports across the world, servicing sailors and others.

'In the 1900s tattooing was briefly an aristocratic fashion,' explains tattoo historian Paul Ramsbottom. 'Lady Randolph Churchill, for example, had a butterfly on her shoulder, and the King of Norway had several tattoos.' A tattooist by trade (whose celebrity clients include the Spice Girls), Ramsbottom has opened his own tattooing museum in Manchester, one of only a handful in the world. Vintage tattooing material is rare and difficult to track down. 'A lot of antique dealers simply don't know what the implements are, they think they are engraving machines,' says Ramsbottom. 'Britain has a fantastic tattooing history, and I believe that there are still many objects to be discovered. I really hope this book will help bring some of them to light.'

The objects featured here are all from Ramsbottom's collection. They celebrate a truly popular art form and are certainly among the most unusual items ever featured in a Miller's guide!

A Coptic tattoo block, 18thC, 2 x 4in (5 x 10cm).
£500–600 *Ram*

Five Victorian painted tattoo flashes, from Mitchell Brothers, largest 7 x 5in (18 x 12.5cm).
£5–15 each *Ram*

Moko or Maori Tattooing, by Major-General Robley, c1896, 11 x 9in (28 x 23cm).
£60–70 *Ram*

A double twin coil set tattoo machine, by Gamages, Holborn, c1900, 7in (18cm) long.
£100–125 *Ram*

A brass twin coil tattoo machine, by Alfred Charles South, signed, c1900, in original box, 8in (20.5cm) long.
£100–120 *Ram*

A brass clockwork tattoo machine, c1900, 7in (17.8cm) high.
£200–250 *Ram*

l. Four tattoo flashes, designed in coloured pencils on paper, c1920, 7 x 11in (18 x 28cm).
£10–20 each *Ram*

A signed business card of 'The Great Omi', originally Horace Ridler, with various photographs, some depicting the famous tattooist George Burchett working on him, card c1945, photo 1930s.
Card £30–40
Photos £8–10 each *Ram*

A British Army officer during WWI, Horace Ridler reputedly lost his family fortune due to high living, and then set about transforming himself into a circus attraction and one of the most famous tattooed men of all time. Adopting a new name, 'The Great Omi', his head, face and whole body were tattooed with swirling blue zebra stripes. His teeth were filed into sharp points, his blue ears pierced with ivory spikes, and his nose with giant tusks. The Great Omi became one of the highest-paid performers of the day, and remains an icon to tattoo enthusiasts worldwide. Material connected with The Great Omi is highly collectable.

r. A brass tattoo machine, by Jacob Razouk of Israel, c1950, 6in (15cm) long.
£60–80 *Ram*

A tattoo machine, by Joe Hartley, Bristol, complete with coil, 1930s, 7in (18cm) long.
£100–120 *Ram*

Three tattoo trade catalogues, 1940–50, largest 9 x 11in (23 x 30cm).
£1–25 each *Ram*

A miniature twin coil tattoo machine, 1950s, 4in (10cm) long.
£30–35 *Ram*

A collection of ink and pencil tattoo flashes, by Caile, Manchester, 1940s, 8 x 6in (20.5 x 15cm).
£5–10 each *Ram*

An American twin coil vibrating tattoo machine, by Pursey Waters, engraved and signed, 1940s, 5 x 7in (12.5 x 18cm).
£50–70 *Ram*

The Story of A Tattooed Girl and *How to do Good Tattooing*, by Cindy Ray, 1960s, 8 x 7in (20.5 x 18cm).
£15–20 *Ram*

TEAPOTS

A miniature teapot, transfer-printed in green with 3 ladies at a table drinking tea, cover missing, 19thC, 3in (7.5cm) high.
£45–55 *ANV*

A Japanese elephant teapot, c1900, 6in (15cm) high.
£125–145 *JaG*

A charabanc/bus teapot, yellow with black details, 1930s, 8in (20.5cm) wide.
£475–525 *PGA*

This model was also made in green and cream.

A Midwinter Stylecraft teapot, with brown lid and decorated with orange flowers, 1950–60, 4in (10cm) high.
£25–30 *GIN*

A Meashamware teapot, with inscription 'Never Be Weary In Well Doing', c1875, 11in (28cm) high.
£300–330 *DHA*

A Worcester dark blue teapot, with silver overlay, c1910, 5in (12.5cm) high.
£900–1,000 *TH*

A yellow teapot, in the shape of a tank, with a soldier's helmeted head for the knop, c1930, 9in (23cm) wide.
£140–165 *DSG*

A Staffordshire teapot, transfer-printed with Noddy and Big Ears, 1960s, 5½in (14cm) high.
£30–35 *WWY*

A Continental child's teapot, transfer-printed in greens, red and yellow with figures in a garden, c1890, 5in (12.5cm) high.
£40–45 *DHA*

A Belleek white and green teapot, on shell feet, with shell knop, 1920s, 5in (12.5cm) high.
£200–250 *TAC*

A Cottage Ware teapot, by Price of Kensington, 1930s, 7½in (19cm) wide.
£25–30 *PC*

A Tony Wood novelty teapot, depicting Lester Piggot in green and black with yellow cap, 1980s, 8½in (21.5cm) high.
£18–20 *MED*

A Barge or Meashamware teapot, inscribed 'A present from a friend', marked 'Mason Cash & Co, Church Cresley' on base, 1875–80, 13in (33cm) high.
£500–550 DHA

A ceramic teapot, commemorating the Diamond Jubilee of Queen Victoria, 1897, 10in (25.5cm) high.
£90–110 DQ

A Japanese Banko teapot, slight damage, c1900, 5in (12.5cm) high.
£125–145 JaG

A pewter five-piece tea set, backstamped 'Goldsmith's Company', c1925, jug 6in (15cm) high, teapot 4½in (11.5cm) high.
£75–85 AND

A Grimwades cube teapot, c1920, 4in (10cm) wide.
£70–80 PGA

A Japanese Banko teapot, with tengu lid, c1900, 5in (12.5cm) wide.
£85–95 JaG

A hand-painted novelty duck teapot, c1930, 9in (23cm) wide.
£225–250 BEV

A Crown Ducal cottage ware teapot, c1930, 4in (10cm) high.
£115–125 BEV

A Royal Venton novelty elephant teapot, by Holdcroft, 1930s, 5½in (14cm) high.
£475–525 PGA

A Royal Worcester miniature teapot, signed by Roberts, black mark, 1950s, 3½in (9cm) high.
£300–350 DKH

l. A Sadler's OKT 42 teapot, with Mabel Lucie Attwell transfer, c1937, 9in (23cm) wide.
£280–320 S

A Mabel Lucie Attwell teapot, by Shelley, 1930s, 5in (12.5cm) high.
£350–375 PGA

A Steiff bear on wheels, with button to left ear, slightly worn, c1910, 18in (45.5cm) long.
£1,100–1,300 *Bon(C)*

A German teddy bear, with glass eyes, possibly by Bing, some repairs, 1915–20, 16in (40.5cm) high.
£750–850 *STK*

A Farnell teddy bear, with orange glass eyes, cotton pads with webbed stitching to hands and 4 stitched claws to feet, some wear, 1920s, 21in (54cm) high.
£700–800 *Bon(C)*

A Bing mohair teddy bear, with glass eyes and long snout, Excelsior stuffed, slight damage, 1920s, 14in (35.5cm) high.
£450–500 *STK*

'Monty', a small mohair bear, with boot button eyes and original factory outfit of shirt and shorts, 1930s, 5in (12.5cm) high.
£130–150 *STK*

A Polish teddy bear, c1930, 8in (20.5cm) high.
£135–165 *GrD*

A mohair teddy cub, with long snout and short arms and legs, c1930, 13in (33cm) high.
£200–250 *STK*

A pink teddy bear, with orange glass eyes, stitched nose and large round ears, mohair sparse, pads replaced, probably Chiltern, 1940s, 14½in (37cm) high.
£120–140 *Bon*

A Chiltern teddy bear, with golden mohair, orange glass eyes and velveteen paw pads, label to foot and bell in body, c1950, 14in (36cm) high.
£500–550 *Bon(C)*

A Merrythought figure of Noddy, with sprung neck, 1950s, 12in (30.5cm) high.
£250–300 *RBB*

A Merrythought golden mohair cheeky bear, with orange plastic eyes and large ears with bells, 1950s, 18in (45.5cm) high.
£200–250 *Bon(C)*

A Fisher Price Fozzie Bear, c1976, 13½in (34.5cm) high.
£10–12 *CMF*

A Chad Valley Chiltern golly, 1970s, 15in (38cm) high.
£25–30 *CMF*

r. A *Muppet Show* figure of Scooter, c1976, 17in (43cm) high.
£10–12 *CMF*

r. A Beanie Baby, Peace, with embroidered sign, 1997–8, 6in (15cm) high.
£5–6 *BeG*

A Swedish painted desk phone, 1904–8, 13in (33cm) high.
£300–350 *EKK*

A Kellogg grab-a-phone, c1906, custom painted in 1920s, signed by artist, 7in (17.5cm) high.
£180–200 *EKK*

This was the first American desk telephone.

A Kellogg solid brass candle-stick telephone, fully restored, 1920s, 12in (30.5cm) high.
£280–310 *EKK*

A green Bakelite 332 telephone, c1938, 9in (23cm) wide.
£300–350 *CAB*

A Western Electric police wall phone, with metal housing, 1930s, 9in (23cm) high.
£150–170 *EKK*

A two-tone green plastic Trimphone, with luminous dial, c1971, 8in (20.5cm) long.
£25–30 *DOM*

A red plastic telephone, c1972, 8in (20.5cm) wide.
£20–25 *GIN*

A Western Electric push-button plastic telephone, with adjustable volume and metal bottom plate, c1981, 9in (23cm) wide.
£25–30 *DOM*

A set of 6 Jungle Collection Mercury phonecards, mint condition, 1988–89.
£50–60 *JCa*

A BT Union Jack phonecard, produced for troops in Bosnia, mint condition, c1995.
£15–20 *JCa*

r. A Brooklyn Chewing Gum phonecard, 1998.
£2–3 *TAC*

A sampler, depicting a house and a verse, by Amelia Bavage, c1838, 12in (30.5cm) square.
£350–400 *DHA*

r. A beadwork panel, mid-19thC, 10 x 9in (25.5 x 23cm).
£90–110 *CHU*

A fine printed wool summer shawl, c1850, 132 x 66in (335.5 x 167.5cm).
£150–180 *JPr*

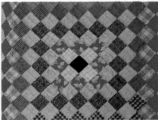

An American patchwork quilt, 19thC, 72in (183cm) square.
£180–200 *OLM*

A Victorian hand-embroidered wall hanging, 22in (56cm) wide.
£45–50 *CHU*

A handmade handkerchief, with woven silk panel inscribed 'Flames, Bapaume 1917', stitched to a velvet panel, overlaid and edged with intricate gold leaf brocade, 24in (61cm) square.
£30–40 *VS*

A cotton quilt, for a single bed, 1930s, 78 x 90in (198 x 228.5cm).
£60–70 *CHU*

A felt tea cosy, with bead-work decoration, c1930, 7in (18cm) high.
£8–10 *CHU*

r. A boxed set of 4 Mabel Lucie Attwell handkerchiefs, 1950s, box 7in (18cm) square.
£25–30 *WWY*

A silk and velvet patchwork cushion, 1940s, 17in (43cm) diam.
£18–20 *CHU*

A pair of North American Indian child's moccasins, c1900, 5in (12.5cm) long.
£65–80 *JPr*

A pair of gentleman's embroidered slippers, and a smoking hat, c1870.
Slippers £75–90
Hat £20–25 *JPr*

A Chodor Turkoman hat, c1900, 7in (18cm) diam.
£130–150 *SAM*

r. A pair of Clarks patterned cloth shoes, with button fastening, 1920s.
£60–70 *PC*

An embroidered satin cloche hat, with grosgrain band, 1920s.
£90–110 *Ech*

A pair of gold and black leather shoes, by Coles of Sheffield, 1930s.
£85–95 *PC*

A pair of Saxone red and white plastic shoes, 1960s.
£4–6 *BOH*

A green satin evening gown, with bias cut skirt and orange marabou feather cape, 1930s.
Evening gown £75–100
Cape £45–55 *TCF*

A pair of Vivienne Westwood red patent leather boots, with mirror disc lace holders, 1990s.
£180–200 *ID*

A Frank Usher pink silk evening dress, the bodice covered in lace and decorated with beads and sequins, 1960s.
£120–150 *JVa*

A Vivienne Westwood hand-crocheted dress, in metallic blue, silver and purple thread, with built-in corset, c1994.
£250–300 *ID*

A Vivienne Westwood harlequin shirt, from the Voyage to Cythera collection, c1989, 30in (76cm) long.
£100–120 *ID*

A German painted wood Noah's Ark and animals, with 8 people, 70 pairs of animals, together with original inventory in 3 languages, minor damage, late 19thC, ark 14in (36cm) long. **£1,300–1,500** *Bon(C)*

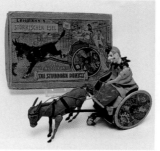

A Lehmann's lithographed tinplate Stubborn Donkey, c1900, 7in (18cm) long, with box and original instructions. **£350–400** *DD*

Two Bayko Light Construction Sets, c1930s, largest 19½in (49.5cm) wide. **£300–350** *CDC*

l. A Dinky Toys set No 60, Aeroplanes, comprising 6 various aircraft, 1930s, in presentation display box, 10in (25.5cm) square. **£1,000–1,200** *WAL*

A child's painted wood wheelbarrow, early 20thC, 37in (94cm) long. **£130–150** *JUN*

A tinplate Dick Tracy squad car, c1940, 20in (51cm) long. **£500–550** *SMAM*

r. Two Pelham Punch and Judy glove puppets, 1950s, Punch 12in (30.5cm) high. **£70–80** *J&J*

A tinplate Noddy and Friends kaleidoscope, 1950s, 8in (20.5cm) high. **£35–40** *MRW*

A Japanese tinplate clockwork musician, c1950, 10in (25.5cm) high. **£500–550** *SMAM*

A Marx tinplate clockwork police motorcycle, with siren, 1950s, 7in (18cm) long. **£150–180** *RAR*

A Tomiyama tinplate battery-powered Firebird Race Car, 1950s, 15in (38cm) long. **£400–440** *RAR*

A Mobo tinplate rocking horse, with wooden seat, 1950s, 41in (104cm) long. **£55–65** *PC*

A Pelham Pinky string puppet, c1960, 13in (33cm) high.
£40–45 *TOY*

A Patch's Pony, by Pedigree, c1968, 8in (20.5cm) high, with box.
£20–25 *CMF*

A Pelham McBoozle puppet, 1960s, 12in (30.5cm) high, in original box.
£55–65 *STK*

A Smurf, Angry, by Schleich, c1964, 2in (5cm) high.
£6–8 *CMF*

Twelve children's play watches, on a display card, 1960s, card 10 x 8in (25.5 x 20.5cm).
£14–16 *MED*

A Womble soft toy, Madame Cholet, 1970s, 9in (23cm) high.
£10–12 *CMF*

A Smurf in a car, by Schleich, 1960s–70s, 3in (7.5cm) long.
£10–12 *CMF*

A Smurf on a leaf skateboard, by Schleich, 1960s–70s, 2⅜in (7cm) high.
£10–12 *CMF*

A plastic Big Mac clockwork toy, c1995, 1¼in (3cm) high.
£2–3 *CMF*

A Japanese tinplate clockwork Mighty Atom robot, by Billiken, c1988, 9in (23cm) high.
£120–150 *TOY*

l. A miniature dapple grey rocking horse, by Stevenson Brothers Ltd, limited edition of 250, c1997, 28in (71cm) long.
£675–750 *STE*

A Minic 50 ME Rolls-Royce Sedanca, c1930s, 5¼in (13.5cm) long.
£320–350 *RAR*

A Minic Ford Royal Mail van, 1950s, 3in (7.5cm) long.
£140–160 *RAR*

A Dinky Toys No. 480 Kodak Bedford van, 1954–6, 3½in (9cm) long, with box.
£80–100 *Bon(C)*

A Dinky Toys No. 4 Racing Cars gift set, including a 23g Cooper-Bristol, 23f Alfa-Romeo, 23h Ferrari, 23j HMW and a 23n Maserati, 1953–54, box 12in (30.5cm) long.
£800–900 *Bon(C)*

A Dinky Toys No. 157 Jaguar XK120 Coupé, 1954–6, 3½in (9cm) long, with box.
£100–120 *Bon(C)*

A Dinky Supertoys No. 968 BBC TV Roving Eye Vehicle, 1959–64, 3¾in (9.5cm) long, with original box.
£80–90 *Bon(C)*

A Wrenn Formula 152 electric model motor racing set, c1961, box 17½in (44.5cm) wide.
£90–100 *PrB*

A Corgi No. 1130 Chipperfields Circus Horse Transporter, c1962, 10in (25.5cm) long.
£110–130 *RAR*

A Corgi Rallye Monte-Carlo gift set, comprising Mini Cooper, Rover 2000 and Citroën DS19, mid-1960s, box 10in (25.5cm) long.
£700–800 *WAL*

A Corgi No. 485 BMC Mini Countryman, 1960s, 3in (7.5cm) long.
£45–50 *DAC*

A hand-held Simon game, by M. B. Electronics, first model, one of only 30, 1970s, 10¾in (27.5cm) diam, boxed.
£25–30 *CGX*

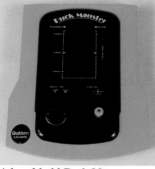

A hand-held Puck Monster computer game, by Gakken, 1970s, 9in (23cm) high.
£15–20 *CGX*

A Grandstand Video Sports Centre game, c1978, 10in (25.5cm) wide.
£40–50 *CGX*

A hand-held Super Space Jack game, by Onko Electronics, 1970s, 10in (25.5cm) high.
£20–30 *CGX*

A Caveman computer game, by Tomy, c1980, 8½in (21.5cm) high.
£12–15 *CGX*

An Intellivision television entertainment centre, by Mattel Electronics, late 1970s, 13½in (34.5cm) wide.
£100–120 *CGX*

A Footballer of the Year, computer game, by Atari, c1986, 5½in (14cm) high.
£4–5 *CGX*

A Cosmic Scramble computer game, c1980, 8½in (21.5cm) high.
£25–30 *CGX*

A Sega Game Gear portable video game system, c1988, 8in (20.5cm) wide.
£35–40 *MEX*

r. A Sonic the Hedgehog game cartridge, for Sega Game Gear, c1988, 3in (7.5cm) high.
£5–7 *MEX*

A Bing for Bassett-Lowke 0 gauge LMS clockwork locomotive and tender, 'George V', c1920, 14in (35.5cm) long.
£255–285 *DQ*

A Bing for Bassett-Lowke 0 gauge LMS 2783 passenger coach, c1925, 13in (33cm) long.
£100–125 *DQ*

A Wrenn Great Western Railways locomotive and tender, 'Devizes Castle', 1930s, 10in (25.5cm) long.
£90–100 *DAC*

A Bassett-Lowke 2525 0 gauge live-steam locomotive and tender, 'Enterprise', c1935, 18in (45.5cm) long.
£400–450 *DQ*

A Hornby 0 gauge Southern Railways passenger coach, late 1930s, 13in (33cm) long, mint condition, boxed.
£300–350 *WaH*

A Hornby 0 gauge No. 1 level crossing, c1940, mint condition, with box.
£30–40 *STK*

A Hornby 0 gauge signal, 1940s, 9in (23cm) high.
£15–20 *STK*

A Bassett-Lowke 0 gauge BR clockwork locomotive and tender, 'Prince Charles', c1952, 16in (40.5cm) long.
£250–275 *WaH*

l. A Hornby 0 gauge printed tinplate signal box, with pierced windows, c1955, 7in (18cm) high.
£30–35 *WaH*

A Meccano model traction engine, 1950s, 13in (33cm) long.
£400–450 *JUN*

A fine scale 0 gauge model of LSWR Adams Radial tank engine, two-rail, electric motor, 1970s, 10in (25.5cm) long.
£500–550 *RAR*

A *Dr Who* battery-operated Dalek, by Marx Toys, 1960s, 6in (15cm) high, in original box.
£70–80 *RAR*

A *Lone Ranger* Tonto doll, by Marx Toys, 1973, 10in (25.5cm) high, in original box.
£40–50 *TOY*

A *Starsky & Hutch* radio-controlled Ford Torino, by Galoob, 1970s, 11in (28cm) long.
£50–55 *OW*

A *Bionic Woman* doll, by Kenner, 1977, 12in (30.5cm) high, in original box.
£85–100 *TOY*

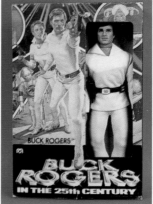

A Buck Rogers doll, from *Buck Rogers in the 25th Century*, 1979, 13in (33cm) high, in original box.
£75–85 *OW*

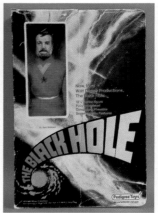

A Dr Hans Reinhardt doll, from *The Black Hole*, by Pedigree Toys, 1979, 12½in (32cm) high, in original box.
£40–50 *OW*

A James Bond *Moonraker* Space Gun, 1979, 12in (30.5cm) long, in original box.
£40–50 *TOY*

A Captain Kirk action figure, from *Star Trek*, 1979, 8in (20.5cm) high, with original card.
£65–75 *OW*

r. A resin puppet, Scott from *Thunderbirds*, dressed in blue, sash replaced, leg repaired, c1985, 21½in (54.5cm) high, with box.
£900–1,000 *DN*

This puppet was possibly made for an advertising campaign.

A *Return of the Jedi* Jabba the Hutt Action Playset, 1983, 13in (33cm) wide, in original box.
£65–75 *TBoy*

A *Double Your Money* quiz game, by Bell Toys, 1950s, 14in (35.5cm) square.
£15–20 *J&J*

A *Magic Roundabout* bagatelle game, 1967, 7in (18cm) diam.
£16–18 *CMF*

A *Crossroads Special* annual, 1970s, 10¾ x 8in (27.5 x 20.5cm).
£8–10 *PC*

A Bruce Forsyth board game, *I'm in Charge*, by Bell Toys, 1960s, 14in (35.5cm) square.
£15–20 *J&J*

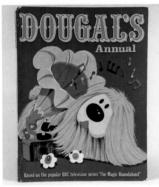

A *Dougal's Annual*, 1973, 12 x 9in (30.5 x 23cm).
£6–8 *CMF*

A Kermit the Frog, from *The Muppet Show*, 1976, 19in (48.5cm) high.
£16–18 *CMF*

l. A pair of red swimming shorts, worn by David Hasselhoff in *Baywatch*, c1990.
£600–675 *FRa*

A *Blue Peter* jigsaw puzzle, 1971, 9½ x 11½in (24 x 29cm).
£2–3 *CMF*

A *Basil Brush Annual*, 1974, 10½ x 8in (26.5 x 20.5cm).
£3–4 *CMF*

A colour photograph, signed by members of the cast of *Baywatch*, c1990, 8 x 10in (20.5 x 25.5cm).
£300–350 *FRa*

A *Coronation Street* bar towel, musical mug and beer mat, c1996, towel 16in (40.5cm) long.
£5–6 *PC*

A Tunbridge ware writing slope, with a view of Eridge Castle, attributed to Humphrey Burrows, c1845, 16in (40.5cm) wide.
£2,200–2,500 *AMH*

A Tunbridge ware rosewood writing slope, c1860, 12in (30.5cm) wide.
£1,000–1,100 *MB*

A French rosewood box, inlaid with ivory, brass and pewter, inscribed 'Lettres', c1870, 9in (23cm) wide.
£325–365 *GeM*

l. A selection of pens, with Tunbridge ware, cranberry glass, tartanware, silver and mother-of-pearl handles, 1870–1910, longest 7½in (19cm).
£30–135 each *VB*

A Burnham No. B48 blue mottled fountain pen, c1954, 5in (12.5cm) long.
£35–40 *RUS*

A Victorian letter box, with lock and key, 29in (73.5cm) high.
£500–550 *ACT*

A silver and mother-of-pearl sealing wax set, Birmingham 1899, 5in (12.5cm) wide.
£325–375 *AMH*

Five Victorian seals, with agate, brass and bloodstone handles, largest 2½in (6.5cm) long.
£30–50 each *VB*

A burr walnut stationery cabinet, c1870, 13in (33cm) high.
£900–1,000 *GeM*

A French brass inkwell, with original glass liner, marked 'Deposé', c1890, 7in (18cm) wide.
£70–80 *STK*

A Scottish glass, silver and granite presentation inkwell, c1900, 10in (25.5cm) diam.
£100–120 *BWA*

An inlaid mahogany inkstand, c1900, 9in (23cm) wide.
£150–175 *MB*

An Arcadian pot with cover, with crest and inscribed 'Kingstown', 1920, 1½in (4cm) high.
£4–5 *MLa*

A Christmas greetings postcard, c1905, 3½ x 5½in (9 x 14cm).
50p–£1 *TAC*

A pair of gentleman's pad garters, 1930s, in original box, 3½in (9cm) wide.
£4–5 *MRW*

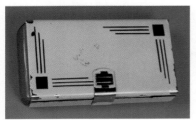

An Art Deco enamelled powder compact, some damage, 1930s, 4¾in (12cm) long.
£4–5 *PC*

l. Sheet music for 'Why Did She Fall for the Leader of the Band', c1935, 12½in (31.5cm) high.
£2–3 *RAD*

A set of cocktail sticks in wooden container, 'Mr Bartender', 1940s–50s, 3½in (9cm) high.
£3–4 *TRE*

A Japanese pelican pepper pot, 1930s, 3in (7.5cm) high.
£3–5 *JMC*

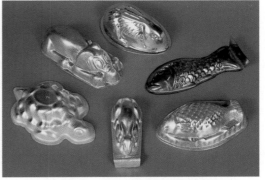

A selection of aluminium jelly moulds, c1950, 5in (12.5cm) long.
£2–3 each *AL*

A collection of figures from *The Empire Strikes Back*, c1982, 2in (5cm) high.
£3–4 each *Ada*

r. A pack of Tetley tea playing cards, 1980s, 2½in (6.5cm) high.
£1–2 *CMF*

Five pairs of platform boots, as worn by Ginger Spice, Geri Halliwell, c1998.
£1,000–2,500 per pair *S*

The 1990s have seen a number of new phrases entering our vocabulary: 'Brit Pop', 'Cool Britannia' and 'Girl Power'. Made for Ginger Spice, Geri Halliwell, these spangly platform boots symbolize all these notions and are a memento of one of the most famous bands of the decade.

A Bank of England £10 error note, Kentfield Chief Cashier signature, with extra paper, 1992.
£80–90 *WP*

This note is not legal tender, but it is worth considerably more than its face value. If you come across an error note or a specimen note, you could be quids in.

A Kinder Surprise chocolate egg, with contents, 1998, 2⅖in (6.5cm) high.
42p *PC*

Created by Ferrero, Kinder eggs were launched in Italy in 1972. Germany followed, then the rest of Europe, and today Kinder eggs, with their surprise toys, are sold in countries across the world, with the exception of the USA and Africa. There are already Kinder societies, collectors' catalogues and a number of enthusiasts' web sites.

A signed colour photograph of Cindy Crawford, 1980s, 10 x 8in (25.5 x 20.5cm).
£100–120 *Fra*

Super models – another phrase that became current in the 1990s – are now as famous as pop stars.

A brick from Boston Garden, with engraved plaque and certificate, 1997.
£40–50 *HALL*

This brick is from an American stadium. When famous buildings are demolished, remnants are often preserved and sold as commemorative collectables. Recent examples include rubble from the Berlin Wall and bricks from the Cavern, the Liverpool music club. Top tip for Collectable of the Future could be fragments of Wembley Stadium, when the celebrated edifice is finally destroyed to make way for a new building.

A Princess Beanie Baby, first edition, produced for the Diana, Princess of Wales Trust, 1997, 8in (20.5cm) high.
£150–200 *PC*

Beanie Babies have been one of the most talked about collectables in recent times. There are Beanie fairs, collecting societies, handbooks and such is demand that these soft toys have even been faked. Certain Beanie Babies, such as the example illustrated here, can fetch three-figure sums. Are Beanie Babies an example of cynical marketing and collecting mania, or will they keep their value in the 21st century? Only time will tell.

A Simpsons doll, by Vivid imaginations, 1997, 9in (23cm) high.
£7–8 *PC*

A true cartoon classic, The Simpsons TV series is popular across the world and watched by adults and children alike.

TEDDY BEARS & SOFT TOYS

r. A Steiff standing bear, with black boot button eyes and growler voice box, attached button in ear and original felt pads, marked 'Steiff', c1915, 13in (33cm) high.
£600–700 *FW&C*

A German golden mohair teddy bear, probably by Bing, with black boot button eyes and straw-stuffed body with growler, c1909, 11in (28cm) high.
£220–260 *Bon(C)*

A clockwork dancing bear, with key-wound movement, natural fur-covered body, black glass eyes, papier mâché paws, one ear missing, early 20thC, 11¾in (30cm) high.
£400–450 *Bea(E)*

A Farnell plush teddy bear, with stitched snout, clear glass eyes, swivel-jointed body, head slightly faded, c1920, 13¾in (35cm) high.
£600–700 *S(S)*

A blue plush teddy bear, with amber glass eyes and swivel jointed body, possibly Australian, c1920, 22½in (57cm) high.
£375–425 *S(S)*

A golden mohair wire jointed teddy bear, possibly Merrythought, 1920s, 13½in (34.5cm) high.
£200–250 *Bon(C)*

A Chiltern Hugmee mohair teddy bear, with glass eyes, c1930, 16in (40.5cm) high.
£300–350 *STK*

A pink mohair rabbit and a white curled wool rabbit, makers unknown, 1930s, largest 11in (28cm) long.
£60–80 each *STK*

A Chiltern brown and cream mohair teddy bear, with orange plastic eyes, 1950s, 18in (46cm) high.
£220–250 *Bon(C)*

A Chiltern black and white mohair panda bear, with orange plastic eyes with black felt lining, c1950, 14in (36cm) high.
£80–100 *Bon(C)*

A Merrythought golly, with white and black disc eyes, red felt smiling mouth and black hair, soft body with sewn-on clothes of black and white striped trousers and bow tie, and red tailed jacket, 1950s, 14in (36cm) high.
£120–140 *Bon(C)*

A Pedigree long golden mohair teddy bear, with orange plastic eyes, black felt nose, inverted Y-shaped mouth, large ears, fully-jointed straw and kapok filled body with velveteen pads, part label to back, c1950, 16in (40.5cm) high.
£90–110 *Bon(C)*

l. A Steiff mohair teddy bear, with glass eyes, c1950, 11in (28cm) high.
£500–600 *STK*

A talking Basil Brush, made by Wendy Boston, 1960s, 15½in (39.5cm) high.
£30–40 *CMF*

Television has inspired a whole generation of soft toys. Basil Brush, created by Peter Firmin, with voice by Ivan Owen, was first given his own BBC TV series in 1968. The wise-cracking, ultra-British fox attracted audiences of 11 million in the 1970s, and his resounding 'Boom! Boom!' became a national catch phrase.

A *Wombles* Uncle Bulgaria, with tartan jacket and hat, 1970s, 8in (20.5cm) high.
£10–12 *CMF*

A *Muppets* Fozzie Bear, with red ribbon, 1980s, 14in (35.5cm) high.
£12–14 *CMF*

TELEPHONES

An Eiffel Tower telephone, with gold-plated 'teardrop' cradle, c1894, 12in (30.5cm) high.
£900–1,000 *EKK*

A house telephone bell, on wooden plaque with trumpet-style plastic mouthpiece and wooden handle, c1900, 17in (43cm) high.
£55–60 *DOM*

l. A Kellogg wall telephone, c1901, 8in (20.5cm) high.
£50–60 *EKK*

A Kellogg black candle-stick telephone, c1908, 12in (30.5cm) high.
£135–155 *EKK*

An JYDSK magneto telephone, in black painted metal case, early 20thC, 13in (33cm) high.
£110–130 *Oli*

l. An Ericsson desk set, with witness receiver, original condition, 1910–12, 10in (25.5cm) high.
£220–250 *EKK*

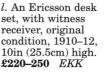

A North Electric 'wide body' chrome desk telephone, c1937.
£225–250 *TCT*

An Ericsson Corporation set N21151 magneto telephone, with metal body and base, wooden top, Bakelite column and handset, handle on side for charging, 1930s, 12in (30.5cm) high.
£40–45 *DOM*

The body of the telephone may be older than the handset.

Three Western Electric candlestick telephones:
l. A half-brass candlestick telephone, c1921.
c. An all-brass candlestick telephone, c1921.
r. An all-brass, non-dial candlestick telephone, c1915, 13in (33cm) high.
£300–350 each *TCT*

r. A Plan 7 telephone, 1938–60, 7½in (19cm) high.
£100–125 *CAB*

r. A Danish two-line desk telephone, with indicator unit, c1935, 7in (18cm) high, in original box.
£230–250 *OTC*

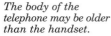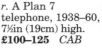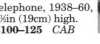

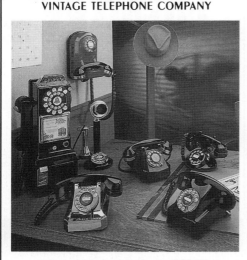

A GEC wooden railway telephone, with Bakelite handset and metal bell, 1940–50, 13in (33cm) high.
£25–35 *DOM*

A Danish Kjøbenhavns Telefon Aktieselskab telephone, with metal body, Bakelite handset with talk button and 2 counters which log number of calls, 1940s–50s, 7in (18cm) high.
£45–50 *DOM*

A black Bakelite telephone, with chrome 'bell on' and 'bell off' buttons, original handset cord, alphabet dial and drawer, 1950s, 6in (15cm) high.
£180–200 *OTC*

A Reliance black Bakelite intercom telephone, with chrome buttons, 1950s, 9in (23cm) long.
£35–40 *DOM*

An ivory Bakelite telephone, model 312L, with call exchange button, drawer and original line cord, c1956, 6in (15cm) high. **£220–250** *DOM*

Although not the rarest of the coloured Bakelites, ivory examples are still very sought-after. Coloured telephones were more expensive for subscribers to rent and were less common than black models.

r. A Type 706L black plastic telephone, c1960, 9in (23cm) high. **£25–30** *CAB*

A Bakelite 'ram's head' wall telephone, c1958, 10in (25.5cm) high. **£65–75** *DOM*

These telephones were nicknamed 'ram's head' because of their design. They were less popular than table telephones so are harder to find today.

A GPO Model 312 black Bakelite telephone, with alpha/numerical dial, dial codes in drawer tray, original cable and call exchange button, working order, c1956, 6in (15cm) high. **£100–120** *DOM*

The pull-out compartments for addresses in the base of these telephones were often known as 'cheese drawers'.

r. A GEC 64d black bell set, 1960s–70s, 7½in (19cm) high. **£20–30** *OTC*

A beige plastic Trim-phone, 1960s, 8in (20cm) long. **£20–25** *CAB*

Phonecards

A Graham's Black Bottle Scotch Whisky BT phonecard, c1986.
£35–40 *JCa*

This was BT's first advertising card. 15,000 were produced.

A Limerick Trial special issue 20 units phonecard, for IMI Conference, Killarney, only 250 issued, mint condition, 1989.
£230–250 *WA*

An NHS Trust Federation Annual Conference BT phonecard, mint condition, 1992.
£350–400 *JCa*

An X-Files Prepaid $10 Phonecard, c1996.
£10–15 *ALI*

A Muirfield Golf Festival £1 (10 units) phonecard, mint condition, 1987.
£125–225 *JCa*

The values of other cards in this series are:
£2 (20 units) cards £150–300
£10 (100 units) £1,200–2,800
This was the first series of pictorial commemorative phonecards. Only 900 £10 cards were issued hence the high value of the few remaining examples.

Four Caribbean phonecards:
British Virgin Islands, 1,000 issued.
£135–155
Barbados, 1,000 issued.
£135–155
Anguilla, 1,000 issued.
£135–155
St Kitts & Nevis, 2,000 issued.
£25–30 *JCa*

A Greek phonecard, c1997.
£2–2.50 *TAC*

r. A set of 18 HK$10 Princess Diana phonecards, 2,000 issued, 1997–8.
£40–50 *JCa*

A BT London Challenge phonecard, November 1987, mint condition.
£450–500 *JCa*

An Ethel Davis Special School BT phonecard, 640 produced, mint condition. August 1991.
£35–40 *JCa*

This was the first privately produced phonecard.

Two Blue Peter BT phonecards, c1993.
40–50p each *CMF*

TEXTILES
Costume

A silk-embroidered waistcoat, c1880.
£350–400 *JPr*

A blue silk cape/cloak, with chenille bobble fringing, c1850.
£110–130 *L&L*

A green and cream checked wool and silk dress, 1850s.
£180–220 *L&L*

A Victorian French red and black silk petticoat.
£65–80 *L&L*

An Alexandra silver-plated skirt lifter, with belt clip, 1880–1900, 7½in (19cm) long.
£18–25 *WAB*

This device was used to clip up long skirts, so that they would not get dirty trailing on the ground.

l. A pair of Edwardian white cotton lawn drawers, trimmed with lace, 27in (68.5cm) long.
£18–20 *CHU*

r. A red paisley wool and silk shawl, c1860, 133 x 66in (338 x 167.5cm).
£450–550 *JPr*

A black velvet coat, with mink collar, 1920s.
£180–200 *BMo*

An Edwardian ivory duchesse satin wedding dress, with pin-tucked detail to bodice and sleeves, inset lace to stand-up collar and bodice, trimmed with pearls to bodice and cuffs, the gored skirt trimmed with swags of lace and ribbons to hemline, and a short train, with net veil.
£120–140 *WW*

An Irish orange silk chiffon evening gown, decorated with silver bugle beads, 1920s.
£300–350 *JVa*

r. A pair of black satin camiknickers, with white lace inserts, 1930s, 28in (71cm) long.
£30–35 *PC*

A pink and black beaded evening dress, 1920s.
£200–220 *L&L*

A black net evening dress, appliquéd with cream stylized flower-heads, highlighted with sequins, fitted underskirt and net shoulder cape similarly trimmed, 1930s.
£130–150 *WW*

A brown window-checked suit, labelled 'Henry Poole, Saville Row', c1939.
£200–250 *BMo*

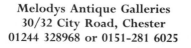
Cross Reference
Fifties
Sixties

A pair of lady's black and gold high-heeled shoes, by Jack Jacobus Ltd, London, with interlaced ribbon design and ankle strap, 1940s.
£20–25 *Har*

A Christian Dior wedding dress, c1959.
£180–220 *TT*

Embroidered Pictures & Samplers

A French needlework picture on silk, depicting a girl feeding swans, with original frame, 18thC, 15 x 17in (38 x 43cm).
£350–400 *MTa*

A sampler, depicting Adam and Eve, with the Tree of Life, lion, unicorn, country house and floral motifs, central text, dated '1822', 19 x 16in (48.5 x 40.5cm).
£450–500 *DD*

A French needlework picture, with a girl and a bird, in an ornate border, 19thC, 13¾ x 13in (35 x 33cm).
£220–240 *MTa*

A map sampler of England, c1880, 11 x 13in (28 x 33cm).
£450–500 *DHA*

Hats

A Victorian green and pink stiffened printed cotton sun bonnet.
£35–45 *L&L*

r. A baron's red velvet coronet, with ermine border to the silver gilt circlet, 6 large spheres and gold braid terminal, together with tin box engraved 'The Right Honourable Lord Wandsworth, coronet', maker WGB, 1901.
£900–1,000 *L*

l. A late Victorian black silk folding opera top hat and red box.
£60–70 *CHU*

l. A Yellow Cab silk hat, with black peak, 1950s.
£75–85 *SMAM*

Linen & Lace

An Italian white linen panel, with drawn threadwork showing Adam and Eve flanking the serpent-entwined apple tree, within an inscription, and a border, the ends decorated with unicorns, 17thC, 30 x 56in (76 x 142cm).
£1,000–1,200 *RA*

A Victorian Irish lace top, featuring Clones lace, linen embroidered openwork and drawn stitch lace, 15in (38cm) long.
£900–1,000 *JVa*

Clones is a region in Ireland and the lace features a rose and shamrock design. Garments such as this were complex and time-consuming to make, hence the high price range of this garment.

A Victorian cream lace collar.
£14–18 *CHU*

A Victorian tape lace collar.
£30–50 *CHU*

This type of collar was known as a bertha and was used around a low necked gown.

A white collar, hand-embroidered on net, c1880, 31in (78.5cm) long.
£80–100 *CHU*

A Victorian cream appliqué lace scarf.
£110–120 *L&L*

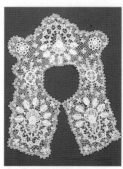

An Irish cream crochet lace collar, made with pure cotton and silk thread, c1880, 18in (45.5cm) long.
£75–85 *AIL*

A Victorian ivory-handled parasol, with Bedfordshire lace cover, 27in (68.5cm) long.
£90–100 *JPr*

r. A white cloth, with crocheted butterfly pattern, c1900, 27in (68.5cm) square.
£24–28 *Ech*

An Irish hand-embroidered white damask linen and crocheted lace tray cloth, c1900, 24 x 34in (61 x 86.5cm).
£25–30 *AIL*

Damask means that the design appears on both sides and double damask means that double the number of threads are used.

A cream linen tray cloth, 1930s, 23 x 32in (58.5 x 81.5cm).
£20–25 *Ech*

An oval white linen tray cloth, c1900, 20in (51cm) wide.
£12–15 *Ech*

A cream nightdress case, with hand-embroidered centre, edged with hand-made bobbin lace and filet lace, and pink ribbon, early 20thC, 15 x 18in (38 x 45.5cm).
£18–20 *CHU*

An Irish linen pillow case, hand-embroidered at both ends with a shamrock design, c1910, 30in (76cm) long.
£20–25 *AIL*

An Irish crocheted cream lace doily, with shamrock design, c1920, 10in (25.5cm) diam.
£10–15 *AIL*

Quilts

A Victorian hexagonal patchwork quilt, in yellows and pinks, not backed, 94in (239cm) square.
£100–120 *L&L*

r. A French cotton quilt, printed with Art Nouveau style flowers in pink and green, on a navy blue background, c1910, 68 x 60in (172.5 x 152.5cm).
£100–120 *OLM*

Vivienne Westwood

Vivienne Westwood is one of our most important *fin de siècle* designers. Early examples of her work can fetch four-figure sums, and 'vintage' Westwood is collected by Europeans and, above all, by the Japanese, who regard her as one of the icons of 20th-century fashion.

Born in 1941, Westwood began designing at the age of 30. 'Let it Rock', her first shop in London's King's Road, opened with her then partner Malcolm McLaren, sold 1950s-style clothing and records. In 1972, the name was changed to 'Too Fast to Live, Too Young to Die', and the couple created clothing for rockers with zips and chains, and slogan T-shirts. In 1974, the shop was called 'Sex', and supplied rubber and bondage ware, and T-shirts decorated with everything from ripped holes to erotic images.

The mid-1970s saw the arrival of punk, largely masterminded by McLaren and styled by Westwood. The shop became known as 'Seditionaries', then 'World's End', and its punk clothing was to transform Westwood into one of the most famous and controversial designers of the period. In 1981 Westwood held her first cat-walk show at Olympia in London. The Pirate Collection established the opulent look of the New Romantics, and since then her original and provocative collections have continued to wield a huge influence on contemporary fashion, setting a new trend for everything from corsets, to crinolines, to elevated platform shoes. Westwood has twice been named British Fashion Designer of the Year, and her work, love it or hate it, is impossible to ignore and has become increasingly collectable.

A Vivienne Westwood Let It Rock label black mohair sweater, with PVC studded collar and PVC glove sleeves, c1971, 22in (56cm) long.
£1,000–1,200 *ID*

Although in poor condition, this sweater is a rare piece, and a period photograph showing singer Iggy Pop wearing this design enhances its appeal.

A Vivienne Westwood Seditionaries cream muslin shirt entitled 'Two Naked Cowboys', with figures in green and pink, c1976, 26in (66cm) long.
£250–300 *ID*

This rude T-shirt from Sex turned into a cause célèbre. In 1975, a member of staff was arrested for wearing it in the street, the shop was raided and McLaren and Westwood were prosecuted, gaining much valuable media coverage.

A pair of Vivienne Westwood Sex label pink open-toed mules, with clear vinyl straps, c1975.
£250–300 *ID*

> **Miller's is a price GUIDE not a price LIST**

A pair of Vivienne Westwood Pirate Collection kid leather pirate boots, with buckled straps, c1981, 14in (35.5cm) high.
£150–170 *ID*

These boots are worn. In mint condition they would be worth double this amount.

A copy of Vivienne Westwood's Destroy muslin shirt, 1970s, 27in (68.5cm) long.
£20–30 *ID*

The Destroy muslin shirt, from Seditionaries, was the archetypal punk top and was much imitated. This is a period copy. Original versions can be identified by the Seditionaries label, sewn inside the lining at the front of the garment.

A Vivienne Westwood Buffalo Collection brown felt hat, c1982, 13in (33cm) diam.
£80–100 *ID*

A Vivienne Westwood
Witches Collection black
and yellow stretch jersey
tube mini skirt, illustrated
by Keith Haring, c1983,
17in (43cm) long.
£200–250 *ID*

A Vivienne Westwood
Portrait Collection red
stretch satin dress,
printed with gold foil
rococo decoration, c1990,
38in (96.5cm) long.
£120–150 *ID*

A Vivienne Westwood
Buffalo Collection
green and brown wool
suit, decorated with a
medieval print and
sliced horn buttons,
mint condition, c1982,
46in (117cm) long.
£600–700 *ID*

A Vivienne Westwood
'hunchback' dress, in
quilted camel cotton
with blue marbled
effect jersey front
panel, blue and russet
geometric motifs with
a low collar creating a
hunchback effect when
dress is worn, c1982,
52in (132cm) long.
£200–300 *ID*

A Vivienne Westwood
orb and chain, 1970s,
orb 3in (7.5cm) wide,
chain 15in (38cm) long.
£40–50 *CRIS*

l. A pair of Vivienne
Westwood gilt frame
earrings, moulded
with orbs with hanging
miniature fauns, 1990s,
2½in (6.5cm) long.
£30–40 *PC*

*The orb has become
Westwood's symbol. As
part of the royal regalia it
represents Westwood as a
British designer and her
commitment to tradition.
The satellite ring
surrounding it stands for
the future, and her belief
that new discoveries in
design come from
studying the past.*

A Vivienne Westwood
stretch satin and denim
boned corset, decorated
with stars, 1990s,
23in (58.5cm) long.
£150–165 *ID*

A Vivienne Westwood gilded *faux* safety pin,
with orb charm, non-piercing to be attached to
the mouth, 1990s, 3½in (9cm) long.
£40–50 *ID*

r. A pair of Vivienne
Westwood elevated
platform shoes, in black
patent and charcoal
grey cloth, 1990s,
8½in (21.5cm) high.
£120–150 *ID*

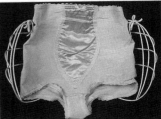

A Vivienne Westwood orb design Swatch
watch, in plastic orb case, 1993.
£250–300 *ID*

r. A Vivienne Westwood
Erotic Zones Collection
wire cage bustle,
attached to a cream
nylon girdle, 1994–95,
15in (38cm) wide.
£100–120 *ID*

TOYS
Computer & Video Games

Electronic computer games appeared in the early 1970s. Noel Bushnell (founder of Atari) invented Computer Space, the first video arcade game, in 1971. Arcade games became hugely successful, favourites including Asteroids, Pacman and Space Invaders. The last, created by Taito in 1978, proved so popular in its native Japan that the national mint had to produce extra 100 yen pieces.

Arcades helped stimulate demand for home models. TV video games became available in the first half of the decade, and 1976 saw the launch of the first hand-held electronic games. Home computers (introduced in 1971) were initially too expensive for many game players, but the market was revolutionized in 1981 by Clive Sinclair. His little ZX81 computer cost just £50 rather than several hundreds, making computers and computer games affordable, and helping to introduce children to the joys of programming.

Today computer games are among the most popular toys. There is a well-established secondary market as people sell and swap games they have completed or grown tired of, but in this as in many other fields, today's second-hand bargain could perhaps become tomorrow's collectable. Enthusiasts are already collecting vintage computer games. 'We get a lot of adult interest, both from England and Germany,' says Wayne Maxted from Computer & Games Exchange in London. 'People like early Atari material, more unusual items such as the Vectrex, and anything cartridge based. Some are dedicated computer buffs, others just want to buy an old item for nostalgic reasons. You also get people who are into 1970s and 1980s style and might buy a hand-held game for its decorative appeal.' This is the first time that computer games of this type have appeared in a Miller's guide, but it seems likely that it won't be the last.

A UFO Invaders Block Buster hand-held computer game, boxed, late 1970s, 10in (25.5cm) long.
£40–50 *CGX*

r. A Neo-Geo cartridge console, c1990, 17in (43cm) wide.
£90–100 *CGX*

This is a home version of a popular pub and arcade machine.

l. A Sinclair ZX81 personal computer, c1981, 6½in (16.5cm) wide.
£70–80 *CGX*

r. An Amiga game, Daley Thompson's Olympic Challenge by Ocean, on 3½in disk, c1998, box 6 x 8in (15 x 20.5cm).
£4–5 *MEx*

A Vectrex computer game player, c1983, 14¾ x 9½in (37.5 x 24cm).
£130–150 *CGX*

An Atari ST computer game, Rainbow Islands by Ocean, c1989, 7 x 6in (18 x 15cm).
£4–5 *MEx*

A Nintendo Game Boy, c1989, 5½in (14cm) long.
£15–20 *MEx*

Diecast Vehicles

A Dinky Toys 25d petrol tank wagon, grey with black open chassis, 'Pool' painted in white, smooth black hubs and black tyres, c1945, 7½in (19cm) long.
£200–220 *S(S)*

Two Chad Valley clockwork diecast Fordson Major tractors, c1952–55, 4½in (11.5cm) long.
£350–380 *DN*

A Dinky Toys 514 Spratt's Guy Van, with red chassis and cab, red and cream body, spare tyre, red wheel hubs, 1953–54, 6in (15cm) long, with box.
£350–400 *Bon(C)*

A Dinky Toys 981 British Railways burgundy horse box, with logos on both sides and rear, 1954–60, 8in (20.5cm) long, with box.
£90–100 *Bon(C)*

A Dinky Toys 430 Breakdown Lorry, the cab and chassis finished in tan, with green back, Dinky Service logo, windows, operational crane, red hub caps, 1954–64, 5½in (14cm) long, with box.
£70–80 *Bon(C)*

A Dinky Supertoys Bedford yellow and black articulated lorry, 1948–54, 6in (15cm) long.
£65–75 *WaH*

An American Husky Extra James Bond 007 Aston Martin, with silver paintwork, 1960s, 2in (5cm) long, in original packaging.
£160–180 *RAR*

A Dinky Toys 149 Sports Cars Gift Set, with 107 Sunbeam Alpine, 108 MG Midget, 109 Austin-Healey, 110 Aston Martin, 111 Triumph TR2, all in competition finish with racing numbers, 1958–61, box 18in (45.5cm) long.
£1,000–1,200 *Bon(C)*

A Tri-Ang Spot-On presentation set, comprising Aston Martin DB3 in light blue, Bentley saloon in two-tone grey, Austin A40 in light green with white roof, BMW Isetta in bright red, and an MGA in beige with cream seats, minor wear, 1964–65, box 10in (25.5cm) wide.
£360–400 *WAL*

l. A Corgi Gift Set 13, comprising a blue Fordson Power Major Tractor, with red wheels, and four furrow plough, c1964, 7in (18cm) long, with box.
£60–75 *RAR*

A Tri-Ang Spot-On Sports Cars presentation set, comprising Jaguar XKSS in light metallic blue with creamy yellow seats, Triumph TR3 in light blue with pale blue seats, Austin-Healey in light yellow with pale blue seats, and an MGA in red with light grey seats, 1963–4, box 8in (20.5cm) square.
£550–650 *WAL*

Spot-On diecast toys were started by Lines Brothers in 1959. Modelled to 1:42 scale they were slightly larger than Dinky Toys at 1:43. Cars included many features such as fully fitted interiors, windows, Flexomatic suspension and were notable for their rounded, almost sculptural design. Boxes were fragile, so complete presentation sets, such as this example, are rare and sought-after. The factory closed down in 1967.

r. A Dinky Toys 202 Fiat Abarth 2000, with red paintwork, c1971, 3½in (9cm) long, mint and boxed.
£25–30 *OTS*

McDonald's Toys

A McDonald's Hercules toy, in original bag, c1996, bag 6½ x 8in (16.5 x 20.5cm).
£3–5 *CMF*

McDonald's toys are worth more in their unopened bags.

Three McDonald's *101 Dalmations* toys, c1996, dog 3¼in (8.5cm) high.
£3–4 each *CMF*

A McDonald's plastic figure of a skier, c1994, 3½in (9cm) high.
£2–3 *CMF*

Model Figures & Animals

A set of 9 Elastolin figures, including Adolf Hitler and 8 soldiers and officers, German, c1936, 3in (7.5cm) high.
£500–550 *PrB*

Forty-seven Elastolin and Lineol-type wild animals, together with an oval painted wood and composition zoo setting with opening gates and curved railings, early 1900s, zoo 30in (76cm) wide.
£600–700 *S(S)*

A Charbens paratrooper, riding a motorcycle, c1950, 6in (15cm) long.
£170–200 *P(Ba)*

A Britains Set 2172 French Colonial Army, Spahi Algérien, comprising a standard bearer and 4 troopers, in original fitted box, with 4 further troopers, 1958–59.
£600–700 *S(S)*

A Britains horse-drawn plough, with harness and farmer, 1950s, 9⅜in (24cm) long.
£30–35 *MED*

Puppets

A Pelham puppet theatre, with 9 electrically-operated puppets, 1950s, 40in (106.5cm) wide.
£750–900 *PAR*

Pelham Puppets

Pelham (1947–92) is perhaps the most famous of all British puppet companies. The firm manufactured a huge variety of models ranging from traditional fairy tale characters to TV favourites and even pop star figures.

Boxes can be helpful in dating puppets. Initially Pelham used brown cardboard boxes, applied with the company's label. By the 1960s boxes were yellow, printed with pictures of puppets and in the '70s these solid yellow containers were given a cello-phane window, so that the puppet was visible.

A Pelham sailor puppet, 1950s, 12in (30.5cm) high, boxed.
£35–40 *ARo*

r. A Pelham lady cow puppet, with green felt skirt, yellow top and red shoes, 1960s, 11in (28cm) high.
£40–50 *ARo*

A Sooty glove puppet, early 1950s, 9½in (24cm) high.
£24–28 *CMF*

A Pelham horse string puppet, white with brown markings, 1960s, 10in (25.5cm) wide.
£25–30 *J&J*

A Pelham Noddy puppet, with red jacket, blue shorts and hat, 1950s, 12in (30.5cm) high.
£50–60 *ARo*

r. A Pelham rabbit string puppet, wearing brown checked trousers, c1963, 10in (25.5cm) high.
£80–100 *J&J*

This is one of a range of dressed animals.

Rocking Horses

A carved wood rocking horse, with original paintwork, real black hair mane and tail, leather studded saddle, on trestle base, 1900s, 40in (101.5cm) high.
£350–400 *AP*

A wooden rocking horse, with original dapple finish, leather bridle, stirrups and leathers and elm cantel, on trestle base, saddle, mane and tail missing, c1900, 42½in (108cm) high.
£750–900 *S(S)*

A rocking horse, with leather saddle, deerskin body and long hair mane, trade label of Wylie Hills of Glasgow, on trestle base, c1900, 44in (112cm) high.
£400–500 *MEA*

r. A brown painted rocking horse, with remains of original leather tack, on overpainted pine twin-pillar safety stand, mane missing, tail sparse, early 20thC, 37½in (95cm) high.
£300–350 *DN*

l. A dapple grey rocking horse, with remains of original leather tack, on pine twin-pillar safety stand, mane missing, early 20thC, 38¼in (97cm) high.
£500–550 *DN*

A push-along two-horse galloper, the red painted wood seat with metal handle and central shaft, the horses with pale dappled grey finish and red painted harness, early 20thC, 41¼in (105cm) long.
£450–500 *S(S)*

A three-wheeled black and white pedal horse, with wooden body and iron frame, c1910, 26in (66cm) high.
£650–750 *JUN*

A Lines Bros rocking horse, partially restored, late 1930s, 36in (91.5cm) high.
£250–275 *PC*

l. A Mobo hollow-cast tinplate walking horse, with dappled grey paintwork, some rusting, 1950s, 33in (84cm) long.
£100–120 *PC*

r. A tin rocking horse, on a metal base, 1950s, 34in (86.5cm) high.
£75–100 *COLL*

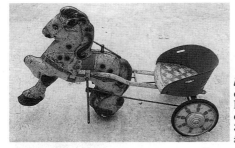

l. A Mobo hollow-cast tinplate horse, pulling a carriage, 1950s, 35in (89cm) long.
£100–120 *PC*

A Mobo hollow-cast tinplate rocking horse, with original black and grey paintwork, mounted on tubular frame with sprung suspension, 1960s, 38in (96.5cm) wide.
£75–100 *CARS*

An oak rocking horse, by Stevenson Brothers, with red saddlecloth, c1985, 48in (122cm) high.
£2,000–2,300 *STE*

A dapple grey rocking horse, with fibreglass body, white mane and tail, leather saddle and tack, on pine twin-pillar safety stand, 1980s, 49½in (126cm) high.
£350–400 *DN*

A wooden rocking horse, with leather tack, black mane and tail, on metal rockers with brass fittings, turned supports and platform base, by Ian Armstrong, Durham, bearing maker's label, 1990s, 45½in (115.5cm) high.
£500–600 *HCC*

A rocking horse, from the Miniature Collection by Stevenson Brothers, limited edition, 1996–97, 19in (48.5cm) high.
£650–750 *STE*

An oak rocking horse, from the Miniature Collection by Stevenson Brothers, limited edition, c1997, 19in (48.5cm) high.
£650–750 *STE*

Science Fiction & TV Toys

A *Black Hole* Kate McCrae figure, by Pedigree, c1979, 12½in (32cm) high.
£25–35 *OW*

A *Buck Rogers* Wilma Deering figure, in original packaging, c1979, 3½in (9cm) high.
£55–65 *OW*

A Dune action figure, 1980s, 3½in (9cm) high.
£5–7 *OW*

A *Nightmare Before Christmas* Sally figure, with detachable arms, legs and head, mint condition, in original packaging, c1993, card 11½in (29cm) high.
£80–120 *TB*

The *Six Million Dollar Man* Bionic Adventure Test Flight Set, by Kenner, c1976, card 16 x 12in (40.5 x 30.5cm).
£25–30 *TOY*

A *Star Trek* Scotty action figure, on resealed card, c1979, figure 3¾in (9.5cm) high.
£10–12 *OW*

Loose this figure would be worth about £5, and if the card were unopened about £35.

l. A *Lone Ranger* Hidden Silver Mine set, by Marx toys, c1973, box 11 x 13in (28 x 33cm).
£15–20 *TOY*

l. A *Star Wars* Bobafett action figure, complete with wookie scalps and all accessories, 1980s, 12in (30.5cm) high.
£90–120 *TBoy*

Without its accessories this figure would be worth in the region of £40.

Smurfs

Originally known as 'Schtroumpfs', the Smurfs were created by Belgian illustrator Peyo Culliford (known as Peyo) who died in 1994. They first appeared in *Le Journal de Spirou* on 23 October 1958. Initially secondary characters, they were soon awarded their own stories and books. The characters appeared in a film – *The Smurfs and the Magic Flute* – and even became recording stars when Dutch singer Vader Abraham scored a huge European hit with the first Smurf single.

Numerous toys, records and books were released in the 1970s, but true Smurf world domination came in 1981, when Hanna Barbera purchased the rights to the Smurfs and turned them into a cartoon TV series for NBC. Over 250 episodes were produced, which now show in an estimated 30 countries. The Smurfs have become internationally famous, their squeaky-voiced CDs sell by the millions, and the little blue figures are recognized and collected across the globe.

A Peyo Spy Smurf, c1969, 2in (5cm) high.
£7–9 *CMF*

A Smurf Mushroom House, with blue roof and yellow door, c1978, 4in (10cm) high.
£15–18 *CMF*

A skipping Smurf, c1982, 2½in (6.5cm) high.
£5–7 *CMF*

A Papa Smurf, c1983, 2in (5cm) high.
£3–4 *CMF*

The Smurfs Sticker Book, 1980s, 10½in (26.5cm) high.
£5–8 *CMF*

A Gargamel figure, c1984, 2¼in (5.5cm) high.
£10–12 *CMF*

An astronaut Smurf, c1985, 2in (5cm) high.
£12–15 *CMF*

A McDonald's Smurf, c1996, 2¼in (5.5cm) high.
£2–3 *CMF*

Tinplate

A Günthermann clockwork tinplate Vis-à-Vis, based on a Peugeot of the 1890s, with blue and brown paintwork, steering wheel, driver and one tyre missing, c1900, 10¼in (26cm) long.
£1,000–1,200 *BKS*

A Lehmann clockwork tinplate yellow Galop racing car, with red driver and wheels, c1928, 5in (12.5cm) long.
£220–250 *RAR*

A Meccano No 1 constructor car, in the form of a No 3 road racer, with black body, tinplate wheel hubs and red seats, complete in original box with paperwork, some wear, 1930s, box 16in (40.5cm) long.
£320–360 *WAL*

A Fairylite clockwork tinplate red and yellow speedboat, 1950s, 6in (15cm) long.
£55–65 *RAR*

l. A tinplate clockwork dancing figure, with yellow jacket and hat and checked trousers, Japanese, 1940s, 8in (20.5cm) high.
£450–500 *SMAM*

Trains

A wooden train, late 19thC,
14in (35.5cm) long.
£55–65 *FOX*

A Bing gauge I clockwork 4-6-2 Pacific
locomotive and tender, hand-enamelled in
black Bavarian State Railway livery, with
red lining, 'GBN' monogram printed and
embossed, c1914, 22in (56cm) long.
£500–600 *S(S)*

r. A lithographic
tinplate railway line-
side hut and half-
tunnel, a Bing
pedestrian footbridge
and corner, with
mounted manual
signals, c1910.
£120–150 *BKS*

A Bing 1921 Series GWR 1st class coach in lake
livery, a Bing LNWR 3rd/brake, and a Bing for
Bassett-Lowke LMS 1st class carriage, c1921,
13in (33cm) long.
£200–220 *BKS*

A Märklin LNWR 0-4-0 clockwork locomotive
and tender No. 2663, 'George V', finished in red
and yellow lined black livery, 1920s.
£170–190 *ONS*

*This locomotive was one of a number of trains
purchased for a child by his father from Gamages
in the 1920s. Seventy years later, the original owner
rediscovered his train set wrapped in a 1920s
newspaper and untouched since he stopped playing
with it. The collection was then put up for auction.*

A Hornby 0 gauge Metropolitan clockwork
locomotive, with intricate litho printing in wood
pattern with red and gold lining, 1927–29,
10in (25.5cm) long.
£220–250 *WaH*

A Bassett-Lowke 0 gauge Enterprise 4-4-0 live
steam locomotive, the spirit-fired boiler with
twin outside cylinder, finished in black, lined
in red, boxed, c1935, engine 9in (23cm) long.
£230–250 *AH*

Four Hornby vans, 5½in (14cm) long, good condition, boxed:
l. A GW gunpowder van, c1926.
£385–400
l.c. An LMS luggage van, c1927.
£110–120
c.r. An LNER brake van, c1924.
£40–50
r. An LMS refrigeration van, c1927.
£60–70 *HOB*

A Hornby 0 gauge Schools Class steam locomotive, 'Eton', with olive green tender inscribed 'Southern 900', excellent condition, late 1930s, 9in (23cm) long, boxed.
£1,000–1,200 *WaH*

r. A Hornby 0 gauge No. 1 green buffer stop, 1940s, 2in (5cm) wide, boxed.
£10–15 *STK*

A Hornby 0 gauge No. 4 clockwork tank locomotive, mint condition, 1940s, 6in (15cm) long, boxed.
£70–80 *STK*

A Trix Trains 00 gauge AH Peppercorn A1 locomotive, finished in LNER green, c1955, 12in (30.5cm) long, boxed.
£100–120 *RAR*

A Trix Twin LNER Train System, 1950s, box 27in (68.5cm) long.
£100–120 *RAR*

A Triang Hornby RS62 'Car-a-Belle' train set, with Jinty tank, 2 bogie car transporter wagons, brake van, 12 Minix cars, track, oil bottle, smoke oil sachet, instructions, mint condition, 1965–70.
£130–150 *DN*

TREEN

A burr walnut snuff box,
c1810, 3in (7.5cm) wide.
£100–125 *MB*

A bog oak saucepan and lid, with
carved shamrock decoration,
18thC, 3¼in (8.5cm) diam.
£35–40 *STA*

A French Napoleonic carved
cocquilla nut snuff box, c1820,
3in (7.5cm) long.
£180–200 *MB*

l. A pair of Welsh wooden love
spoons, 19thC, 8½in (21.5cm) long.
£620–680 *AEF*

A Tunbridge ware inlaid
rosewood clothes brush,
c1860, 4in (10cm) long.
£55–65 *MB*

A carved wooden quaiche, c1850,
4½in (11.5cm) diam.
£100–130 *BWA*

*A quaiche is a shallow, wooden
drinking cup, formerly much used
in Scotland.*

A Dutch carved wood
snuff shoe, 19thC,
5in (12.5cm) long.
£270–300 *AEF*

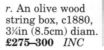

A Mauchline ware
sycamore glove
stretcher, c1860,
7in (18cm) long.
£60–70 *MB*

| Cross Reference |
| Kitchenware |

r. An olive wood
string box, c1880,
3¼in (8.5cm) diam.
£275–300 *INC*

Two Tartan ware egg cups, in McDuff
and Stewart tartans, late 19thC,
3¾in (9.5cm) diam.
£35–60 each *MRW*

A Tunbridge ware box,
with coromandel veneer,
decorated with a butterfly,
c1870, 7¾in (20cm) wide.
£600–700 *AMH*

A Tunbridge ware lined
jewellery box, with
parquetry-inlaid top, c1880,
5½in (14cm) wide.
£180–200 *VB*

TV SOAP COLLECTABLES

The term 'soap opera' derives from the American soap manufacturers, who were among the first to sponsor these serialized, domestic dramas, predominantly targeted at an audience of housewives. In Britain, soap operas first took off on the radio, most famously with *The Archers* – 'an everyday story of country folk' – premiered nationally in January 1951, and now the longest running of all radio serials. Television soon began to compete. The 1950s saw the invention of continuous narrative series such as *The Grove Family* (1954–57) and *Emergency Ward 10* (1957–66). In December 1960, Granada launched *Coronation Street*, now a British institution and probably the longest running TV soap opera in the world. Today, every major soap has its fan club, and enthusiasts collect merchandise and memorabilia connected with their favourite stars and series.

A black and white souvenir photo-card of Gwen Berryman, Mrs Doris Archer of *The Archers*, 1950s, 5½ x 3⅜in (14 x 9.5cm).
£8–10 *FRa*

A signed photo of *Dallas* star Linda Gray (Sue Ellen), 1980s, 10 x 8in (25.5 x 20.5cm).
£40–50 *FRa*

A collection of *Coronation Street* black and white portraits, with facsimile signatures, 1970s–80s.
£20–30 *VS*

An Emmerdale Family Album, by Michael Heatley, c1994, 7 x 9in (18 x 23cm).
£15–20 *KEN*

Two *EastEnders* black and white postcards, of Pam St Clement and Wendy Richard, signed, 1980s, 5¾ x 4in (14.5 x 10cm).
£4–5 each *FRa*

A Staffordshire Tableware *Coronation Street* mug, 1990s, 3½in (9cm) high.
£3–5 *PC*

r. An *EastEnders* ceramic teapot, in the form of the Queen Victoria pub, c1997, 9in (23cm) high.
£20–25 *KEN*

l. A *Coronation Street* poster, entitled 'Ladies of the Rovers', by Stuart McIntyre, signed, c1996, 17 x 24in (43 x 61cm).
£40–50 signed
£20–25 unsigned *KEN*

WRITING

A pair of glass inkwells, with brass tops, c1870, 2in (5cm) high.
£60–70 *STK*

A bowfronted post box, c1880, 11in (28cm) high.
£700–800 *GeM*

A patent glass inkwell, c1900, 3¾in (9.5cm) high.
£15–20 *WAB*

A brass stamp holder, with chain to hang from waistcoat, c1910, 4¼in (11cm) long.
£20–25 *WAB*

FURTHER READING

Miller's Pens & Writing Equipment: A Collector's Guide
Miller's Publications, 1999

top: A Tunbridge ware pencil, c1850, 4½in (11.5cm) long.
£250–260
bottom: A Tunbridge ware pen, c1870, 7½in (19cm) long.
£120–130 *AMH*

A silver duck-shaped pen wiper, c1880, 2in (5cm) wide.
£40–50 *VB*

A walnut desk inkstand, the glass inkwells with brass collars and matching glass bowl, c1880, 9in (23cm) wide.
£100–125 *MB*

A Tunbridge ware inlaid rosewood paper knife, c1880, 12in (30.5cm) long.
£40–50 *MB*

A silver and tortoise-shell paper knife, Birmingham 1899, 14¾in (37.5cm) long.
£200–225 *WeH*

A white metal telescopic propelling pencil, with scroll design body, c1920, 4¼in (10.5cm) long.
£70–80 *RUS*

A Parker Duofold Senior black and pearl propelling pencil, c1929, 5½in (14cm) long.
£100–120 *RUS*

A Yardolette lady's silver pencil, London 1948, 4in (10cm) long.
£40–50 *ABr*

A Cunard SS *Samaria* pencil, 1950s, 5in (12.5cm) long.
£12–15 *BAf*

DIRECTORY OF SPECIALISTS

If you require a valuation for an item, it is advisable to check whether the dealer or specialist will carry out this service and if there is a charge. Please mention Miller's when making an enquiry. Having found a specialist who will carry out your valuation it is best to send a description and photograph of the item to the specialist together with a stamped addressed envelope for the reply. A valuation by telephone is not possible. Most dealers are only too happy to help you with your enquiry; however, they are very busy people and consideration of the above points would be welcomed.

London

Angling Auctions,
P O Box 2095,
W12 8RU
Tel: 0181 749 4175
Angling auctions.

A. H. Baldwin & Sons Ltd,
Numismatists,
11 Adelphi Terrace,
WC2N 6BJ
Tel: 0171 930 6879
Coins and commemorative medals.

Linda Bee,
Art Deco Stand L18–21,
Grays Antique Market,
1–7 Davies Mews,
W1Y 1AR
Tel: 0171 629 5921
Costume and perfume bottles.

Behind the Boxes,
98 Kirkdale, Sydenham,
SE26 4BG
Tel: 0181 291 6116
Art Deco.

Nigel Benson
20th Century Glass,
Kensington Church
Street Antique Centre,
58–60 Kensington
Church Street,
W8 4DB
Tel/Fax: 0171 729 9875
Mobile: 07971 859848
Glass.

Beverley,
30 Church Street,
Marylebone, NW8 8EP
Tel: 0171 262 1576
Art Deco furniture, glass, figures, metalware and pottery.

Bloomsbury Book
Auctions,
3–4 Hardwick Street,
Off Rosebery Avenue,
EC1R 4RY
Tel: 0171 833 2636
Book auctions.

Christie's South
Kensington Ltd,
85 Old Brompton Road,
SW7 3LD
Tel: 0171 581 7611
Auctioneers.

Collectors' Lot,
25 Eccleston Place,
SW1W 9NF
Tel: 0171 881 8170
Publications.

Comic Book Postal
Auctions Ltd,
40-42 Osnaburgh Street,
NW1 3ND
Tel: 0171 424 0007
Comic book auctions.

Dix-Noonan-Webb,
1 Old Bond Street,
W1X 3TD
Tel: 0171 499 5022
Auctioneers.

Liz Farrow t/as Dodo,
Admiral Vernon Market,
Portobello Road, W11
Sats only 9–4pm.
Posters and old advertising items.

Liz Farrow, t/as Dodo,
Stand F073/83,
Alfie's Antique Market,
13–25 Church Street,
NW8 8DT
Tel: 0171 706 1545
Tues–Sats only 10.30–5.30pm. Posters and old advertising items.

Francis Joseph
Publications,
15 St Swithins Road,
SE13 6RW
Tel: 0181 318 9580
Publishers.

Michael C. German,
38B Kensington Church
Street,
W8 4BX
Tel: 0171 937 2771
Walking canes.

Richard Gibbon,
Stand G067 Alfies
Antique Market,
13–25 Church Street,
NW8 8DT
Tel: 0171 723 0449
Costume jewellery.

Grays Doll &
Teddy Centre,
1–7 Davies Mews,
W1Y 2LP
Tel: 0171 629 7034
Dolls and teddies.

Harlequin House
Puppets & Masks,
3 Kensington Mall,
W8 4EB
Tel: 0171 221 8629
Best collection of Pelham puppets, also antique rod puppets from Polka Theatre Wimbledon, old ventriloquist's dummies, Czech puppets, Punch & Judy. Open Tues, Fri and Sat 11.00–5.30pm. Nearest tube Notting Hill Gate, top of Kensington Church St.

Adrian Harrington
64a Kensington
Church Street,
W8 4DB
Tel: 0171 937 1465
Antiquarian books, prints and maps.

Peter Harrington,
100 Fulham Road,
SW3 6HS
Tel: 0171 591 0220/0330
Antiquarian books.

Harrison's Books,
Stand J20/21
Grays Mews
Antiques Market,
1–7 Davies Street,
W1Y 2LP
Tel: 0171 629 1374
Angling books.

Herzog, Hollender
Phillips & Company
The Scripophily Shop,
PO Box 14376,
NW6 1ZD
Tel/Fax: 0171 433 3577
e-mail:hollende
r@dial.pipex.com
http://Currency.dealers-on-line.com/Scripophily Shop.

David Huxtable,
Alfies Antique Market,
Stand S03/05 (Top Floor),
13–25 Church Street,
Marylebone,
NW8 8DT
Tel: 0171 724 2200
Old advertising collectables.

Murray Cards
(International) Ltd,
51 Watford Way,
Hendon Central,
NW4 3JH
Tel: 0181 202 5688
Cigarette and trade cards.

Pars Antiques,
Stand A14–15,
Grays in the Mews,
1–7 Davies Street,
W1Y 1AR
Tel: 0171 491 9889
Antiquities. Roman glass.

Stevie Pearce,
G144, Ground Floor,
Alfies Antique Market,
13–25 Church Street
Marylebone, NW8 8DT
Tel: 0171 723 1513/
0171 723 2526
Costume jewellery and fashion accessories 1900–1970.

Phillips,
Blenstock House,
101 New Bond Street,
W1Y 0AS
Tel: 0171 629 6602/
468 8233
Auctioneers.

Pin Ball Geoff,
1B Shelford Place,
Stoke Newington,
N16 9HX
Tel: 0171 254 6700/0138
Pin ball machines.

Radio Days,
87 Lower Marsh,
Waterloo, SE1 7AB
Tel: 0171 928 0800
Costume and textiles, collectables.

The Reel Thing,
17 Royal Opera Arcade,
Pall Mall, SW1Y 4UY
Tel: 0171 976 1830
Vintage sporting items.

Geoffrey Robinson,
GO77–78 (Ground floor),
Alfies Antique Market,
13–25 Church Street,
Marylebone, NW8 8DT
Tel: 0171 723 0449
Art Deco and post-war lighting, glass and chrome. Small furniture etc.

Alvin Ross,
Alfies Antique Market,
Stand G9–11, 13–25
Church Street,
Marylebone, NW8 8DT
Tel: 0171 723 1513
Pelham puppets.

Rumours,
10 The Mall, Upper
Street, Camden Passage,
Islington, N1 0PD
Tel: 01582 873561
Moorcroft pottery.

Totem,
168 Stoke Newington,
Church Street,
N16 0JL
Tel: 0171 275 0234
*LPs, MCs, CDs bought,
sold and exchanged.*

Vintage Cameras Ltd,
256 Kirkdale,
Sydenham, SE26 4NL
Tel: 0181 778 5416
*Antique and
classic cameras.*

Nigel Williams,
Rare Books,
22 & 25 Cecil Court,
WC2N 4HE
Tel: 0171 836 7757
*Books – first editions,
illustrated, children's
and detective.*

Wimpole Antiques,
Stand 349, Grays
Antique Market, South
Molton Lane,
W1Y 2LP
Tel: 0171 499 2889
Jewellery.

Wonderful World
of Animation,
30 Bramham Gardens,
SW5 0HF
Tel: 0171 370 4859
(US) 001 212 888 3712
*http://www.animationa
rtgallery.com
Animated art.*

Yesterday Child
Angel Arcade,
118 Islington High Street,
N1 8EG
Tel: 0171 354 1601
*Antique dolls and dolls,
house miniatures.*

Bedfordshire

Christopher Sykes,
The Old Parsonage,
Woburn, Milton Keynes,
MK17 9QM
Tel: 01525 290259
*Corkscrews and wine
related items.*

Berkshire

Collect It!
P O Box 3658,
Bracknell, RG12 7XZ
Tel: 01344 868280
Magazine for collectors.

Mostly Boxes,
93 High Street, Eton,
Windsor, SL4 6AF
Tel: 01753 858470
Antique wooden boxes.

Special Auction Services,
The Coach House,
Midgham Park,
Reading, RG7 5UG
Tel: 0118 971 2949
Commemorative auctions.

Cambridgeshire

Antique Amusement Co,
Mill Lane,
Swaffham,
Bulbeck,
CB5 0NF
Tel: 01223 813041
*Vintage amusement
machines also auctions
of amusement machines,
fairground art and
other related collectables.*

Cloister Antiques,
1a Lynn Road,
Ely, CB7 4EG
Tel: 01353 668558
*Sewing, writing, heavy
horse, smoking.*

James Fuller & Son,
51 Huntingdon Road,
Chatteris, P16 6JE
Tel: 01354 692740
Architectural antiques.

Warboys Antiques,
Old Church School,
High Street,
Warboys,
Huntingdon,
PE17 2SX
Tel: 01487 823686
*Sporting antiques
and tins.*

Cheshire

Collector's Corner,
PO Box 8,
Congleton, CW12 4GD
Tel: 01260 270429
*Rock and Pop
collectables, Sci-Fi,
TV and Beatles
memorabilia.*

Dollectable,
53 Lower Bridge Street,
Chester, CH1 1RS
Tel: 01244 344888/
01244 679195
Antique dolls.

On The Air,
42 Bridge Street Row,
Chester, CH1 1NN
Tel: 01244 348468
Vintage radios.

Sweetbriar Gallery,
Robin Hood Lane,
Helsby, WA6 9NH
Tel: 01928 723851
Paperweights.

Charles Tomlinson,
Chester
Tel: 01244 318395
Scientific Instruments.

Treasures in Textiles,
Melodys Antique
Galleries,
30/32 City Road,
Chester
Tel: 01244 328968
*Antique textile and
vintage clothing.*

Derbyshire

Chuck Overs,
The Cottage,
Warslow Road,
Longnor, SK17 0LA
Tel: 01298 83806
Radios.

Dorset

Ancient & Gothic,
PO Box 356,
Christchurch, BH23 1XQ
Tel: 01202 478592
Antiquities.

Books Afloat,
66 Park Street,
Weymouth, DT4 7DE
Tel: 01305 779774
*Books, shipping
memorabilia, models,
old postcards, paintings.*

Dalkeith Auctions,
Dalkeith Hall,
Dalkeith Steps, Rear of
81 Old Christchurch Rd,
Bournemouth, BH1 1YL
Tel: 01202 292905
*Auctions of postcards,
cigarette cards,
ephemera and
collectors items.*

Hardy's Collectables,
862 Christchurch Road,
Boscombe,
Bournemouth, BH7 6DQ
Tel: 01202 422407
Poole Pottery.

The Nautical Centre,
Harbour Passage,
Hope Square,
Weymouth, DT4 8TR
Tel: 01305 777838
Open Tues–Fri.

*Thousands of nautical
souvenirs and
memorabilia, sextants,
logs, flags, clocks,
telescopes, badges,
blocks, compasses, bells,
lights. Also maritime
items wanted.*

Old Button Shop
Antiques,
Lytchett Minster,
Poole, BH16 6JF
Tel: 01202 622169
Buttons and collectables.

Essex

GKR Bonds Ltd,
PO Box 1,
Kelvedon, CO5 9EH
Tel: 01376 571711
*Old bonds and
share certificates.*

Haddon Rocking
Horses Ltd,
5 Telford Road,
Clacton-on-Sea,
CO15 4LP
Tel: 01255 424745
*http://www.haddonhorse
.u-net.com
Rocking horses.*

Megarry's and
Forever Summer,
Jericho Cottage,
The Duckpond Green,
Blackmore, CM4 0RR
Tel: 01277 821031 and
01277 822170
*Antiques, Arts & Crafts,
Teashop and garden.
Summer opening hours:
10–6pm every day except
Wed. Winter opening
hours: 11–5pm, every
day except Wed. Member
Essex Antiques Dealers
Association. Car parking.*

Off World,
Unit 20, Romford
Shopping Halls,
Market Place,
Romford, RM1 3AT
Tel: 01708 765633
Sci-Fi Toys.

Old Telephone Company
The Old Granary,
Battlesbridge Antiques
Centre, Nr Wickford,
SS11 7RF
Tel: 01245 400601
Period telephones.

Saffron Walden Saleroom,
1 Market Street,
Saffron Walden,
CB10 1JB
Tel: 01799 513281
Auctioneers.

Gloucestershire

Bread & Roses,
Durham House Antique
Centre, Sheep Street,
Stow-on-the-Wold,
GL54 1AA
Tel: 01451 870404/
01926 817342
Kitchenware.

Creative Phonecards,
PO Box 12,
Tetbury, GL8 8WB
Tel: 01454 238600
Telephone cards.

Oriental Gallery
Tel: 01451 830944
*Oriental ceramics and
works of art.*

**Park House Antiques
& Toy Museum,**
Park Street,
Stow-on-the-Wold,
GL54 1AQ
Tel: 01451 830159
Fax: 01451 870809
*Come and see one of the
best private collections of
old toys in the country.
Admission £1.50 OAP's
£1. Summer 10–1pm
and 2–5pm. Winter
11–1pm and 2–4pm.
Closed Tues and all May.
We buy old toys and
teddy bears.*

David Partridge,
Gable End House,
Pitchcombe,
Stroud, GL6 6LN
Tel: 01452 812166
*Militaria – specialist in
antique firearms.*

Samarkand Galleries,
8 Brewery Yard,
Sheep Street,
Stow-on-the-Wold,
GL54 1AA
Tel: 01451 832322
*email:
mac@samarkand.co.uk
web site:
www.samarkand.co.uk
Antique rugs from near
East and central Asia.
Antique nomadic
weavings. Decorative
carpets. Tribal artefacts.
Contact: Brian
MacDonald FRGS.*

**Specialised Postcard
Auctions,**
Corinium Galleries,
25 Gloucester Street,
Cirencester, GL7 2DJ
Tel: 01285 659057
Postcard auctions.

Telephone Lines Ltd,
304 High Street,
Cheltenham,
GL50 3JF
Tel: 01242 583699
*Antique and Bakelite
telephones.*

Greater Manchester

British Tattoo Museum,
First Floor, 7 Thomas St,
Central Manchester,
M4 1EZ
Tel: 0161 839 0090

Hampshire

Bona Arts Decorative Ltd,
The Hart
Shopping Centre,
Fleet, GU13 8AZ
Tel: 01252 372188
*www.bona.co.uk
Art Deco, glass, lighting,
furniture and ceramics
including Clarice Cliff.*

Cobwebs,
78 Northam Road,
Southampton,
SO14 0PB
Tel: 01703 227458
*Ocean liner memorabilia.
Also naval and
aviation items.*

Goss & Crested China Co,
62 Murray Road,
Horndean, PO8 9JL
Tel: 01705 597440
Goss and crested china.

The Old Toy Shop
Tel/Fax: 01425 476899
*Clockwork, steam and
electric vintage toys and
memorabilia and figures.*

Romsey Auction Rooms,
86 The Hundred,
Romsey, SO51 8BX
Tel: 01794 513331
Toys. Auctions.

Romsey Medal Centre,
5 Bell Street,
Romsey, SO51 8GY
Tel: 01794 512069
*Orders, decorations
and medals.*

**Solent Railwayana
Auctions,**
31 Newtown Road,
Warsash, SO31 9FY
Tel: 01489
578091/584633
*Railway relics and
model railway items.
Also Railwayana
auctions.*

Hertfordshire

Beau Mo'nde Costume,
By George Antique Centre,
23 George Street,
St Albans, AL3 4ES
Tel: 01727 853032/855572
Costumes and textiles.

Forget Me Knot Antiques,
Over the Moon,
27 High Street,
St Albans, AL3 4EH
Tel: 01727 848907
Jewellery.

Isle of Wight

Nostalgia Toy Museum,
High Street,
Godshill, PO38 3HZ
Tel: 01938 526254
Diecast toys.

Kent

20th Century Marks,
12 Market Square,
Westerham, TN16 1AW
Tel: 01959 562221
*20th century furniture,
glass, ceramics,
lighting, art etc.*

Beatcity,
56 High Street,
Chatham, ME4 4DS
Tel: 01634 844525/
0370 650890
Beatles and Rock & Roll.

Candlestick & Bakelite,
PO Box 308,
Orpington, BR5 1TB
Tel: 0181 467 3743/3799
Telephones.

Claris's Tearooms,
1–3 High Street,
Biddenden, TN27 8AL
Tel: 01580 291025
*Moorcroft, Dennis China,
Kingsley Enamels, Okra
Glass, TY Beanie
Babies™, Merrythought
Bears, Boyds Bears,
Hantel miniatures.*

Delf Stream Gallery,
14 New Street,
Sandwich, CT13 9AB
Tel: 01304 617684
Art pottery.

Dragonlee Collectables
Tel: 01622 729502
Noritake.

Stuart Heggie,
14 The Borough,
Northgate,
Canterbury, CT1 2DR
Tel: 01227 470422
*Vintage cameras, optical
toys and photographic
images.*

J & M Collectables,
Tel: 01580 891657
*Postcards, crested china,
Osborne plaques, Ivorex
and small collectables.*

Old Tackle Box,
PO Box 55, High Street,
Cranbrook, TN17 3ZU
Tel/Fax 01580 713979
Old fishing tackle.

Pretty Bizarre,
170 High Street,
Deal, CT14 6BQ
Tel: 0973 794537
Art Deco.

Neville Pundole,
8a & 9 The Friars,
Canterbury, CT1 2AS
Tel: 01227 453471
*Moorcroft and
contemporary pottery.*

Serendipity,
168 High Street,
Deal, CT14 6BQ
Tel: 01304 369165/366536
Staffordshire pottery.

St Clere Antiques,
PO Box 161,
Sevenoaks, TN15 6GA
Tel: 01474 853630
*St Clere – Carltonware
The UK's leading
Specialists in Carlton
Ware. Selling and buying
Carlton 1890–1992. Mail
orders taken. Visa and
Mastercard accepted.
Contact Helen and
Keith Martin.*

Stevenson Brothers,
The Workshop, Ashford
Road, Bethersden,
Ashford, TN26 3AP
Tel: 01233 820363
Rocking horses.

Variety Box,
16 Chapel Place,
Tunbridge Wells,
TN1 1YQ
Tel: 01892 531868
*Tunbridge ware,
silver ware, glass,
fans, hat pins, writing,
sewing and other
collectors items.*

The Warehouse,
29–30 Queens Gardens,
Worthington Street,
Dover, CT17 9AH
Tel: 01304 242006
Toys.

Wenderton Antiques,
Tel: 01227 720295
(by appt only)
Kitchenware.

Wot a Racket,
250 Shepherds Lane,
Dartford, DA1 2PN
Tel /Fax: 01322 220619
Sporting.

Lancashire

Farmhouse Antiques,
Corner Shop,
23 Main Street,
Bolton-by-Bowland,
Clitheroe, BB7 4NW
Tel: 01200 447294/
441457
*Probably the largest
stock of antique textiles
in Lancashire.
Open Saturday, Sunday
and bank holidays all
year round. 12–4.30pm
or ring for appointment.
01200 441457. Trade
enquiries welcome.*

Glasform Ltd,
123 Talbot Road,
Blackpool, FY1 3QY
Tel: 01253 626410
*www.btinternet.com /-
glasform
Glasform@btinternet.
comGlass*

Pendelfin Studio Ltd,
Cameron Mill,
Housin Street,
Burnley, BB10 1PP
Tel: 01282 432301
Pendelfins.

Tracks,
PO Box 117,
Chorley, PR7 2QZ
Tel: 01257 269726
*Beatles and rare
pop memorabilia.*

Leicestershire

Pooks Motor Bookshop,
Fowke Street,
Rothley, LE7 7PJ
Tel: 0116 237 6222
email: pooks.motorbooks,
@virgin.net
Books and Automobilia.

Lincolnshire

20th Century Frocks,
65 Steep Hill
(opposite Jews House),
Lincoln, N1 1YN
Tel: 01522 545916
*Vintage clothing and
accessories bought
and sold
Costume – all periods,
also handbags, compacts,
accessories.
Open Tuesday, Thursday,
Friday and Saturday
Open 11am–5pm.*

Anthony Jackson,
Rocking Horse Maker
& Restorer,
20 Westry Corner,
Barrowby, Grantham,
NG32 1DF
Tel: 01476 567477
Rocking horses.

Junktion,
The Old Railway Station,
New Bolingbroke,
Boston, PE22 7LB
Tel: 01205 480068/480087
*Advertising and
packaging, automobilia,
toys.*

Frank Munford,
390 Newark Road,
Lincoln, LNX 8RX
Tel/Fax: 01522 878362
email:frank.munford
@virgin.net.
*Collector / dealer of Brooke
Bond tea cards, ephemera
and memorabilia and
other cereal / trade cards.
Buy–sell–exchange
Tel 01522 878362 anytime
after 9.00am and before
8.00pm please.*

Janie Smithson,
Tel/Fax 01754 810265.
Mobile 0831 399180
Kitchenware.

Middlesex

Albert's
Cigarette Card Specialists,
308 Nelson Road,
Twickenham, TW2 7AJ
Tel: 0181 893 9339
Cigarette cards.

Joan & Bob Anderson,
Tel: 0181 572 4328
Midwinter ceramics.

Hobday Toys,
Tel: 01895 636737
*Tinplate toys, trains
and dolls' houses.*

John Ives,
5 Normanhurst Drive,
Twickenham, TW1 1NA
Tel: 0181 892 6265
*Reference books on
antiques and collecting.*

When We Were Young,
The Old Forge,
High Street,
Harmondsworth Village,
UB7 0AQ
Tel: 0181 897 3583
*Collectable items
related to British
childhood characters
and illustrators.*

Norfolk

Roger Bradbury Antiques,
2 Church Street,
Coltishall, NR12 7DJ
Tel: 01603 737444
Oriental pottery.

Cat Pottery,
1 Grammar School Road,
North Walsham,
NR28 9JH
Tel: 01692 402962
Animal pottery.

Church Street Antiques,
2 Church Street,
Wells-next-the-Sea,
NR23 1JA
Tel: 01328 711698
*Open Tues–Sun inclusive
10am–4pm Hat pins,
linen and lace,
textiles, kitchenware,
collectables, jewellery.*

Northampton

The Old Brigade,
10A Harborough Road,
Kingsthorpe, NN2 7AZ
Tel: 01604 719389
Militaria.

Nottingham

T. Vennett-Smith,
11 Nottingham Road,
Gotham, NG11 0HE
Tel: 0115 983 0541
*Ephemera and
sporting auctions.*

Vintage Wireless Shop,
The Hewarths, Sandiacre,
Nottingham, NG10 5NQ
Tel: 0115 939 3139
*Early wireless and
television sets.*

Millennium
Collectables Ltd,
PO Box 146,
Eastwood Hall,
Eastwood, NG16 3SS
Royal Doulton.

Oxfordshire

Dauphin Display
Cabinet Co,
PO Box 602,
Oxford, OX44 9LU
Tel: 01865 343542
Display stands.

Stone Gallery,
93 The High Street,
Burford, OX18 4QA
Tel/Fax 01993 823302
*Specialist dealer in
antique and modern
paperweights, gold and
silver designer jewellery
and enamel boxes.*

Teddy Bears,
99 High Street,
Witney, OX8 6LY
Tel: 01993 702616
Teddy bears.

Vine Antiques,
Tel: 01235 812708
Stevengraphs.

Pembrokeshire

Pendelfin,
Arch House,
St George Street,
Tenby, SA70 7JB
Tel: 01834 843246
Pendelfins.

Rutland

House of Burleigh,
The Old Shop Cottage,
2 Braunston Road,
Knossington,
Oakham,
LE15 8LN
Tel: 01664 454570/454114
Ceramics.

Shropshire

Mullock & Madeley,
The Old Shippon,
Wall-under-Heywood,
Nr Church Stretton,
SY6 7DS
Tel: 01694 771771
Sporting auctions.

Somerset

Antiques & Collectables
Magazine,
30a Monmouth Street,
Bath, BA1 2AN
Tel: 01225 311077
Publications.

Bath Dolls' Hospital,
2 Grosvenor Place,
London Road,
Bath, BA1 6PT
Tel: 01225 319668
Doll restoration.

Bonapartes,
1 Queen Street,
Bath, BA1 1HE
Tel: 01225 423873
Military figures.

Lynda Brine,
Assembly Antique Centre,
5–8 Saville Row,
Bath, BA1 2QP
Tel: 01225 448488
Perfume bottles.

Glenville Antiques,
120 High Street,
Yatton, BS19 4DH
Tel: 01934 832284
Collectables.

Philip Knighton,
11 North Street,
Wellington,
TA21 8LX
Tel: 01823 661618
*Wireless, gramophones
and all valve equipment.*

Le Boudoir Collectables,
Bartlett Street
Antique Centre,
Bath, BA1 2QZ
Tel: 01225 311061
*Perfume bottles, fairings,
jewellery, smoking,
crested china.*

T. J. Millard Antiques,
Assembly Antiques,
5–8 Saville Row,
Bath, BA1 2QP
Tel: 01225 448488
Boxes and games.

Joanna Proops,
Antiques & Textiles,
34 Belvedere,
Bath, BA1 5HR
Tel: 01225 310795
Textiles.

Richard Twort,
Tel: 01934 641900
Mobile 0411 939789
*Meteorological
instruments.*

Staffordshire

Brian Bates &
Paul Haskell
Tel: 01782 680667/
01634 669362
*Old mechanical
slot machines,
'Alwins', Bandits,
Fortune Tellers,
Mutoscopes, etc.*

Keystones,
PO Box 387,
Stafford,
ST16 3FG
Tel: 01785 256648
Denby pottery.

Gordon Litherland,
25 Stapenhill Road,
Burton-on-Trent,
DE15 9AE
Tel: 01283 567213
*Bottles, breweriana
and pub jugs and
commemoratives.*

Peggy Davies Ceramics,
28 Liverpool Road,
Stoke-on-Trent,
ST4 1VJ
Tel: 01782 848002
*Ceramics. Limited
edition Toby jugs
and figures.*

The Potteries
Antique Centre,
271 Waterloo Road,
Cobridge, Stoke-on-
Trent, ST6 3HR
Tel: 01782 201455
Ceramics.

Room at the Topp
1st Floor, Antiques
Warehouse,
Glass Street, Hanley,
Stoke-on-Trent, ST1 2ET
Tel: 01782 271070
1950s collectables.

Trevor Russell,
PO Box 1258,
Uttoxeter, ST14 8XL
*Fountain pens
and repairs.*

The Tackle Exchange,
95B Trentham Road,
Dresden, Stoke-on-Trent,
ST3 4EG
Tel: 01782 599858
Old fishing tackle.

Suffolk

Jamie Cross,
PO Box 73,
Newmarket, CB8 8RY
Tel: 01638 750132
Mobile 0802 366631
*We buy and sell German,
Italian and British WWI
and WWII medals,
badges and decorations.*

W. L. Hoad,
9 St. Peter's Road,
Kirkley,
Lowestoft, NR33 0LH
Tel: 01502 587758
Cigarette cards.

Surrey

David Aldous-Cook,
PO Box 413,
Sutton, SM3 8SZ
Tel: 0181 642 4842
*Reference books on
antiques and
collectables.*

Childhood Memories,
The Farnham Antique
Centre, 27 South Street,
Farnham, GU9 7QU
Tel: 01252 724475/793704
*Antique teddies, dolls
and miniatures.*

Church Street Antiques,
10 Church Street,
Godalming, GU7 1EH
Tel: 01483 860894
*Art Deco ceramics,
traditional antique
silverware, glass
and ceramics.*

Gooday Gallery,
20 Richmond Hill,
Richmond, TW10 6QX
Tel: 0181 940 8652
*Art Deco, Art
Nouveau, tribal.*

Richard Joseph
Publishers Ltd,
Unit 2, Monk's Walk,
Farnham, GU9 8HT
Tel: 01252 734347
Publishers.

West Promotions,
PO Box 257,
Sutton, SM3 9WW
Tel: 0181 641 3224
Banking collectables.

Sussex

Art Deco Etc,
73 Upper Gloucester Rd,
Brighton, BN1 3LQ
Tel: 01273 329268
Poole pottery.

Tony Horsley,
Tel: 01273 550770
*Candle extinguishers,
Royal Worcester and
other porcelain*

Libra Antiques,
81 London Road,
Hurst Green,
Etchingham, TN19 7PN
Tel: 01580 860569
Lighting.

Ann Lingard,
Ropewalk Antiques,
Rye, TN31 7NA
Tel: 01797 223486
Kitchenware.

Mint Arcade,
71 The Mint,
Rye, TN31 7EW
Tel: 01797 225952
Cigarette cards.

Utility Plus,
66 High Street,
West Ham,
Pevensey, BN24 5LP
Tel: 01323 762316
0850 130723
50s kitchenware.

Wallis & Wallis,
West Street Auction
Galleries,
Lewes, BN7 2NJ
Tel: 01273 480208
*Specialist auctioneers of
militaria, arms, armour,
coins and medals. Also
die-cast and tinplate
toys, teddy bears, dolls,
model railways, toy
soldiers and models.*

Tyne & Wear

Antiques at H & S
Collectables,
No1 Ashburton Road,
Corner Salters Rd,
Gosforth, NE3 4XN
Tel: 0191 284 6626
*Curios, Victoriana,
Maling specialist.*

Warwickshire

Amese Militaria Fairs,
PO Box 194,
Warwick, CV34 5ZG
Tel: 0115 947 4137 or
01926 497340
*'The International',
Birmingham.
The U.K's largest one
day fair for antique
arms, medals and
militaria.*

The Antique Shop,
30 Henley Street,
Stratford-upon-Avon,
CV37 6QW
Tel: 01789 292485
*Dolls, teddy bears,
fishing tackle, glass,
porcelain, jewellery,
oriental, silver and
collectables.*

Chris James,
Medals & Militaria,
Warwick Antiques
Centre, 22–24 High St,
Warwick, CV34 4AP
Tel: 01926 495704
*Specialists in antique
arms, edged weapons,
medals, militaria &
aviation items. For sale
and purchased.*

Malcolm Welch Antiques
PO Box 1122,
Rugby, CV23 9YD
Tel: 01788 810 616
*Buttons and buckles,
advertising items, paper
items including
postcards, etc.*

West Midlands

Antiques Magazine,
HP Publishing,
2 Hampton Court Road,
Harborne,
Birmingham, B17 9AE
Tel: 0121 681 8000
Publications.

Birmingham Railway
Auctions & Publications,
7 Ascot Road, Moseley,
Birmingham, B13 9EN
Tel: 0121 449 9707
*Railway auctions and
publications.*

Jenny & Martin Wills,
Tango Art Deco,
22 Kenilworth Road,
Knowle,
Solihull, B93 0JA
Tel: 01564 776669
Tel/Fax: 0121 704 4969
Art Deco.
Open Fridays and
Saturdays 9–6pm.

Worcestershire

BBM Jewellery & Coins
(W. V. Crook),
8–9 Lion Street,
Kidderminster,
DY10 1PT
Tel: 01562 744118
Antique jewellery, coins.

John Neale,
11A Davenport Drive,
The Willows,
Bromsgrove, B60 2DW
Tel: 01527 871000
Vintage toy trains.

Yorkshire

Antique &
Collectors Centre,
35 St Nicholas Cliff,
Scarborough, YO11 2ES
Tel: 01723 365221
Website:
collectors.demon.co.uk
email: sales@collectors.
demon.co.uk
International dealers
in stamps, postcards,
silver, gold, medals,
cigarette cards and
many more collectables.

BBR,
Elsecar Heritage Centre,
Wath Road, Elsecar,
Barnsley, S74 8HJ
Tel: 01226 745156
Advertising, breweriana,
pot lids, bottles, Doulton
and Beswick.

Briar's C20th
Decorative Arts,
Skipton Antiques &
Collectors Centre,
The Old Foundry,
Cavendish Street,
Skipton, BD23 2AB
Tel: 01756 798641
Art Deco ceramics and
furniture, specialising in
Charlotte Rhead pottery.

The Camera House,
Oakworth Hall, Colne
Road (B6143),
Oakworth,
Keighley, BD22 7HZ
Tel: /Fax01535 642333
Anytime

Website: www.the-camera-
house.co.uk
email: info@the-camera-
house.co.uk. Cameras and
photographic equipment
for the user and collector
from 1850. Purchases,
sales, part exchanges,
repairs, cine, slide video
transfers. Valuations for
Probate and Insurance.
Open Wed–Fri 10–5 Sat
10–3 or by appointment.
Prop. C Cox.

Country Collector,
11–12 Birdgate,
Pickering, YO18 7AL
Tel: 01751 477481
Art Deco ceramics, Blue
& White, pottery and
porcelain.

Crested China Co,
The Station House,
Driffield, YO25 7PY
Tel: 01377 257042
Goss and crested china.

Echoes,
650a Halifax Road,
Eastwood,
Todmorden, OL14 6DW
Tel: 01706 817505
Antique costume, textiles
including linen, lace
and jewellery.

G. M. Haley,
Hippins Farm,
Black Shawhead,
Nr Hebden Bridge,
HX7 7JG
Tel: 01422 842484
Military toys.

John & Simon Haley,
89 Northgate,
Halifax, HX6 4NG
Tel: 01422 822148/360434
Old toys and
money boxes.

Muir Hewitt,
Halifax Antiques Centre,
Queens Road Mills,
Queen's Road/
Gibbet Street,
Halifax, HX1 4LR
Tel: 01422 347377
Clarice Cliff.

Linen & Lace,
Shirley Tomlinson,
Halifax Antiques Centre,
Queens Road/
Gibbet Street,
Halifax, HX1 4LR
Tel: 01422 366657
Mobile 0411 763454
Antique linen, textiles,
period costume
and accessories.

Old Copper Shop and
Posthouse Antiques,
69 & 75 Market Place,
South Cave,
HU15 2AS
Tel: 01430 423988
General stock.

Sheffield Railwayana
Auctions,
43 Little Norton Lane,
Sheffield, S8 8GA
Tel: 0114 274 5085
Railwayana, posters and
models auctions.

Rep of Ireland

Michelina &
George Stacpoole,
Main Street, Adare,
Co Limerick
Tel: 00 353 6139 6409
Pottery, ceramics, silver
and prints.

Whyte's Auctioneers,
30 Marlborough St,
Dublin 1,
Tel: 00 353 1 874 6161
Ephemera and militaria.

Scotland

Edinburgh Coin Shop,
11 West Crosscauseway,
Edinburgh, EH8 9JW
Tel: 0131 668 2928
0131 667 9095
Coins, medals, militaria
and stamps.

Rhod McEwan
Golf Books,
Glengarden, Ballater,
Aberdeenshire,
AB35 5UB
Tel: 013397 55429
Rare and out-of-print
golfing books.

Timeless Tackle,
1 Blackwood Crescent,
Edinburgh, EH9 1QZ
Tel: 0131 667 1407
Old fishing tackle.

Wales

A.P.E.S. Rocking Horses,
20 Tan-y-bwlch
Mynydd Llandygai,
Bangor, Gwynedd,
LL57 4DX
Tel: 01745 540 365
Rocking horses.

The Emporium,
112 St Teilo St,
Pontarddulais,
Nr Swansea,
SA4 1QH
Tel: 01792 885185
Brass and cast iron.

Paul Gibbs Antiques,
25 Castle Street,
Conway,
Gwynedd, LL32 8AY
Tel: 01492 593429
/596533
Art pottery. Teapots.

Islwyn Watkins,
1 High Street,
Knighton,
Powys, LD7 1AT
Tel: 01547 520145
18th and 19th Century
Pottery. 20th Century
country and Studio
pottery, small country
furniture, treen and
bygones.

Australia

Gary Wanstall &
Robyn Valja,
408–410 King Street,
Newtown,
New South Wales 2042
Tel: 02 9519 306
Toys.

USA

20th Century Vintage
Telephones,
2780 Northbrook Place,
Boulder, Colorado
80304,
Tel: 001 44 (303) 442 3304
Telephones.

The Dunlop Collection,
P.O. Box 6269,
Statesville,
NC 28687
Tel: (704) 871 2626 or
Toll Free Telephone
(800) 227 1996
Paperweights.

Mike Roberts,
4416 Foxfire Way,
Fort Worth,
Texas 76133
Tel: 001 817 294 2133
Electric fans.

DIRECTORY OF COLLECTORS' CLUBS

This directory is in no way complete. If you wish to be included in next year's directory or if you have a change of address or telephone number, please inform us by 1st November, 1999.

Antiquarian Horological Society
New House, High Street, Ticehurst,
Sussex TN5 7AL Tel: 01580 200155
Antique Collectors' Club
5 Church Street, Woodbridge, Suffolk IP12 1DS
The Arms and Armour Society Hon Secretary
Anthony Dove, PO Box 10232, London SW19 2ZD
Association of Bottled Beer Collectors
c/o 66 High Street, Puckeridge, Ware SG11 1RX
Tel: 01920 822405
Association of Comic Enthusiasts: ACE!
8 Silverdale, Sydenham, London SE26 4SJ
Avon Magpies Club Mrs W. A. Fowler,
36 Castle View Road, Portchester, Fareham,
Hampshire PO16 9LA Tel: 01705 642393
Badge Collectors' Circle
c/o Mary Setchfield, 3 Ellis Close, Quorn,
Nr Loughborough, Leicestershire LE12 8SH
Tel: 01509 412094
Beanie Baby Official Club
PO Box 381, Horsham, W. Sussex RH13 5FP
British Art Medal Society
c/o Philip Attwood, Dept of Coins and Medals,
The British Museum, London WC1B 3DG
Tel: 0171 323 8170 Extn 8227
British Association of Sound Collections
c/o Alan Ward, National Sound Archive,
29 Exhibition Road, London SW7 2AS
Tel: 0171 589 6603
The British Beermat Collectors' Society
Hon Sec, 69 Dunnington Avenue, Kidderminster,
Worcestershire PY10 2YT
The British Button Society
Mr Keith Riddle, The Old Dairy,
Newton Kettering, Northants NN14 1BW
Tel: 01536 461818
British Compact Collectors' Society
SAE to PO Box 131, Woking, Surrey GU24 9YR
British Matchbox Label and Booklet Society
Arthur Alderton (Hon. Sec), 122 High Street,
Melbourn, Cambridgeshire SG8 6AL
Tel: 01763 260399
The British Model Soldier Society
Hon Secretary, 22 Lynwood Road, Ealing,
London W5 1JJ
The British Numismatic Society
Dr J. D. Bateson, Hunterian Museum, Glasgow
University, University Avenue, Glasgow,
Scotland G12 8QQ
British Stickmakers' Guild
c/o Brian Aries, 44a Eccles Road, Chapel-en-le-
Frith, Derbyshire SK12 6RG Tel: 01298 815291
British Teddy Bear Association
PO Box 290, Brighton, Sussex BN2 1DR
British Watch & Clock Collectors Association
Tony Woolven, 5 Cathedral Lane, Truro, Cornwall
TR1 2QS Tel: 01872 241953

The Buttonhook Society c/o Paul Moorehead,
2 Romney Place, Maidstone, Kent ME15 6LE
Byngo Collectors Club 23 Longhedge,
Caldecotte, Buckinghamshire MK7 8LA
The Cambridge Paperweight Circle
c/o Roy Brown, 34 Huxley Road, Welling, Kent
DA16 2EW Tel: 0181 303 4663
Carlton Ware Collectors Club 5 Southbrook
Mews, London SE12 8LG Tel: 0181 318 9580
CarltonWare Collectors International
Helen Martin, PO Box 161, Sevenoaks, Kent
TN15 6GA Tel: 01474 853630
Carnival Glass Society (UK) Ltd
PO Box 14, Hayes, Middlesex UB3 5NU
The Cartophilic Society of Great Britain
Mr A. W. Stevens, 63 Ferndale Road, Church
Crookham, Aldershot, Hampshire GU13 0LN
Tel: 01252 621586
Charlotte Rhead Newsletter
c/o 49 Honeybourne Road, Halesowen, West
Midlands B63 3ET Tel: 0121 560 7386
Chintz Club of America Jane Fehrenbacher
and Carolyn Fox, The Chintz Collector, PO Box
50888, Pasadena, California 91115, U.S.A.
Tel: 001 (626) 441 4708 email: chintz4u@aol.com
**The City of London Photograph and
Gramophone Society** 63 Vicarage Way,
Colnbrook, Buckinghamshire S13 0JY
Clarice Cliff Collectors' Club c/o Leonard R
Griffin, Fantasque House, Tennis Drive, The
Park, Nottingham, Nottinghamshire NG7 1AE
Comic Enthusiasts' Society
17 Hill Street, Colne, Lancashire BB8 0DH
Tel: 01282 865468
The Comics Journal
c/o Bryon Whitworth, 17 Hill Street, Colne,
Lancashire BB8 0DH Tel: 01282 865468
Commemorative Collectors' Society
c/o Steven Jackson, Lumless House,
Gainsborough Road, Winthorpe, Newark, Notts
NG24 2NR Tel: 01636 671377
Corgi Collector Club
Susan Pownall, PO Box 323, Swansea, Wales
SA1 1BJ Tel/Fax 08706 071204
Costume Society
Lindsay Robertson, 32 Nore Road, Portishead,
Bristol, Gloucestershire BF20 9HN
The Crested Circle 42 Douglas Road,
Tolworth, Surbiton, Surrey KT6 7SA
Cricket Memorabilia Society
c/o Tony Sheldon, 29 Highclere Road, Crumpsall,
Greater Manchester M8 4WH
Tel/Fax 0161 740 3714
**The Crunch Club (Breakfast Cereal
Collectables)** John Cahill, 9 Weald Rise,
Tilehurst, Reading, Berkshire RG30 6XB
Tel: 0118 942 7291

Doll Club of Great Britain 16E Chalwyn
Industrial Estate, St Clements Road, Parkstone,
Poole, Dorset BH15 3PE
Egg Cup Collectors Club of Great Britain
Audrey Diamond Tel: 01202 744009
Embroiderers' Guild, c/o Mrs F Parsons,
Apartment 41, Hampton Court Palace,
East Molesey, Surrey KT8 9AU
Tel: 0181 943 1229
The English Playing Card Society
c/o Major Donald Welsh, 11 Pierrepont Street,
Bath, Somerset BA1 1LA
Tel: 01225 465218
The European Honeypot Collectors' Society
John Doyle, The Honeypot,18 Victoria Road,
Chislehurst, Kent BR7 6DF
Tel/Fax 0181 467 2053
Fan Circle International Sec: Mrs Joan
Milligan, Cronk-y-Voddy, Rectory Road,
Coltishall, Norwich, Norfolk NR12 7HF
Festival of Britain Society c/o Martin Packer,
124 Havant Road, North End, Portsmouth,
Hampshire PO2 0BP
Tel: 01705 665630/0181 471 2165
The Flag Institute 9 Laurel Grove, Chester,
Cheshire CH2 3HH
Friends of Blue c/o Terry Shepherd, 45a
Church Road, Bexley Heath, Kent DA7 4DD
Friends of Broadfield House Glass Museum
Compton Drive, Kingswinford, West Midlands
DY6 9NS Tel: 01384 273011
Friends of Fred Homepride Flour Men
Jennifer Woodward Tel: 01925 826158
The Furniture History Society c/o Dr. Brian
Austen, 1 Mercedes Cottages, St. John's Road,
Haywards Heath, Sussex RH16 4EH
Tel: 01444 413845
Goss Collectors' Club Mrs Schofield,
Derbyshire Tel: 0115 930 0441
Goss & Crested China Club Pat Welbourne,
62 Murray Road, Horndean, Hants PO8 9JL
Tel: 01705 597440
The Hat Pin Society of Great Britain
PO Box 74, Bozent, Wellingborough, Northants
NN29 7JH
Historical Model Railway Society
59 Woodberry Way, London E4 7DY
Honiton Pottery Collectors' Society
c/o Robin Tinkler, 12 Beehive Lane, Great
Baddow, Chelmsford, Essex CM2 9SX
Tel: 01245 353477
The Hornby Railway Collectors' Association
2 Ravensmore Road, Sherwood, Nottingham,
Nottinghamshire NG5 2AH
Hurdy-Gurdy Society c/o Doreen Muskett,
The Old Mill, Duntish, Dorchester, Dorset
DT2 7DR
International Bank Note Society
36B Dartmouth Park Hill, London NW5 1HN
International Bond and Share Society,
c/o Peter Duppa-Miller, Beechcroft, Combe Hay,
Bath, Somerset BA2 7EG

International Collectors' of Time Assoc
173 Coleherne Court, Redcliffe Gardens,
London SW5 0DX
**International Correspondence of
Corkscrew Addicts**
Don MacLean, 4201 Sunflower Drive,
Mississauga, Ontario L5L 2L4, Canada
King George VI Collectors' Society (Philately)
98 Albany, Manor Road, Bournemouth, Dorset
BH1 3EW Tel: 01202 551515
Knife Rest Collectors Club
Doreen Hornsblow, Braughingbury, Braughing,
Hertfordshire SG11 2RD Tel: 01920 822654
The Lace Guild The Hollies, 53 Audnam,
Stourbridge, West Midlands DY8 4AE
Legend Lane Collector's Club
Albion Mill, London Road, Macclesfield,
Cheshire SK11 7SQ Tel: 01625 424661
The Maling Collectors' Society
PO Box 1762, North Shields NE30 4YJ
Manor Ware Club c/o 66 Shirburn Road,
Upton, Torquay, Devon TQ1 4HR
Tel: 01803 328298
**The Matchbox International Collectors'
Association** c/o Stewart Orr, The Toy Museum,
13a Lower Bridge Street, Chester, Cheshire
CH1 1RS Tel: 01244 346297
Mauchline Ware Collectors' Club
Unit 37 Romsey Industrial Estate, Greatbridge
Road, Romsey, Hampshire SO51 0HR
Memories UK Mabel Lucie Attwell Club
Abbey Antiques, 63 Great Whyte, Ramsey,
Nr Huntingdon, Cambridgeshire PE17 1HL
Tel: 01487 814753
Merrythought International Collectors Club
Ironbridge, Telford, Shropshire TF8 7NJ
Tel: 01952 433116
Model Railway Club The Secretary, Keen
House, 4 Calshot Street, London N1 9DA
website: www.themodelrailwayclub.org
Moorcroft Collectors' Club W. Moorcroft PLC,
Sandbach Road, Burslem, Stoke-on-Trent,
Staffordshire ST6 2DQ Tel: 01782 214323
Musical Box Society of Great Britain
PO Box 299, Waterbeach, Cambridgeshire CB4 4PJ
National Horse Brass Society 12 Severndale,
Droitwich Spa, Worcestershire WR9 8PD
New Baxter Society c/o Museum of Reading,
Blagrave Street, Reading, Berkshire RG1 1QH
Old Bottle Club of Great Britain
Alan Blakeman, BBR, Elsecar Heritage Centre,
Wath Road, Elsecar, Barnsley, Yorks S74 8HJ
Tel: 01226 745156
**Ophthalmic Antiques International
Collectors' Club** 3 Moor Park Road,
Northwood, Middlesex HA6 2DL
Orders and Medals Research Society
123 Turnpike Link, Croydon, Surrey CR0 5NU
The Oriental Ceramic Society
The Secretary, 30b Torrington Square,
London WC1E 7JL Tel: 0171 636 7985/
Fax 0171 580 6749

Pen Delfin Family Circle Matthew Baldock, Shop 28, Grove Plaza, Stirling Highway, Peppermint Grove, Australia 6011 Tel: 09 384 9999

Pen Delfin Family Circle Ronnie Marnef, Fazantenlaan 29, 2610 Antwerp, Belgium Tel: 03 440 5668

Pen Delfin Family Circle Nancy Falkenham, 1250 Terwillegar Avenue, Oshawa, Ontario, Canada L1J 7A5 Tel: 0101 416 723 9940

Pen Delfin Family Circle Irene Svensson, Svebi AB, Box 143, S-562 02 Taberg, Sweden Tel: 036 656 90

The Family Circle of Pen Delfin Susan Beard, 230 Spring Street N.W., Suite 1238, Atlanta, Georgia 30303, U.S.A Tel: Freephone US only 1-800 872 4876

Pen Delfin 'Family Circle' Collectors' Club Cameron Mill, Howsin Street, Burnley, Lancashire BB10 1PP Tel: 01282 432301

Pewter Society Llananant Farm, Penallt, Monmouth NP5 4AP

Photographic Collectors Club of Gt Britain 5 Station Industrial Estate, Prudhoe, Northumberland NE42 6NP

Poole Pottery Collectors Club Gloria Peek, The Quay, Poole, Dorset BH15 1RF Tel: 01202 666200

The Postcard Club of Great Britain c/o Mrs D Brennan, 34 Harper House, St James's Crescent, London SW9 7LW Tel: 0171 771 9404

Pot Lid Circle c/o Keith Mortimer, Buckinghamshire Tel: 01753 886751

Quimper Association Odin, Benbow Way, Cowley, Uxbridge, Middlesex UB8 2HD

Railwayana Collectors Journal 7 Ascot Road, Moseley, Birmingham, West Midlands B13 9EN

Robert Harrop Collectors Club Robert Harrop, Coalport House, Lamledge Lane, Shifnal, Shropshire TF11 8SD Tel: 01952 462721

Royal Doulton International Collectors' Club Minton House, London Road, Stoke-on-Trent, Staffordshire ST4 7QD

The Royal Numismatic Society c/o Mr Joseph Cribb, Department of Coins and Medals, British Museum, London WC1B 3DG Tel: 0171 636 1555 extn 404

Royal Winton International Collectors' Club Dancers End, Northall, Beds LU6 2EU Tel: 01525 220272

Scientific Instrument Society Wg Cdr G. Bennett, 31 High Street, Stanford in the Vale, Faringdon, Oxfordshire SN7 8LH Tel: 01367 710223 email: sis@hidex.demon.co.uk

The Shelley Group 4 Fawley Road, Regents Park, Southampton, Hampshire SO2 1LL

Silhouette Collectors' Club c/o Diana Joll, Flat 5, 13 Brunswick Square, Hove, Sussex BN3 1EH Tel: 01273 735760

The Silver Spoon Club c/o Mr & Mrs T R Haines, Glenleigh Park, Sticker, St Austell, Cornwall PL26 7JD Tel/Fax 01726 65269

The Silver Study Group The Secretary, London Tel: 0181 202 0269

Studio Szeiler Collectors Circle Miss Gillian Vigus, Gwent, Wales Tel: 01291 620715

Susie Cooper Collectors Group Allison Dobbs, PO Box 7436, London N12 7QF

The Sylvac Collectors Circle 174 Portsmouth Road, Horndean, Waterlooville, Hants PO8 9HP Tel: 01705 591725

Telecommunications Heritage Group PO Box 561, Croydon, Surrey CR2 6YL

The Thimble Society of London c/o Bridget McConnel, Shop 134, Grays Antique Market, 58 Davies Street, London W1Y 2LP Tel: 0171 493 0560

Toby Fillpot Memorial Club Vadim Linetski (Membership sec), 609a High Road, Leyton, London E10 6RF Tel: 0181 558 3676

The Tool and Trades History Society c/o Chris Hudson, 60 Swanley Lane, Swanley, Kent BR8 7JG Tel: 01322 662271

Torquay Pottery Collectors' Society Jill & Paul Griffin, Torre Abbey, Avenue Road, Torquay, Devon TQ2 5JX

Train Collectors' Society c/o Joe Swain, Lock Cottage, Station Foot Path, Kings Langley, Hertfordshire WD4 8DZ

The Transport Ticket Society c/o Courtney Haydon, 4 Gladridge Close, Earley, Reading, Berkshire RG6 7DL Tel: 01734 579373

The Trix Twin Railway Collector's Association c/o Mr C B Arnold, 6 Ribble Avenue, Oadby, Leicester, Leics LE2 4NZ

UK Perfume Bottles Collectors Club Lynda Brine, Stand 14, Assembly Antique Centre, 5-8 Saville Row, Bath, Somerset BA1 2QP Tel: 01225 448488

Unofficial McDonalds Collectors Newsletter c/o Ian Smith, 14 Elkstone Road, Chesterfield, Derbyshire S40 4UT

USSR Collectors Club Bob & June Moore, PO Box 6, Virginia Water, Surrey GU25 4YU Tel: 01344 843091

Victorian Military Society 20 Priory Road, Newbury, Berkshire RG14 7QN Tel: 01635 48628

The Vintage Model Yacht Group c/o Russel Potts, 8 Sherard Road, London SE9 6EP Tel: 0181 850 6805

The Wedgwood Society of Great Britain c/o Dr W. A. M. Holdaway, 89 Andrewes House, The Barbican, London EC2Y 8AY

Wireless Preservation Society The National Wireless Museum, Arreton Manor, Newport, Isle of Wight PO30 3AA Tel: 01983 567665

Writing Equipment Society c/o Dr M. L. Greenland, Cartledge Cottage, Cartledge Lane, Holmesfield, Dronfield, Derbyshire S18 7SB

DIRECTORY OF MARKETS & CENTRES

London

Alfies Antique Market,
13–25 Church Street,
NW8 8DT
Tel: 0171 723 6066

Antiquarius Antique
Market,
131/141 King's Road,
Chelsea, SW3 5ST
Tel: 0171 351 5353

Bond Street Antiques
Centre, 124 New Bond
Street, W1Y 9AE
Tel: 0171 351 5353

Grays Antique Market,
South Molton Lane,
W1Y 2LP
Tel: 0171 629 7034

The Mall Antiques Arcade,
Camden Passage,
359 Upper Street, N1 8DU
Tel: 0171 351 5353

Northcote Road Antique
Market, 155a Northcote
Road, Battersea, SW11 6QB
Tel: 0171 228 6850

St James's Antiques
Market, 197 Piccadilly,
W1V 0LL
Tel: 0171 734 4511

Berkshire

Barkham Antique Centre,
Barkham Street,
Barkham, Nr Wokingham
RG40 4PJ
Tel: 0118 976 1355

Halls Corner Antiques,
207 Halls Road,
Tilehurst, Reading
RG30 4PT
Tel: 0118 942 3700
*Opposite the Bear Inn,
near the water tower,
5 mins from J12 M4. Open
10.30am–6pm Mon–Sat,
Sunday 11.30am–5pm.
Wide range of antique and
collectable items from
Georgian, Victorian and
Edwardian furniture,
traditional pine furniture,
Art Deco, '50s, silver,
ceramics, clocks,
collectables, Doulton,
Hummels, prints,
watercolours and oils,
kitchenalia, garden effects.*

Stables Antiques Centre,
1a Merchant Place
(off Friar St), Reading
RG1 1DT
Tel: 0118 959 0290
Open 10am–5pm.

Buckinghamshire

Antiques at Wendover,
Old Post Office, 25 High
St, Wendover HP22 6DU
Tel: 01296 625335

Marlow Antique Centre,
35 Station Road,
Marlow SL7 1NW
Tel: 01628 473223
*Antique and collectable
items, 30 dealers. Georgian,
Victorian and Edwardian
furniture, pine, decorative
furniture, silver, glass,
china, Art Deco, bedsteads,
cameras, old tools, garden
items, jewellery, pens, cuff
links, vintage toys,
secondhand books.
Mon–Sat 10am–5.30pm,
Sun 11am–4.30pm.*

Cambridgeshire

Fitzwilliam Antiques
Centre,
Fitzwilliam Street,
Peterborough PE1 2RX
Tel: 01733 565415

Cheshire

Davenham Antique Centre
& Tea Room, 461 London
Road, Davenham,
Northwich CW9 8NA
Tel: Shop 01606 44350
Office: 0161 973 3385

Derbyshire

Alfreton Antique Centre,
11 King St,
Alfreton DE55 7AF
Tel: 01773 520781
*40 dealers on 2 floors.
Antiques, collectables,
furniture, books, postcards
etc. Open Mon–Sat
10am–4.30pm, Sun &
Bank Holidays 11am–3pm.*

Bakewell Antiques &
Collectors' Centre, King
St, Bakewell DE45 1DZ
Tel: 01629 812496
e-mail: bacc@chappells-
antiques.co.uk
website: www.Chappells-
antiques.co.uk
*30 dealers inc. BADA &
LAPADA members. Quality
furniture, ceramics, silver,
plate, metals, treen, clocks,
barometers, books, pictures,
maps, prints, textiles,
kitchenalia, lighting and
furnishing accessories from
the 17th–20th centuries.
Open Mon–Sat 10am–5pm,
Sun 11am–5pm, closed
Christmas, Boxing & New
Year's Day.*

Heanor Antiques Centre,
Ilkeston Road,
Heanor DE75 7AG
Tel: 01773 531181
*Over 70 dealers. Open
daily 10.30am– 4.30pm.*

Matlock Antiques,
Collectables & Crafts,
7 Dale Road,
Matlock DE4 3LT
Tel: 01629 760808

Devon

The Quay Centre,
Topsham,
Nr Exeter EX3 0JA
Tel: 01392 874006
*Riverside warehouse on
Topsham Quay with 80
dealers on 3 floors. Antiques,
collectables and traditional
furnishings. Ample parking.
Open 7 days, 10am–5pm All
major cards accepted.*

Dorset

Antiques For All,
Higher Shaftesbury Road,
Blandford Forum
DT11 7TA
Tel: 01258 458011

Castle Antiques &
Collectables Centre,
12A Castle Street,
Christchurch BH23 1DT
Tel: 01202 875167

Essex

Gallerie Antiques,
62–70 Fowler Road,
Hainault IG6 3XE
Tel: 0181 501 2229

Gloucestershire

Cirencester Arcade &
Ann's Pantry,
25 Market Place,
Cirencester GL7 2PY
Tel: 01285 644214
*Antiques, furnishings, gifts,
etc. Restaurant / tea rooms.
Private room for hire.*

Gt Manchester

The Ginnell Gallery
Antique Centre,
18–22 Lloyd Street
M2 5WA
Tel: 0161 833 9037
*Extensive stock of antiques
and collectables covering
periods from 1200 BC to 1970
AD, Art Deco to fishing tackle
and comprehensive book
section. Large stock of 1950s
& 1960s glass and ceramics.
8,000 sq. ft. inc. restaurant.*

Hampshire

Dolphin Quay Antique Centre,
Queen Street,
Emsworth PO10 7BU
Tel: 01243 379994/0800 389142
Tel/Fax: 01243 379251
*www.antiquesbulletin.com /
dolphinquay*
*Marine, naval antiques, paintings,
watercolours, prints, antique clocks,
decorative arts, furniture, sporting
apparel, luggage, specialist period
lighting, conservatory and garden
antiques, fine antique and country
furniture, French / antique beds.
Open 7 days a week (including Bank
Holidays) Mon–Sat 10am– 5pm,
Sun 10am–4pm.*

Lymington Antiques Centre,
76 High Street,
Lymington SO41 9AL
Tel: 01590 670934

Secondhand Rose,
20 Stakes Road,
Purbrook PO7 5LX
Tel: 01705 374994
Open Mon–Sat 9am–6pm.

Herefordshire

The Hay Antique Market,
6 Market Street,
Hay-on-Wye HR3 5AF
Tel: 01497 820175

Mulberry's Antiques & Collectables,
30/32 St Owen St,
Hereford HR1 2PR
Tel: 01432 269925
*Two floors, wide range of antiques
and collectables – furniture,
porcelain, silver, jewellery, textiles,
pre-1930s clothing & accessories,
objets d'art, prints, oils and
watercolours.
Trade welcome.*

The Old Merchant's House Antique
Centre & Victorian Tearooms,
10 Corn Square,
Leominster HR6 8LR
Tel: 01568 616141.
*Wide variety of antiques, collectables
and memorabilia.
Tearooms. Open Mon–Sat,
10am–5pm.*

Hertfordshire

Herts & Essex Antiques Centre,
The Maltings, Station Road,
Sawbridgeworth CM21 9JX
Tel: 01279 722044.
*30 antique shops and 90 showcases.
Over 10,000 items of antiques,
furniture, jewellery, porcelain,
collectables, stamps, coins,
postcards, costume, paintings, glass,
ceramics and ephemera. All in well-
lit showrooms serviced by friendly
staff. Open every day (except
Monday). Tues–Fri 10am–5pm,
Sat–Sun 10am–6pm (including most
Bank Holidays).*

Kent

Copperfields Antique &
Craft Centre,
3c/4 Copper-fields,
Spital Street,
Dartford DA9 2DE
Tel: 01322 281445
*Open Mon–Sat 10am–5pm.
Antiques, collectables,
stamps, Wade, SylvaC,
Beswick, Royal Doulton,
clocks, Victoriana,
1930s–60s, Art Deco,
crafts, hand-made toys,
dolls' houses & miniatures,
jewellery, glass, china,
furniture, Kevin Francis
character jugs, silk, lace
and lots more. American-
style bistro.*

Malthouse Arcade,
Malthouse Hill,
Hythe CT21 5BW
Tel: 01303 260103.

Sidcup Antique & Craft
Centre, Elm Parade,
Main Rd, Sidcup
DA4 9DR
Tel: 0181 300 7387
*Over 100 dealers and
crafts people in one
unique setting. Coffee
shop. Open 7 days a
week 10am–5pm. Easy
parking nearby.*

Lancashire

GB Antiques Centre,
Lancaster Leisure Park,
(former Hornsea Pottery),
Wyresdale Road,
Lancaster
LA1 3LA
Tel: 01524 844734
*Over 140 dealers in
40,000 sq. ft. of space.
Porcelain, pottery, Art
Deco, glass, books and
linen. Large selection of
furniture. Open 7 days a
week 10am–5pm.*

Kingsmill Antique Centre,
Queen Street, Harle Syke,
Burnley BB10 2HX
Tel: 01282 431953

Leicestershire

Oxford St Antiques Centre,
16–26 Oxford Street,
Leicester
LE1 5XU
Tel: 0116 255 3006
*30,000 sq. ft. of showrooms
on 4 floors. Extensive
range of Victorian,
Edwardian and later
furniture etc. On-site
parking. Open Mon–Fri
10am–5.30pm, Sat
10am–5pm, Sun
2pm–5pm.*

**BATH
ANTIQUES MARKETS**
THE MARKET SPECIALISTS

BATH ANTIQUES MARKET
Guinea Lane, off Lansdown Road, Bath, Somerset
Tel: 01225 337638 (Weds)
Wednesday: 6.30am - 2.30pm

TAUNTON ANTIQUES CENTRE
27-29 Silver Street, Taunton, Somerset
Tel: 01823 289327 (Mon)
Mondays: 9am - 4pm

BERMONDSEY ANTIQUES MARKET
Corner of Long Lane & Bermondsey Street, London SE1
Tel: 0171-351 5353
Fridays: 5am - 2pm

ROGER'S ANTIQUES GALLERY
65 Portobello Road, London W11
Tel: 0171-727 1262 (Sat. only)
Saturday: 7am - 4pm

BATH ANTIQUES MARKET
Chenil House, 181-183 King's Road, London SW3 5EB
Enquiries out of market hours: 0171-351 5353

Lincolnshire

St Martins Antiques Centre,
23a High St, St Martins,
Stamford PE9 2LE
Tel: 01780 481158

Sue's Collectables,
61 Victoria Road,
Mablethorpe LN12 2AF
Tel: 01507 472406
*Open daily 10am–5pm.
20,000 collectable items inc.
old glass lampshades, gas
& electrical fittings,
Bakelite, breweriana,
kitchenalia, chalk figures,
Christmas lights &
decorations. Pendelfins
bought and sold.*

Nottinghamshire

Newark Antiques Centre,
Regent House, Lombard St,
Newark NG24 1XP
Tel: 01636 605504

Occleshaw Antiques Centre,
The Old Major Cinema,
11 Mansfield Road,
Edwinstowe NG21 9NL
Tel: 01623 825370
*e-mail:
paul@nut.talkland.com
Large centre with wide
range of furniture, jewellery,
militaria, cameras and
collectables. Services:
bookbinding, restoration,
French polishing etc.*

Portland Street Antiques
Centre, Portland Street,
Newark NG24 4XF
Tel: 01636 702836

Top Hat Antiques Centre,
70–72 Derby Road,
Nottingham NG1 5FD
Tel: 0115 941 9143

Oxfordshire

Antiques on High,
85 High Street,
Oxford OX1 4BG
Tel: 01865 251075
*35 dealers with a wide range
of quality stock. Open weekdays 10am–5pm, Suns &
Bank Holidays 11am–5pm.*

Deddington Antiques
Centre, Market Place,
Bull Ring, Deddington,
Nr Banbury OX15 0TW
Tel: 01869 338968

Didcot Antiques Centre,
220 Broadway,
Didcot OX11 8RS
Tel: 01235 510819
*25 dealers, ceramics, glass,
silver, jewellery, furniture,
pictures, Art Deco, Dinky &
Corgi, Steiff & collectable
toys, wind-up gramophones,*

*railwayana, metalware,
textiles, smoking accessories
etc. Bookshop, tearoom,
parking. Tues–Sat
10am–5pm, Sun 11am–4pm.*

Lamb Arcade Antiques
Centre, 83 High Street,
Wallingford OX10 0BS
Tel: 01491 835166
*Furniture, silver, porcelain,
glass, books, boxes, crafts,
rugs, jewellery, brass bedsteads, linens, pictures,
stringed instruments,
sports and fishing items,
decorative items. Open
10am–5pm Sat to 5.30pm,
Bank holidays 11am–5pm.
Coffee shop and wine bar.*

Shropshire

Stretton Antiques Market,
Sandford Avenue,
Church Stretton SY6 6BH
Tel: 01694 723718

Somerset

Bartlett Street Antiques,
7 Princes Buildings,
George St, Bath BA1 2QX
Tel: 01225 401717

Bartlett Street Antiques
Centre, 5-10 Bartlett St,
Bath, BA1 2QZ
Tel: 01225 466689

Bath Antiques Market,
Guinea Lane,
(off Landsdown Road),
Bath BA1 5NB
Tel: 01225 337638

Fountain Antiques Centre,
3 Fountain Buildings,
Lansdown Road,
Bath BA1 5DU
Tel: 01225 428731/471133

Staffordshire

Rugeley Antique Centre,
161 Main Road, Brereton,
Nr Rugeley WS15 1DX
Tel/Fax: 01889 577166
*Open Mon–Sat 9am–5pm,
Sun / Bank Holidays
12 noon–4.30pm.*

Tutbury Mill Antiques
Centre, Tutbury Mill Mews,
Tutbury DE13 9LU
Tel: 01283 520074
*Open Mon–Sat 10.30am–
5.30pm, Sun 12 noon–5pm.*

Surrey

The Antiques Centre,
22 Haydon Place,
Corner of Martyr Road,
Guildford GU1 4LL
Tel: 01483 567817
Closed Mon & Wed.

Esher Antiques Centre,
128–132 High Street,
Esher
KY10 9QJ
Tel: 01372 471166

Fern Cottage Antique
Centre, 28/30 High Street,
Thames Ditton
KT7 0RY
Tel: 0181 398 2281

Maltings Monthly Market,
Bridge Square,
Farnham GU9 7QR
Tel: 01252 726234

Packhouse Antique Centre,
Hewett's Kiln,
Tongham Road,
Runfold, Farnham
GU10 1PQ
Tel: 01252 781010

Serendipity Antique
Centre, 7 Petworth Road,
Haslemere GU27 2JB
Tel: 01428 642682
Closed Sundays.

Sussex

Antiques & Collectors Mkt,
Old Orchard Building,
Old House, Adversane,
Nr Billingshurst
RH14 9JJ
Tel: 01403 783594

Roundabout Antiques
Centre, 7 Commercial Sq,
Haywards Heath
RH16 7DW
Tel: 01273 835926
Open Mon–Sat 9.30am–
5.30pm, Suns 1.00–5.00pm.

Tyne & Wear

The Antique Centre,
142 Northumberland St,
Newcastle-upon-Tyne
NE1 7DQ
Tel: 0191 232 9832
Mon–Sat 10am–5pm.

Wales

Afonwen Craft & Antique
Centre, Afonwen Caerwys,
Nr Mold CH7 5UB
Tel: 01352 720965
Open all year Tues–Sun,
9.30am–5.30pm, closed Mons,
open Bank Holiday Mondays.
The largest Craft and Antique
Centre in North Wales. 14,000
sq. ft. of showrooms, antiques,
collectables from fine jewellery
to furniture. Restaurant.

Offa's Dyke Antique
Centre, 4 High Street,
Knighton, Powys LD7 1AT
Tel: 01547 528635

Romantiques Antique
Centre, Bryn Seion Chapel,
Station Road, Trevor,
Nr Llangollen LL20 7PF
Tel: Daytime 0378 279614
Evening 01978 752140
Open 10am–5pm 7 days.
2,500 sq. ft. displaying a
wide range of antiques and
collectables. Parking. Trade
welcome. Services: furniture
restoration, upholstery, clock
repairs and valuations.

Second Chance Antiques
& Collectables Centre,
Ala Road, Pwllheli,
Gwynedd LL53 5BL
Tel: 01758 612210

Warwickshire

Barn Antiques Centre,
Station Rd, Long Marston,
Nr Stratford-upon-Avon
CV37 8RB
Tel: 01789 721399
Open 7 days 10am–5pm.
Antique furniture, pine,
linen, lace, old fireplaces &
surrounds, collectables,
pictures and prints, silver,
china, ceramics and objets
d'art, reproduction clocks,
furniture, country kitchens.

Malthouse Antiques Centre,
4 Market Place,
Alcester B49 5AE
Tel: 01789 764032
Open 7 days. Good selection
of furniture, ceramics,
pictures & collectables.

Stables Antiques Centre,
Hatton Country World,
Dark Lane, Hatton,
Warwicks CV35 8XA
Tel: 01926 842405
25 independent dealers.
Café. Open daily
10am–5pm.

Stratford Antiques Centre,
59–60 Ely Street,
Stratford-upon-Avon,
CV37 6LN
Tel: 01789 204180

West Midlands

Birmingham Antique
Centre, 1407 Pershore
Road, Stirchley,
Birmingham B30 2JR
Tel: 0121 459 4587

Worcestershire

Worcester Antiques
Centre,
Reindeer Court,
Mealcheapen Street,
Worcester WR1 4DF
Tel: 01905 610680

Yorkshire

Halifax Antiques Centre,
Queens Road/Gibbet St,
Halifax HX1 4LR
Tel: 01422 366657

The Mall Antique Centre,
400 Wincolmlee,
Hull HU2 0QL
Tel: 01482 327858
60 local antique dealers.
Georgian, Victorian,
Edwardian, reproduction,
1930s furniture, silver,
china, clocks, hardware,
etc. Weekdays 9am–5pm,
Sat & Sun 10am–4pm.

Sheffield Antiques
Emporium & The Chapel,
15–19 Clyde Road,
Sheffield S8 0YD
Tel: 0114 258 4863
Over 70 dealers, antiques
and collectables, clocks,
Art Deco, French furniture,
books, pine, fabrics,
porcelain etc. Upholstery,
furniture and pottery
restoration, re-caning.
Refreshments. Open 7 days.

Stonegate Antiques Centre,
41 Stonegate,
York YO1 8AW
Tel: 01904 613888

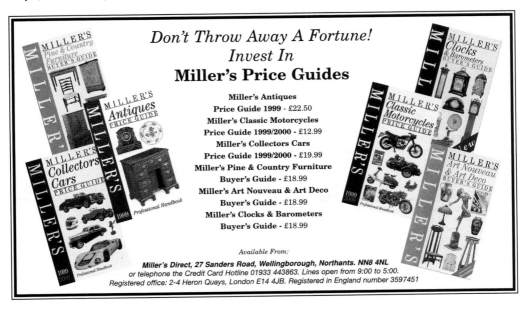

KEY TO ILLUSTRATIONS

Each illustration and descriptive caption is accompanied by a letter code. By referring to the following list of Auctioneers (denoted by *) and Dealers (•), the source of any item may be immediately determined. Inclusion in this edition in no way constitutes or implies a contract or binding offer on the part of any of our contributors to supply or sell the goods illustrated, or similar articles, at the prices stated. Advertisers in this year's directory are denoted by (†).

If you require a valuation for an item, it is advisable to check whether the dealer or specialist will carry out this service and if there is a charge. Please mention Miller's when making an enquiry. Having found a specialist who will carry out your valuation it is best to send a photograph and description of the item to the specialist together with a stamped addressed envelope for the reply. A valuation by telephone is not possible.

Most dealers are only too happy to help you with your enquiry. However, they are very busy people and consideration of the above points would be welcomed.

A&A • Antiques & Art, 116 State Street, Portsmouth NH 03802 USA Tel: 603-431-3931

AAN • Appledore Antiques Tel: 01233 758272

AAV * Academy Auctioneers & Valuers, Northcote House, Northcote Avenue, Ealing, London W5 3UR Tel: 0181 5797466

ABr • Avril Brown, Bartlett Street, Bath, Somerset BA1 2QZ Tel: 01225 310457/446322

ACA • Acorn Antiques, Durham House Antiques Centre, Stow-on-the-Wold, Glos GL54 1AA Tel: 01451 870404

ACT • Alscot Bathroom Co, The Stable Yard, Alscot Park, Stratford-upon-Avon, Warwicks CV37 8BL Tel: 01789 450861

Ada • Dale Adams, Fountain Antiques Market, 6 Bladud Buildings, Bath, Somerset BA1 5LS Tel: 01225 339104

ADE •† Art Deco Etc, 73 Upper Gloucester Road, Brighton, Sussex BN1 3LQ Tel: 01273 329268

AEF • A & E Foster, Little Heysham, Naphill, Bucks HP14 4SU Tel: 01494 562024

AGA *† Angling Auctions, PO Box 2095, London W12 8RU Tel: 0181 749 4175

AH * Andrew Hartley, Victoria Hall Salerooms, Little Lane, Ilkley, Yorkshire LS29 8EA Tel: 01943 816363

AHa •† Adrian Harrington, 64a Kensington Church Street, London W8 4DB Tel: 0171 937 1465

AIL • Antique Irish Linen, Dublin Tel: 00 353 1 451 2775

AL •† Ann Lingard, Ropewalk Antiques, Rye, Sussex TN31 7NA Tel: 01797 223486

ALI • Alien Enterprises, Stratford Model Centre, The Minories, Stratford-upon-Avon, Warwickshire CV37 6QW Tel: 01789 299701

AMH • Amherst Antiques, 23 London Road, Riverhead, Sevenoaks, Kent TN13 2BU Tel: 01732 455047

AND • Joan & Bob Anderson, Middlesex Tel: 0181 572 4328

ANG •† Ancient & Gothic, PO Box 356, Christchurch, Dorset BH23 1XQ Tel: 01202 478592

ANN • Antique Newspapers, PO Box 396, Jersey, Channel Islands GY1 3FW Tel: 01 481 712 990

ANP • Annette Power, The Collector, 9 Church Street, Marylebone, London NW8 8EE Tel: 0171 723 4167

AnS •† The Antique Shop, 30 Henley Street, Stratford-upon-Avon, Warwicks CV37 6QW Tel: 01789 292485

ANT • Anthemion, Bridge Street, Cartmel, Grange-over-Sands, Cumbria LA11 7SH Tel: 015395 36295

ANV • Anvil Antiques, Cavendish Street, Cartmel, Cumbria LA11 6QA Tel: 015395 36362

AP * Andrew Pickford, The Hertford Saleroom, 42 St Andrew Street, Hertford, Hertfordshire SG14 1JA Tel: 01992 583508

ARE • Arenski, 189 Westbourne Grove, London W11 2SB Tel: 0171 229 4297

ARo •† Alvin Ross, Alfies Antique Market, Stand G9–11, 13–25 Church Street, Marylebone, London NW8 8DT Tel: 0171 723 1513

ARP • Arundel Photographica, The Arundel Antiques Centre, 51 High Street, Arundel, Sussex BN18 9AJ Tel: 01903 882749

ASe • Alan Sedgwick e-mail: Alan.Sedgwick@BTInternet.com

ASM • Art Smith, Antiques at Wells Union, Route 1, 1755 Post Road, Wells, ME 04090 USA Tel: 207 646 6996

ATH • Apple Tree House Tel: 01694 722953

ATQ • Antiquarius Antique Market, 131/141 King's Road, Chelsea, London SW3 5ST Tel: 0171 351 5353

AWT • Antique Associates at West Townsend, 473 Main Street, PO Box 129W, West Townsend, MA 01474 USA Tel: (001) 508-597-8084

B&R •† Bread & Roses, Durham House Antique Centre, Sheep Street, Stow-on-the-Wold, Glos GL54 1AA Tel: 01451 870404/01926 817342

BAf •† Books Afloat, 66 Park Street, Weymouth, Dorset DT4 7DE Tel: 01305 779774

BaH • Calamus, The Shambles, Sevenoaks, Kent TN13 1AL Tel: 01732 740603

BAL •† A. H. Baldwin & Sons Ltd, Numismatists, 11 Adelphi Terrace, London WC2N 6BJ Tel: 0171 930 6879

BaN • Barbara Ann Newman, London House Antiques, 4 Market Square, Westerham, Kent TN16 1AW Tel: 01959 564479/Mobile 0850 016729

Bar • Chris Barge Antiques, 5 Southside Place, Inverness, Scotland IV2 3JF Tel: 01463 230128

BBR *† BBR, Elsecar Heritage Centre, Wath Road, Elsecar, Barnsley, Yorkshire S74 8HJ Tel: 01226 745156

BCA • Beaulieu Cars Automobilia, Beaulieu Garage, Brockenhurst, Hampshire SO42 7YE Tel: 01590 612999

BDA • Briar's C20th Decorative Arts, Yorkshire Tel: 01756 798641

Bea * Bearnes, Rainbow, Avenue Road, Torquay, Devon TQ2 5TG Tel: 01803 296277

Bea(E)* Bearnes, St Edmund's Court, Okehampton Street, Exeter, Devon EX4 1DU Tel: 01392 422800

BeG • Bears Galore, 8 The Fairings, High Street, Tenterden, Kent TN30 6QX Tel: 01580 765233

BELL • Bell Antiques, Moore Road, Bourton-on-the-Water, Glos GL54 2AZ Tel: 01451 822498

Ber • Berry Antiques, Berry House, 11–13 Stone Street, Cranbrook, Kent TN17 3HF Tel: 01580 712345

BEV •† Beverley, 30 Church Street, Marylebone, London NW8 8EP Tel: 0171 262 1576

BEX • Daniel Bexfield Antiques, 26 Burlington Arcade, London W1V 9AD Tel: 0171 491 1720

BGA • By George Antique Centre, 23 George Street, St Albans, Hertfordshire AL3 4ES Tel: 01727 853032

BHa • Judy & Brian Harden, Gloucestershire Tel: 01451 810684

BIG * Bigwood Auctioneers Ltd, The Old School, Tiddington, Stratford-on-Avon, Warwickshire CV37 7AW Tel: 01789 269415

BIL • Box in the Lanes, Cabinet 112 (Basement), Bartlett Street Antiques Centre, Bath, Somerset BA1 2QZ Tel: 0468 720338

BKK • Bona Art Deco Store, The Hart Shopping Centre, Fleet, Hampshire GU13 8AZ Tel: 01252 616666

BKS * Brooks (Auctioneers) Ltd, 81 Westside, London SW4 9AY Tel: 0171 228 8000

BMo •† Beau Mo'nde Costume, By George Antique Centre, 23 George Street, St Alban's, Hertfordshire AL3 4ES Tel: 01727 853032/855572

BOH • Bohemia, 11 Warner Street, Accrington, Lancashire Tel: 01254 231119

Bon * Bonhams, Montpelier Street, Knightsbridge, London SW7 1HH Tel: 0171 393 3994

Bon(C)* Bonhams, 65–69 Lots Road, Chelsea, London SW10 0RN Tel: 0171 393 3900

BONA •† Bonapartes, 1 Queen Street, Bath, Somerset BA1 1HE Tel: 01225 423873

BOW • David Bowden, S.319 Gray's Antique Market, 58 Davies Street, London W1Y 2LP Tel: 0171 495 1773

BQ • The Button Queen, 19 Marylebone Lane, London W1M 5FE Tel: 0171 935 1505

Bri * Bristol Auction Rooms, St John's Place, Apsley Road, Clifton, Bristol, Glos BS8 2ST Tel: 0117 973 7201

BRT • Britannia, Stand 101, Gray's Antique Market, 58 Davies Street, London W1Y 1AR Tel: 0171 629 6772

BRU • Brunel Antiques, Bartlett Street Antiques Centre, Bath, Somerset BA1 2QZ Tel: 01225 310457/446322

BrW • Brian Watson Antique Glass, The Grange, Norwich Road, Wroxham, Norwich, Norfolk NR12 8RX Tel: 01603 784177

BS • Below Stairs, 103 High Street, Hungerford, Berkshire RG17 0NB Tel: 01488 682317

BSA •† Bartlett Street Antique Centre, 5–10 Bartlett Street, Bath, Somerset BA1 2QZ Tel: 01225 446322/310457

BTC •† Beatcity, 56 High Street, Chatham, Kent ME4 4DS Tel: 01634 844525/0370 650890

BUR •† House of Burleigh, The Old Shop Cottage, 2 Braunston Road, Knossington, Oakham, Rutland LE15 8LN Tel: 01664 454570/454114

BUSH• Bushwood Antiques, Stags End Equestrian Centre, Gaddesden Lane , Hemel Hempstead, Herts HP2 6HN Tel: 01582 794700

BWA • Bow-Well Antiques, 103 West Bow, Edinburgh, Scotland EH1 2JP Tel: 0131 225 3335

BWC •† British Watch & Clock Collectors Association, 5 Cathedral Lane, Truro, Cornwall TR1 2QS Tel: 01872 241953

BYG • Bygones Reclamation (Canterbury), Nackington Road, Canterbury, Kent Tel: 01227 767453

ByI • Bygones of Ireland, Westport Antiques Centre, Lodge Road, Westport, Co Mayo, Republic of Ireland Tel: 00 353 98 26132

C * Christie, Manson & Wood Ltd, 8 King Street, St James's, London SW1Y 6QT Tel: 0171 839 9060

CA • Crafers Antiques, The Hill, Wickham Market, Suffolk IP13 0QS Tel: 01728 747347

CAB •† Candlestick & Bakelite, PO Box 308, Orpington, Kent BR5 1TB Tel: 0181 467 3743/3799

CaC * Cato Crane & Co, Liverpool Auction Rooms, 6 Stanhope Street, Liverpool, Merseyside L8 5RF Tel: 0151 709 5559

CAG * Canterbury Auction Galleries, 40 Station Road West, Canterbury, Kent CT2 8AN Tel: 01227 763337

CaH • The Camera House, Oakworth Hall, Colne Road (B6143), Oakworth, Keighley, Yorks BD22 7HZ Tel/Fax: 01535 642333

CARS • C.A.R.S. (Classic Automobilia & Regalia Specialists), 4–4a Chapel Terrace Mews, Kemp Town, Brighton, Sussex BN2 1HU Tel: 01273 60 1960

CAT • Lennox Cato, 1 The Square, Edenbridge, Kent TN8 5BD Tel: 01732 865988/ Mobile 0836 233473

CATH • Cathac Books, 10 Duke Street, Dublin 2, Republic of Ireland Tel: 00 3531 6718676

CB • Christine Bridge Antiques, 78 Castelnau, London SW13 9EX Tel: 07000 445277

CBP *† Comic Book Postal Auctions Ltd, 40–42 Osnaburgh Street, London NW1 3ND Tel: 0171 424 0007

CCC •† Crested China Co, The Station House, Driffield, Yorkshire YO25 7PY Tel: 01377 257042

CCI § Carlton Ware Collectors International, Helen Martin, PO Box 161, Sevenoaks, Kent TN15 6GA Tel: 01474 853630

CCO • Collectable Costume, Fountain Antique Centre, 3 Fountain Buildings, Lansdowne Road, Bath, Somerset BA1 5DU Tel: 01225 428731

CDC * Capes Dunn & Co, The Auction Galleries, 38 Charles Street, Off Princess Street, Greater Manchester M1 7DB Tel: 0161 273 6060/1911

CEX • Corn Exchange Antiques Centre, 64 The Pantiles, Tunbridge Wells, Kent TN2 5TN Tel: 01892 539652

CGC * Cheffins Grain & Comins, 2 Clifton Road, Cambridge, Cambs CB2 4BW Tel: 01223 358721/213343

CGX • Computer & Games Exchange, 65 Notting Hill Gate Road, London W11 3JS Tel: 0171 221 1123

CHe • Chelsea Clocks & Antiques, Antiquarius, Stand H3–4, 135 Kings Road, London SW3 4PW Tel: 0171 352 8646

CHU • Church Street Antiques, 2 Church Street, Wells Next the Sea, Norfolk NR23 1JA Tel: 01328 711698

CMF •† Childhood Memories, The Farnham Antique Centre, 27 South Street, Farnham, Surrey GU9 7QU Tel: 01252 724475/793704

CoA • Country Antiques (Wales), Castle Mill, Kidwelly, Carms, Wales SA17 4UU Tel: 01554 890534

COB •† Cobwebs, 78 Northam Road, Southampton, Hampshire SO14 0PB Tel: 01703 227458

CoH * Cooper Hirst, The Granary Saleroom, Victoria Road, Chelmsford, Essex CM2 6LH Tel: 01245 260535

CoHA • Corner House Antiques, High Street, Lechlade, Glos. GL7 3AE Tel: 01367 252007

COLL • Collinge Antiques, Old Fyffes Warehouse, Cowry Road, Llandudno Junction, Wales LL31 9LU Tel: 01492 580022

CORO• Coromandel, PO Box 9772, London SW19 3ZG Tel: 0181 543 9115

CP •† Cat Pottery, 1 Grammar School Road, North Walsham, Norfolk NR28 9JH Tel: 01692 402962

CPA • Cottage Pine Antiques, 19 Broad Street, Brinklow, Nr Rugby, Warwickshire CV23 0LS Tel: 01788 832673

CRIS • Cristobal, Unit G125–127, Alfies Antique Market, 13–15 Church Street, London NW8 8DT Tel: 0171 724 7789

CS •† Christopher Sykes, The Old Parsonage, Woburn, Milton Keynes, Bedfordshire MK17 9QM Tel: 01525 290259

CSA •† Church Street Antiques, 10 Church Street, Godalming, Surrey GU7 1EH Tel: 01483 860894

CSK *† Christie's South Kensington Ltd, 85 Old Brompton Road, London SW7 3LD Tel: 0171 581 7611

CTO •† Collector's Corner, PO Box 8, Congleton, Cheshire CW12 4GD Tel: 01260 270429

CWo • Collectors World, Stand G101, G130/143 Alfies Antique Market, 13–25 Church Street, Marylebone, London NW8 8DT Tel: 0171 723 0564/Mobile 0860 791588

DA * Dee, Atkinson & Harrison, The Exchange Saleroom, Driffield, Yorkshire YO25 7LD Tel: 01377 253151

DAC • Didcot Antiques Centre, 220 Broadway, Didcot, Oxfordshire OX11 8RS Tel: 01235 510819

DaH • Dale House Antiques, High Street, Moreton-in-Marsh, Glos GL56 0AD Tel: 01608 650763

DAN • Andrew Dando, 4 Wood St, Queen Square, Bath, Somerset BA1 2JQ Tel: 01225 422702

DBA • Douglas Bryan Antiques, The Old Bakery, St David's Bridge, Cranbrook, Kent TN17 3HN Tel: 01580 713103

DBr • David Brown, 23 Claude Street, Larkhall, Lanarkshire, Scotland ML9 2BU Tel: 01555 880333

DD * David Duggleby, The Vine St Salerooms, Scarborough, Yorkshire YO11 1XN Tel: 01723 507111

DDM * Dickinson Davy & Markham, Wrawby Street, Brigg, Humberside DN20 8JJ Tel: 01652 653666

DeA • Delphi Antiques, Powerscourt Townhouse Centre, South William Street, Dublin 2, Republic of Ireland Tel: 00 353 1 679 0331

DEE • Dee's Antique Pine, 89 Grove Road, Windsor, Berkshire SL4 1HT Tel: 01753 865627/850926

DgC • Dragonlee Collectables, Kent Tel: 01622 729502

DHA • Durham House Antiques Centre, Sheep Street, Stow-on-the-Wold, Glos GL54 1AA Tel: 01451 870404

DIC • D & B Dickinson, The Antique Shop, 22 & 22a New Bond St, Bath, Somerset BA1 1BA Tel: 01225 466502

DKH • David K. Hakeney, 400 Wincolmlee, Hull, Humberside HU2 0QL Tel: 01482 228190

DLP •† The Dunlop Collection, PO Box 6269, Statesville, NC 28687 USA Tel: (704) 871 2626/Toll Free: (800) 227 1996

DN * Dreweatt Neate, Donnington Priory, Donnington, Newbury, Berkshire RG13 2JE Tel: 01635 31234

DN(H) * Dreweatt Neate Holloways, 49 Parsons Street, Banbury, Oxfordshire OX16 8PF Tel: 01295 253197

DNW *† Dix-Noonan-Webb, 1 Old Bond Street, London W1X 3TD Tel: 0171 499 5022

Do • Liz Farrow t/as Dodo, Admiral Vernon Market, Portobello Road, London W11

Doc * Dockree's, Cheadle Hulme Business Centre, Clemence House, Mellor Rd, Cheadle Hume, Cheshire SK8 5AT Tel: 0161 485 1258

DOL •† Dollectable, 53 Lower Bridge Street, Chester, Cheshire CH1 1RS Tel: 01244 344888/679195

DOM • Peter Dome, Sheffield

DOR • Dorset Reclamation, Cow Drove, Bere Regis, Wareham, Dorset BH20 7JZ Tel: 01929 472200

DPO • Doug Poultney, 219 Lynmouth Ave, Morden, Surrey SM4 4RX Tel: 0181 330 3472

DQ • Dolphin Quay Antique Centre, Queen Street, Emsworth, Hampshire PO10 7BU Tel: 01243 379994/0800 389142 Tel/Fax: 01243 379251

DRJ • DS & RG Johnson, The Motorhouse, Thorton Hall, Thorton, Bucks MK17 0HB Tel: 01280 812280

DRU • Drummonds of Bramley, Birtley Farm, Horsham Road, Bramley, Guildford, Surrey GU5 0LA Tel: 01483 898766

DSG •† Delf Stream Gallery, 14 New Street, Sandwich, Kent CT13 9AB Tel: 01304 617684

DUD • Dudley Howe, SO55/56/57 Alfies Antique Market, 13–25 Church Street, London NW8 8DT Tel: 0171 723 6066

E * Ewbank, Burnt Common Auction Room, London Road, Send, Woking, Surrey GU23 7LN Tel: 01483 223101

EAS • Eastgate Antiques, Stand 7/9 Alfies Antique Market, 13–25 Church Street, London NW8 8DT Tel: 0374 206289

EBB • Ella's Button Box, South View, Twyford, Bucks MK18 4EG Tel: 01296 730910

Ech •† Echoes, 650a Halifax Road, Eastwood, Todmorden, Yorkshire OL14 6DW Tel: 01706 817505

ED • Elite Designs, Sussex Tel: 01424 434856

EDC • Edward's China, 2–10 Market Lane, Stoke-on-Trent, Staffordshire

EH * Edgar Horn, Fine Art Auctioneers, 46–50 South Street, Eastbourne, Sussex BN21 4XB Tel: 01323 410419

EIM • Christopher Eimer, PO Box 352, London NW11 7RF Tel: 0181 458 9933

EKK • Ekkehart, USA Tel: 001 415 571 9070

ELG • Enid Lawson Gallery, 36a Kensington Church Street, London W8 4DB Tel: 0171 937 8444

EMC • Sue Emerson & Bill Chapman, Bourbon-Hanby Antiques Centre, Shop No 18, 151 Sydney Street, Chelsea, London SW3 6NT Tel: 0171 351 1807

EON • Eugene O'Neill Antique Gallery, Echo Bridge Mall, 381 Elliot Street, Newtown Upper Falls, MA 02164 USA Tel: (617) 965 5965

ET • Early Technology, 84 West Bow, Edinburgh, Scotland EH1 2HH Tel: 0131 226 1132

FAM • Fountain Antiques Centre, 3 Fountain Buildings, Lansdown Road, Bath, Somerset BA1 5DU Tel: 01225 428731/471133

FB • Francis Bowers Chess Suppliers, 34 Middle Road, Whaplode, Spalding, Lincolnshire PE12 6TW Tel: 01406 370166

FD • Frank Dux Antiques, 33 Belvedere, Bath, Somerset BA1 5HR Tel: 01225 312367

FHF * Frank H. Fellows & Sons, Augusta House, 19 Augusta Street, Hockley, Birmingham, West Midlands B18 6JA Tel: 0121 212 2131

FMu • Frank Munford, 390 Newark Road, Lincoln, Lincolnshire LNX 8RX Tel: 01522 878362

FOX • Foxhole Antiques, Swan & Foxhole, Albert House, Stone Street, Cranbrook, Kent Tel: 01580 712720

FRa • Frasers, 399 The Strand, London WC2 Tel: 0171 836 9325

FrG • The French Glasshouse, P14/16 Antiquarius, 135 King's Road, Chelsea, London SW3 4PW Tel: 0171 376 5394

FW&C * Finan, Watkins & Co, The Square, Mere, Wiltshire BA12 6DJ Tel: 01747 861411

G&CC •† Goss & Crested China Co, 62 Murray Road, Horndean, Hampshire PO8 9JL Tel: 01705 597440

GAK * G. A. Key, 8 Market Place, Aylsham, Norfolk NR11 6EH Tel: 01263 733195

GAZE * Thomas Wm Gaze & Son, Diss Auction Rooms, Roydon Road, Diss, Norfolk IP22 3LN Tel: 01379 650306

GBr • Geoffrey Breeze Antiques, 6 George Street, Bath, Somerset BA1 2EH Tel: 01225 466499

GEM • Gem Antiques, 28 London Road, Sevenoaks, Kent TN13 1AP Tel: 01732 743540

GeM • Gerald Mathias, R5/6 Antiquarius, 135 King's Road, Chelsea, London, SW3 4PW Tel: 0171 351 0484

GeW • Geoffrey Waters Ltd, F1–F6 Antiquarius Antiques Centre, 135–141 King's Road, London SW3 4PW Tel: 0171 376 5467

GH * Gardiner Houlgate, The Old Malthouse, Comfortable Place, Upper Bristol Road, Bath, Somerset BA1 3AJ Tel: 01225 447933

GIN • Ginnell Gallery Antique Centre, 18–22 Lloyd Street, Gt. Manchester M2 5WA Tel: 0161 833 9037

GIO • Giovanna Antiques, Bourbon-Hanby Antiques Centre, Shop16, 151 Sydney St, London SW3 6NT Tel: 0171 565 0004

GKR •† GKR Bonds Ltd, PO Box 1, Kelvedon, Essex CO5 9EH Tel: 01376 571711

GLA •† Glasform Ltd, 123 Talbot Road, Blackpool, Lancashire FY1 3QY Tel: 01253 626410

GLT • Glitterati, Assembly Antique Centre, 6–8 Saville Row, Bath, Somerset BA1 2QP Tel: 01225 333294

GN • Gillian Neale Antiques, PO Box 247, Aylesbury, Bucks. HP20 1JZ Tel: 01296 423754

GNR • Gnome Reserve, West Putford, Nr Bradworthy, Devon EX22 7XE Tel: 01409 241435

GOL • The Golden Sovereign, The Copper House, Great Bardfield, Essex CM7 4SP Tel: 01371 810507

GrD •† Grays Dolls, Grays in the Mews, 1–7 Davies Street, London W1Y 2LP Tel: 0181 367 2441/0171 629 7034

GS • Ged Selby Antique Glass, by appointment Tel: 01756 799673

GSP * Graves, Son & Pilcher, Hove Auction Rooms, Hove Street, Hove, Sussex BN3 2GL Tel: 01273 735266

GSW • Georg S. Wissinger Antiques, 21 & 44 West Street, Chipping Norton, Oxfordshire Tel: 01608 641369

GV • Garth Vincent, The Old Manor House, Allington, Nr Grantham, Lincolnshire NG32 2DH Tel: 01400 281358

GWA • GB Antiques Centre, Lancaster Leisure Park, (the former Hornsea Pottery), Wyresdale Road, Lancaster, Lancs LA1 3LA Tel: 01524 844734

HAK •† Paul Haskell, Kent Tel: 01634 669362

HALL • Hall's Nostalgia, 21 Mystic Street, Arlington, MA 02474 USA Tel: 001 781 646 7757

HAM * Hamptons Antique & Fine Art Auctioneers, 93 High Street, Godalming, Surrey GU7 1AL Tel: 01483 423567

Har • Patricia Harbottle, Geoffrey Vann Arcade, 107 Portobello Road, London W11 2QB Tel: 0171 731 1972 Saturdays

HaR • A. Harris, Middlesex Tel: 0181 931 6591/Mobile 09561 46083

HarC •† Hardy's Collectables, 862 Christchurch Road, Boscombe, Bournemouth, Dorset BH7 6DQ Tel: 01202 422407/ Mobile 07970 613077

HAX * Halifax Property Services, Fine Art Department, 53 High Street, Tenterden, Kent TN30 6BG Tel: 01580 763200

HBo •† Harrison's Books, Stand J20/21 Grays Mews Antiques Market, 1–7 Davies Street, London W1Y 2LP Tel: 0171 629 1374

HCC * H C Chapman & Son, The Auction Mart, North Street, Scarborough, Yorks YO11 1DL Tel: 01723 372424

HEG •† Stuart Heggie, 14 The Borough, Northgate, Canterbury, Kent CT1 2DR Tel: 01227 470422

HEI • Heirloom Antiques, 68 High Street, Tenterden, Kent TN30 6AU Tel: 01580 765535

HEL • Helios Gallery, 292 Westbourne Grove, London W11 2PS Tel: 01225 336097/ Mobile 0973 730843

HEM • Hemswell Antique Centre, Caenby Corner Estate, Hemswell Cliff, Gainsborough, Lincolnshire DN21 5TJ Tel: 01427 668389

HHa • Henry Hay, Alfies Antique Market, Stand S54, 13–25 Church Street, Marylebone, London NW8 8DT Tel: 0171 723 6105

HOB •† Hobday Toys, Middlesex Tel: 01895 636737

HofB • Howards of Broadway, 27A High Street, Broadway, Worcestershire WR12 7DP Tel: 01386 858924

HOK * Hamilton Osborne King, 4 Main Street, Blackrock, Co Dublin, Republic of Ireland Tel: 353 1 288 5011

HON • Honans Antiques, Crowe Street, Gort, County Galway, Republic of Ireland Tel: 00 353 91 31407

HUX •† David Huxtable, Alfies Antique Market, Stand S03/05 (Top Floor), 13–25 Church Street, Marylebone, London NW8 8DT Tel: 0171 724 2200

HYD * H Y Duke & Son, Dorchester Fine Art Salerooms, Dorchester, Dorset DT1 1QS Tel: 01305 265080

ID • Identity, Portobello Green Market, Under the Canopy, London W11 Tel: 0171 792 4604

INC • The Incurable Collector, Surrey Tel: 01932 860800

IS • Ian Sharp Antiques, 23 Front Street, Tynemouth, Tyne & Wear NE30 4DX Tel: 0191 2960656

IW •† Islwyn Watkins, 1 High Street, Knighton, Powys, Wales LD7 1AT Tel: 01547 520145

J&J • J & J's, Paragon Antiques & Collectors Market, 3 Bladud Buildings, The Paragon, Bath, Somerset BA1 5LS Tel: 01225 313176

J&L No longer trading

JAG • JAG Applied Arts, 58–60 Kensington Church St Antique Centre, Unit 6, London W8 4DB Tel: 0171 938 4404

JaG • Japanese Gallery, 66d Kensington Church Street, London W8 4BY Tel: 0171 229 2034/ 0171 226 3347

JAL • J. A. Allen, 4 Lower Grosvenor Place, London SW1W 0EL Tel: 0171 834 0090

JAS • Jasmin Cameron, M16 Antiquarius, 131–141 King's Road, London SW3 5ST Tel/Fax: Shop 0171 351 4154/Mobile 0374 871257/ Home 01494 774276

JCa • J Cards, PO Box 12, Tetbury, Glos GL8 8WB Tel: 01454 238600

JER • Jeremiah Fine Art, G012 Alfies Antique Market, 13–25 Church St, London NW8 8DT

JH * Jacobs & Hunt, 26 Lavant Street, Petersfield, Hampshire GU32 3EF Tel: 01730 233933

JHa • Jeanette Hayhurst Fine Glass, 32a Kensington Church Street, London W8 4HA Tel: 0171 938 1539

JHo • Jonathan Horne, 66C Kensington Church Street, London W8 4BY Tel: 0171 221 5658

JMC • J & M Collectables, Kent Tel: 01580 891657

JO • Jacqueline Oosthuizen, 23 Cale Street, Chelsea, London SW3 3QR Tel: 0171 352 6071

JoC • Jo Campbell, Jo's Antiques, Rt. 1, Box 2390, Mount Pleasant, Texas USA Tel: 903 572 3173

JON • Jon Bird, Kent Tel: 01227 273952

JP • Janice Paull, 16A High Street, Kenilworth, Warwickshire CV8 1LZ Tel: 01926 851311

JPr •† Joanna Proops Antiques/Textiles, 34 Belvedere, Bath, Somerset BA1 5HR Tel: 01225 310795

JUN •† Junktion, The Old Railway Station, New Bolingbroke, Boston, Lincolnshire PE22 7LB Tel: 01205 480068/480087

JV • June Victor, S041–43, Alfies Antique Market, 13–25 Church St, London NW8 8DT Tel: 0171 723 6066

JVa • Jenny Vander, 20–22 Market Arcade, George Street, Dublin 2, Republic of Ireland Tel: 00 353 1 677 0406

JVM • Malchione Antiques & Sporting Collectibles, 110 Bancroft Road, Kennett Square, PA 19348 USA Tel: 610-444-3509

KEN • Alan Kenyon, PO Box 33, Port Talbot, Glamorgan Tel: 01639 895359

KES •† Keystones, PO Box 387, Stafford, Staffordshire ST16 3FG Tel: 01785 256648

KEY • Key Antiques, 11 Horsefair, Chipping Norton, Oxfordshire OX7 5AL Tel: 01608 643777

L * Lawrence Fine Art Auctioneers, South Street, Crewkerne, Somerset TA18 8AB Tel: 01460 73041

L&E * Locke & England, Black Horse Agencies, 18 Guy Street, Leamington Spa, Warwickshire CV32 4RT Tel: 01926 889100

L&L •† Linen & Lace, Shirley Tomlinson, Halifax Antiques Centre, Queens Road/ Gibbet Street, Halifax, Yorkshire HX1 4LR Tel: 01422 366657/Mobile 0411 763454

LA • Lane Antiques, 40 Pittshanger Lane, Ealing, London W5 1QY Tel: 0181 810 8090

LAY * David Lay (ASVA), Auction House, Alverton, Penzance, Cornwall TR18 4RE Tel: 01736 361414

LB • Lace Basket, 116 High Street, Tenterden, Kent TN30 6HT Tel: 01580 763923/763664

LBr • Lynda Brine, Assembly Antique Centre, 5–8 Saville Row, Bath, Somerset BA1 2QP Tel: 01225 448488

LCA • La Chaise Antiques, 30 London Street, Faringdon, Oxfordshire SN7 7AA Tel: 01367 240427

LCC • The London Cigarette Card Co Ltd, Sutton Road, Somerton, Somerset TA11 6QP Tel: 01458 273452

LeB •† Le Boudoir Collectables, Bartlett Street Antique Centre, Bath, Somerset BA1 2QZ Tel: 01225 311061

LEG • Legend Lane, Albion Mill, London Road, Macclesfield, Cheshire SK11 7SQ Tel: 01625 424661

LIB • Libra Antiques, 81 London Road, Hurst Green, Etchingham, Sussex TN19 7PN Tel: 01580 860569

LPA • L. P. Furniture, (The Old Brewery), Short Acre Street, Walsall, West Midlands WS2 8HW Tel: 01922 746764

LT * Louis Taylor Auctioneers & Valuers, Britannia House, 10 Town Road, Hanley, Stoke-on-Trent, Staffordshire ST1 2QG Tel: 01782 214111

LUC • R. K. Lucas & Son, The Tithe Exchange, 9 Victoria Place, Haverfordwest, Wales SA16 2JX Tel: 01437 762538

MAC • Mall Antique Centre, 400 Wincolmlee, Hull, E. Yorks HU2 0QL Tel: 01482 327858

MANS • William Mansell, 24 Connaught Street Marble Arch, London W2 2AF Tel: 0171 723 4154

MAP • Marine Art Posters, 71 Harbour Way, Merchants Landing, Victoria Dock, Port of Hull, Yorkshire HU9 1PL Tel: 01482 321173

MAR * Frank R. Marshall & Co, Marshall House, Church Hill, Knutsford, Cheshire WA16 6DH Tel: 01565 653284

MAr •† Mint Arcade, 71 The Mint, Rye, Sussex TN31 7EW Tel: 01797 225952

MAU • Sue Mautner, Stand P13, Antiquarius, 135 Kings Road, London SW3 4PW Tel: 0171 376 4419

MAV • May Avenue, Antiquarius V13, 131–141 King's Road, Chelsea, London SW3 4PW Tel: 0171 351 5757

MB •† Mostly Boxes, 93 High Street, Eton, Windsor, Berkshire SL4 6AF Tel: 01753 858470

MBo • Michael E. Bound, Portobello, London

MCA * Mervyn Carey, Twysden Cottage, Benenden, Cranbrook, Kent TN17 4LD Tel: 01580 240283

MCN • MCN Antiques, 183 Westbourne Grove, London W11 2SB Tel: 0171 727 3796

MEA * Mealy's, Chatsworth Street, Castle Comer, Co Kilkenny, Republic of Ireland Tel: 00 353 56 41229

MED * Medway Auctions, Fagins, 23 High Street, Rochester, Kent ME1 1LN Tel: 01634 847444

MEG • Megarry's and Forever Summer, Jericho Cottage, The Duckpond Green, Blackmore, Essex CM4 0RR Tel: 01277 821031/822170

MER • Mere Antiques, 13 Fore Street, Topsham, Exeter, Devon EX3 0HF Tel: 01392 874224

MEx • Music Exchange, 21 Broad Street, Bath, Somerset BA1 5LN Tel: (Music) 01225 333963 (Records) 01225 339789

MiA • Old Mill Antiques Centre, Mill Street, Low Down, Bridgnorth, Shropshire Tel: 01746 768778

Mit * Mitchells, Fairfield House, Station Road, Cockermouth, Cumbria CA13 9PY Tel: 01900 827800

MJa • Mark Jarrold, The Grey House, Tetbury Street, Minchinhampton, Glos GL6 9JH Tel: 01453 887074

MJW • Mark J. West, Cobb Antiques Ltd, 39a High Street, Wimbledon Village, London SW19 5YX Tel: 0181 946 2811

ML • Magic Lanterns at By George, 23 George Street, St Albans, Hertfordshire AL3 4ES Tel: 01727 865680/853032

MLa • Marion Langham, London Tel: 0171 730 1002

MLL • Millers Antiques Ltd, Netherbrook House, 86 Christchurch Road, Ringwood, Hampshire BH24 1DR Tel: 01425 472062

MON • Monty Lo, Stand 369, Gray's Antique Market, 58 Davies Street, London W1Y 1AR Tel: 0171 493 9457

MoS • Morgan Stobbs, 17 High Street, Eton, Berkshire SL4 6AR Tel: 01753 840631

MR * Martyn Rowe, Truro Auction Centre, City Wharf, Malpas Road, Truro, Cornwall TR1 1QH Tel: 01872 260020

MRo •† Mike Roberts, 4416 Foxfire Way, Fort Worth, Texas 76133 USA Tel: 001 817 294 2133

MRW •† Malcolm Welch Antiques, PO Box 1122, Rugby, Warwickshire CV23 9YD Tel: 01788 810 616

MSB • Marilynn and Sheila Brass, PO Box 380503, Cambridge, MA 02238-0503 USA Tel: 617 491 6064

MTa • Maggie Tallentire, Cousy 82160 Caylus, Tarn et Garonne, France Tel: 0033(0)5 63 24 05 27

MUL •† Mullock & Madeley, The Old Shippon, Wall-under-Heywood, Nr Church Stretton, Shropshire SY6 7DS Tel: 01694 771771

MURR • Murrays' Collectables Tel: 01202 309094

NAR • Colin Narbeth & Son Ltd, 20 Cecil Court, Leicester Square, London WC2N 4HE Tel: 0171 379 6975

NC •† The Nautical Centre, Harbour Passage, Hope Square, Weymouth, Dorset DT4 8TR Tel: 01305 777838

NCA • New Century, 69 Kensington Church Street, London W8 4DB Tel: 0171 937 2410

No7 • No 7 Antiques, Shropshire Tel: 01630 647118

Nor • Sue Norman, L4 Antiquarius, 135 King's Road, London SW3 5ST Tel: 0171 352 7217

NP • Neville Pundole, 8A & 9 The Friars, Canterbury, Kent CT1 2AS Tel: 01227 453471

NWi • Neil Wilcox, 113 Strawberry Vale, Twickenham, Middlesex TW1 4SJ Tel: 0181 892 5858

OCH • Gillian Shepherd, Old Corner House Antiques, 6 Poplar Road, Wittersham, Tenterden, Kent TN30 7PG Tel: 01797 270236

OD • Offa's Dyke Antique Centre, 4 High Street, Knighton, Powys, Wales LD7 1AT Tel: 01547 528635

Oli * Olivers, Olivers Rooms, Burkitts Lane, Sudbury, Suffolk CO10 6HB Tel: 01787 880305

OLM • The Old Mill, High Street, Lamberhurst, Kent TN3 8EQ Tel: 01892 891196

ONS * Onslow's, The Depot, 2 Michael Road, London SW6 2AD Tel: 0171 371 0505/Mobile 0831 473 400

OPG/PP Octopus Publishing Group Ltd, 2–4 Heron Quays, London E14 4JB (Pro-Photo).

ORI • Oriental Gallery, Gloucestershire Tel: 01451 830944

ORIG • The Originals, GO 87/88, Alfies Antique Market, 13–25 Church Street, London NW8 8DT Tel: 0171 723 6066

OTA •† On The Air, 42 Bridge Street Row, Chester, Cheshire CH1 1NN Tel: 01244 348468

OTB •† Old Tackle Box, PO Box 55, High Street, Cranbrook, Kent TN17 3ZU Tel/Fax: 01580 713979

OTC •† Old Telephone Company, The Old Granary, Battlesbridge Antiques Centre, Nr Wickford, Essex SS11 7RF Tel: 01245 400601

OTS •† The Old Toy Shop, Hampshire Tel/Fax: 01425 476899

OTT • Otter Antiques, 20 High Street, Wallingford, Oxon, Oxfordshire OX10 0BP Tel: 01491 825544

OVE •† Chuck Overs, The Cottage, Warslow Road, Longnor, Derbyshire SK17 0LA Tel: 01298 83806

OW •† Off World, Unit 20, Romford Shopping Halls, Market Place, Romford, Essex RM1 3AT Tel: 01708 765633

P *† Phillips, Blenstock House, 101 New Bond Street, London W1Y 0AS Tel: 0171 629 6602/468 8233

P(B)/ * Phillips, 1 Old King Street, Bath,
PB Somerset BA1 2JT Tel: 01225 310609

P(Ba) * Phillips Bayswater, 10 Salem Road, Bayswater, London W2 4DL Tel: 0171 229 9090

P(C) * Phillips Cardiff, 9–10 Westgate Street, Cardiff, Wales CF1 1DA Tel: 01222 396453

P(EA) * Phillips, 32 Boss Hall Road, Ipswich, Suffolk IP1 59J Tel: 01473 740494

P(G) * Phillips Fine Art Auctioneers, Millmead, Guildford, Surrey GU2 5BE Tel: 01483 504030

P(HSS) * Phillips, 20 The Square, Retford, Notts DN22 6XE Tel: 01777 708633

P(M) * Phillips, 158 Queen Street, Woollahra, Melbourne, NSW 2025 Australia Tel: (612) 9326 1588

P(NE) * Phillips North East, St Mary's, Oakwellgate, Gateshead, Tyne & Wear NE8 2AX Tel: 0191 477 6688

P(S) * Phillips, 49 London Road, Sevenoaks, Kent TN13 1AR Tel: 01732 740310

PA * No longer trading

PAC •† Potteries Antique Centre, 271 Waterloo Road, Cobridge, Stoke-on-Trent, Staffordshire ST6 3HR Tel: 01782 201455

PAR • Park House Antiques & Toy Museum, Park Street, Stow-on-the-Wold, Gloucestershire GL54 1AQ Tel: 01451 830159

PARS •† Pars Antiques, Stand A14–15, Grays in the Mews, 1–7 Davies Street, London W1Y 1AR Tel: 0171 491 9889

PBr • Pamela Brooks, Leicestershire Tel: 0116 230 2625

PC Private Collection

PER • Persiflage, Stand F00 6–8, Alfies Antique Market, 13–25 Church Street, London NW8 8DT Tel: 0171 723 6066

PFK * Penrith Farmers' & Kidd's plc, Skirsgill Salerooms, Penrith, Cumbria CA11 0DN Tel: 01768 890781

PGA •† Paul Gibbs Antiques, 25 Castle Street, Conway, Gwynedd, Wales LL32 8AY Tel: 01492 593429/596533

PHa •† Peter Harrington, 100 Fulham Road, London SW3 6HS Tel: 0171 591 0220/0330

PING •† Pinball Geoff, 1B Shelford Place, Stoke Newington, London N16 9HX Tel: 0171 254 6700

PKT • Glitter & Dazzle, Pat & Ken Thompson Tel: 01329 288678

PLB • Planet Bazaar, 151 Drummond Street, London NW1

PLY * The Plymouth Auction Rooms, Edwin House, St John's Rd, Cattedown, Plymouth, Devon PL4 0NZ Tel: 01752 254740

PO • Pieter Oosthuizen, De Verzamelaar, Bourbon-Hanby Antiques Centre, 151 Sydney Street, London SW3 6NT Tel: 0171 359 3322/Fax: 0171 376 3852

POSH • Posh Tubs, Moriati's Workshop, High Halden, Ashford, Kent TN26 3LZ Tel: 01233 850155

POW • Sylvia Powell Decorative Arts, 18 The Mall, Camden Passage, London N1 0PD Tel: 0171 354 2977/0181 458 4543

PPe • Past Perfect, 31 Catherine Hill, Frome, Somerset BA11 1BY Tel: 01373 453342

PPH • Period Picnic Hampers Tel: 0115 937 2934

PrB •† Pretty Bizarre, 170 High Street, Deal, Kent CT14 6BQ Tel: 0973 794537

PSA • Pantiles Spa Antiques, 4, 5, 6 Union House, The Pantiles, Tunbridge Wells, Kent TN4 8HE Tel: 01892 541377

Q2 • Q2, Antiquarius Antique Market, 131/141 King's Road, Chelsea, London SW3 5ST Tel: 0171 351 5353

RA • Roberts Antiques, Lancashire Tel: 01253 827798

Rac • Rochester Antiques Centre, 93 High Street, Rochester, Kent ME1 1LX Tel: 01634 846144

RAD • Radio Days, 87 Lower Marsh, Waterloo, London SE1 7AB Tel: 0171 928 0800

RAM • Ram Chandra (Gabriella Rijal), Gray's Portobello, 138 Portobello Road, London W11 2DZ Tel: 0181 740 0655

Ram •† Rambo's Tattoo Studio, 42 Shudehill, Gt. Manchester M4 1EY Tel: 0161 839 0090

RAR * Romsey Auction Rooms, 86 The Hundred, Romsey, Hampshire SO51 8BX Tel: 01794 513331

RAT •† Room at the Topp, 1st Floor, Antiques Warehouse, Glass Street, Hanley, Stoke on Trent, Staffordshire ST1 2ET Tel: 01782 271070

RAW • The Original Reclamation Trading Co, 22 Elliot Road, Love Lane Estate, Cirencester, Glos GL7 1YS Tel: 01285 653532

RBA •† Roger Bradbury Antiques, Church Street, Coltishall, Norfolk NR12 7DJ Tel: 01603 737444

RBB * Russell, Baldwin & Bright, Fine Art Salerooms, Ryelands Road, Leominster, Herefordshire HR6 8NZ Tel: 01568 611122

RCh • Rayner & Chamberlain, London Tel: 0181 293 9439

RdeR • Rogers de Rin, 76 Royal Hospital Road, London SW3 4HN Tel: 0171 352 9007

RDG • Richard Dennis Gallery, 144 Kensington Church Street, London W8 4BN Tel: 0171 727 2061

RECL • Reclamation Services Ltd, Catbrain Quarry, Painswick Beacon, Above Paradise, Painswick, Glos GL6 6SU Tel: 01452 814064

Riv • Riverbank Antiques, Wells Union, Route 1, PO Box 3009, Wells, ME 04090 USA Tel: 207 646 6314

RMC •† Romsey Medal Centre, 5 Bell Street, Romsey, Hampshire SO51 8GY Tel: 01794 512069

RRA • Rambling Rose Antiques, Marcy & Bob Schmidt, Frederick, MD USA Tel: 301 473 7010

RTh •† The Reel Thing, 17 Royal Opera Arcade, Pall Mall, London SW1Y 4UY Tel: 0171 976 1830

RTo   *   Rupert Toovey & Co Ltd, Star Road, Partridge Green, Sussex RH13 8RJ Tel: 01403 711744

RTw   •†   Richard Twort, Somerset Tel: 01934 641900/Mobile 0411 939789

RuC   •   Ruskin Coins and Antiquities, Oxford Antique Trading Co, 40 Park End Street, Oxford, Oxfordshire OX1 1JD Tel: Mobile 0585 542744

RUM   •†   Rumours, 10 The Mall, Upper Street, Camden Passage, Islington, London N1 0PD Tel: 01582 873561

RUS   •   Trevor Russell, PO Box 1258, Uttoxeter, Staffordshire ST14 8XL

RWB   •   Roy W. Bunn Antiques, 34–36 Church Street, Barnoldswick, Colne, Lancashire BB8 5UT   Tel: 01282 813703

RYA   •   Robert Young Antiques, 68 Battersea Bridge Road, London SW11 3AG Tel: 0171 228 7847

S   *   Sotheby's, 34–35 New Bond Street, London W1A 2AA   Tel: 0171 293 5000

S(NY)   *   Sotheby's, 1334 York Avenue, New York, NY 10021 USA   Tel: 001 212 606 7000

S(S)   *   Sotheby's Sussex, Summers Place, Billingshurst, Sussex RH14 9AD Tel: 01403 833500

SAF   *†   Saffron Walden Saleroom, 1 Market Street, Saffron Walden, Essex CB10 1JB Tel: 01799 513281

SAM   •   Samarkand Galleries, 8 Brewery Yard, Sheep Street, Stow-on-the-Wold, Glos GL54 1AA   Tel: 01451 832322

SAS   *†   Special Auction Services, The Coach House, Midgham Park, Reading, Berkshire RG7 5UG   Tel: 0118 971 2949

SCO   •   Peter Scott, Stand 39, Bartlett Street Antiques Centre, Bath, Somerset BA1 2QZ Tel: 01225 310457/0117 986 8468/ Mobile 0850 639770

SCR   •†   Herzog, Hollender Phillips & Company, The Scripophily Shop, PO Box 14376, London NW6 1ZD Tel/Fax: 0171 433 3577

SER   •†   Serendipity, 168 High Street, Deal, Kent CT14 6BQ   Tel: 01304 369165/366536

SFL   •   The Silver Fund, 139A New Bond Street, London W1Y 9FB   Tel: 0171 499 8501

SHa   •   Shapiro & Co, Stand 380, Grays Antique Market, 58 Davies Street, London W1Y 1LB Tel: 0171 491 2710

SLL   •   Sylvanna Llewelyn Antiques, Unit 5, Bourbon-Hanby Antiques Centre, 151 Sydney Street, Chelsea, London SW3 6NT Tel: 0171 351 4981

SMAM   •   Santa Monica Antique Market, 1607 Lincoln Boulevard, Santa Monica, California 90404 USA   Tel: 310 314 4899

SMI   •†   Janie Smithson, Lincolnshire Tel/Fax 01754 810265/Mobile 0831 399180

SnA   •   Snape Maltings Antique & Collectors Centre, Saxmundham, Suffolk IP17 1SR Tel: 01728 688038

SOL   •†   Solent Railwayana Auctions, 31 Newtown Road, Warsash, Hampshire SO31 9FY Tel: 01489 578093/584633

Som   •   Somervale Antiques, 6 Radstock Road, Midsomer Norton, Bath, Somerset BA3 2AJ   Tel: 01761 412686

SPa   •   Sparks Antiques, 4 Manor Row, High Street, Tenterden, Kent TN30 6HP Tel: 01580 766696

SPE   •   Sylvie Spectrum, Stand 372, Gray's Market, 58 Davies Street, London W1Y 1LB Tel: 0171 629 3501

SpM   •   Sparkle Moore, G116 Alfies Antique Market, 13–25 Church Street, London NW8 8DT   Tel: 0171 723 6066

SpP   *   Specialised Postcard Auctions, 25 Gloucester Street, Cirencester, Gloucestershire GL7 2DJ Tel: 01285 659057

SPU   •   Spurrier-Smith Antiques, 28, 39, 41 Church Street, Ashbourne, Derbyshire DE6 1AJ   Tel: 01335 343669/342198

SRA   *†   Sheffield Railwayana Auctions, 43 Little Norton Lane, Sheffield, Yorkshire S8 8GA Tel: 0114 274 5085

SSW   •   Spencer Swaffer, 30 High Street, Arundel, Sussex BN18 9AB Tel: 01903 882132

STA   •   Michelina & George Stacpoole, Main Street, Adare, Co Limerick, Republic of Ireland Tel: 00 353 6139 6409

StC   •†   St Clere Antiques, PO Box 161, Sevenoaks, Kent TN15 6GA   Tel: 01474 853630

STE   •†   Stevenson Brothers, The Workshop, Ashford Road, Bethersden, Ashford, Kent TN26 3AP   Tel: 01233 820363

STG   •†   Stone Gallery, 93 The High Street, Burford, Oxfordshire OX18 4QA Tel/Fax 01993 823302

STK   •   Stockbridge Antiques, 8 Deanhaugh Street, Edinburgh, Scotland EH4 1LY Tel: 0131 332 1366

SUC   •   Succession, 18 Richmond Hill, Richmond, Surrey TW10 6QX   Tel: 0181 940 6774

SUS   •   Susannah, 142/144 Walcot Street, Bath, Somerset BA1 5BL   Tel: 01225 445069

SVB   •   Steve Vee Bransgrove, 6 Catherine Hill, Frome, Somerset BA11 1BY Tel: 01373 453225

SWB   •†   Sweetbriar Gallery, Robin Hood Lane, Helsby, Cheshire WA6 9NH Tel: 01928 723851

SWN   •   Swan Antiques, Stone Street, Cranbrook, Kent TN17 3HF   Tel: 01580 712720

SWO   *   G E Sworder & Sons, 14 Cambridge Road, Stansted Mountfitchet, Essex CM24 8BZ Tel: 01279 817778

TAC   •   Tenterden Antiques Centre, 66–66A High Street, Tenterden, Kent TN30 6AU Tel: 01580 765655/765885

TAN   •   Tanglewood Antiques, Tanglewood Mills, Coke Street, Derby, Derbyshire DE1 1NE Tel: 01332 346005

TAR   •   Lorraine Tarrant Antiques, 3 Market Place, Ringwood, Hants BH24 1AN Tel: 01425 461123

TAY   *   Taylors, Honiton Galleries, 205 High Street, Honiton, Devon EX14 8LF Tel: 01404 42404

TBoy   •   Toy Boy, Alfies Antique Market, 13–25 Church Street, Marylebone, London NW8 8DT   Tel: 0171 723 6066

TC   •   Timothy Coward, Devon   Tel: 01271 890466

TCF   •†   20th Century Frocks, 65 Steep Hill (opposite Jews House), Lincoln, Lincolnshire N1 1YN   Tel: 01522 545916

TCG   •   20th Century Glass, Kensington Church Street Antique Centre, 58–60 Kensington Church Street, London W8 4DB Tel: 0171 729 9875/

TCT   •†   20th Century Vintage Telephones, 2780 Northbrook Place, Boulder, Colorado 80304 USA Tel: 001 44 (303) 442 3304

TEN   *   Tennants, Auction Centre, Harmby Road, Leyburn, Yorks DL8 5SG Tel: 01969 623780

TH   •† Tony Horsley, Sussex Tel: 01273 550770

THA   • Town Hall Antiques, Market Place, Woburn, Bedfordshire MK17 9PZ Tel: 01525 290950

THOM   • S & A Thompson, Stand V12 Antiquarius, 131/141 Kings Rd, London SW3 5ST Tel: 0171 352 8680

TIH   • Time In Our Hands, The Platt, Wadebridge, Cornwall PL27 7AD Tel: 01208 815210

TMA   * Brown & Merry, Tring Market Auctions, Brook Street, Tring, Hertfordshire HP23 5EF Tel: 01442 826446

TMi   • T. J. Millard Antiques, Assembly Antiques, 5–8 Saville Row, Bath, Somerset BA1 2QP Tel: 01225 448488

TOM   •† Charles Tomlinson, Chester Tel: 01244 318395

TOT   •† Totem, 168 Stoke Newington, Church Street, London N16 0JL Tel: 0171 275 0234

TOY   • The Toy Store, 7 Thomas Street, Manchester City Centre, Greater Manchester M4 IEU Tel: 0161 839 6882

TP   • The Collector, Tom Power, 9 Church Street, Marylebone, London NW8 8EE Tel: 0171 723 4167/0181 361 6111

TPCS   §† Torquay Pottery Collectors' Society, Torre Abbey, Avenue Road, Torquay, Devon TQ2 5JX

TRE   • No longer trading

TRL   * Thomson, Roddick & Laurie, 60 Whitesands, Dumfries, Scotland DG1 2RS Tel: 01387 255366 and 24 Lowther Street, Carlisle, Cumbria CA3 8DA Tel: 01228 28939/39636

TRU   • The Trumpet, West End, Minchinhampton, Glos GL6 9JA Tel: 01453 883027

TT   •† Treasures in Textiles, Melodys Antique Galleries, 30/32 City Road, Chester Tel: 01244 328968

TUO   • The Unique One, 2802 Centre Street, Pennsauken NJ 08109 USA Tel: 001 (609) 663 2554

TVM   • Teresa Vanneck-Murray, Surrey

TWa   • Time Warp, c/o Curioser & Curioser, Sydney Street, Brighton, Sussex BN1 Tel: 01273 821243

UTP   • Utility Plus, 66 High Street, West Ham, Pevensey, Sussex BN24 5LP Tel: 01323 762316/0850 130723

VB   •† Variety Box, 16 Chapel Place, Tunbridge Wells, Kent TN1 1YQ Tel: 01892 531868

VCL   •† Vintage Cameras Ltd, 256 Kirkdale, Sydenham, London SE26 4NL Tel: 0181 778 5416

VGC   • Vintage Gas Cooker Collection, 4 Church Street, Cirencester, Glos GL7 1LE Tel: 01285 654351

VH   • Valerie Howard, 2 Campden Street, Off Kensington Church Street, London W8 7EP Tel: 0171 792 9702

VINE   •† Vine Antiques, Oxfordshire Tel: 01235 812708

VS   *† T. Vennett-Smith, 11 Nottingham Road, Gotham, Notts NG11 0HE Tel: 0115 983 0541

VSt   • Vera Strange Antiques, 811 Christchurch Road, Boscombe, Bournemouth, Dorset BH7 6HP Tel: 01202 429111

W&S   • Pat Woodward and Alma Shaw, Unit G43, Ground Floor, Gloucester Antiques Centre, In The Historic Docks, Severn Road, Gloucester GL1 2LE

WA   *† Whyte's Auctioneers, 30 Marlborough St, Dublin 1, Republic of Ireland Tel: 00 353 1 874 6161

WAB   •† Warboys Antiques, Old Church School, High Street, Warboys, Huntingdon, Cambs PE17 2SX Tel: 01487 823686

WAC   • Worcester Antiques Centre, Reindeer Court, Mealcheapen Street, Worcester, Worcestershire WR1 4DF Tel: 01905 610680

WaH   • The Warehouse, 29–30 Queens Gardens, Worthington Street, Dover, Kent CT17 9AH Tel: 01304 242006

Wai   • Peter Wain, Glynde Cottage, Longford, Market Drayton, Shropshire TF9 3PW Tel: 01630 639613

WAL   *† Wallis & Wallis, West Street Auction Galleries, Lewes, Sussex BN7 2NJ Tel: 01273 480208

WaR   • Wot a Racket, 250 Shepherds Lane, Dartford, Kent DA1 2PN Tel: 01322 220619

WBH   * Walker, Barnett & Hill, Waterloo Road Salerooms, Clarence Street, Wolverhampton, West Midlands WV1 4JE Tel: 01902 773531

WEE   • Weedon Bec Antiques, 66 High Street, Weedon, Northants NN7 4QD Tel: 01327 349910

WeH   • Westerham House Antiques, The Green, Westerham, Kent TN16 1AY Tel: 01959 561622/562200

WilP   * Wilson Peacock, The Auction Centre, 26 Newnham Street, Bedford, Bedfordshire MK40 3JR Tel: 01234 266366

WIM   • Wimpole Antiques, Stand 349, Grays Antique Market, South Molton Lane, London W1Y 2LP Tel: 0171 499 2889

WL   * Wintertons Ltd, Lichfield Auction Centre, Wood End Lane, Fradley, Lichfield, Staffordshire WS13 8NF Tel: 01543 263256 Photos: Courtesy of Crown Photos: Tel: 01283 762813

WO   • Woodville Antiques, The Street, Hamstreet, Ashford, Kent TN26 2HG Tel: 01233 732981

WP   •† West Promotions, PO Box 257, Sutton, Surrey SM3 9WW Tel: 0181 641 3224

WRe   • Walcot Reclamations, 108 Walcot Street, Bath, Somerset BA1 5BG Tel: 01225 444404

WW   * Woolley & Wallis, 51–61 Castle Street, Salisbury, Wiltshire SP1 3SU Tel: 01722 424500

WWY   •† When We Were Young, The Old Forge, High Street, Harmondsworth Village, Middlesex UB7 0AQ Tel: 0181 897 3583

YAG   • The York Antiques Gallery, Route 1, PO Box 303, York, ME 03909 USA Tel: 207-363-5002

YAN   • Yanni's Antiques, 538 San Anselmo Avenue, San Anselmo, CA 94960 USA Tel: 001 415 459 2996

YC   •† Yesterday Child, Angel Arcade, 118 Islington High Street, London N1 8EG Tel: 0171 354 1601

INDEX TO ADVERTISERS

INDEX

Italic page numbers denote colour pages; **bold** numbers refer to information and pointer boxes.

MYSTERY OBJECTS

A primitive oak chair, used for cockfighting, c1800.
£300–330 *ANV*

A rosewood hemming clamp, c1840, 7in (18cm) high.
£225–250 *GeM*

A treacle-glazed ceramic sash window stop, c1865, 5in (13cm) high.
£80–100 *DSG*

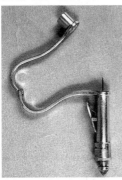

A brass ear piercer, 1920s, 3in (7.5cm) long.
£25–35 *WAB*

l. A silver-plated skirt lifter, 1880–1900, 3¾in (9.5cm) long.
£35–45 *WAB*

r. A plastic square egg cooker, 1970s, 3¾in (9.5cm) high.
£10–15 *WAB*

Key to Front Cover Illustrations

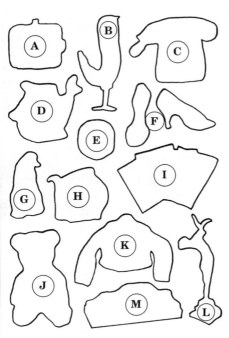

A. An Agfa Clack camera, c1955. **£4–5** *VCL*

B. A blown-glass bird, by Allessandro Pianon, c1962, 12⅘in (32.5cm) high. **£800–1,000** *OPG/PP*

C. A Type 706L red telephone, c1960, 9in (23cm) high. **£25–30** *CAB*

D. A Kevin Francis Toby jug, designed for Spitting Image, c1985, 5⅓in (13.5cm) high. **£100–125** *ANP*

E. A tin of French face powder, 'Le Trèfle Incarnat', 1930s, 2⅘in (7cm) diam. **£12–15** *PC*

F. A pair of Rayne gold kid shoes, 1950s. **£15–18** *Ech*

G. A Russian hand-painted penguin group, 1950s, 6in (15cm) high. **£60–70** *MRW*

H. A Clarice Cliff Stamford shape teapot, decorated in Green Chintz pattern, 1931–33, 6in (15cm) wide. **£700–750** *BEV*

I. Four *The Beatles'* monthly magazines, 1960–70s, 8in (20.5cm) high. **£2–3 each** *BTC*

J. A Pedigree mohair bear, c1950, 16in (41cm) high. **£200–240** *Bon(C)*

K. A green military style jacket, 19thC. **£100–150** *BWA*

L. An Art Deco gilt cast-spelter figure, on a marble plinth, c1920, 17in (43cm) high. **£250–300** *CARS*

M. A Dinky Toys Citroën Presidentielle, c1972, 8in (20cm) long. **£350–400** *CSK*